THE ALFRED HITCHCOCK STORY

THE ALFRED HITCHCOCK STORY

KEN MOGG

With contributions by

Dan Auiler

David Barraclough

Steven L. DeRosa

Martin Grams Jr.

Philip Kemp

J. Lary Kuhns

TAYLOR PUBLISHING COMPANY
Dallas, Texas

Published by arrangement with Titan Books Ltd. of 42–44 Dolben Street, London SE1 0UP, England.

No part of this book may be reproduced in any form or by any means—including photocopying and electronic reproduction—without written permission from the publisher.

Designed by David Timmons

Published by Taylor Publishing Company
1550 West Mockingbird Lane
Dallas, Texas 75235
www.taylorpub.com

Library of Congress Cataloging-in-Publication Data:

Mogg, Ken.
    The Alfred Hitchcock story / Ken Mogg.
        p.   cm.
    Filmography: p.
    Includes bibliographical references.
    ISBN 0-87833-163-8
    1. Hitchcock, Alfred, 1899–1980.
    2. Motion picture producers and directors—Great Britain Biography.
    I. Title
PN1998.3.H58M65   1999
                                                99-35294
                                                CIP

10 9 8 7 6 5 4 3 2 1
Printed in the United States of America

CONTENTS

Hitchcock said of *Rear Window* that no considerations of morality could have stopped him from making it, such was his love of pure film. I take this Nietzschean–sounding remark to imply that for Hitchcock, ordinary morality is restrictive or deadening, but that creating pure film involves an imaginative approach to life. In short, I see Hitchcock as a Romantic artist, and his most self-revealing film the gloriously amoral *The Trouble With Harry*.

In turn, this book takes Hitchcock's films to be about the life force—or rather the life-and-death force, the cosmic *Will*. The latter term was coined by Friedrich Nietzsche's predecessor, Arthur Schopenhauer, whose *The World as Will and Representation* (1819; 1844) anticipated Freud's notion of the Unconscious, and whose very title, it seems to me, sums up *Vertigo*, with its twin aspects of upwards striving and illusion. I make no apology for citing several vitalist philosophers in these pages: Schopenhauer, Nietzsche, and Henri Bergson. However, it's true that Hitchcock's understanding of the life force does seem to vary from film to film: sometimes that force seems little more than the zeitgeist, the spirit of the period, as in *Jamaica Inn* and *Notorious*.

Again, it has become commonplace in Hitchcock scholarship to say that he was deeply affected by German expressionism—witness an early film like *The Lodger*. Well, a direct line runs from Schopenhauer and Nietzsche to the German filmmakers: for instance, the physical appearance of Doctor Caligari in *The Cabinet of Dr. Caligari* (1919) is literally an image of Schopenhauer, being based on a photograph of the philosopher in his old age. But *The Lodger* also shows the influence of both Freud and, if obliquely, the novelist Charles Dickens. Freud has already been mentioned (and is discussed later). As for Dickens, his stories deeply impressed *Caligari*'s scriptwriter Carl Mayer precisely because of the *animism* with which they invested both people and objects. For his part, Hitchcock studied four Dickens novels at school. The novels' mixture of the comic-grotesque with a dark undercurrent patently informs such films as *The Wrong Man* and *Frenzy*, though in *The Wrong Man*, the grotesque is strictly confined to the events and coincidences.

Lastly, Professor John Carey's *The Intellectuals and the Masses* (1992) notes that in Britain by the 1930s, the Nietzschean assumption that most people are dead had become "a standard item in the repertoire of any self-respecting intellectual." Hitchcock's *Rich and Strange* (American title: *East of Shanghai*) from that period posits the same idea, though allowing its ordinary couple, Fred and Emily, an ambiguous reprieve at the end. I can't emphasize enough the importance of Hitchcock's membership, in the late 1920s, in the Film Society in London.

Here he rubbed shoulders with some of the leading intellectuals of the day—for whom both Nietzsche's and Bergson's vitalist ideas were currently fashionable—and announced his ambition to create art movies that were also popular movies.

The ordering of films in this book follows that of Jane E. Sloan in her *Alfred Hitchcock: A Filmography and Bibliography* (1993), an ordering that is sometimes questionable. Thus *The Manxman* was certainly the last of Hitchcock's pre-sound films—not the third last, as Sloan indicates. In some cases, we have silently amended a film's release date as given by Sloan. Likewise, we have had occasion to deviate from some of the running times she gives for the sound films, bearing in mind that different countries often release slightly different prints of films. For instance, various countries appear to have cut *Torn Curtain* from its original 128 minutes. (Sloan, unhelpfully, gives a running time of "approximately 120 minutes.") Also, our filmography omits some of the more dubious alternate titles of films.

I thank heartily my fellow writers of this book, who responded at short notice when asked to contribute their expertise. And to our readers I say: May you find our book both stimulating and a work of lasting reference.

Ken Mogg,
June 1999

FOREWORD

Genius! Spirit, pixie, brilliance, intellect, skill, soul, wit, horse sense, mastery, flair, strategist, wizard. There are additional definitions of genius, but I feared if I put them all down there might not be room to say anything else about Mr. Alfred Hitchcock, Sir Alfred, Mr. Hitchcock, Hitch. Naturally, genius was the first word to pop into my head when asked to write of Mr. Hitchcock. There were endless synonyms in my trusty *Roget's Thesaurus* and, along with the ones already noted, all fit him to a T.

This book will chronicle Mr. Hitchcock's unparalleled contributions to the film industry and its history, all of which will fortunately be studied, treasured, and most importantly enjoyed by present and future generations. I hope to give a brief glimpse from my vantage point of the man behind the legend.

I met Mr. and Mrs. Hitchcock socially a few years before the making of *Psycho*. We always hit it off, mainly due, I suppose, to our wild sense of humor and mutual passion for movies. In the late summer of 1959, a messenger delivered an envelope containing a book and a note that read, in essence, 'Dear Janet, please consider the part of Mary Crane. The role will be enhanced dramatically in the finished version. Anthony Perkins is set to play Norman Bates.' And it concluded with his customary signature profile.

That was the beginning of my professional relationship with the man. I went to his home for tea and to be introduced to his *modus operandi*. It was awesome. In his mind, and sketched on the pages of his script, the film was already shot. He showed me the model sets and moved the miniature camera through the tiny furniture toward the wee dolls, exactly the way he intended to do in *reel* life. He was meticulously thorough down to the minutest detail.

I was told I had *carte blanche* to play Marion (the name was changed from the novel) as I envisioned her, except I had to move when his camera dictated. He would be ready and willing to help if I had a problem motivating the move, or, of course, if I was completely off base in my interpretation of this pivotal character. I am aware many actors felt this approach was a threat to their freedom of expression. Perhaps I

would have also, under a different leader. But how could anyone question his method when his results were so spectacular? 'If it ain't broke, don't fix it!'

I treated this ultimatum as a challenge. As an actress I should be able (actually it's my obligation) to rethink my first instinct in order to blend with my director's need and concept. Fortunately we molded perfectly. It was one of the most relaxed and pleasurable atmospheres in which I've worked. No tension, no tantrums, a great deal of interesting conversation, much laughter, and many practical jokes. But believe me, when the cinematographer was ready, we were all business, completely focused on the scene.

I began to see the why of having his camera absolute. By not having one superfluous frame of film, he kept the story taut and mounted the suspense. The shower sequence took seven shooting days and tallied over seventy set-ups, and he knew precisely what portion of a second he would use of each angle.

He was such a mischievous imp. And oh so smart! Mr. H deliberately wove a web of mystery and speculation about

this film. Always the quintessential salesman, he had rumors flying by the first week of shooting. The set was closed, which always aroused interest. The crew respected the secrecy, but when I was actually in the shower, wearing moleskin over the necessary parts and a bathing suit where I was out of camera, I noticed each crew member had several new assistants. When I had finished my three weeks, he hired a professional artist's model to be on the set nude, obviously fueling the buzz he had created.

I am certain he followed the same pattern of perfection in every one of his endeavors. He was fearless in pursuing the unexplored, the unusual. And humanity is the heir to his legacy. No one can ever take him away from us.

His genius will live forever.

Janet Leigh

Janet Leigh
Beverly Hills
February 1999

THE ALFRED HITCHCOCK STORY

THE EARLY YEARS
1899—1933

S ir Alfred Joseph Hitchcock was born on August 13, 1899, the third child of a Catholic family living in the London suburb of Leytonstone, near the Waltham Forest. The birth took place at home, a small flat above his father's wholesale poultry and grocery store (which, sadly, no longer exists), and it was from here that the young Hitchcock first ventured out into Greater London.

Leytonstone, where Hitch spent his formative years, was a lower middle class area at the turn of the century, and the locality has much the same character in 1999 as it did in 1899. It was at the police station just steps away from his birthplace that Hitchcock's father once sent him with a note instructing the officer to lock the young man up for five minutes, so that he would learn "what happened to bad little boys." As incredible as this story may seem, it is nonetheless one that he told numerous times throughout his life.

Such was the external setting during these early years in which an internal landscape that would translate into more than fifty years of cinematic nightmares began to take shape. We know little of real substance about Hitchcock's relationship with his mother and father, Emma and William, or his older siblings, William and Nellie. He never spoke about them to the press. Hitchcock's father died when Hitch was fifteen and we can sur-

Left: *Young Alfred.*
Above: *Hitch (on the horse) seen outside his father's grocery store.*

mise (if only from the police station story) that he was at times a severe man with an odd sense of humor.

After his father's death on December 12, 1914, it was imperative that Hitch pick a trade. It is interesting to note that he did not assume his father's occupation (his brother took over the business), but strove for a more artistic career from the outset. Admittedly engineering was hardly Left Bank, but it was also not wholesale

poultry mongering, and the crafts learned in the evening classes he attended gave Hitchcock the necessary tools for his later entrée into films. In particular, his sketching was immediately recognized as above average by his employers, the Henley Telegraph and Cable Company, and this later transported him from desk work to their advertising and marketing department. As the First World War continued, the eighteen-year-old Hitchcock was excused from military service after a medical exam, although he did enlist in the volunteer corps of the Royal Engineers.

The concerns of the world did not

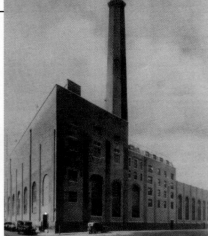

Far Left: *Hitchcock's first completed feature as a director,* The Pleasure Garden.
Left: *The Gainsborough studios in Islington.*
Bottom: Blackmail *was shot as both a silent and a "100% talkie."*

entirely overwhelm young Alfred—he remained an avid theater-goer and in the early twenties saw many of the actors and productions which would later shape his own work. Of particular significance is his recollection of the pivotal (for Hitchcock) production of J. M. Barrie's *Mary Rose* (1925). This play haunted Hitch throughout his entire career, but, despite his acquisition of the film rights, he never managed to bring the work to the screen. In addition to the stage, of course, was the far less expensive cinema. Hitchcock spoke reverentially of the great films he saw in this period and how influential some of the directors were to his own work. Later in life, Hitch pretended that he saw few movies, although in truth he always remained a fervent cinemagoer—he simply stopped going to public cinemas. Hitchcock's daybooks list private weekly screenings of all the latest films.

Hitch was probably seen as something of a creative force at Henley, as the company's first in-house newsletter featured his darkly humorous short story "Gas." It's a tale evidently influenced by his love of Edgar Allan Poe (1809–1849), an author Hitchcock had discovered in his mid-teens, along with G. K. Chesterton (1874–1936) and, set to loom large in his future career, John Buchan (1875–1940). Despite his success at Henley, Hitch made a daring stab at breaking into the then nascent British film industry. He kept up with industry news, and after reading Famous Players-Lasky's forthcoming productions list, made a set of title cards for a silent film, which he then took to the company. Unfortunately, the film had been cancelled, but the producers were nevertheless impressed and gave Hitch his first job in the movies. At the age of twenty-one, Hitchcock was on his way.

Having helped finish direction on the Seymour Hicks production *Always Tell Your Wife* (after the original director, Hugh Croise, was fired), Hitchcock's first solo effort was *Number 13* for Famous Players-Lasky. Only a still remains from this unfinished film, which became a victim of the British cinema's volatility when funds ran out during production. Hitchcock immediately went to work for the independent producers who became the new tenants at Islington studios, and within months was assistant director to Graham Cutts, Britain's most prominent director of the period. In 1924, the studio was acquired by Gainsborough Pictures; headed by Michael Balcon, the company would be Hitch's employer for his first five (completed) films. Work with Cutts took Hitch to UFA studios in Germany, where he had a chance to observe the legendary director F. W. Murnau on the set of *The Last Laugh* (1924; "almost the perfect film . . . [it] had a tremendous influence on me," Hitch later recalled).

As important as these developments were to Hitchcock professionally, even more significant was the close working relationship he formed with a talented

editor, writer, and sometime actress (he may have even seen her as a young woman in the 1918 film, *King Richard's Court*) Alma Reville. Alma was born on August 14, 1899 (just a day after Hitchcock), in Nottingham, later moving to Islington, and had worked in the film industry from a very young age. When Hitchcock began his career as a title card designer, she already had a fine reputation as a cutter and writer. She used to joke that Hitch waited to propose marriage until he had a job higher in rank than her own. He made that proposal to a seasick Alma on a return ferry from Germany in late 1923, and after a lengthy engagement and Alma's conversion to Catholicism, the couple married on December 2, 1926. Eighteen months later, on July 7, 1928, Alma gave birth to their only child, Patricia.

Hitchcock was industrious and well organized, but only to a point, which in interviews he attributed to his earlier Jesuit schooling. As he told Peter Bogdanovich: "Their education is very strict, and orderliness is one of the things that came out of that, I suppose, although my orderliness is spasmodic. I remember when I was eighteen or nineteen and as senior estimator at that electrical engineering firm [Henley], the requests for estimates used to come in, and I was kind of lazy so I'd pile them up on my desk and they'd go up to a big stack. And I used to say, 'Well, I've got to get down to this,' and then I polished them off like anything—and used to get praised for the prodigious amount of work I'd done on that particular day. This lasted until complaints began to come in about the delay in answering. That's the way I still feel about working. Certain writers want to work every hour of the day—they're very facile. I'm not that way. I want to say,

'Let's lay off for several hours—let's play.' And then we get down to it again. I'm sure the Jesuits did not teach that."

By 1925, Graham Cutts had begun to worry about this "upstart crow," and his relationship with his assistant director deteriorated. This ultimately proved a stroke of luck for Hitchcock, as, with producer Michael Balcon's support, Hitch then embarked on his own directing career in earnest, with a complicated and somewhat baroque soap opera entitled *The Pleasure Garden*. The film was produced in Germany, away from Gainsborough Pictures' immediate control, giving Hitchcock rather more independence than most first-time directors enjoy. Viewed today, the story is hardly a prime example of Hitch's talent, but the film's visuals are often quite striking and indicative of how his career would develop.

However, Hitch's success was in no way guaranteed. The studio shelved his first two films after lackluster receptions at trade screenings, in particular from Gainsborough's head of distribution, C. M. Woolf. His third was met with equal disdain by the studio, with Woolf again being his fiercest critic. Fortunately, Balcon brought in Ivor Montagu to help recut the film, and with some reluctance it was eventually released. *The Lodger* proved a smash hit, helping to define public expectations of a Hitchcock film for the next fifty years. Hitch would occasionally stray from the film's themes, but always

Above: *Filming* Rich and Strange.
Below: *Hitch directing* The Mountain Eagle. *Alma can be seen to the right.*

returned to a popular mix of avant-garde and conventional storytelling.

In addition to his film work, Hitchcock was quite active in two societies that would have major consequences for him. As a member of the influential Film Society, he saw the best of European and American cinema, pictures not usually shown commercially in Britain. The director admitted their profound effect on his work and how membership in the club, which also included Ivor Montagu, helped shape his career. His association with the Hate Club, a loose organization that discussed (often with some animosity), those elements of society which interfered with art and artistic cinema, was also of some importance—at the very least to perhaps explain his love/hate relationship with film critics. Hitchcock never liked them, but nevertheless recognized the power of creating what we now call *synergy*, using newspapers, radio, and eventually television to build audiences for films.

With timing that was distinctly Hitchcockian (in other words, just as he was on the brink of professional disaster), fortune spun around and

handed him *Blackmail*, promoted as Britain's first full-length talkie (although that claim is still disputed). Its historical importance aside, the film was remarkably good and furthermore a big box-office success, providing the fading Hitchcock with a new lease on life.

Blackmail was based on a popular stage play by Charles Bennett, whom Hitch met briefly but did not work with extensively on the film (for which Benn Levy wrote the dialogue). However, the success of *Blackmail* faded as Hitchcock, in a pattern that is repeated throughout his career, spent his recently acquired power and reputation on experimental and witty films which seldom appealed to the public at large. Nonetheless, the small pictures he directed between 1928 and 1933 are in many cases excellent. And Hitchcock's own public profile remained high, thanks to the articles he often contributed to film publications and the efforts of his personal publicity company, Hitchcock Baker Productions.

After a four-year run of fairly dismal reviews, Hitchcock accepted an offer from Michael Balcon to join him at his current studio, Gaumont-British. Hitch took with him a project he had been developing with Charles Bennett—a spy thriller, to be called *The Man Who Knew Too Much*.

Dan Auiler

THE PLEASURE GARDEN

First screening March 1926

Production company:
Gainsborough-Emelka GBA

Duration approximately 85 minutes

Black and white

Silent

Patsy Brand (Virginia Valli), a dancer in the chorus of The Pleasure Garden theater, befriends Jill Cheyne (Carmelita Geraghty), just up from the country, and helps her get work at the theater. Jill proves talented but ruthless, determined to be a star. Engaged to Hugh Fielding (John Stuart), who is about to go to Asia for two years, she invites the attentions of wealthy admirers who may help her, including a supposed Russian prince (C. Falkenburg). Meanwhile, Patsy meets Hugh's friend Levett (Miles Mander), who smooth-talks her into marrying him. They spend their honeymoon at Lake Como in Italy. Afterwards, both Levett and Hugh leave for the Tropics, where Levett begins living with a native girl (Nita Naldi). Patsy learns the truth about her husband when, hearing that he's ill with fever, she rushes to join him. Jill is about to marry the Russian, and refuses to help with the fare. Confronted, Levett becomes half-mad and drowns the native girl. Later, he lunges at Patsy with a scimitar, but is shot by the local doctor. Patsy finally finds love and consolation with Hugh, nursing him through an attack of fever and returning with him to London.

A good, offbeat melodrama, *The Pleasure Garden* pulses with life and sexuality that sometimes take odd forms. In one scene, Jill models a costume for her boss, Oscar Hamilton (the name echoes that of the legendary theatre manager Oscar Hammerstein, 1847–1919), and is fussed over by a butterfly-like male couturier who has been sitting alongside Hamilton on a sofa, with an arm around his shoulder. It's a pre-echo of Vandamm's chummy friendship with his male secretary Leonard, seen decades later in *North by Northwest*.

A German influence affects *The Pleasure Garden* in matters of both design and character detail—especially detail that's sometimes rather frank. Hitchcock had already worked in Germany alongside Graham Cutts on *The Blackguard*, and now he found himself back there directing his first solo feature, with fiancée Alma Reville assisting him. *The Blackguard* had been shot at UFA's Neubabelsberg studio in Berlin; *The Pleasure Garden* was filmed largely at the Emelka Studios, Munich, described by actor Miles Mander as "a miniature Universal City" located on a fifty-acre estate surrounded by forest.

The story, however, was by the prolific English novelist Mrs. Oliver Sandys, and it allowed Hitchcock to include much that would later become recognizable as the Hitchcock touch. The show business world of the opening scenes is lovingly detailed, literally and figuratively from all angles, right down to the symbolic moment when Jill first arrives at the stage door, to be promptly relieved of the con-

Patsy (Virginia Valli) and Levett (Miles Mander).

tents of her purse by one of the shady types loitering there. The theater's very name, The Pleasure Garden, suggests both the sensual delights it offers and the false Eden it represents—and which the film shows may be a microcosm of the world at large.

Just one or two moments are allowed to offer any glimpse of real tranquility, such as the sequence filmed on location at Lake Como, with its photography by Baron Ventigmilia, described by the trade paper *The Bioscope* as "enchanting." Here, Patsy, on her honeymoon, prays that her marriage may be a happy one—a prayer which goes unanswered, though she's given a second chance later. What the Catholic writer Father Neil Hurley has labelled Hitchcock's typical "open-ended pessimism" was thus already apparent in *The Pleasure Garden*.

The film's even-handed approach extends to its depiction of the two girls, one brunette and one blonde (but both played by top American actresses, as part of producer Michael Balcon's policy of maximizing box-office appeal). In an anticipation of the two male leads in *The Ring*, they propel each other to their respective destinies. Patsy is nicer, Jill has more God-given talent. Hitchcock simply tells their two stories, which are ultimately one story.

THE MOUNTAIN EAGLE

**First screening October 1926
(trade shows)**

**Production company:
Gainsborough-Emelka GBA**

**Duration approximately 89 minutes
(cut for the U.S.)**

Black and white

Silent

In a mountain village in Kentucky, Beatrice Brent (Nita Naldi), a schoolteacher, incurs the enmity of Pettigrew (Bernard Goetzke), the unpopular local storekeeper and Justice of the Peace. Pettigrew thinks that Beatrice has encouraged advances by his crippled son, Edward (John Hamilton), whom she's been giving evening lessons. However, when Pettigrew questions Beatrice, he senses her charm and attempts liberties, which she repels. Furious, he publicly accuses her of wantonness. Edward, who saw what took place, goes into hiding. The villagers drive Beatrice out, but fortunately she is saved from the mob's further anger by a handsome young man known as Fearogod (Malcolm Keen), who takes her to his remote cabin. Later, to end any scandal, he and Beatrice return to the village and compel Pettigrew to marry them (planning to get a divorce later, if necessary). Pettigrew is enraged by this new humiliation, especially when he recalls that he and Fearogod had once loved the same woman, who had died in giving birth to Edward. Taking advantage of his son's disappearance, Pettigrew goes to the cabin and arrests Fearogod on a trumped-up charge of murder. A year passes while Fearogod languishes in prison. Finally, he escapes and rejoins his wife, who by now has a baby. But at the height of winter the baby becomes ill. Fearogod carries it across the snow to the doctor in the village, then prepares for a showdown with Pettigrew. Some doubt as to which of the men is going to attack the other first is settled by an onlooker firing a gun, which wounds Pettigrew in the shoulder. The sudden return of Edward convinces the older man of the futility of pressing charges against Fearogod. Instead, the two long-time rivals shake hands.

This synopsis, based on one in *The Bioscope*, is about all we know of the plot of *The Mountain Eagle*. All prints of the film have disappeared, and the passage in the English version of Truffaut's *Hitchcock*, in which Truffaut says, "I have the scenario here," is sadly misleading. The original French reads, "J'ai là un résumé du scénario"—a mere synopsis again. No script was found in Hitchcock's papers. What did turn up were some thirty stills, which can certainly help to tell us what the film was like.

For example, the first of a pair of stills shows Fearogod and Beatrice in his log cabin: they are smiling and she is winding lengths of woollen yarn around his held-out arms. The next still is practically identical—except that the smiles have gone and Fearogod's arms are now held rather higher because someone is snapping handcuffs on his wrists. Ironic transitions like this would become a feature of Hitchcock's films. There are several in *North by Northwest*, such as the moment when a man's gasp of apparent recognition at a photograph proves to be caused by the knife embedded in his back.

The Mountain Eagle was the second of the two films that Hitchcock and Michael Balcon made together in Germany, and was partly shot on location in the Tyrol. The nominal Kentucky setting, and the use again of international stars (Nita Naldi from America, Bernard Goetzke from Germany, Malcolm Keen from Britain) helped get the film what limited distribution it had. Despite records of press previews in Britain, it's unclear whether it was ever publicly shown there. Nonetheless, the film was favorably mentioned in *Modern*, February 19, 1927, as "one of the finest pictures of the year." On the other hand, when it was released in Germany under the title *Der Bergadler*, the *Reichsfilmblatt* referred to its "some-times arduously constructed" script and "dragging" direction.

As already indicated, *The Mountain Eagle* did foreshadow Hitchcock ingredients to come—including the trial marriages of *Secret Agent* and *Spellbound* and the showdown of rivals that was the intended ending of *Topaz*. But perhaps the film that it most anticipated wasn't one by Hitchcock at all: Delmer Daves's darkly psychological melodrama, *The Red House* (1947), likewise set in the American backwoods.

Left: *Alma Reville prepares Bernard Goetzke for a take.*
Right: *Beatrice (Nita Naldi) and Fearogod (Malcolm Keen).*

THE LODGER: A STORY OF THE LONDON FOG

First screening September 1926

Production company: Gainsborough Pictures

Duration approximately 100 minutes

Black and white

Silent

On the Thames Embankment in London a young woman lies dead. She is the seventh victim of a serial killer known as "The Avenger", who kills only blonde girls and always on Tuesday nights. The whole of London is soon agog over this latest news. Two people following the case with special interest are Mr. and Mrs. Bunting of the West End. Their daughter Daisy (played by "June") is herself a blonde, a model, currently stepping out with Joe (Malcolm Keen), a police detective. One evening, a gentlemanly stranger (Ivor Novello) arrives at the Buntings' front door and indicates the Room to Let sign. The Buntings receive him gladly for they need the money. But in the ensuing days their satisfaction turns to anxiety. The Lodger's strange ways, and Daisy's increasing friendliness towards him, worry her parents. Could he possibly be The Avenger? The jealous Joe thinks so, and arrests him on suspicion, but The Lodger escapes. Later that night, The Lodger is pursued by a mob, only to be saved by the arrival of Joe, who has just heard that the real Avenger has been caught red-handed. Daisy and The Lodger marry.

The Lodger comes from Mrs. Belloc Lowndes's best-selling 1913 novel based on the Jack the Ripper case. In view of how the Ripper's brutal murders had shocked and enthralled Londoners in 1888, it's fitting that Hitchcock's film begins with a lengthy sequence showing the reaction of present-day Londoners to The Avenger's crimes. The people in the film treat the news of the killings with a mixture of frenzied concern, jocularity, and business-as-usual aplomb—but not indifference. It's as if the city has taken out an extra lease on life. Indeed, well before the end of the film, London becomes a

major character. Something that helps establish this is the visual gag that Hitchcock later described to Truffaut, in which the back windows of a careering London news van appear like two rolling eyes. In turn, there's a faint suggestion that those eyes are mirroring our own—that the city *is* the viewer. That idea provides another reminder of the influence of German Expressionism on Hitchcock.

Hitchcock had just returned from Germany. As he happily set about filming the city where he was born and grew up

(and where he had explored every major bus route by the time he was ten), he was literally in his element. The Gainsborough Studios themselves were located in north London, in an old power station in Islington. Here Graham Cutts had recently directed one of his biggest successes, *The Rat*, starring the glamorous Welsh actor, playwright, and songwriter, Ivor Novello. Now Novello brought his rather boyish good looks, and limited acting skills, to what its director would later call "the first true Hitchcock film."

In Hitchcock's phrase, it's a film with lots of psychology. To begin with, the general vitality stimulates us, alerts us to possibilities (as in the beginning of *Psycho*). Freud might have called this the arousing of the viewer's psychic energy. Such a notion would have been timely. In 1926, Freud's influence was just reaching the London stage in a new play called *The Lash*, in which a forgotten childhood trauma proves to hold the solution to a present-day mystery.

Further, *The Lodger* has an explanatory flashback of its own. Based on a passage in the novel that suggests The Avenger is a Jekyll-and-Hyde figure, it shows The Lodger dancing with his blonde sister at her coming-out ball. Ostensibly the flashback clears The Lodger of his sister's murder, but on closer examination it carries the opposite possibility. At the very least, it implies a brother-sister complex of juicy ripeness!

Daisy's attraction to The Lodger adds another psychological element. When Joe remarks of the new tenant, "I'm glad he's not one for the girls!" a close-up of Daisy shows that her interest in The Lodger has only been more aroused. It seems she wants to mother him. It was an attribute that Hitchcock would often give his heroines thereafter, even having Emily in *Rich and Strange* say, "A wife is more than half a mother!"

But all this psychology was one reason *The Lodger*'s producers felt uneasy, initially shelving the film for two months, before calling on a young film critic and producer, Ivor Montagu, to re-edit it. Montagu was tremendously impressed by what he saw but felt that the film was too wordy. He reduced the number of captions from around 400 to eighty, and had Hitchcock shoot some re-takes. Then he asked the painter and poster-artist E. McKnight Kauffer to design the credits and the caption backgrounds. Some of these show an influence of the new art deco movement, but they are always skillfully integrated with the film's own motifs. (Montagu continued his association with Hitchcock during the next two pictures and later, in the thirties.)

Though the distributors still felt that the Germanic look of the film told against it, *The Lodger* was finally released—to immediate acclaim. *The Bioscope* raved: "It is possible that this film is the finest British production ever made. . . . The tempo of the whole film has seldom been

Previous Page (Bottom Left): *The original novel was reissued with a "tie-in" cover.*
Previous Page (Right): *The Lodger (Ivor Novello) with Daisy ("June").*

Above: *The mysterious Lodger. Hitchcock had to change his originally ambiguous ending once star Ivor Novello was cast in the role.*
Left: *A signed portrait of Ivor Novello, who also appeared in the first of the film's three remakes in 1932.*

equalled . . . Mr. Hitchcock builds up his evidence against the lodger relentlessly and logically. It is a directorial triumph." *The Lodger* was the box office success of 1926.

Certainly the thriller form was a natural for the screen. The film's most intimate moment comes when Daisy is taking a bath, and The Lodger calls her to the locked door. As they whisper together, the scene plays like a furtive love scene with only the door separating the pair, one of whom we're aware is naked beneath her towel. A further tease is the build-up to this moment, which has implied that The Lodger has murderous intentions!

Thus a key to *The Lodger* is its ambiguity. At the climax, word comes that the killer has been captured elsewhere. Since the real Ripper murders were known to have provoked copycat killings, Hitchcock's original audiences may easily have felt some doubt as to The Lodger's innocence. In fact, there's an exactly matching moment in *Shadow of a Doubt* which shows conclusively that its police have been hoodwinked. Incidentally, the three times (to date) *The Lodger* has been remade the producers have on each occasion followed the original novel and shown The Lodger to be guilty.

DOWNHILL

American title:
When Boys Leave Home

First screening May 1927

Production company:
Gainsborough Pictures

Duration approximately 105 minutes

Black and white

Silent

Roddy Berwick (Ivor Novello) scores the winning try in an important rugby match at his private school. Later he's made School Captain. But his delight is short-lived, for a local waitress accuses him of misconduct. Out of loyalty to his friend, Tim Wakely (Robin Irvine), Roddy doesn't deny the charge, and is expelled. Worse, his father, Sir Thomas Berwick (Norman McKinnel), thinks he must be guilty—so Roddy leaves home. He finds work as a minor actor in a theater. Things look up when he inherits £30,000 and successfully woos and marries the leading actress (Isabel Jeans). But secretly she keeps up an affair with her leading man (Ian Hunter), and when Roddy's money runs out, discards him. Next he works in a Paris music hall as a gigolo, but quits in disgust. Finally, he ends up delirious in a dockside room in Marseilles. Some sailors take pity on him and ship him back to London. He cuts a shabby figure on arriving home. Meanwhile, his father has learned the truth about the waitress's accusation, and joyfully welcomes his son's return. In an Old Boys' (old-timers') rugby match, Roddy scores another try.

"Down, down, down, until I could go no further down," Ingrid Bergman cries in *Under Capricorn*, a film which also hinges on the consequences of someone taking the blame for the misdeed of another. But whereas *Under Capricorn* puts its romantic emphasis on the theme of sacrifice, *Downhill* questions the very nature of reality, and shows it to be a matter of worlds within worlds. *Downhill* has three parts, called respectively The World of Youth, The World of Make-Believe, and The World of Lost Illusions. The story may be slight, but Hitchcock made the most of it.

It began as a play by "David L'Estrange" (pseudonym of Ivor Novello and actress Constance Collier), whose previous success had been the play and film, *The Rat*. Hitchcock and regular scriptwriter Eliot Stannard made cuts and other changes. In the stage performance, which had a short run in the West End and longer in the provinces, Novello thrilled his fans by washing his legs after the rugby match. "The scent of good honest soap crosses the footlights," wrote an appreciative James Agate. Hitchcock couldn't manage that, but he did include a shot of Novello naked from the waist up. Later, in both *The Ring* and *The Manxman*, he remembered to include similar shots of a robust Carl Brisson.

Several sequences play with the worlds-within-worlds idea. The Paris music hall is managed by someone whom a caption calls "Madame, La Patronne, expert in human nature"—which suggests the sordid reality beneath all illusions. Aspects of the sequence prefigure the

Julia (Isabel Jeans, right; with Hannah Jones).

Stork Club scenes in *The Wrong Man*. The main idea—that mortality is everywhere, however we deny it—was conveyed by having harsh sunlight break in on the hall's patrons after a night of abandon. (One gentleman has just had a seizure.) In a taut foreshadowing, Hitchcock had earlier shown the front of the hall by night and by day—first alluring, then drab.

But the most brilliant scene is the one in which we first see Roddy starting on his new life after leaving home. In close-up he looks reasonably cheerful in evening dress, but then we realize that he's a waiter. The couple at the table now get up and move onto the dance floor. Roddy pockets something from the table before he too joins a line of the dancers. As the camera continues panning, we grasp that the whole scene represents a musical review taking place on a theater stage. Of course, the master touch is the cigarette case that Roddy pockets. It apparently belongs to the show's leading lady, whom Roddy later visits in her dressing room. Was leaving it behind, we wonder, part of the show's script? An accident? Or something else again?

One trade review of *Downhill* noted: "Selling angle: the name of Hitchcock."

C.M. WOOLF and MICHAEL BALCON
present
IVOR NOVELLO
in
"DOWNHILL"
with
ISABEL JEANS
A Gainsborough Picture Directed by Alfred Hitc...

EASY VIRTUE

First screening August 1927

Production company:
Gainsborough Pictures

Duration approximately 105 minutes

Black and white

Silent

Larita Filton (Isabel Jeans), wife of an habitual drunkard, gains notoriety following an encounter in the studio of a young portrait painter, who takes pity on her and kisses her. When the husband discovers them together, the artist commits suicide, leaving Larita money in his will. Consequently, the husband easily obtains a divorce on the grounds of his wife's misconduct. Larita leaves for the Mediterranean, where she meets John Whittaker (Robin Irvine), the son of a wealthy English family, who is attracted to her. Without knowing anything of her past life, he proposes and is accepted. The newly married couple return to England to live with John's parents and his two sisters in their ancestral country mansion. But the elder Mrs. Whittaker (Violet Farebrother) is resentful—she had intended a different bride, Sarah (Enid Stamp Taylor), for her son. Larita begins to feel estranged. When she appeals to John to take her back to the South of France, he is distant. Then Mrs. Whittaker discovers old photos of Larita in The Tatler, *thereby learning of her notoriety, and it's only a matter of time before a new divorce case is headed for court.*

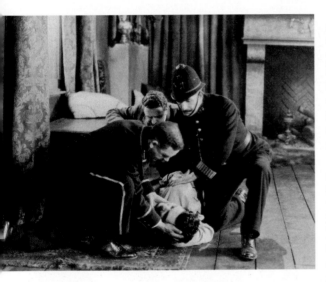

Hitchcock said that his film *Rebecca* owed much to the play *His House in Order* (1906), by Sir Arthur Wing Pinero. Drama critic Benedict Nightingale has suggested the same ancestor for Noël Coward's play *Easy Virtue* (1925). "But," he adds, "Coward is more contemptuous of the smugness, insularity, and hypocrisy of the 'respectable' people than Pinero dared be." In filming *Easy Virtue*, Hitchcock introduced into his work an occasional criticism of the upper classes that would continue to inform his films up to *Marnie* and beyond.

Only once do we see Larita find any happiness, and that is on what the film pointedly calls "the tolerant shores of the Mediterranean." This brief interlude begins beside a tennis court—a less stressful court than the one Larita has just come from—and is one of successive scenes emphasizing the sunlight and airi-

ness of the Corniche region. Claude McDonnell's photography of these scenes rivals Baron Ventigmilia's views of Lake Como in *The Pleasure Garden*. (Ventigmilia photographed Hitchcock's first three films; McDonnell shot the next two.)

By contrast, the courtroom scenes that begin and end the film are gloomy and austere, while the ancestral Whittaker home known as "Moat House" is positively sepulchral in the scene where the family sits down to dinner beneath murals of gaunt-looking saints. Neither the Whittakers nor society at large shows much saintliness. A large woman on the jury at the first divorce proceedings hears evidence of the artist's feelings towards Larita, and writes on a pad: "Pity is akin to love." Momentarily, we suppose she's sympathetic to Larita, but ultimately she presses her fellow jurors for a verdict of misconduct. This ungenerous woman leads in turn to the elder Mrs. Whittaker, the first of Hitchcock's many formidable mother-figures. A monster of social prejudice, who wears sleeveless gowns that draw attention to her muscular arms, Mrs. Whittaker simply can't understand the more humane attitude of

someone like Sarah, whom John was supposed to marry. Sarah attempts to reconcile Larita with her husband. She tells Mrs. Whittaker, "I feel terribly sorry for both of them." For this shot, Hitchcock places Sarah above Mrs. Whittaker. He makes a further comment later when Larita, preparing to go away for good, kisses Sarah and says that she should have been the one to marry the feckless John. The kiss suggests Hitchcock's belief in a free-flowing Eros as the surest means of keeping us all human.

The Bioscope wrote: "In spite of an excellent performance by Isabel Jeans, and Hitchcock's always-apparent resourcefulness and occasional brilliance, this was not one of his more effective films." But that verdict, too, seems ungenerous today.

Above Left: *The artist (Eric Bransby Williams) is found to have committed suicide, in a scene censored from existing prints of the film.*
Below: *Larita (Isabel Jeans) and John (Robin Irvine).*

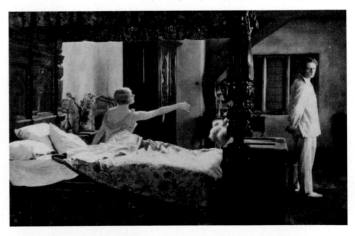

THE RING

First screening October 1927

**Production company:
British International Pictures (BIP)**

Duration approximately 110 minutes

Black and white

Silent

"One Round" Jack Sander (Carl Brisson) is a young boxer in a circus sideshow booth. His sweetheart Mabel (Lilian Hall-Davis) sells the tickets out front. Hearing of Jack's prowess, a boxing promoter visits the booth with his champion, Bob Corby (Ian Hunter). Not knowing who Bob is, Mabel invites him to go a round with Jack. For the first time ever, Jack is defeated. Bob feels attracted to Mabel, and secretly gives her an arm bangle. However, when the promoter offers to make Jack the champion's sparring partner, the way is open for Jack and Mabel to marry. An uneasy three-way relationship follows. Jack and Bob remain sparring partners, but it becomes an open secret that Mabel is having an affair with the champion. Meanwhile, Jack's own career advances. After he and Mabel quarrel, and she walks out on him, he confronts Bob at a nightclub and demands satisfaction in the ring. The big fight duly takes place at a packed Albert Hall. Mabel watches nervously. Eventually, with the fight going against Jack, she whispers to him her support. He rallies and wins on a KO. Later, a discarded bangle is found at the ringside.

A misconception has it that Hitchcock wasn't interested in documentary detail. A careful look at any of his silent films, and several of the later ones, dispels that notion. In particular, the first reel of each of the silent pictures is typically a triumph of sustained scene-setting. *The Ring* opens with atmospheric shots of a drum being beaten, roundabouts whirling, a girl shrieking on a swing—shots with a documentary impact that might have made John Grierson, a distinguished British documentarian, proud.

And impact *The Ring* as a whole certainly has. This is not simply a matter of its boxing subject—about which Hitchcock was knowledgeable, being a regular attendee at prize fights—nor just of the remarkable original screenplay he'd written himself, but also of the contributions made by practically everyone involved. Working for a new company, British International Pictures, in its studios at Elstree in Hertfordshire, Hitchcock was back in top form.

Photography was by Jack Cox, who would work with Hitchcock for the next five years (and rejoin him briefly on *The Lady Vanishes* in 1938). He was equal to all of the director's demands, including use of the new Schüfftan process, with its ingenious combining of real and mirror images. Supervised by art director C. W. Arnold, this technique allowed hard-to-get shots, like those in the Albert Hall sequence showing tiers of balconies emerg-

Above: *"One Round" Jack Sander (Carl Brisson) is flanked by his trainer (Gordon Harker, left) and the circus showman (Harry Terry, right).*
Left: *Hitchcock considered Harker "a brilliant character actor."*

GORDON HARKER

ing from darkness. The still-shot of the Albert Hall auditorium that's behind the opening titles employs a different effect, that of *Stimmung*, mood achieved by means of lighting. The distant, lit-up boxing ring surrounded by unseen watchers has intimations of destiny.

One reason the film works so well as a treatment of that idea is that it represents a classic *crucible* situation—defined by novelist Sol Stein as "an emotional or physical environment that bonds two people [who] won't declare a truce." The crucible here is the closed world of boxing or, rather, the respective worlds of the circus boxing troupe and championship boxing, which are all these people know. Emphasizing the closure effect, but also commenting on it, Hitchcock added layers of symbolism, punning on both *ring* and *round*.

The circular Albert Hall of the film's climax may be far removed from the boxing tent (and circus ring) of the opening scenes—but in another way both worlds reflect each other. Certainly, to the boxers themselves, it's all one. At a party in Jack's London flat, where the champagne has flowed freely, two girls do a wild dance then retire to their respective corners and are revived by their seconds. At a nightclub, Jack and Bob come to blows and Bob appears to be "counted out" by the slide of a trombone being played nearby. However, at the Albert Hall, champagne is poured over the boxers' heads to spur them on.

The film shows various bonds being forged. One type of bonding is represented by the wedding ring that Jack puts on Mabel's finger, another by the snake-like bangle that Bob had earlier given her— the latter effectively a symbol of original sin. (Related snake imagery occurs in *The Pleasure Garden* and *The Paradine Case*.) But Hitchcock appears to bear no malice towards the worldly Bob. During the title-fight, Bob is depicted as the total professional—at one point, he helps Jack to his feet after the bell. When the fight ends, Bob gives Mabel a wry smile and nods acknowledgment of his (double) defeat.

One feels that Hitchcock loves these characters. Mabel is played by the delightful Lilian Hall-Davis. Importantly, not only does her erring character repent her misdemeanors, but her previous flightiness may be seen to have set the various events in motion, thus propelling her husband to the heavyweight crown.

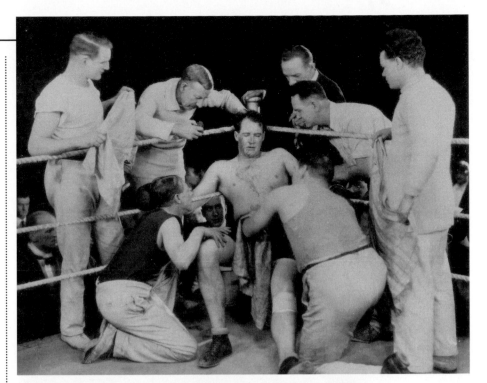

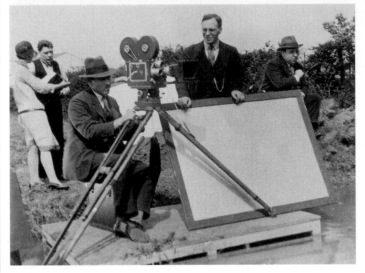

Top: Bob Corby (Ian Hunter) during the climactic fight.
Left: Hitchcock (far right) on location. Jack Cox is seated behind the camera.

Danish actor and trained boxer Carl Brisson seems thoroughly to understand the part of Jack, who must endure a long humiliation before his eventual triumph. And, as Bob Corby, Ian Hunter is splendid. Corby, who seems to be based on Australian boxer Les Darcy (1895–1917), is a go-getter, a bit of a rogue, perhaps a lost soul—but someone the viewer always respects. There's also a fine comic performance by Gordon Harker (in his film debut) as Jack's trainer.

In the final analysis, the greatness of *The Ring* is a cumulative matter. Individual details are striking enough— the fight referee who looks like the conductor Toscanini, for example—but in addition there's a broader sense of life. To Truffaut, Hitchcock mentioned a key

image: a billboard featuring the rise of "One Round" Jack from minor fighter to championship contender. As the seasons pass, the boxer's name, in bigger and bigger letters, rises to the top of the display. Meanwhile, trees blossom in spring, snow falls in winter. It's this imagery of the passing seasons that is so important. Hitchcock said he took great care over it.

The film was a success with the critics but not at the box office. The *Evening Standard* reviewer must have overestimated audiences of the time, writing that *The Ring* "succeeds in . . . being the purest film art and a fine popular entertainment." The *Daily Herald* reviewer thought the film "challenges comparison with the best that America can produce."

BEHIND THE SCENES COLLABORATORS

Above: Jack Cox behind the camera on the set of Champagne.
Below: British producer Michael Balcon.

Right from the start of his career, Hitchcock had every intention of making his personal mark. "Actors come and go," he remarked in 1925, within weeks of directing his first film, "but the name of the director should stay clearly in the mind of the audience." He succeeded so well that during his lifetime—and perhaps even still today—Hitchcock became the best-known movie director in the world. No filmmaker has gained more from the auteur theory: a Hitchcock film is widely taken as being entirely his achievement, an impression Hitch did little to contradict.

Nonetheless, Hitchcock owed a lot to his collaborators, as he well knew; he chose them carefully and, in many cases, kept them for film after film. In the latter part of his career, Hitchcock's status within the industry allowed him to build up a regular team, not only ensuring a consistent standard of work, but supplying the reassuring sense of familiarity that his nervous temperament craved. These trusted colleagues included editor George Tomasini, cinematographer Robert Burks, assistant director (later associate producer) Herbert Coleman, title designer Saul Bass, and composer Bernard Herrmann. Most or all of them worked on the great run of mid- to late fifties Hitchcock masterpieces that included *Rear Window*, *Vertigo*, and *North by Northwest*. By the time *Torn Curtain* was screened, the team had broken up, through death or dispersal, and it's noticeable that from then on the quality of Hitchcock's films declined.

Robert Burks, who worked on every Hitchcock film (with the notable excep-tion of *Psycho*) from *Strangers on a Train* to *Marnie*, was perhaps his most signifi-cant collaborator during this period. Hitchcock could be extremely demand-ing; according to the screenwriter John Michael Hayes, Burks "gave Hitchcock marvelous ideas" but also "had a very tense time. . . . By the end of each picture [he] was emotionally worn out." A supremely versatile technician, Burks's range could encompass both the sunny, glossy look of *To Catch a Thief* (for which he won an Oscar) and the dark, moody realism of *The Wrong Man*; the subtle monochrome of *Strangers on a Train* and the saturated surrealism of *Vertigo* and *Marnie*. The one film Burks didn't work on was *Psycho*. Setting out to shoot fast and economically, television-style, Hitchcock evidently felt Burks' craftsmanlike approach would take too long, and brought in his regular television cinematographer, John L. Russell.

Hitchcock did retain his then regular editor on *Psycho*: George Tomasini, whose virtuoso cutting of the famous shower sequence (seventy shots in forty-five seconds) is a justly celebrated *tour de force*. Credit should also go to Saul Bass, who storyboarded the sequence. Bass was also responsible for the stark, dynamic titles that brilliantly set the mood of the film (as did his titles for *Vertigo* and *North by Northwest*). The other memo-rable contribution to *Psycho* was of course Bernard Herrmann's jagged strings-only score. (Ironically, Hitchcock had planned for the shower scene, ulti-mately accompanied by the best-remem-bered section of the score, to be without music until he heard Herrmann's treat-ment of it.) The finest of Hitchcock's musical collaborators, Herrmann worked on eight of his films. As versatile as Burks, he could switch from the cynical geniality of *The Trouble With Harry* to the brood-ing desolation of *Vertigo*, in each case cre-ating a strikingly original sound.

Hitchcock, as his regular screenwriter of the thirties Charles Bennett noted, "had a monstrous ego that matched his appetite," and preferred collaborators who didn't compete with him. The associ-ation with Herrmann, who never lacked ego himself, ended in a clash over *Torn Curtain*. It was a sad rift: though Hitchcock worked with other fine film composers—Franz Waxman, Dimitri Tiomkin, Miklos Rozsa and (at Gaumont) the workmanlike Louis Levy—

none shared his pessimistic, oneiric vision as fully as Herrmann.

Of Hitchcock's collaborators on his British films, the most significant (besides the writers) were Ivor Montagu and the cinematographers Jack Cox and Bernard Knowles. Knowles photographed four of Hitchcock's Gaumont thrillers, lending them a strong sense of location and often grimy reality. Cox, whose sensitive eye for landscape redeemed the otherwise dull *The Manxman*, brought his subtle framing and lighting to all of Hitchcock's films for BIP (bar *Elstree Calling*), and was reunited with Hitch for the finest of his thirties films, *The Lady Vanishes*. After his tactful editing had saved *The Lodger* and helped launch Hitchcock's reputation, Ivor Montagu joined the director again in the thirties as associate producer.

As with *The Lodger*, part of Montagu's job was, as he put it, "to act as cushion between company and creator," in particular protecting Hitch against the enmity of the powerful distributor, C. M. Woolf.

Throughout his career, Hitchcock relied on a succession of helpers, usually women, to act as a combination of personal assistant, associate producer, secretary, moral support, and protective buffer against the world. Chief of these was his wife, Alma Reville, assistant director and continuity girl on his directorial debut, *The Pleasure Garden*. Subsequently, Alma often took joint script credit, and even after she ceased to do so in 1950 she remained in the background as a sounding board and final arbiter. Joan Harrison joined Hitchcock in 1934, accompanied him to America, and later produced many of his television shows. Starting out with Hitchcock as second unit director in the early fifties, Herbert Coleman graduated to working closely with Hitch as associate producer, often making key casting decisions. When he left, Peggy Robertson took over; she and Hitchcock's personal secretary, Suzanne Gauthier, made it their job to weave a protective cocoon around the director, shielding him from irritation and anxiety.

Lastly, a mention must go to the two producers who each had a strong influence on Hitchcock's career. Michael Balcon gave Hitch his initial break as a director at Gainsborough, championed him against hostile elements within the company, and a few years later launched him on his first great period at Gaumont-British. Recognizing Hitchcock's expertise, Balcon sensibly left him alone to get on with his job, rarely intervening unless invited. By contrast, David O. Selznick interfered constantly, and Hitchcock was relieved when their association ceased after *The Paradine Case*. But it was Selznick who brought Hitchcock to America, providing him with the base to become established as a director in Hollywood. From 1950 onwards, Hitchcock was able to rely on his ideal producer: himself.

Philip Kemp

Above left: Producer David O. Selznick in discussion with Hitch.
Above right: Composer Bernard Herrmann and Hitchcock clown for the camera.
Left: Robert Burks (standing next to a seated Hitchcock) at work on the remake of The Man Who Knew Too Much.

THE MANXMAN

First screening January 1928

Production company:
British International Pictures (BIP)

Duration approximately 100 minutes

Black and white

Silent

The Isle of Man. Fisherman Pete Quilliam (Carl Brisson) arrives back in port to be greeted by his friend since boyhood, lawyer Philip Christian (Malcolm Keen). Both men admire Kate Cregeen (Anny Ondra), daughter of old Caesar (Randle Ayrton), the village pub owner. But Caesar glowers at Pete because of his poverty, making him realize that his present chances of marrying Kate are slim. He vows to go abroad and seek his fortune. Extracting from Kate a promise to wait for him, he asks Philip to watch over her. Time passes, then news comes that Pete has been killed in South Africa. Kate and Philip begin an affair. When Pete returns, very much alive, he suspects nothing. Pete and Kate marry, but the child she soon bears is Philip's—though Pete thinks it his. Unable to keep up the deception, Kate tries to drown herself. For this offense, she is brought before Philip, newly appointed Deemster (judge). But Caesar, who knows the truth, publicly denounces Philip. The latter resigns office to depart with the woman he loves and their baby. Pete returns to the fishing fleet.

Three men, runs a well-know Hindu parable, were asked to describe an elephant in the dark. One, touching its trunk, said "this animal is like a water pipe;" another, touching its ear, said, "this animal is like a fan;" a third, touching its legs, described the animal as a pillar. *The Manxman* opens with a shot of the triskele (three-legged) symbol of the isle of Man, and proceeds to tell a story that perfectly illustrates how none if its three main characters sees—at least until too late—the whole truth. The gaze of each

has been clouded by worldy ambition.

Unfortunately, to make a popular film of Sir Hall Caine's best-selling novel (1894) was, by 1928, likely to present problems, especially for a progressive director like Hitchcock. The basic story, from Tennyson's narrative poem *Enoch Arden* (1864), had been around too long. A film of the novel had appeared in 1916, and there had been two cinema versions of *Enoch Arden* made by D. W. Griffith back in 1910 and 1911, and another version made in 1915. So when BIP's John

Maxwell insisted despite everything that the film go ahead, Hitchcock may well have wondered, what could a new *Manxman* hope to achieve? The story was without humor, if not totally hackneyed. The fact is that during the making of the film, Hitch showed signs of being bored.

Nevertheless, Eliot Stannard had fashioned a credible screenplay along the somewhat philosophical lines indicated previously, with several strong scenes. The director had brought Stannard with him from Gainsborough, no doubt appreciating both his professionalism and his prowess as talker and drinking companion. Nor could Hitch complain about his film's cast, which in addition to Malcolm Keen starring in his third Hitchcock film, and Carl Brisson in his second, included the beautiful Anny Ondra, a German-Czech. This lively, cheerful girl (who returned to Germany when sound arrived) was about to become the prototypical Hitchcock screen blonde. Both Hitch and Alma found her captivating.

It is a charming scene in the film, with Kate in her little girl's dress waving in dappled sunlight to the approaching Philip. *Faux naif* on Hitchcock's part, of course, but effective. Yet the

Left: *A little "local color." Malcolm Keen and Carl Brisson can be seen standing next to each other at the front of the crowd in this location shot.*

Caine passage may give the best clue to Hitch's lack of engagement with his film. The characters in *The Manxman* do indeed often seem like children and none of them are greatly sympathetic to an audience. Pete is a Holy Fool; Kate and Philip are often like puppets of their collective and individual fates.

The story makes a point of showing how each character's worldly ambition is, partly at least, imposed from without. Though Kate promises Pete that she'll wait for him, it's clear that her father's influence draws her to Philip with his prospects of status and wealth. Philip is driven by an ambitious spinster aunt. Pete's poverty, which goads him to make his fortune abroad, is shown to stem from the inroads into the fishing fleet's catch made by foreign trawlers.

There is much that is sophisticated about *The Manxman*. Nonetheless, the presentation almost by that very fact is phony, and at times too cut-and-dried. It was not a success with the public when it received a belated general release in January 1930. It certainly has its defenders—Charles Barr calls it "one of the finest of all [Hitchcock's] films"—but the jury remains out.

Left: *The triangular relationship: Carl Brisson, Malcolm Keen, and Anny Ondra.*

Below: *A romance develops between the Manxman Pete Quilliam (Carl Brisson) and Kate Cregeen (Anny Ondra).*

THE FARMER'S WIFE

First screening March 1928

Production company:
British International Pictures (BIP)

Duration approximately 100 minutes

Black and white

Silent

The young wife of Farmer Sweetland (Jameson Thomas) is dying. Her last words, whispered to the housekeeper Araminta Dench (Lilian Hall-Davis), are, "Don't forget to air your master's pants." Time passes, and Sweetland's daughter marries. Araminta, efficient as always, oversees the wedding breakfast and dispenses presents to the guests. Afterwards, Sweetland confides to her his intention of re-marrying, and asks her to help him draw up a list of candidates. Four names go on it. Sweetland thinks that the first candidate, Louisa Windeat (Louise Pounds), will "come like a lamb to the slaughter," but is rebuffed when the widow sternly tells him that she values her independence. The same general result follows his proposals to various spinsters: the prim Thirza Tapper (Maud Gill), the simpering postmistress Mary Hearn (Olga Slade), and the buxom barmaid Mercy Bassett (Antonia Borough). At first Sweetland is angry, then despairing. Ultimately, he sees that his own enchanting Araminta, who has served him so well, is the one he should have thought of first. His glum handyman, Churdles Ash (Gordon Harker), appears to agree, saying, "The next best thing to no wife is a good one."

As is so often in Hitchcock's films, life and sexuality are the subject matter of *The Farmer's Wife*, in which rural images carry a voluptuous charge. Sweetland's elderly neighbor Coaker speaks of pulling turnips, "as round and white as a woman's bosom." The intention of the filmmakers is less prurient than it is to share a matter of profound importance, to let the viewer "enter in" (as the housekeeper Araminta's phrase has it). The film is an antecedent of the equally sagacious *The Trouble With Harry*.

Born in India, writer Eden Phillpotts spent an important part of his long life in Devon, the setting of his novel *Widdicombe Fair* (1913) which he and his daughter adapted for the stage as *The Farmer's Wife* (1916; revised 1924). For a time, the play held the record for the longest run in London, a record now held by Agatha Christie's thriller *The Mousetrap*. That seems apt, not just because Christie herself was a Devonian, but because *The Farmer's Wife* has the loose-seeming shape of a typical Christie detective story, with its alarums and excursions and final disclosure. Indeed, the two centerpieces of *The Farmer's Wife* are a wedding breakfast and a tea party whose main plot function is to let us get to know the women on Sweetland's list of candidates, or suspects.

As the bachelor

Left: Cast and crew of The Farmer's Wife *break for tea. Gordon Harker (as Churdles Ash) is in the deckchair.*

Below: Farmer Sweetland (Jameson Thomas) with Araminta Dench (Lilian Hall-Davies). According to Hitch, Davies "had an [unfounded] acute inferiority complex in regard to her ability to play certain parts."

farmhand Churdles Ash, comic actor Gordon Harker gave one of his best performances. Hitchcock had originally spotted him in an Edgar Wallace play, then cast him as Jack's trainer in *The Ring*. Churdles's unsociable outlook parodies what Sweetland must overcome in himself before, "humble as a worm," he proposes to the patient Araminta. At Thirza Tapper's tea afternoon, Churdles's main job is to announce the arriving guests—but at one point he takes time out to sample the refreshments. First he drinks his tea from a saucer, tilting his head well back to avoid waste. Then, just as thoughtfully, he shakes the saucer dry on the carpet before he starts in on a plate of cakes.

However, a flustered Thirza arrives, and orders, "Fruit, in the garden!" Churdles rises grumpily, one hand holding up his trousers that have refused to stay fastened.

In a nice touch, Churdles figures also in the moment when Sweetland finally loses his complacency. Returning from Mercy Bassett, the farmer peers through his parlor window and overhears Churdles say that the master will throw a tantrum if he's had another rebuff. Now Sweetland checks both his ire and his willfulness: "I be tamed to hearing no," he prefaces his proposal to Araminta. For her part, she is immediately, and delightfully, transfigured as she dons the party frock given her by the previous wife.

The Farmer's Wife was sufficiently well received to be remade as a sound film in 1940.

CHAMPAGNE

First screening August 1928

**Production company:
British International Pictures (BIP)**

Duration approximately 104 minutes

Black and white

Silent

New York. When her millionaire Father (Gordon Harker) frowns on her affair with The Boy (Jean Bradin), The Girl (Betty Balfour) simply borrows one of her Father's airplanes and rejoins her lover at sea (he is on a liner, sailing for Europe), crash-landing the plane in the process. Soon The Boy proposes, but bad weather on the rest of the trip forces him to stay in his cabin. The Girl reports that she's arranged with the captain to marry them, but The Boy expostulates, "You've arranged—don't I arrange anything?" This and later events are observed by The Man (Theo von Alten), a mysterious stranger whom The Girl first meets in the ship's lounge. On arriving in Paris, the lovers, still at odds, separate for a time. More bad news is brought by The Father in person—he is bankrupt. The Girl, who is good natured (if rather spoiled), goes to work as a flower girl in a cabaret. But when her Father eventually admits that he isn't bankrupt at all, and has only been testing her, the chastened Girl is reunited with The Boy, who has come seeking her.

The most interesting character in *Champagne* may be The Man. Introduced by a subjective shot through the bottom of an upended champagne glass, he turns out to be not the Vile Seducer we might suppose but someone paid by the millionaire to keep watch on his daughter. Even when this is disclosed at the end, The Man continues his watching. Again he upends a champagne glass, and through it he observes The Girl and her fiancée embracing. Clearly The Man is also a surrogate for the audience.

What, then, does he know? What do *we* know? The necessarily equivocal answer is that none of us is quite sure, though we may fantasize. The theme of *Champagne* is what the critic Robin Wood euphemistically calls Order versus Chaos. In the cabaret, with its art deco friezes and pillars, The Man tells The Girl, "anything could happen to you in a

Left: *The Girl (Betty Balfour) encounters some disreputable characters as she searches for work in Paris.*

Below: *Betty Balfour in an apt publicity shot.*

place like this"—and the recurring shot of the champagne glass briefly returns. Then, The Man appears to escort The Girl past dancing couples and into a private booth, where he tries to rape her. But in the next shot, the two of them are still conversing over drinks in the ballroom. So whose fantasy have we just seen? The Man's? The Girl's? Ours? All of those?

The cabaret scene in its entirety, which recalls the one in *Downhill*, is brilliant, worthy of the brothel scenes in Luis Buñuel's *Belle de Jour* (1967), which it much resembles. (For example, the shot of the champagne glass, which triggers various fantasies, functions in that respect exactly like the recurring sound of harness bells in Buñuel's film.)

Comedienne Betty Balfour makes a spirited heroine, her character quite convincing when she attempts to emulate Lindbergh and fly across the Atlantic! Fittingly, Eliot Stannard wrote the script—he had scripted Balfour's first success, *Squibs* (1921), in which she played a

Mary Pickford-like flower girl—though the original idea of *Champagne* is attributed to Walter Mycroft, film critic of the *Evening Standard* and story editor at BIP, later head of the studios. Sadly, Hitchcock seems to have found Balfour too head-strong, which may be why he never cast her in his films afterwards (despite her blondeness!). Perhaps also he was distracted at the time by good news on his home front—the birth of a daughter, Patricia, on July 7, 1928.

It was time to pop a champagne cork or two—something that Hitch was seldom averse to doing. The sparkling liquid flows freely in *Champagne*, one more symbol of the sexuality and spirit that is the true subject of all his films right up to the last, *Family Plot*. (George in that film, with its several risqué lines, may be "too pooped to pop", but the final image is of a coruscating diamond.) Hitchcock later dismissed *Champagne* as "dreadful," yet *The Bioscope* called it "bright entertainment."

BLACKMAIL

First screening June 1929 (sound version), August 1929 (silent version)

Production company: British International Pictures (BIP)

Duration approximately 80 minutes

Black and white

Silent/Sound

Scotland Yard detective Frank Webber (John Longden) helps arrest and interrogate a suspect. Later, he takes his girlfriend Alice White (Anny Ondra) to a crowded restaurant. But they quarrel, and leave separately—Alice with another man. The latter is an artist (Cyril Ritchard), whom Alice had evidently encouraged previously. He asks her back to his studio, where he tries to rape her. In self-defense she kills him with a knife. Then, in the early morning, she stumbles home to her parents' tobacconist's shop, unaware that a man, Tracy (Donald Calthrop), has seen her. Frank is put on the murder investigation. In the artist's studio he finds—and promptly conceals—evidence of Alice's involvement. He goes to the shop to confront her, and the pair are joined by Tracy, who makes blackmail demands. But word comes that the police suspect Tracy of the murder, and Frank tells them where he is. Tracy bolts, only to be spotted by the police as he attempts to hide in the British Museum. Chased onto the roof, he falls through it to his death, leaving Alice and Frank to live with their respective guilt.

The sound version of *Blackmail* was particularly well served by Hitchcock's knowledge of some of the new broadcasting techniques and by his extensive theater-going experience. For example, this version ends to the accompaniment of ringing laughter, an effect used previously in the famous Pirandello play *Right You Are! (If You Think So)* to comment on its characters' assumption that truth is simple and knowable. (The play had its first London performance in 1925, when it starred Claude Rains.) In *Blackmail*, Hitchcock puts with the sound of laughter an image of a jester pointing directly at the audience. Whether this is another case of our being implicated in original sin (see *The Ring*), the fact is that none of the film's three main characters is innocent. Even Frank, whose concealing of evidence appears to have an honorable motive—protecting Alice—is selfishly driven: he wants to get his girl back, and keep her.

Some silent films of 1929 had the final reel quickly reshot and were released with sound. But Hitchcock had seen sound coming. According to Charles Barr, *Blackmail* "was in order; (1) shot silent; (2) reshot, not just in the last reel, with

Above: *Tracy (Donald Calthrop, left) with Frank Webber (John Longden). In 1936, Hitch claimed that Calthrop "has more to give as a motion picture actor than most people I have ever handled."*
Left: *Hitch wanted to end the film with Alice (Anny Ondra) locked up, but commercial common sense dictated otherwise.*

dialogue; (3) released as a talkie; (4) released as a silent." The reason for the separate, belated release of the silent version was that many cinemas had not yet converted to sound. Both versions used the same sets, though there were many subtle differences between the two (for example, the silent version has an insert shot of the shop bell that isn't in the sound version).

A misconception about *Blackmail* is that it was the first British talkie. It wasn't: that distinction probably belongs to *The Clue of the New Pin*, based on an Edgar Wallace novel, whose distributor advertised it in *The Bioscope* of January 9, 1929 as the first British All-Talkie, and released it in March of that year. It fea-

Above: Alice in the artist's studio. The image of a jester reappeared at the end of the talkie version.

tured Donald Calthrop, who in Hitchcock's film plays Tracy. It also had a twenty-five-year-old John Gielgud in a bit part.

But no one denies *Blackmail*'s quality. Lady Eleanor Smith in *The Bystander* called it "An English Triumph," and advised her readers: "*Blackmail* should please everybody—the highbrows because it is intelligent and sensible drama unspoiled by blatant absurdities, and the lowbrows because it is a thrilling film packed throughout with excitement and incident."

As usual, Hitchcock had employed many talented colleagues. The original play, by Charles Bennett, had starred Tallulah Bankhead as Alice. Hitch now brought in playwright Benn Levy to help him adapt the dialogue—Eliot Stannard was apparently considered not suitable, and after scripting all but one of Hitchcock's first nine pictures he never worked with him again. The British Museum climax was suggested to Hitch by Michael Powell, who was familiar with the Reading Room and its glass dome. In turn, Powell may have got the idea from seeing John Longden in *Palais de Dance* (Maurice Elvey, 1928), in which the glass-domed locale had been similarly exploited.

Another misconception about *Blackmail* is that the famous scene on the morning after the artist's killing, in which a gossipy neighbor repeatedly uses the word *knife*, is all a matter of technique. Striking as the scene may be, it works for other, deeper reasons. It draws attention to itself for a purpose, being a study in the psychology of Alice, who has gone all night without sleep. At such times, the mind plays tricks—here the word *knife* seems to lunge at Alice, still aghast at last night's events. The scene's showiness also sets up the audience for what's coming, including Tracy's breathtaking show of bravado as he virtually takes over the premises, even using White's own chair. The growing tension until the moment when the parlor window shatters and Tracy flees, represents the sort of crucible situation that Hitchcock would sometimes make the subject of a whole film, such as *Rope*. Adding to the impact of the knife effect is the depiction of the gossipy neighbor herself, played by Phyllis Monkman, with her knitted striped jacket, cloche, and shopping basket, and her talk of previous murders, such as the real-life "Brides in the Bath" case (in which George Joseph Smith married three times, each time drowning his new bride in the bath and then collecting her life insurance. He was hanged in 1915).

Hitchcock's fine ear for dialogue was matched, right from the start, by his ear for sound in general, including music. The scene in the artist's studio shows brilliance in this respect. A slithery, mournful music sets in after the murder, prefaced by some sour piano notes distinct from the innocuous notes played earlier by Alice and from the lilting tune the artist had played and sung while Alice was getting changed. (Cyril Ritchard was in fact a singer/dancer and a light comedian, and his song "Miss Up-to-Date" came from one of his stage shows.) The slithery music is heard again later when Alice wanders through the streets. Hitchcock must have liked the effect, because he used very similar music in *Frenzy* for the scene at night where Rusk disposes of Babs's body.

Blackmail deserves books to itself, but even a brief overview should include a tribute to Anny Ondra's delightful acting (though her voice was that of Joan Barry, used because of Ondra's accent). Her character is more engaging and convincing than that of Kate in *The Manxman*, and her performance is both deeper and more sensual.

JUNO AND THE PAYCOCK

First screening June 1929

Production company:
British International Pictures (BIP)

Duration 85 minutes

Black and white

Dublin in the 1920s. Though he struts like a peacock, Jack Boyle (Edward Chapman) is really an idler who leaves the care of home and family to his wife Juno (Sara Allgood). His neighbor, Joxer Daly (Sidney Morgan), is equally feckless. In a bar, the pair hear about the finding of the bullet-riddled body of a young Republican Army soldier, apparently betrayed by an informer. Jack goes home, where Juno tells him that their daughter Mary (Kathleen O'Regan) is bringing a visitor. Meanwhile, their son Johnny (John Laurie), who once lost an arm for the Republican cause, mopes. The visitor is lawyer Charles Bentham (John Longden), with whom Mary is clearly smitten. Charles has good news: Jack has inherited £2,000. For several days, the Boyles celebrate and incur debt by buying furniture and even a gramophone. Then all the bad news arrives at once. The inheritance has fallen through. Charles has abandoned Mary, who reveals that she is pregnant by him. And two men in trenchcoats come for Johnny, accusing him of being the dead man's betrayer. Juno and Mary walk out on the improvident Jack.

If *The Farmer's Wife* appeared to ridicule several of its female characters, *Juno and the Paycock* is its foil: both "Captain" Boyle (whom we're told even a river voyage would make seasick) and his crony Joxer were described by one drama critic as "moral cretins," and *none* of the play's men emerge "with much moral plausibility." Meanwhile, the women pay for men's misdeeds while trying to uphold a decent humanity. Juno Boyle speaks what is evidently the playwright's view: "Ah, what can God do agen the stupidity o' men!"

Hitchcock filmed Sean O'Casey's famous play because he liked its blend of humor and tragedy, but he wasn't able to disguise its stage origins. Not even help from Alma—credited as scenarist—could hide those. So Hitch felt guilty when the film received widespread acclaim (trade journal *Kinematograph Weekly* went so far as to rank it "amongst the screen masterpieces of the world"). A different kind of tribute was paid the film when a print was burned by Irish nationalists in the streets of Limerick in 1930. O'Casey's anti-extremist barbs had struck home.

Today, the main interest of *Juno and the Paycock* is historical. The film itself, despite Sara Allgood's excellent performance, is stodgy, especially when compared with the preceding *Blackmail* (in which Allgood had played Mrs. White). Hitchcock evidently sensed this. For example, Juno represents both the first *and* the last of his films' positive "Great Mother" figures. Thereafter he would strive to give his films more psychology, even paranoia, with a result being the eventual emergence of the *negative* Great

Mother figures in films like *Rebecca*, *Notorious*, and ultimately *Psycho*. Much more interesting!

Along with *The Skin Game* and *Rope*, *Juno and the Paycock* is one of the most intellectual plays that Hitchcock filmed. Both Johnny and his mother express a

hope that their new wealth will allow them to move somewhere they're not known. But of course escape is never so easy. Behind the opening credits we see cramped-up Dublin buildings—with no trace of sky—photographed as if through the frame of a window. The view in effect is doubly constricted, both objectively and subjectively. Later, views out of windows recur, accompanied several times by the sound of machine-gun fire. Also, in a comic moment, Joxer hides from Juno by scrambling onto a window ledge, but gets caught in a sudden downpour. All of this suggests that retribution will come, or the outside world will exert its rigors, in spite of every effort to the contrary.

It is the crucible situation again (see *The Ring*). Revealingly, Joxer is given the line from Burns—"Man's inhumanity to man makes countless thousands mourn"—that Hitchcock once quoted to critic Richard Schickel to sum up the human condition. However, Juno and Mary's departure at the end does lend the film a slightly upbeat note.

Above: Juno (Sara Allgood) with son Johnny (John Laurie). John Laurie also played a small role in The 39 Steps.
Left: The Boyles gather to hear Charles's (John Longden) news.

ELSTREE CALLING

First screening February 1930

**Production company:
British International Pictures (BIP)**

Duration 86 minutes

Black and white/Pathécolour

The first British musical film consists of a series of all-star vaudeville and review items drawn in part from stage shows then running in London. A couple of the dance numbers have been stencil-colored. The film is hosted in mock-formal vein by comedian Tommy Handley, wearing evening dress, as if it were being transmitted on television from BIP's film studio at Elstree. At one point, Handley reads the weather forecast. Though Adrian Brunel was the film's supervisory director, Alfred Hitchcock is credited with "sketches and other interpolated items." According to the British Film Institute's Monthly Film Bulletin, *November 1975, this means in effect that Hitchcock directed the brief sketch "Thriller," in which Jameson Thomas plays a cuckolded husband, the burlesque of* The Taming of the Shrew, *which features Donald Calthrop and Anna May Wong, and the scenes of Gordon Harker struggling to tune his home-made television set, watched by Hannah Jones as his wife.*

Hold tight to your cat's-whiskers!" Tommy Handley's words launch a film that has more going for it than just the few moments directed by Hitchcock. Indeed, writing in 1975, critic Geoff Brown thought the film, "on balance, livelier than the [rather more] streamlined Revues, Parades and Follies with which Hollywood celebrated the coming of sound." Hitchcock had a nostalgia for the music hall, and the film provides a chance to see at least its vestiges: the two numbers sung and danced with a good deal of abandon by Lily Morris for example, or the patter and songs of the Scottish comedian Will Fyffe.

On release, *Kinematograph Weekly*, while allowing that it was "a good box office proposition," thought that the film "seems short of inspiration in its presentation methods." The blame for that may lie with executive producer John Maxwell. Allowing just ten days between the end of shooting and the film's trade show, Maxwell threw out Adrian Brunel's elaborate montage plans. Apart from Handley's interspersed remarks, the main continuity the film now has is provided by a couple of running gags. One of these involves Donald Calthrop as he endeavors to stage, by hook or by crook, a production of Shakespeare. The other shows Gordon Harker's repeated attempts to tune in to Elstree on his television set, not helped by a neighbor who keeps popping in to report that the set upstairs is working perfectly.

Gordon Harker, here unshaven and grumpy, was making his fourth appearance for Hitchcock. Hannah Jones, as his beady-eyed little wife, was by now no less

a Hitchcock regular, having already appeared in *Downhill*, *Champagne*, and *Blackmail*. The gag involving the recalcitrant television set was simply an elaboration of one involving a crystal-set owned by the elderly couple, Patsy's landlords, in *The Pleasure Garden*. Already, then, Hitchcock was sticking to his adage that if you've found a promising bit of business, bring it back and refine it!

The sketch called "Thriller" is mainly of interest because the cuckolded husband is played by Jameson Thomas from *The Farmer's Wife*. The style of the piece, which runs no more than two minutes, anticipates the burlesque tone of *Number Seventeen*.

Donald Calthrop finally gets to play in Shakespeare near the end of the film, in the Hitchcock-directed burlesque of *The Taming of the Shrew*. Slightly surreal, this involves Calthrop as Petruchio riding around on a motorbike and sidecar in the jaunty manner of Douglas Fairbanks, and cracking a whip. Then Calthrop directs similar treatment at Katharina, the shrew, played by Anna May Wong (who had starred with Fairbanks in *The Thief of Baghdad*). But she has armed herself with a store of custard pies . . .

Below: A typical scene from Elstree Calling. Kinematograph Weekly *thought that "(i)n spite of the array of talent, the picture cannot be called entirely satisfactory."*

MURDER!

First screening October 1930

**Production company:
British International Pictures (BIP)**

Duration 100 minutes

Black and white

In a British provincial town, an actress in a touring company is found murdered. A fellow actress, Diana Baring (Norah Baring), is charged with the crime. At her trial, jury member Sir John Menier (Herbert Marshall) fails to convince the other jurors of her innocence. She is sentenced to hang, and is held in prison. Sir John, who is a distinguished actor-manager in London, hunts for evidence that will free her. He enlists the help of Ted Markham (Edward Chapman), stage manager of the touring company, and his wife Doucie (Phyllis Konstam), and together they revisit the scene of the crime. Sir John finds himself staying overnight in humble lodgings, a novel experience for him these days. Evidence turns up pointing to Handel Fane (Esmé Percy), a female impersonator, as the real murderer. Fane has left the company to work as a trapeze artist in a circus. Inspired by a scene in Hamlet, *Sir John tricks him into revealing his guilt. Fane commits suicide in spectacular fashion—before a stunned crowd—and in due course Sir John is able to offer a part in his new play to Diana, who has always idolized him.*

We are apt to forget," writes J. B. Priestley, "how many playhouses there were at one time in England." Whole circuits existed where touring companies performed their repertoires consisting of melodramas, rough farces, comedies—and, invariably, Shakespeare. But gradually these circuits dwindled. After World War I, a new type of actor-manager appeared, who hated touring and depended entirely on West End runs. In effect, Sir John in *Murder!* is a satirical portrait of one such actor-manager, based on Hitchcock's friend Sir Gerald du Maurier; and the touring company we see represents a tatty, down-at-the-heel remnant of the sort of companies that had once flourished.

Murder! is based on the 1929 novel *Enter Sir John* by Clemence Dane and Helen Simpson. Dane, whose real name was Winifred Ashton, was the inspiration, a few years later, for Nöel Coward's most famous character, Madame Arcati in *Blithe Spirit*. In *Enter Sir John*, the authors lampoon their title character by having a reviewer suggest that Sir John

should "go out into the highways and hedges of real life for a model, instead of depending on his shaving-glass." Hitchcock seized on that passage, which is the key to his film.

"This is not a play but life," Sir John says, awakened from his narcissism. The trouble is, everywhere Sir John turns, people insist on playing roles! Even his fellow jurors behave as a chorus and smother the spark of insight he has had concerning Diana's innocence. Sir John must exercise all of his considerable intellect—and the lessons of his art—before he can uncover the truth, which proves in any case to be not a simple matter. The alleged villain, Fane, was driven to commit murder by the vindictiveness of the woman who threatened to reveal that he was a "half-caste" (homosexual). Hitchcock takes pains in the film to imply that gender is itself a matter of role-playing.

Sexual ambiguity always fascinated Hitchcock. In the aquarium scene in *Sabotage*, a rather sissy-looking youth (a young Charles Hawtrey) tells his girl-friend how, "after laying a million eggs,

the female oyster changes her sex." In *Murder!*, Hitchcock dwells on related matters. The various members of the touring company nearly all have characteristics of both sexes. There's Tom Druitt, for example, a married man with a squeaky voice like a woman's. And Doucie, whom we first see in jodhpurs, is described by her husband as a versatile performer. Recently she was "pure Tallulah"—meaning Tallulah Bankhead, the bisexual actress. In the courtroom scenes, we see both mannish women and effeminate men.

Hitchcock scholar William Rothman feels that *Murder!* is the director's masterpiece among the early films. A full analysis might show how very astute that assessment is. Hitchcock also shot a German version of the film, called *Mary*, with a cast headed by Alfred Abel, but reports indicate that it was the inferior of the two.

Left: Sir John (Herbert Marshall) visits Diana (Norah Baring) in prison.

Top: Sir John with Ted Markham (Edward Chapman). Chapman had also been seen in the previous year's Juno and the Paycock.

THE SKIN GAME

First screening June 1931

**Production company:
British International Pictures (BIP)**

Duration 89 minutes

Black and white

Three men approach a tree in a meadow and begin chopping it down. The meadow belongs to nouveau riche developer and industrialist Hornblower (Edmund Gwenn), whose land-clearing plans include demolishing the cottage of an elderly couple, the Jackmans. The couple ask nearby landowner Hillcrist (C. V. France) to intervene. The Hillcrist estate has been in the family for centuries, and the land containing the Jackman cottage had until recently been part of it. "Leave this to me," declares Hillcrist, appalled at the thought of factory chimneys rising nearby. But at a public auction, Hornblower outwits him and obtains even more land. An embittered and snobbish Mrs. Hillcrist (Helen Haye) turns to blackmail. She learns that Hornblower's daughter-in-law Chloe (Phyllis Konstam) has a tarnished past. Though Chloe is a friend of the Hillcrists' daughter Jill (Jill Esmond), Mrs Hillcrist confronts Hornblower with her knowledge, forcing him to sell at a loss the land he has just bought. An attempt by Chloe to drown herself now adds a further perspective to recent events—this "skin game" as Hillcrist ruefully calls it. In the meadow, the tree falls.

Many of Hitchcock's films, in their outlook, bear a resemblance to the philosophy of the German Arthur Schopenhauer (1788–1860), whose work had been promoted by such writers as George Bernard Shaw. Schopenhauer, who believed in a life force, taught that people are driven by a basic egoism plus varying amounts of compassion and malice. Objectivity, he felt, is something few of us are capable of—though great art may point the way. There's more than a touch of that outlook in *The Skin Game* where, for example, Jill Hillcrist denies that "the big point of view" exists. "We're all out for our own," she says.

But the author of *The Skin Game*, John Galsworthy, was himself one of the

Right: Hitchcock directs Edmund Gwenn, in the first of his four films for the director.
Below: Hornblower (Gwenn), Hillcrist (C. V. France), and Jill (Jill Esmond).

most generous and even-handed of men. At Oxford, he'd read law and been called to the Bar: hence, perhaps, his sense of fair play, his readiness to do justice to each side of any dramatic conflict. That's certainly the case in *The Skin Game* which, when staged in 1920, had been Galsworthy's first real commercial success. Neither Hillcrist nor Hornblower is presented unfairly. Hillcrist speaks out in favor of the Jackmans, saying that "[t]heir heart's in that cottage." Hornblower replies: "Have a sense of proportion, man. My works supply thousands of people, and *my* heart's in *them*." Significantly, when Hillcrist proceeds in his feud with Hornblower, it's made clear that he has personal motives—such as his dislike of his opponent—that outweigh his concern for the Jackmans, genuine though that concern may be.

Hitchcock's casting was inspired. As Hillcrist he chose stage actor C. V. France, who projected the patrician seriousness of Galsworthy himself—whom, moreover, he resembled physically! And as Hillcrist's potential nemesis, Hornblower, Hitchcock cast distinguished stage and screen actor Edmund Gwenn, who in 1920 had appeared in an earlier film version of the play. Gwenn's chipper, confident performance wins the character his fair share of audience sympathy, thus helping to set the scene for high drama.

Technically, *The Skin Game* is Hitchcock's most accomplished sound film to this time. He'd kept in touch with both the American and European cinemas, and learned much. His admiration for Jean Cocteau's avant-garde *Le sang d'un poète* (1930) led him to imitate that film's famous opening and closing shots of a factory chimney being demolished — only Hitchcock, in a nice touch, showed a tree being felled. The symbolism is complex. The felled tree represents not just progress but a life force inseparable from destructiveness. Shades of *Vertigo*, in fact.

Hitch even included some charming rural footage from *The Farmer's Wife*. Already he was well aware of the importance of having an audience *feel* matters being discussed onscreen, not just think about them. *Picturegoer* wrote: "This extremely powerful and dramatic picturization of Galsworthy's play proves that Hitchcock is one of England's most brilliant directors."

HITCHCOCK'S CAMEO APPEARANCES

In fact, so well known are his fleeting roles that some filmgoers think he appeared in every one of his fifty-six movies. This was not quite the case, particularly during the British period of his career when his "acting" was, at best, intermittent.

Hitch's first appearance came in his third film, *The Lodger*, where he took on two prestigious roles, playing a man in the newsroom towards the beginning of the movie and later an onlooker in the crowd that beats the Lodger. At the time, a life-long acting career was hardly Hitch's intention. He explained to Truffaut that "[I]t was strictly utilitarian; we had to fill the screen." After *The Lodger*, Hitchcock appeared in just six more of his British movies: *Easy Virtue* (as a man beside a tennis court); *Blackmail* (as a passenger travelling on the London Underground who is being irritated by a young boy); *Murder!* (as a passer-by late in the film); *The 39 Steps* (again simply as a passer-by, when Hannay takes Annabella back to his flat); *Young and Innocent* (as a photographer outside the courthouse when Robert makes his escape) and *The Lady Vanishes* (playing "man at railway station" back in London). Hitchcock-the-director obviously decided that Hitchcock-the-actor could not be trusted with larger roles.

Upon moving to Hollywood, Hitch embarked more seriously on an acting career and was rarely missing from his own movies. As he again explained to Truffaut in the sixties: "Later on, it became a superstition and eventually a gag. But by now it's a rather troublesome gag, and I'm very careful to show up in the first five minutes so as to let the peo-

ple look at the rest of the movie with no further distraction."

His more ingenious cameo appearances can be found in three films relying on confined sets: *Lifeboat*, where Hitch is the before-and-after man in a Reduco slimming advertisement in the newspaper being read by Gus; *Rope*, where his famous profile is an image on a flashing neon sign seen through the apartment window; and *Dial M for Murder*, where he can be seen in a school reunion dinner photo. In fact, the only films

Clockwise from upper left: I Confess, Blackmail, Under Capricorn, Lifeboat.

not to feature Hollywood's most famous bit-part player are the two war-time shorts, *Bon Voyage* and *Aventure Malgache*. A cameo appearance filmed for *The Wrong Man* was later cut, when Hitch felt it worked against the film's documentary feel (he does however still appear, giving an onscreen introduction to the film's true story). And although he does feature in both *Saboteur* and *The Trouble With Harry*, according to Hitchcock historian Jane Sloan he is not easily identifiable in existing prints.

Hitch's final cameo appearance came in his last film, *Family Plot*, where he can be seen in silhouette behind an office window at the Registrar of Births and Deaths.

Those American Hitchcock cameo performances in full are:

Rebecca (standing outside a phone booth occupied by Jack Favell)

Foreign Correspondent (reading a newspaper just after Johnnie arrives in London)

Mr. and Mrs. Smith (as a passer-by in the street)

Suspicion (seen mailing a letter as Lina meets a friend in town)

Saboteur (as a man at a newsstand)

Shadow of a Doubt (playing bridge on the train carrying Uncle Charlie)

Lifeboat (as the man in the Reduco newspaper advertisement)

Spellbound (walking out of a crowded elevator in the Empire State Hotel lobby)

Notorious (drinking champagne at Alex's party)

The Paradine Case (as a man with a cello at the railway station)

Rope (his profile is part of a red flashing neon sign)

Under Capricorn (standing outside Government House [or governor's manse])

Stage Fright (as a passer-by who stares at Eve in her Doris Tinsdale disguise)

Strangers on a Train (boarding a train with a double bass when Guy first arrives at Metcalf)

I Confess (walking across the top of a flight of steps early in the film)

Dial M for Murder (in Tony's school reunion dinner photo)

Rear Window (winding the clock in the composer's apartment)

To Catch a Thief (sitting next to Robie at the back of a bus)

Clockwise from upper left: The Birds, Topaz *(with Peggy Robertson),* Rear Window, Family Plot.

The Trouble With Harry (walking past a roadside stand)

The Man Who Knew Too Much (in a crowd at the market watching the acrobats)

The Wrong Man (introducing the film)

Vertigo (as a passer-by carrying a horn case when Scottie goes to visit Gavin Elster)

North by Northwest (missing a bus at the beginning of the film)

Psycho (wearing a cowboy hat outside the realty office where Marion works)

The Birds (walking into a pet shop with two terriers, passing Melanie Daniels)

Marnie (seen in the corridor of the hotel where Marnie is staying)

Torn Curtain (holding a baby in a Copenhagen hotel lobby)

Topaz (getting out of a wheelchair to meet someone at the airport in New York)

Frenzy (in the crowd listening to a politician's speech)

Family Plot (as the silhouette behind an office window).

Finally, a little known cameo occurs in "Dip in the Pool," a Hitchcock–directed episode of the television series *Alfred Hitchcock Presents*, in which Mr. Renshaw is seen reading a copy of the *Alfred Hitchcock Mystery Magazine*, featuring a front cover photo of the director.
David Barraclough

NUMBER SEVENTEEN

First screening July 1932

Production company:
British International Pictures (BIP)

Duration 65 minutes

Black and white

One windy night, after chasing his hat along a suburban street, Gilbert Allardyce (John Stuart) thinks he sees a light moving about inside a house bearing a For Sale notice. The door proves unlocked. Upstairs, he finds the apparently dead body of a man, and nearby, frightened, a Cockney merchant sailor, Ben (Leon M. Lion), who says he is merely sheltering after losing his ship. Events escalate rapidly as it becomes apparent that the house, located above a railway, is being used by jewel thieves as an escape point to the Continent. One thief, Sheldrake (Garry Marsh), is already hiding in the house's bathroom. Various other crooks arrive: Brant (Donald Calthrop), his reluctant companion Nora (Anne Grey), and Henry Doyle (Barry Jones). Eventually they all jump on a passing train, which Ben manages to board too. Allardyce falls off but gives chase by commandeering a bus. When the train goes out of control, it crashes in spectacular fashion onto the Dover-Calais ferry, but Ben escapes injury. Furthermore, he has retrieved the stolen diamonds. Allardyce, also known as Barton, and who is really an undercover detective, arrives in time to save Nora from drowning.

Called *Joyous Melodrama* when it was first produced on the London stage in 1925, *Number Seventeen* in its play and film versions defies short synopsis. Hitchcock hadn't wanted to film it. For one thing, a silent version existed, made in Germany in 1928 by Géza von Bolvary (who then directed a version of Hitchcock's *Champagne*, using its star, Betty Balfour). Also, he'd wanted to film a quite different comedy about London, John van Druten's *London Wall*. Forced to make *Number Seventeen*, Hitch decided to have fun with it. He satirized the play's absurdities and tried out various thriller techniques (subjective effects, use of red herrings), the culmination of which

Above: *Hitchcock watches his daughter, Patricia, on the set of* Number Seventeen.
Left: *Rose (Anne Casson) and Allardyce (John Stuart) are left hanging. Kinematograph Weekly felt the film was "(d)istinguished more for Alfred Hitchcock's brilliant camera work and intelligent coordination of music and action, than for conciseness of narrative."*

would be seen in *Psycho*, nearly thirty years later.

Of course, being little more than a "quota quickie," the film isn't always very good—merely fun. Hitchcock afterwards decried his "careless" approach, and certainly the film's plot construction is rudimentary. At one point, a Mr. Ackroyd and his daughter Rose (Ann Casson) turn up from next door, and for a time it appears Rose will be the film's heroine. In a famous scene, it's she and Allardyce who

hang suspended from a collapsed balcony-rail that threatens to plunge them to their deaths. However, they manage to extricate themselves. Then, just minutes later, Mr. Ackroyd is knocked out and left seriously injured in the bathroom, and Allardyce tells Rose to "fetch a doctor"—which is the last we see or hear in the film of either father or daughter.

The original play was conceived as a vehicle for the actor who plays Ben, Leon M. Lion, who also produced it. Lion

Top left: Anne Grey, Anne Casson, and John Stuart.
Bottom: Brant (Donald Calthrop) and Sheldrake (Garry Marsh) on the train featured in the film's climax.

eventually put money into Hitchcock's film version. At about the same time, he rented the Garrick Theatre in London where he successfully staged a series of Galsworthy plays (including *Escape*, one of Hitch's favorites). But it was as Ben that Lion appears to have first made his reputation. The play promised to become a hardy annual. J. Jefferson Farjeon, its author, wrote other plays and novels featuring the character, who, in his scarf and cropped hair, is supposed to be in the endearing Cockney mold. Nonetheless, one can see why film historian William Everson isn't enamored of him. He does tend to "[seem] in the way all the time."

The best things about *Number Seventeen* are its liveliness and wit, and the chase sequence that Hitch dreamed up to resolve the troublesome plot. Ben is established as partial to alcohol, and on the train he finds himself amidst crates of Emu Tonic Wine (a surreal touch). After imbibing generously, he proceeds across the swaying carriages to where he'd seen Nora and the crooks jump aboard. The train's movement doesn't seem in the least to upset the tipsy Ben—a variant, this, on the gags involving shipboard drunks that Hitch used in *Champagne* and *Rich and Strange*. Earlier, the dialogue had dealt with related matters. Grateful to Allardyce for a nip of brandy from a flask, Ben thinks he hears himself being offered

more. In fact, Allardyce is dissatisfied with one of Ben's statements, and has said, "Have another think." Replies Ben: "Don't mind if I do." And when Allardyce's hand goes to his pocket, and Ben's eyes greedily follow, it comes out not with the expected brandy flask but with just . . . a handkerchief.

There's a follow-up to that piece of business. The crook Brant makes a threatening gesture with a gun, then gratuitously sneezes—and an absurdly brandished handkerchief is again the payoff. In later films, Hitchcock would refine and perfect these matters of a film's texture, until crit-

ics could suggest that there's *no* detail in a Hitchcock film that doesn't relate to another detail, each playing its part in the whole.

The chase scene, filmed largely with a model train and bus, using miniature sets, is a highpoint in Hitchcock's work at this time. Granted, there's an even more poetic use of model shots in *Young and Innocent*, but for sheer visceral excitement the chase in *Number Seventeen* takes some beating. Soundtrack, lighting, and camera movement all contribute. The highly realistic clanking of the train carriages, and the whine of the bus's motor, are the almost musical ground whose note of urgency allows effects like a witty cut-in of a billboard telling the bus's shaken passengers to, "See the countryside by Green Line." As the night turns to dawn, the bus careens through a sleeping town complete with dreaming spire. It all climaxes of course with the spectacular piling of the train onto the cross-channel ferry—something that the Hitchcockian comedy-thriller *Silver Streak* (1976) emulated in its own fashion when it had an out-of-control train slam into the Chicago rail terminal.

At the climax, when Allardyce saves Nora from drowning, it is the second time he's saved her life: he'd earlier deflected a bullet that was heading her way. Hitchcock characterizes Nora as both mysterious (someone who had initially seemed mute) and a lady. In effect, she's a prototype of Madeleine in *Vertigo*.

RICH AND STRANGE

American title: East of Shanghai

First screening March 1932

Production company:
British International Pictures (BIP)

Duration 87 minutes

Black and white

No sooner has accountant Fred Hill (Henry Kendall) told wife Emily (Joan Barry) that he wants "some life" than a letter comes from Fred's uncle giving the couple money for a world cruise. Happily fleeing Suburbia, the pair arrive first in Paris where they take in the Folies Bergère. Then life on board ship goes to their heads and each begins an affair. Emily is attracted to the fatherly Commander Gordon (Percy Marmont), who is en route to his plantation in the Tropics. Fred, having got over seasickness, promptly succumbs to the charms of a sultry princess (Betty Amann). Between Port Said and Singapore, both affairs ripen. But when Gordon disembarks, Emily decides not to go with him, sensing that her husband of eight years needs her. Sure enough, Fred learns that the "princess" is a mere adventuress and has departed, taking his money. A reunited husband and wife now head home on a cargo boat—only to find themselves marooned after it founders in the South China Sea. Rescued by a junk, they eventually reach a wintry England. Yet to Fred and Emily, Suburbia never looked so good.

Top: *Hitchcock is seen in the center, during filming at Elstree.*
Left: *Emily (Joan Barry) and Fred (Henry Kendall).*

Dig a little in *Rich and Strange*, and you'll find essential Hitchcock. The dashed hopes of *Vertigo* and *Psycho*, the out-of-control relationships of *Under Capricorn*, the naïve couple from *Torn Curtain*, the idea in *Rear Window* of the need to get outside oneself and look in—all are anticipated here. John Grierson wrote that the film showed a knowledge of the outside world that was "almost nil," but Hitchcock had at least partly foreseen, and met, that criticism. The film, resembling a private memoir, is *about* its characters' solipsism. Fred and Emily might almost be a rueful Alfred and Alma looking back, and both of the latter are credited with working on the script.

Then again, Hitchcock was probably more detached about the project than has been supposed. *Rich and Strange* faithfully adapts a 1930 novel by Australian writer Dale Collins. Researching this matter, Charles Barr found that Hitch and Alma had met Collins and his wife socially, and suggests that the story may have begun as a possible film project which was realized first as a novel, then somewhat later as a film. From this it seems clear that the Hitchcocks' recent cruise to West Africa and the Caribbean made only an incidental contribution to the film. John Russell Taylor quotes Hitch as saying darkly that the cruise merely gave them a sense of how, being cooped up for a while on a ship, everyone comes to hate one another. (There's a hint of that when Emily inquires her husband's whereabouts from a steward, who answers deadpan that Fred has gone ashore with the princess.)

For the film itself, Hitch stayed in England but sent a second unit with a silent camera on a cruise, the ports of call of which were those in the script. Taylor reports this used up so much of the budget that Hitch couldn't afford important stars; fortunately, he was able to recruit capable people from the West End stage. Among them was Elsie Randolph, a vivacious young review performer. She was cast against type as Miss Imery, a bespectacled spinster, whose costume for the ship's fancy-dress evening is that of Bo Peep—Miss Imery herself is often rather cruelly made to look as lost as Bo Peep's flock. Hitch certainly appreciated Randolph's performance. Forty years later, he cast her as Gladys, the receptionist of the Coburg Hotel, in *Frenzy*.

Miss Imery serves as foil to the goings-on that occur around her. When Fred exclaims that he wants "some life—life, I tell you," he sounds the film's keynote. Life and sexuality are again Hitchcock's very topic. The film begins with an image of a large clock in Fred's office, hanging over the workers in their separate cubicles. Time is getting away—a fact which the viewer will be reminded of again. On the voyage, shots of the ship's foaming wake measure progress. In Singapore, Emily gazes down absently at the passing road as she decides not to leave with Gordon. In the South China Sea, when Fred and Emily find themselves marooned, shots of the rising water emphasize urgency. Miss Imery's lost sheep, then, represent lost opportunities, lost moments.

But that's only half the point. Hitchcock wants to teach his couple—and us—a deeper lesson. The film provides a classic instance of its director's outflanking technique, whereby assumptions are exposed as insufficient, viewpoints questioned, and a wiser outlook hinted at. Fred is the main butt of the lesson here. He had assumed that he knew what *life* meant. But in the East his viewpoints don't match the prevailing ones. We're shown the detachment of the Chinese: when one of their number slowly drowns, his foot caught in a rope ladder thrown over the side of the sinking ship, no one moves to save him—mainly

Above: *The sultry "princess" (Betty Amann) comes between Fred and Emily at the fancy-dress party.*
Left: *Hitchcock was not particularly keen to use Joan Barry, who had provided the voice for Anny Ondra in* Blackmail.

because it would do no good, but also from a cultivated nonchalance. Meanwhile, Fred and Emily watch in horror. Successive close-ups of their heads turning, as they seek out help, recall matching close-ups when they'd merely gawked at the tourist sites in Paris. At least they've now awakened to a more basic sense of *life*.

Hitchcock isn't finished. One sees why Grierson might feel an inadequacy in the depiction of the film's Chinese. But Hitchcock, as if acknowledging this, dwells on the inadequacy of *Fred's* (and to some extent Emily's) responses. Fred's xenophobia resurfaces. "These Chinese breed like rabbits," he says smugly. Settling back to enjoy life on the junk, he compares it to yachting. Immediately the film cuts to one of the crew pushing on a massive tiller. On returning home, the couple are seemingly little changed by their experiences.

However, they have each other, something that subsequent Hitchcock films will show is the most crucial thing. Also, they've faced death together, and we've heard Fred say, "I'm scared, Em." To the list of films given previously that *Rich and Strange* foreshadows, add *The Birds*, with its own exemplary terror. Neither the critics nor the public much liked *Rich and Strange* when it appeared ("[Hitchcock] admirers will have difficultly knowing what to say," remarked *Variety*), but its director always retained a fondness for it. Seen today, it looks almost post-modern.

WALTZES FROM VIENNA

American title:
Strauss's Great Waltz

First screening 1933

Production company:
A Tom Arnold Production

Duration 80 minutes

Black and white

Johann Strauss Jr. (Esmond Knight), known as Schani, is the son of the famous conductor and composer, and plays the violin in his father's orchestra. He hasn't had any of his own compositions performed or published because Strauss Sr. (Edmund Gwenn) sternly discourages it. Not dismayed, Schani gives singing lessons to his gifted sweetheart Rasi (Jessie Matthews), a pastry chef's daughter, and dedicates all his songs to her. Then he meets a Countess (Fay Compton) who has written some verses and asks his help in setting them to music. When her husband, the Prince (Frank Vosper), hears from a servant that a young man is upstairs with his wife, he storms into the music room, but the name of Strauss placates him. Later, Rasi isn't so easily placated, for she senses a rival. However, the Countess essentially has Schani's best interests at heart. With a publisher friend, she successfully plots to have the elder Strauss delayed one night so that Schani's new composition, "The Blue Danube," may receive a performance. Schani conducts the waltz himself, becoming the sensation of Vienna. Soon afterwards, though the Prince's suspicions have briefly been aroused again, everyone is finally reconciled.

Hitchcock would have preferred to film Dennis Wheatley's first novel, *Forbidden Territory* (1933), a thriller set inside Communist Russia, but his producer insisted he stick with *Waltzes from Vienna*, "a musical without music," as its director once inaccurately called it. (What he meant, probably, was that the film has no big production numbers.) Contrary to reports, the film works well. "It was an innovative, charming film," wrote Maurice Yacowar in 1977, "and it retains much of its charm." That sentiment was echoed the following year by Hitchcock's biographer, John Russell Taylor, who likewise found the film "rather charming."

Nonetheless, Hitchcock had his rea-

Left: Edmund Gwenn, who'd starred previously in The Skin Game.
Above: Filming at Lime Grove Studios in Shepherd's Bush.

sons for remembering *Waltzes from Vienna* unfavorably, once calling it, "My lowest ebb." He had just left BIP after serving out his contract by producing—but not directing—another of that company's low-budget films, *Lord Camber's Ladies*, starring Gertrude Lawrence and Gerald du Maurier. Now he accepted an offer by independent producer Tom Arnold to make a film of a stage spectacle by Guy Bolton that had run for a year in London, about the elder and younger Strausses. (The original source was German, the basis for the 1933 film *Waltzerkrieg*.) He soon regretted it. This wasn't, he decided, his type of material, and he took out his frustrations on the film's hapless stars by indulging even

more than usual in practical jokes and cruel sarcasm. Poor Jessie Matthews, Britain's ascendant young musical performer, suffered as much as anyone at his hands. To make matters worse, the budget was tight, and Hitchcock was anxious to keep to schedule. Often cast and crew worked far into the night.

Filming took place at the Gaumont-British facilities at Lime Grove Studios in Shepherd's Bush, London. After one very trying day, Hitchcock told his despondent cast, "I hate this stuff. Melodrama is the only thing I can do." Naturally, word of that outburst got around, which doubtless affected both the way the film was regarded by its makers and the way the critics approached it. In Britain, its general release was delayed until March 1934. But again contrary to report, not all the reviews were hostile. Though Jessie Matthews received disappointing notices (*The Spectator* called her character "Johann's feather-witted sweetheart") and *The Times* took Hitchcock to task for treating her as "a not-too-important part of the film's design," perhaps the most balanced review was Caroline Lejeune's in *The Observer*. After admitting a certain week-in week-out quality of the film, she noted "touches of felicitous design" and how "[n]o one can produce as efficient a script as Hitch. . . . Every scene is annotated with a line drawing beforehand."

The fact is that Hitchcock's meticulous pre-planning stood him in good stead. Whatever the troubles during shooting, *Waltzes from Vienna* is an intelligent film about musical inspiration—and life. A reason for Rasi, Jessie Matthews's character, to be kept within bounds is that the two women in the story stand for com-

plementary aspects of Schani himself, and to that extent it would be wrong for Rasi to overshadow the Countess. Significantly, both women have one song with Schani. Rasi sings "With All My Heart" at the start of the film, and she is indeed both sweetheart and inspiration to Schani. But she is also someone who is inexperienced, just as he is initially. It takes his meeting with the Countess—with whom he sings a duet about the sun—to force Schani to adopt a mature view about where his life is heading and the need to oppose his father. The two women in *Waltzes from Vienna* roughly correspond to the two heroines in *Number Seventeen*—though the latter film is much the sketchier.

The basic situation in some respects resembles that of *Rear Window*. Rasi wants Schani to settle down and take a steady job in her father's bakery. The Countess wants him to realize his potential as a great popular composer. To do that, Schani will have to defy his jealous father. Similar conflicts of ambition oper-

ate in *Rear Window*, which climaxes in the violent confrontation of photographer hero Jeff with his would-be nemesis Thorwald—effectively an evil-father figure. Also, during both films we follow the gradual composition of a piece of music ("The Blue Danube", "Lisa") to its realization in a full orchestral version at the story's climax. Eventually all disharmonies are resolved. In *Rear Window*, Jeff and his fiancée reach a *modus vivendi* for their future together (rather than apart). In *Waltzes from Vienna*, Schani is set to marry Rasi and may not need to work in her father's bakery—where, however, he'd earlier had a moment of musical inspiration. Either way, it looks like he may get to eat his pastry and have it too.

In America, where the film was not released until 1935 (following the success of *The Man Who Knew Too Much*), the reviews were negative or unenthusiastic. *Variety* thought it "should never have crossed the ocean." The *New York Times* called it a "[d]iscreet and sober little romance." In truth, today's Hitchcock aficionado will find in it much that is admirable—not least the skillful filming of the performance of "The Blue Danube."

Above Left: *Johann Strauss Jr. (Esmond Knight). Esmond Knight was recreating his role from the West End production.*
Below: *Rasi (Jessie Matthews) and Johann. Shortly after its release, Hitchcock claimed that "Waltzes from Vienna gave me many opportunities for working out ideas in the relation of film and music."*

CLASSIC BRITISH MOVIES
1934—1939

Early 1934 saw Hitchcock installed at the Gaumont-British offices in Shepherd's Bush. Embarking on a five-picture deal with the studio, he and writer Charles Bennett worked on a project based around the popular Bulldog Drummond stories. As was often the case with Hitch and his writers, conversation strayed from the source material and pretty soon they were creating an entirely different plotline, one involving kidnapping and an international spy ring, which evolved into *The Man Who Knew Too Much*.

Expectations for the finished film were high, but Hitchcock had the misfortune to once again encounter the manipulations of his only real professional enemy, C. M. Woolf. Now head of distribution at Gaumont-British, Woolf labelled the film disastrous and announced to the stunned Hitchcock that it would be re-shot by Maurice Elvey. Michael Balcon was out of the country and fortunately Woolf agreed to wait until his return. Ivor Montagu again stepped in and insisted that Woolf screen the film for the trades to gain a second opinion. The reaction was good (*Kinematograph Weekly* hailed it "a glorious melodrama. It is artless fiction,

Left: The Man Who Knew Too Much *trade show ad.*
Above: *Hitch poses with Peter Lorre.*

staged on a spectacular scale."), and Woolf reluctantly agreed to release the film, but only as the second or B picture to the main feature.

Nevertheless, *The Man Who Knew Too Much*, released in December 1934, was a huge critical and popular success and built the foundation for Hitchcock's extraordinary success throughout the rest of the decade. Hitch had finally established himself as the preeminent British director of suspense films.

The film's success (albeit with poor financial returns due to Woolf's mismanagement) gave Hitch greater confidence for his next film, *The 39 Steps*. He again collaborated with Charles Bennett, and their partnership lasted until Bennett left for America in 1937, a couple of years before Hitch's own departure. Bennett had been raised on the stage and was both a successful actor and playwright. His

easygoing nature, ability to gossip with the best, and unerring sense of story structure made him the perfect companion for Hitchcock.

Toward the end of his life, Bennett still recalled with affection those years with Hitchcock, remembering the long lunches at the Mayfair Hotel, which was not far from Hitchcock's flat on Cromwell Road, where the pair often worked. Bennett's nature spoiled Hitch, who was as eager not to work as he was to actually get things done. This pattern would remain with Hitchcock throughout his career, yet he loved the scripting stage of filmmaking, with its hours of discussion, trying to dream up the perfect thriller.

It also brought into the Hitchcock vernacular the term MacGuffin. Hitch's longtime friend and writer Angus MacPhail used the term for the element in the story that all the characters seek but which remained deliberately mysterious to the audience. The word came from an old joke (quoted by Spoto) that MacPhail told about two men travelling on a train

John Gielgud, Hitchcock, and Peter Lorre, on the set of Secret Agent.

to Scotland. In the overhead luggage rack was an odd-looking package:

"What have you there?" asked one of the men.

"Oh, that's a MacGuffin," replied his companion.

"What's a MacGuffin?"

"It's a device for trapping lions in the Scottish Highlands."

"But there aren't any lions in the Scottish Highlands!"

"Well, then, I guess that's no MacGuffin!"

Over the years Hitchcock often used the term, explaining that this plot trick was something audiences really did not care about, since they were actually more concerned with the characters and their relationship. *The 39 Steps* is a perfect example of his use of the MacGuffin, dragging the story along without any real explanation.

Hitchcock abandoned the light touch of *The 39 Steps* for his next pictures, two further spy films. First came *Secret Agent*, an altogether darker examination of the spy game (but again starring Madeleine Carroll). During production Hitch became disenchanted, partly due to John Gielgud, whom he found difficult to work with at times, but also because Peter Lorre's morphine addiction was beginning to affect his performance. Uncharacteristically, Hitch even abandoned his typically well-planned script for a day and improvised on the set. Spoto, in

his biography of Hitchcock, described the moment: "Some idea of the unconventional atmosphere that prevailed during shooting is suggested by the scene involving Carroll, [Robert] Young, and a Swiss coachman, played by the famous French actor Michel Saint-Denis. The whole brief scene was invented extemporaneously when Saint-Denis visited his old friend Gielgud on the set. No one was quite sure where the scene would be inserted in the finished film . . ."

By the time he began production on his next film, Hitch was at his greatest weight. At over 300 pounds, he was obviously enjoying his success, perhaps rather more

than he should have been. The positive critical response to *The 39 Steps* and *Secret Agent* led to Hitchcock being a little more daring with *Sabotage*, which continued his exploration of the darker corners of the espionage world. His decision to kill young Stevie in a bus explosion angered audiences and reviewers alike, with film critic Caroline Lejeune particularly vocal in her criticism. Only a few months earlier, she had written a fascinating sketch of Hitchcock at work: "On the set he's a sadist. He revels in spiritual debagging. Nothing delights him more than to take a film star with a good opinion of himself, work him until he sweats, and

Hitchcock prepares a scene with Madeleine Carroll and John Gielgud for Secret Agent.

Filming Sabotage.

Hitch and Sylvia Sidney on the set of Sabotage.

then publicly can the sequence. His language is fierce, and his humor rarely drawing room. He respects nobody's feelings; but everybody respects him.

"Hitch's genius is for draughtsmanship. He is an instinctive visualizer. His film scripts are minor works of art, every shot blocked on the margin of the page in rough design. When a script is finished, he loses interest in the picture. He would rather get on with the next job."

With *Sabotage*, Lejeune felt Hitchcock had violated a basic trust between the filmmaker and audience. Hitch now ran for cover, reworking *The 39 Steps* in the more youthful, lighter vein of *Young and Innocent*. When Gaumont-British closed down in mid-production, Hitchcock found himself back working for Gainsborough Pictures, this time under producer Edward Black. *Young and Innocent* proved to be his last British film with Charles Bennett, who had signed a contract with Universal Studios and moved permanently to Beverly Hills. After completing filming, the Hitchcocks made their own first trip to America, touring New York City and parts of the state in August 1937, as well as entertaining tantalizing offers from producer David O. Selznick.

When Hitch returned to London in September, he quickly edited *Young and Innocent* and began production on *The Lady Vanishes*, again for Gainsborough. During this period, the tempo of cables from Selznick increased following the release and smashing success of *Young and Innocent*. After wrapping production

A poster for Hitch's ex-employer Graham Cutts's Aren't Men Beasts! *can be seen in the background of this shot from Sabotage.*

Relaxing on the set of Young and Innocent: *Nova Pilbeam, Hitch, Derrick de Marney (standing), and Percy Marmont.*

Above left: *Michael Redgrave, Margaret Lockwood, and Hitch at work on* The Lady Vanishes.
Above: *Hitch and Alma land in America.*
Left: *Hitch greets Charles Laughton, star of* Jamaica Inn, *his last British movie before moving to America.*

on *The Lady Vanishes*, and before beginning what would be his final British film for over thirty years, *Jamaica Inn* (made for Mayflower Pictures), Hitch returned once more to the States. This time he made the journey across country to Hollywood, where, on July 14, 1938, he signed a contract with Selznick. Hitch then returned home on the S. S. *Normandie*, to go

through the rather perfunctory motions of directing *Jamaica Inn*. The experience was challenging for everyone involved, and the film received a decidedly mixed critical reaction, although it enjoyed moderate box-office success.

In March 1939 the Hitchcock family, which included a cook, maid, Joan Harrison, and two small dogs, boarded

the *Queen Mary* for America. During the voyage, Hitch, Alma, and Harrison spent their time working on the treatment for his first film for Selznick. Not a version of the *Titanic* tragedy, as the trades had already announced, but, like *Jamaica Inn*, an adaptation of a Daphne du Maurier novel, *Rebecca*.

Dan Auiler

THE MAN WHO KNEW TOO MUCH

First screening December 1934

Production company:
Gaumont-British Picture
Corporation, Ltd.

Duration 85 minutes

Black and white

Bob Lawrence (Leslie Banks) and wife Jill (Edna Best) holiday at St Moritz. Jill narrowly loses a clay pigeon shooting contest to her opponent Ramon (Frank Vosper). That evening, the Lawrences dine with a French skier, Louis Bernard (Pierre Fresnay), who is secretly an anti-terrorist agent. When Bernard is shot, before dying he tells Jill of the planned assassination of a foreign diplomat in London. Then an urgent message is handed to the Lawrences warning them to keep silent and informing them that their teenage daughter Betty (Nova Pilbeam) has been kidnapped. The distraught couple return to London. Unable to go the police, they begin their own search for Betty. With Uncle Clive (Hugh Wakefield), Bob locates the kidnappers' hideout above a seedy tabernacle in Wapping. Bob is captured by the gang but Clive escapes, and gets word to Jill that the assassination attempt will occur at the Albert Hall. After Jill manages to foil the aim of the marksman, Ramon, the police tail him to the hideout. In a shoot-out, all of the gang, including their leader Abbot (Peter Lorre), are killed. Betty and her father are reunited with Jill.

In the Bulldog Drummond novel *Temple Tower* (1929), by H. C. McNeile ("Sapper"), there's a passing reference to Drummond and his wife Phyllis having a baby. Seizing on that passage, and probably also thinking of some recent headlines from America (the 1932 Lindbergh baby kidnapping case), Hitchcock and screenwriter Charles Bennett asked themselves what Drummond would do if his child were kidnapped. The resulting story eventually became the screenplay of *The Man Who Knew Too Much*. During the writing, Hitchcock also invoked his favorite author, John Buchan. From *The Three Hostages* (1924), he and Bennett drew the idea of international terrorists who use both kidnapping and hypnotism to further their schemes. And, for the film's

Above: Recreating the Alps in the studio. Hitch can be seen in the center.

title, Hitch recalled a 1922 collection of tales by G. K. Chesterton, another author he admired. With all this resourcefulness, and plenty of ideas of its own, *The Man Who Knew Too Much* launched a spectacular new era of the Hitchcock thriller.

The story goes that Hitchcock and Bennett had already written "Bulldog Drummond's Baby" when *Waltzes from Vienna* was being filmed. One day

Michael Balcon, the man who had given Hitch his start as a director, and who had recently become head of production at both Islington (Gainsborough) and Shepherd's Bush (Gaumont-British), visited him on the set. When Hitch told him of the script he had in his drawer, Balcon was enthusiastic and immediately signed the thirty-four-year-old director to come and work for him at Gaumont-British. A

Top: The Siege of Sydney Street was an obvious influence on the film's climax.
Above left: Bob Lawrence (Leslie Banks, right) with "Uncle" Clive (Hugh Wakefield). Banks later acted in Hitchcock's Jamaica Inn.
Above right: Lawrence is menaced by Abbott (Peter Lorre). Scriptwriter Charles Bennett later wrote that "Peter carried his personal gentleness into his characterizations, and this was a great part of his magic. [He] could kill . . . and still remain amusingly lovable."

year later, the film was released. Some exhibitors initially disliked it, but the reviews helped change their minds. In *The Spectator*, Caroline Lejeune wrote: "I am very happy about this film. It seems to me, because of its very recklessness, its frank refusal to indulge in subtleties, to be the most promising work Hitchcock has produced since *Blackmail*."

A highlight, everyone agreed, was the thrilling climax based on London's Sydney Street siege of 1911, in which a group of anarchists fought a gun battle with police. The scene compares favorably with the similar one in Howard Hawks's gangster film, *Scarface* (1932).

Indeed, the Hawks film seems to have been in Hitchcock's mind, influencing, for example, his conception of Abbot, who is given an impressive scar of his own, running down his forehead and through his right eyebrow. Also, Hitchcock would have noted in *Scarface* the hint of incest between Tony Camonte (Paul Muni) and his sister (Ann Dvorak), not so different, after all, from the brother-sister relationship in *The Lodger*. The relationship in *The Man Who Knew Too Much* of Abbot to his companion Nurse Agnes (Cicely Oates) is decidedly strange—it sometimes seems like that of mother and son, and yet is different from that. At the climax, the

anarchists barricade themselves upstairs in their hideout behind a steel door (also seen in Tony Camonte's steel shutters) and prepare to do battle. Nurse Agnes fights alongside Abbot until the moment she's shot. Whereupon, Abbot's horror and grief are every bit as great as Tony Camonte's had been at the death of his sister, likewise killed by a police bullet.

Peter Lorre, who had recently fled Nazi Germany, where he'd played the child-murderer in Fritz Lang's *M* (1931), makes Abbot at once likeable and repellent. In an early scene, Abbot asks a fellow anarchist to ensure that the dumpy housekeeper, Mrs. Brockett, attends them for the evening instead of going home to give her husband his supper. The man, Rawlinson, orders Mrs. Brockett to remove her skirt. Abbot, seeing her in her bloomers, chuckles loudly. (This incident was drawn from an actual account of the Sydney Street anarchists!) Mischievously, the film adds a joke of its own. Rawlinson seems to pinch Mrs. Brockett on the bottom, but then we see that he was merely reaching for some *hors d'oeuvre* on a plate behind her.

Abbot's sense of humor, like the film's, is acceptable in itself. What makes him so chilling is his narcissism, though he is not alone in that. In fact, the film pivots on the idea of isolation as something to be overcome, community as perhaps the main goal. In a fine scene, Jill and Uncle Clive look at Betty's abandoned toys, and both try hard not to become demoralized. The bachelor Clive plays with the train set because he feels out of his depth, though he does his best to console Jill. With his monocle, and services background, he's the equivalent of Bulldog Drummond's staunch ally, Algy Longworth. But Jill remarks that he's not been a good uncle, too self-absorbed in fact, and we recall that Betty had found her preferred "uncle" in the late Louis Bernard. However, the film will show the Lawrences learning from their ordeal, and seeming to grow closer. Clive is given his share of the pain—and, we must hope, his share of the growing.

Despite Caroline Lejeune's opinion that the film refuses "to indulge in subtleties," close analysis shows many of them. Its main theme of infant-versus-adult makes for a moving experience. Its thrills, humor and rapid mood-switches make for great entertainment. Hitchcock himself remade the film in 1956.

THE 39 STEPS

First screening September 1935

**Production company:
Gaumont-British Picture
Corporation, Ltd.**

Duration 81 minutes

Black and white

In a London music hall, Richard Hannay (Robert Donat), a Canadian, catches the act of Mr. Memory (Wylie Watson) until the moment when mysterious gunshots cause the audience to stampede to the exits. Outside, an attractive foreigner calling herself Annabella Smith (Lucie Mannheim) asks Hannay if she may accompany him home. But in Hannay's flat, intruders murder Annabella. She had indicated that an espionage ring is based in Scotland, and Hannay now knows that he must go there— if only to clear himself of the murder. The upshot is that he finds himself on the Scottish moors surrealistically handcuffed to a young woman, Pamela (Madeleine Carroll), fleeing from some phony policemen sent after them by the spy chief, Professor Jordan (Godfrey Tearle), because they know too much. At an inn, Pamela overhears their pursuers say that the Professor is meeting someone at the London Palladium—Mr. Memory. Onstage at the Palladium, Mr. Memory seems about to expose the spies when the Professor shoots him. The Professor tries to flee across the stage but is caught. Pamela and Hannay (with handcuffs still dangling from one wrist) hear Mr. Memory's dying words.

One of the great crowd-pleasers, and a considerable box office success, *The 39 Steps* turns out to be built on a motif of sexual frustration, like several Howard Hawks comedies, for example. Happily, Hannay is a gentleman, and imperturbable. There is also a deeper motif. Hannay's adventures educate him in a knowledge that might be called *Bergsonian*, after the philosopher Henri Bergson (1859–1941), who taught that "real time" must be grasped intuitively. Hannay's foil is Mr. Memory, who knows only facts.

Both Robert Donat and Madeleine Caroll had just returned from Hollywood. Donat was born in Manchester and received elocution lessons at an early age.

Below: Hitch and Alma on the set with star Madeleine Carroll, the first true Hitchcock blonde.

In films since 1932, his supporting role to Charles Laughton in Alexander Korda's *The Private Life of Henry VIII* (1933) made him famous. The following year, he successfully played a swashbuckler in Rowland V. Lee's *The Count of Monte Cristo*. In *The 39 Steps*, he is the typical Hitchcock innocent-man figure thrust into a bizarre situation that brings out his true mettle. Donat is up to all the script's demands.

Almost as good is Madeleine Carroll. She had a B.A. from Birmingham University, but gave up teaching for acting. Before working for Hitchcock, she'd appeared in such films as *Escape* (1930), the Ivor Novello vehicle *Sleeping Car* (1933), and John Ford's *The World Moves On* (1934). A still from the Ford film shows her looking positively Garbo-esque. But several reports indicate that it took Hitchcock to bring out more than just the lady-like side of Carroll. Hitch gleefully devised indignities for her to undergo, especially in the scenes on the moors. Perhaps he went too

Richard Hannay (Robert Donat) on the run from the police in Scotland. Both scriptwriter Charles Bennett and Hitchcock liked the double chase (involving both police and spies) element of the original novel.

far. Years afterwards, the actress gave an interview to film scholar Brian McFarlane that was frankly uncomplimentary about some of Hitch's methods of directing her.

Charles Bennett wrote the screenplay from John Buchan's celebrated 1915 shocker. The episode of the cottage isn't in the novel, and was derived from a rather risqué joke that Bennett and Hitch had once heard. At first sight, the film doesn't much resemble the book at all. Mr. Memory is one of the film's own creations, based on a real music-hall performer called Datas. But in the novel there's an episode where the master-spy obtains access to, and memorizes, top secret naval documents by impersonating the First Sea Lord.

Even more than *The Man Who Knew Too Much*, *The 39 Steps* is notable for the speed of its transitions and its general zippiness, something that went down well in America. In the *New York Times*, Andre Sennwald hailed Hitchcock: "Perhaps the identifying hallmark of his method is its apparent absence of accent in the climaxes, which are upon the spectator like a slap in the face before he has set himself for the blow. In such episodes as the murder of the woman in Hannay's apartment, the icy ferocity of the man with

the missing finger when he casually shoots Hannay, or the brilliantly managed sequences on the train, the action progresses through seeming indifference to whip-like revelations."

The train sequence begins with the famous transition from the shot of Hannay's landlady screaming (she's just found the body) to the sound of the train's whistle as it plunges into a tunnel. A paradox is that such slowing-down may itself facilitate the progress of the story. In Professor Jordan's house, Hitchcock wants to establish the man in his *milieu*, and show the respect and privilege that surround him. So the film makes the occasion a Sunday-morning birthday celebration for the Professor's teenage daughter, to which selected guests from the neighborhood have been invited. A brilliantly choreographed shot lasting about a minute and a half lets the audience meet the various guests, register their excitement that the "Portland Place Murderer" may be on the run nearby, and then watch them make their farewells and depart. None of this seems forced, with the single take lending events an almost leisurely note.

Much can be read into the relationship of the Professor and his wife. It is clearly a loving one: see the scene where they anxiously say farewell to each other before the Professor leaves for London. The Jordans are probably the most deeply bonded of all the couples shown or referred to in the film.

In short, the film's tone would seem to allow any interpretation of its view on marriage—pro or con—that a spectator

Hannay at the farmer's cottage (Donat, John Laurie, and Peggy Ashcroft).

Pamela's feelings for Hannay begin to thaw when they spend a night at the inn. Hitch recognized the "sexual connotation" of their being handcuffed together for part of the film.

JOHN BUCHAN (1875–1940)

One of Hitchcock's favorite authors, the gifted John Buchan was the son of a Scottish minister and himself an elder of the Church of Scotland for thirty years. Besides writing his many books, which include biographies of Cromwell and Sir Walter Scott, Buchan served as an officer and war correspondent in the First World War, and was elected to Parliament as a Conservative candidate in 1927. He was made Baron Tweedsmuir of Elsfield in 1935 and appointed Governor-General of Scotland the same year. Literary influences on Buchan include the poetry of John Keats, *Pilgrim's Progress* by John Bunyan, and novels by Stevenson, Rider Haggard, and Kipling, among others. On seeing Hitchcock's film version of *The Thirty-Nine Steps*, Buchan was at first affronted, later praising. The novel itself, one of Buchan's earliest, has been questioned for its "imperialistic" assumptions, and it has some anti-Semitic and homophobic passages. But there is no denying Buchan's general literary skills of scene-setting and atmosphere, his romantic characters and exciting plots. Many influences of Buchan's writing on Hitchcock are detectable, from the Nietzschean villain of *The Power House* (1912; see Tobin in *Saboteur*) to the recurring idea that civilization is "a very thin crust" (e.g., *Huntingtower*, 1922), as alluded to in the remake of *The Man Who Knew Too Much*.

wants to give it; a lot depends in any case on what stage of the film is singled out. There's a gradual progression away from the cynicism of the opening music-hall scene where the manager pleads for order after a brawl erupts, "Gentlemen, gentlemen, you're not at home!" The scene in the crofter's cottage explicitly raises the issue of freedom, and very possibly the filmmakers would agree with the poet Robert Frost, who wrote that freedom is "feeling easy in one's harness." The film's climax occurs in a theater where everything is at once circumscribed yet life-invoking. Mr. Memory has rather cut himself off from life's flow through his unimaginative use of memory. But Hannay has been exposed to a quickening process in every sense (epitomized by his impromptu speech at a political rally). As he and Pamela respectfully attend to Mr. Memory's dying words, the chorus line in the background kicks up its legs to the tune of "Tinkle, Tinkle, Tinkle" from the suitably named Victor Saville film *Evergreen* (1934).

The climax. The police close in on Professor Jordan (Godfrey Tearle), after he shoots Mr. Memory.

SECRET AGENT

First screening January 1936

Production company: Gaumont-British Picture Corporation, Ltd.

Duration 83 minutes

Black and white

London, 1916. Distinguished soldier and novelist Edgar Brodie (John Gielgud) is renamed "Richard Ashenden" and sent to Geneva. His mission: to kill an unknown German agent who is leaving for Arabia. Ashenden is given two assistants; the first, Elsa Carrington (Madeleine Carroll), will pose as his wife. The other, known variously as the General and "the Hairless Mexican" (Peter Lorre), will do the actual killing. Complicating matters is the attention Elsa has been receiving from an American, Robert Marvin (Robert Young). Then matters go disastrously wrong when Ashenden and the General assassinate the wrong man, pushing the innocent Caypor (Percy Marmont) off the Langenthal Alp. Elsa takes this particularly badly. Failing to convince Ashenden, with whom she has shared an affection, to abort the mission, she reacts by leaving with Marvin—just as word comes that Marvin is in fact the German spy. Ashenden and the General follow the pair onto the Constantinople train. Elsa pleads for no more killing, but events are taken out of their hands when the train is bombed and crashes. Marvin is fatally wounded in the crash, but takes a chance to kill the General before dying himself.

Unlike *The 39 Steps*, *Secret Agent* isn't based on sexual frustration. Indeed, Ashenden and Elsa eventually sleep together, with him telling her afterwards, "There are times, Mrs. Ashenden, when it's almost a pleasure to be alive." But, by design, *Secret Agent* lacks the obvious liveliness of its predecessor. Its sardonic tone wasn't always appreciated by 1930s audiences. Today, the film still challenges "our complacent assumptions about the possibility of purity or heroism in war" (Maurice Yacowar).

The film came about after Michael Balcon acquired the rights to a play called *Ashenden*, which a film critic, Campbell Dixon, had based on Somerset Maugham's

Above: Madeleine Carroll, Peter Lorre, Alfred Hitchcock, and Robert Young relax between takes.

short story, "The Hairless Mexican." By combining the original story with another in the "Ashenden" series, called "The Traitor," and adding a love interest taken from the play, Hitchcock and Charles Bennett arrived at the basis of their film. Neither story was in anything like the heroic vein of John Buchan. "The Traitor" tells how Ashenden causes the happily married Caypor to return to England where he is arrested as a spy. "The Hairless Mexican" shows Ashenden and the title character going to Geneva to execute a Greek agent—and killing the wrong man by mistake.

Hitchcock and Bennett then changed and added material. For a dramatic climax, a train smash was introduced. For the film's central scene of Caypor's death, in which the man's dog several miles away appears to sense what is happening, the screenwriters remembered one of G. K. Chesterton's Father Brown stories. (Called "The Oracle of the Dog," it has a scene in which a dog lets out a great howl of woe at what is later found to be the exact time of its master's murder.) And the part of the Hairless Mexican was built up for Peter Lorre, to become easily the film's most intriguing character. In the story, he has smooth skin like a woman's, and no eyebrows or eyelashes. Ashenden comments, "with that frightful appearance can he really be the lady's man he pretends?" (It's worth remembering that author Somerset Maugham was gay, and that Lorre's performance in the film is sometimes described as campy.)

Anticipating in some respects Bruno in *Strangers on a Train*, the General (as the Hairless Mexican is also known) represents the dark side of the hero. In this case, he may be said to represent the allure that espionage holds for a relative innocent like Ashenden. After Ashenden has agreed to Elsa's request that he abandon the mission, the General arrives and tells him that the Germans are using a nearby chocolate factory in their operations. Ashenden can't resist the temptation to investigate. Elsa pleads with him not to go, but he follows the General out. At the door, the General gives Elsa a knowing smile. In a perceptive review, *Kinematograph Weekly* noted how "this espionage drama differs vastly from the orthodox in treatment. Instead of unfolding the tale with the directness usually associated with entertainment of this type, the producer reflects the story in the psychological reactions of the leading characters."

The chocolate-factory sequence is another of the film's big suspense pieces. It works well enough, if in a rather mechanical way because there's no romance involved. Also, its main point seems to be that there's a childish side to espionage (symbolized by the chocolate!), something which adds to the premeditated effect. But there are balancing scenes. One such is an improvised encounter between Elsa, Marvin, and a coach driver (famous stage actor Michel Saint-Denis, who was visiting John Gielgud on the set). The extempore lines are sophisticated, and Madeleine Carroll is relaxed and delightful.

Above all, Hitchcock and Bennett saw that espionage has its *realpolitik* aspect. In a scene set in a London steamroom between intelligence boss "R" (Charles Carson) and his uniformed adjutant (Tom Helmore, who would play Gavin Elster in *Vertigo*), the colonel thinks nothing of dispatching the Royal Flying Corps to shoot up a train carrying both the fleeing German spy and several British agents, as well as innocent civilians.

The scene on the train is masterly. At one moment Marvin tells Elsa that he

Top: *Caypor (Percy Marmont), the General (Peter Lorre), and Edgar Brodie (John Gielgud). Graham Greene disliked Hitch's "inadequate sense of reality" and complained that "nothing is left of that witty and realistic fiction [Ashenden]."*
Above left: *Madeleine Carroll, in her second and last film for Hitchcock.*
Above right: *Peter Lorre in makeup. Charles Bennett thought Lorre's was a "superb performance; hateful but, as always, whimsically lovable."*

never loved her, then immediately kisses her. It is thus far from obvious that his words mean what they say. Marvin's conversation has consistently used reverse-meanings, such as when he had phoned Elsa to ask, "Hello, is that the ugliest woman in the world?" But both Marvin and the General are finally dedicated professional spies. The film's ending is ironic. In the wreckage of the derailed train, the General places a loaded pistol and a single bullet in front of the mortally injured Marvin. This seems to be the traditional invitation to one's enemy to take his own life (see Professor Jordan's offer to Hannay in *The 39 Steps*). But Marvin

can't help himself. Even as he requests water, he picks up the pistol and shoots the General. His unshakeable sense of his duty recalls that of the dying Mr. Memory in *The 39 Steps*—and foreshadows that of the Nazi U-boat captain in *Lifeboat*, relentlessly steering the boat and its Allied occupants, his rescuers, towards a German supply ship.

Arguably, this ending is superior to the one Hitchcock originally wanted—the censor, however, took objection to it at script stage—in which the General would have shot Marvin as he drank the offered water. Either way, *Secret Agent* is another superior spy film by Hitchcock.

SABOTAGE

American title: The Woman Alone

First screening December 1936

Production company:
Gaumont-British Picture
Corporation, Ltd.

Duration 76 minutes

Black and white

When a saboteur disables London's Battersea Power Station, the city is briefly plunged into darkness. The man responsible, Mr. Verloc (Oscar Homolka), returns home to the shabby East End cinema he runs with his wife Winnie (Sylvia Sidney). The couple are childless, but Winnie is devoted to her schoolboy brother Stevie (Desmond Tester), and struggles to make ends meet. She becomes friendly with Ted (John Loder), from the greengrocer's shop next door, who is actually an undercover Scotland Yard man. Suspecting that he is being watched, Verloc, whose next task is to leave a timebomb at Piccadilly Station, gives the parcel to an unwitting Stevie to deliver. But the boy is delayed by the Lord Mayor's Show Day procession, and the bomb explodes on a bus, killing Stevie and everyone else aboard. Later, a dazed Winnie stabs Verloc with a carving knife as she serves him dinner. The bomb's maker, a bird shop proprietor known as the Professor (William Dewhurst), comes to the cinema and finds Verloc's body. When the police follow him there, he blows the place up. But Winnie has left with Ted. In his wisdom, Ted decides to say nothing to the authorities about how Verloc died.

As in *Juno and the Paycock*, it is the women and children in *Sabotage* who end up paying for men's misdeeds. But this time Hitchcock also gives us the character of Ted, who makes a gesture for reasonableness. In a film set in and around a cinema, two movie-related moments are expressive. A screening of one of Disney's Silly Symphonies asks, "Who killed Cock Robin?"—and as the answer shows one of Cock Robin's rivals, *another* Cock Robin. Later, after the dazed Winnie has killed her husband, and Ted is pleading with her to run away with

him, a poster behind them asks ironically, *Aren't Men Beasts!* (the title of a recently shot BIP farce made by Hitchcock's former mentor, Graham Cutts).

There is thus a pessimism to *Sabotage*, based on the famous novel *The Secret Agent* (1907) by Joseph Conrad, as there had also been to Hitchcock's previous film, *Secret Agent*, based on stories by Somerset Maugham. (Revealingly, an influence on both Conrad and Maugham was the philosopher Schopenhauer, often called a pessimist.) Conrad has Winnie Verloc say, "life doesn't stand much looking into," and shows that Verloc himself is only a pawn in an international anarchists' plot. The film repeats that idea when Ted's Scotland Yard boss tells him

that there are people behind the sabotage "that you and I'll never catch." To offset the film's dark side, Hitchcock relied on the vitality of its London settings and the conviction of the performances, even the most minor.

Those performances range from Sylvia Sidney's as Winnie to Martita Hunt's as the Professor's daughter. The American Sidney, who had just co-starred with Spencer Tracy in Fritz Lang's *Fury* (1936), found Hitchcock's direction restrictive, especially in the short takes used for the scene where she knifes her husband. But Hitchcock knew exactly what he was doing. He deliberately gave her a slightly boyish quality to suggest that in some ways Winnie feels closer to her brother

than to Verloc. Her sailor's outfit, and the scene where she helps Stevie mend his toy yacht, hint at something missing from her life. Verloc himself senses this. As played by Oscar Homolka, who was formerly with Max Reinhardt's famous theatrical troupe in Germany, he is a tragic figure. Caught up in the anarchists' world, he has begun to grow weary. In the aquarium, he tells his boss that he doesn't want to be involved in any loss of life, but is overruled. He had half foreseen this. In the scene where he lies on his bed after his rather inept attempt at sabotage, he shows both indolence and complacency. (Uncle Charlie in *Shadow of a Doubt* is depicted in a similar manner.) His almost

willed death is perfectly in keeping.

John Loder brings some vigor to the part of Ted, wittily defining an act of God as "activated by actual action," but the film requires that for much of the time even Ted isn't in control, that the action is dictated from elsewhere. The strongest note of protest at the folly of men and their actions is sounded by the Professor's haggard-looking daughter, whose lover had left her, apparently on hearing she was pregnant. (This again echoes *Juno and the Paycock*.) Near the end of the film, she rounds on her father, demanding that he recover the birdcage that had contained a bomb and might be used in evidence. "How could you be so mad?" she

asks. Actress Martita Hunt would go on to play the eccentric Miss Havisham in both stage and screen versions of *Great Expectations*.

All this pessimism and psychology did not go down well in some quarters. In America, *Variety* saw it as "a weakness, because average American audiences expect Scotland Yard sleuthing to develop. When it doesn't, the film disappoints." But Mark Van Doren's review in *Nation* was full of praise: Hitchcock "is the best film director now flourishing," his film "nothing but detail and all of it good."

One detail was the sound of Verloc's creaking shoe as he moves toward Winnie just before the stabbing. The sound suggests his fear—he's walking on tiptoe—but also it seems to act on Winnie like a goad. During Hitchcock's first sound film, *Blackmail*, a take had been ruined by a pair of squeaky boots. Hitchcock had commented that the sound might be used to create suspense in some later film—*Sabotage*, as it turned out. For the sequence with the bomb, Hitchcock piled detail on detail. Stevie is held up first by a street salesman who uses him to demonstrate to a delighted crowd the merits of a toothpaste and a hair tonic, and then dismisses him with a brusque "hop it, you little basket!" A street procession further delays the boy. The sequence works much like the one in *Psycho* of Marion's unwitting drive to her death in Norman Bates's motel. "The more you go into detail," Hitchcock said, "the more an audience identifies with the character."

Sabotage was the last Hitchcock film produced by Michael Balcon, who soon afterwards left Gaumont-British to set up an MGM production program in Britain, before moving to independent production at Ealing Studios.

HITCHCOCK AND HIS WRITERS

To Alfred Hitchcock, the real creative work on a film was produced in the office with a writer, and Hitch always collaborated on his screenplays. This naturally strengthens his position as an auteur, which he seemingly relished. "A lot of people embrace the auteur theory," said Hitchcock. "But it's difficult to know what someone means by it. I suppose they mean that the responsibility for the film rests solely on the shoulders of the director. But very often the director is no better than his script."

From selection of the basic material to the hiring (and firing) of every writer and the final revision of the final shooting-script, Hitchcock was involved in almost all aspects of the screenplay's development. Although he rarely did any actual writing, especially on his Hollywood productions, Hitch guided his writers through each draft, insisting on strict attention to detail and underscoring the importance of storytelling through visual rather than verbal means.

Hitch's first film job was as a designer of silent movie titles for Famous Players-Lasky, where he worked closely with the studio's writers. During this apprentice-

ship, Hitchcock learned the fundamentals of constructing a movie scenario, and he might have found his calling had his visual flair, technical proficiency, and exposure to the German cinema not made him ideally suited to the role of director.

Hitchcock's run of classic British movies in the thirties appropriately coincided with the beginning of his long association with screenwriter Charles Bennett. (It was Bennett's stage play, *Blackmail*, which Hitchcock had adapted for his first talkie.) In 1934, Bennett and Hitchcock collaborated on *The Man Who Knew Too Much*, the first in a string of innovative thrillers combining the wit, freshness, and originality that became Hitchcock trademarks. Bennett's true genius lay in story construction, and his scenarios were built on many devices now regarded as Hitchcockian: the "MacGuffin," the double-chase, the charming villain, and the use of exotic locales woven dramatically into the plot. With Bennett, Hitchcock's cinematic vision came into clear focus, and he created the blueprint for Hitch's later screenwriting collaborations.

On the BBC program *Omnibus* in 1986, Bennett described a typical workday with Hitchcock: "In the morning, I used to get up and pick up Hitch in Cromwell Road, where he lived, at ten o'clock exactly. And he would be sitting on the curb waiting for me, with Joan Harrison, who was our secretary. And then we would go to the studio where we would discuss the script and what I was

Above: *Secret Agent, scripted by Bennett. Three different endings were written for this film.*
Below: *Blackmail was based on a stage play by Hitch's great thirties scriptwriter, Charles Bennett.*

doing with it. Then at about one o'clock, everything would stop, and we'd go to lunch, always at the Mayfair Hotel, and have a wonderful lunch. Then come back, and at that point Hitch would usually go to sleep in the office, and I would do a little work, and possibly doze off too—slightly. But eventually, at about five o'clock, we would go back to Hitchcock's flat where we would start having nice cocktails for the evening, and talk more and more and more about the script. And I think more work was done on the script in the evening over cocktails than any other time."

Bennett and Hitchcock met each day until they had completed a detailed treatment of about 70 to 100 pages. Only when this treatment was finished would the dialogue be considered (at which point Hitchcock nearly always brought in other writers). It was with their five scripts together in the 1930s—*The Man Who Knew Too Much*, *The 39 Steps*, *Secret Agent*, *Sabotage*, and *Young and Innocent* (they later reunited for *Foreign Correspondent*)—that Hitchcock reached the zenith of his British period.

In 1939, Hollywood beckoned, and Hitchcock was soon working with a number of distinguished American authors, including Robert E. Sherwood and Dorothy Parker. However, these early

efforts largely featured stories set in England, or were reworkings of his British style. Hitch did not really establish an American voice until his collaboration with playwright Thornton Wilder in 1943 on *Shadow of a Doubt*. Hitchcock was delighted to secure Wilder's services (it was to be his only film script work), and proudly described the finished product as

"one of those rare occasions when suspense and melodrama combined well with character."

Even more fruitful was his association with Ben Hecht, who had a knack for crackling dialogue and strong characterizations, honed from his years as a Chicago newspaper reporter. Complemented by Hitchcock's plot twists and ability to draw suspense from almost any situation, Hecht wrote two of the director's finest scripts of the forties, *Spellbound* and *Notorious* (as well as providing some uncredited assistance on *Foreign Correspondent*, *Lifeboat*, and *The Paradine Case*). "[Hecht] was an extraordinary screenwriter and a marvellous man," Hitchcock told a French interviewer in 1972. "We would discuss a screenplay for hours and then he would say, 'Well, Hitchie, write the dialogue you want and then I'll correct it.' Ben was like a chess player, he could work on four scripts at the same time." However, the collaboration did not last. As well as being one of Hollywood's busiest and most expensive screenwriters, Hecht was as notorious a self-promoter as Hitch.

Following his collaboration with Hecht, Hitchcock never worked with another writer whose reputation was on a par with, let alone exceeded, his own. Similarly, Hitchcock's films were fre-

Top: The Man Who Knew Too Much *was Bennett and Hitchcock's first collaboration on an original screenplay.*
Above: *Alma was Hitch's most frequent collaborator.*
Right: Foreign Correspondent *was the last Hitchcock film Bennett worked on. He received an Oscar nomination for his work on this picture.*

quently adapted from lesser known novels and plays. He had learned a valuable lesson from his first Hollywood production, *Rebecca*, which was billed in its theatrical trailer as "David O. Selznick's production of Daphne du Maurier's celebrated novel . . . directed by Alfred Hitchcock." After that, whatever the source material, Hitchcock's name would not be overshadowed by the original author's.

Following a disappointing commercial run at Warner Brothers and for his own company Transatlantic Pictures, Hitchcock moved to Paramount, where he teamed up with writer John Michael Hayes. The Hitchcock/Hayes collaboration resulted in four motion pictures in two years—*Rear Window*, *To Catch a Thief*, *The Trouble with Harry*, and *The Man Who Knew Too Much*—and proved one of Hollywood's most successful director/screenwriter pairings.

"What I brought to Hitch was character, dialogue, movement, and entertainment," remembered Hayes in a 1994 interview with the present author. "He supplied the suspense element. You see, if a writer goes to work with Hitchcock, he doesn't need to bring suspense with him, because Hitch has that." Hayes left an indelible mark on

On Shadow of a Doubt, *Hitch worked with the great American novelist Thornton Wilder, having been attracted by Wilder's play* Our Town.

the director's canon, just as Charles Bennett did before him, providing a perfect mix of style, sophistication, and crisp dialogue. "It was a wonderful experience," said Hayes. "I learned a lot from Hitch about gourmet food, cigars, and wine, in addition to learning about screenwriting. When we worked together there was a certain brightness to his movies, and we should have done more." Unfortunately, Hayes committed the gravest of sins, challenging Hitchcock over a credit dispute on *The Man Who Knew Too Much*. Hayes won the battle, but Hitch severed the relationship. He would never again settle on another writer with whom he completed more than one consecutive film.

Hitchcock ended the 1950s working with screenwriters Samuel Taylor and Ernest Lehman, each of whom wrote one of the director's masterworks. According to Taylor, who scripted *Vertigo*, Hitchcock understood the difference between plot and story, observing that while the director's films were often looked down upon because of his chosen genre, the characters' stories were of great significance. "He preferred telling an inconsequential yarn," recalled Taylor for *Omnibus*, "but bringing to it all the artistry he had."

Above: *Leading Hollywood scriptwriter Ben Hecht worked on both* Spellbound *and* Notorious.
Right: *Hitch's partnership with John Michael Hayes, perhaps his best since working with Charles Bennett, began with* Rear Window.

Above: "What made us a good team," claimed Hayes, "was that he had such brilliant technique and knowledge of the visual, and ego and conviction; and I think I was able to bring him a warmth of characterization." The seduction scene in To Catch a Thief.
Above right: Ernest Lehman wanted "to do a Hitchcock picture to end all Hitchcock pictures . . . with glamour, wit, excitement, movement, big scenes, a large canvas, [and an] innocent bystander caught up in great derring-do." The result was the classic North by Northwest.
Right: Sean Connery rehearses the script for Marnie with script supervisor Lois Thurman.

Ernest Lehman set out to write the "Hitchcock picture to end all Hitchcock pictures," creating in *North by Northwest* Hitch's greatest chase film. "He didn't go around like some imperious film producer-director," Lehman told A&E's *Biography* in 1996. "He was very quiet, very unassuming, but everybody was afraid of his disapproval, and that's what made them do their best for him. You feared doing something that was below his standards."

The 1960s were particularly troublesome for Hitch and his writers: *The Birds* screenwriter, Evan Hunter, was dismissed from *Marnie* when he refused to write the film's rape scene; after completing *Marnie*, Jay Presson Allen adapted J. M. Barrie's *Mary Rose*, but the studio dis-

couraged Hitchcock from proceeding with the film; and Brian Moore was so dissatisfied with his script for *Torn Curtain* that he requested his name be removed from the picture. Nearly every project Hitchcock started required multiple writers, and a number were abandoned at script stage. Joseph Stefano later commented, "In a strange way, the rest of his movies were an attempt to top *Psycho*. He never got back to that nice leisurely going from one film to another that he had done before."

In the end, Hitchcock maintained no allegiance with any of his writers. Even Ernest Lehman, who reunited with the director for *Family Plot*, was replaced by David Freeman on *The Short Night*, the project Hitchcock was preparing before his death in 1980. Perhaps the single most important collaborator of Hitchcock's career was his wife Alma Reville. For nearly fifty years, when not directly involved in the writing of one of his movies, Alma was in the wings as Hitchcock's in-house story editor. Many of Hitchcock's writers have remarked that the director did not believe in giving flattery, and agreed that the greatest compliment one could receive from Hitchcock was that "Alma liked the screenplay very much."

Steven L. DeRosa

YOUNG AND INNOCENT

American title: The Girl Was Young

First screening November 1937

Production company:
Gainsborough Pictures

Duration 80 minutes

Black and white

Robert Tisdale (Derrick de Marney), a young screenwriter, finds a murdered woman on a Kent beach. She has been strangled with the belt from a raincoat. When the police learn that Robert had known the woman, an actress named Christine Clay, and that she has left him £1,200 in her will, they become suspicious—the more so when he tells them that his raincoat has been stolen. He faints, and is brought around with first aid administered by Erica Burgoyne (Nova Pilbeam), the teenage daughter of the local chief constable (Percy Marmont). Robert is arraigned for murder. Given an inept lawyer, he determines to escape. While on the run in the nearby countryside, he re-encounters Erica, and persuades her of his innocence. She hides him in an abandoned mill, and he enlists her aid in hunting the real murderer. From a tramp named Old Will (Edward Rigby), they learn of a man with twitching eyes who had given Will a raincoat minus its belt. Erica finally spots the man, a drummer playing in a hotel dance band. He is identified as Christine's estranged husband and confesses to having killed her out of jealousy.

At dawn on June 8, 1931, the body of an attractive woman—possibly murdered—was found washed up on a lonely beach about twenty miles out of New York. The incident made headlines in both America and Britain. Several novelists eventually used it in their books. One was Agatha Christie, in the opening chapter of *Why Didn't They Ask Evans?* (1934)—though the body was now a man's. Another was Josephine Tey, whose new Inspector Grant mystery, *A Shilling for Candles* (1936), was promptly filmed by Hitchcock as *Young and Innocent.* Despite his unfair estimation of the novel as "very, very bad," *Young and Innocent*

Above: Hitchcock filming his own cameo.

became Hitch's favorite among his British films.

In 1937 Gaumont-British suddenly closed down, except as a distributor, necessitating a move for the Hitchcock film from Lime Grove to Pinewood in the middle of shooting. Gaumont's sister company, Gainsborough, took it over, so Hitch now found himself working under producer Edward Black for the company that had given him his start as a director. It proved a happy return for him. He particularly enjoyed guiding the performance of seven-

teen-year-old Nova Pilbeam, his child star of *The Man Who Knew Too Much*. In deference to her youth, the press was told that Hitchcock "will put the soft pedal on the sex stuff, and will concentrate on the thrills." (The fact that Pilbeam's co-lead, stage actor Derrick de Marney, was more than a dozen years her senior, does suggest a certain paternal slant to the film.) Hitch found her "entirely natural," and a line at the end about the importance of being human effectively pays tribute to that emergent quality in her.

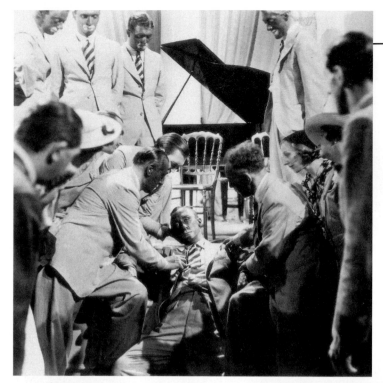

has something native in its people, background, humors and ways of thought; and all of those things unforced." Sadly, the American distributors excised ten minutes. The main casualty was the surreal and very funny children's birthday party scene, which Hitch had managed to lend a sinister note, both literally—the music that's playing on the radio—and figuratively, as Aunt Mary (Mary Clare) becomes suspicious about why Erica and Robert seem so anxious to get away.

Seen today, the film justifies Hitch's own high estimation of it. Beneath the sunny surface is a sly suggestiveness, anticipating aspects of David Lynch's *Blue Velvet* (1986). Both films focus on a youth poised between a married woman—a public entertainer—and a teenager, the daughter of a policeman. In *Young and Innocent*, the murdered actress may have been Robert's mistress. Likewise, in Lynch's film, young Jeffrey (Kyle MacLachlan) cheats on Sandy (Laura Dern), with whom he is investigating a bizarre murder, and sleeps with the married Dorothy (Isabella Rossellini).

Everyone remembers *Young and Innocent*'s climactic crane shot which descends, *deus ex machina*-fashion, from above a crowded dance floor to reveal in close-up the villain with his twitching eyes. The shot required what was then Pinewood's biggest sound stage. But there's another fine shot, worthy of equal acclaim. Erica and Robert, on the run, have stopped their car under cover of night beside a railway shunting yard near a town. Hitchcock here employs a model shot, with a tangible and quite lovely mood. The shot has several ingredients: an elaborate sideways tracking movement as a steam train rushes under a moonlit bridge where we've just seen a car cross; light playing on housefronts from the car's headlamps and from a nearby signal box; the sounds of the speeding train, of shunting, and of a tolling bell; and a final downwards tilt of the camera as, arriving near the parked car, it shows us the focal point of the tableau, the young couple. "The night," we hear Robert say, "always exaggerates things, doesn't it? Personally, I like the night. It's much more alive than the day."

In an often magical film, that is perhaps its most Shakespearean moment.

Even the weather was obliging. Hitch had just written an article for the *New York Times* lamenting that "the greatest difficulty we have in making films in England is to combat the climate." Now he seemed mistaken. Though a unit was specifically sent to Cornwall to obtain footage for the opening storm scene at night, the bulk of the film is palpably set in sunlight on the flat uplands of Kent with its long straight Roman roads—all of this consistent with Pilbeam's character, Erica, and her innocence.

Another benign aspect of the film, noted by critic Penelope Gilliatt, is how it "detectably embod[ies] some parody of

stage and screen comedies of the time." The china mender Old Will is called "more or less of a tramp," and seems to have reminded Hitch of Charlie Chaplin. Thus the free-for-all that breaks out at the roadhouse Tom's Hat resembles the one in *Easy Street* (1917); and the scene set in Nobby's flophouse recalls *Triple Trouble* (1918). Hitch would increasingly allude to other films in this way.

Chaplinesque, too, is how *Young and Innocent* spans various social levels, from the most patrician (spot the Roman busts in Uncle Basil and Aunt Mary's house!) to the most humble. The *Film Weekly* reviewer loved the film's Englishness: "It

First screening August 1938

**Production company:
Gainsborough Pictures**

Duration 97 minutes

Black and white

Iris Henderson (Margaret Lockwood), vacationing in central Europe, is about to return home to London and be married. At the railway station, she is speaking with a kindly middle-aged governess, Miss Froy (Dame May Whitty), when a falling window box knocks her out. When she wakes up, she's on the train, a concerned Miss Froy opposite her. Soon afterwards, Miss Froy disappears—and no one seems to have ever seen her. Desperate, Iris asks a dapper English musicologist, Gilbert (Michael Redgrave), whom she had earlier met and loathed, to help her search the train. They encounter a neurosurgeon, Dr. Hartz (Paul Lukas), who says Iris is hallucinating. Actually, Hartz has kidnapped Miss Froy—a British spy—and swathed her in bandages, ready to smuggle her off the train as a patient. Almost the only people aboard who aren't conspiring with Hartz are the English passengers, including a cricket-mad pair, Charters and Caldicott (Basil Radford and Naunton Wayne). When found out, Hartz arranges to have the train's front section diverted onto a branch line: on board are the English passengers. During a shootout, Miss Froy slips away. But eventually Iris and Gilbert, now firm friends, rejoin her in London.

W hen Hitchcock took over an abandoned project called *Lost Lady* (an adaptation of Ethel Lina White's 1936 novel *The Wheel Spins*), he asked screenwriters Frank Launder and Sidney Gilliat to add several scenes. The revised screenplay became *The Lady Vanishes*, one of its director's best comedy-thrillers. Among the new scenes was the luggage-van episode in which Iris and Gilbert literally come to grips with Signor Doppo (Philip Leaver), the sinister magician whose main act is called The Vanishing Lady. The entire scene is brilliant—yet has almost no plot reason for being in the film. In this and some other respects, it's

Sally Stewart, Margaret Lockwood, Hitch, and Googie Withers between takes on the hotel set.

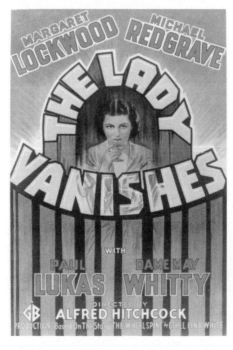

like the children's birthday party episode in *Young and Innocent*, or the McKittrick Hotel scene in *Vertigo* (another vanishing lady act). But plot isn't everything, of course. These scenes remind us that Hitchcock wants to give us much more than a bare story.

In the case of *The Lady Vanishes*, Hitchcock had a proven basic story to begin with. Among the first to tell it had been Mrs. Belloc Lowndes in her 1913 novel *The End of Her Honeymoon*. Later it was re-told by Alexander Woollcott and made into both a film (*So Long at the Fair*

[1950]) and an episode of *Alfred Hitchcock Presents* ("The Vanishing Lady" [1955]). Its essence is that two people visit the Paris Exposition of 1889; when the death of one of them is hushed up, it's because the death was caused by plague. Curiously, a piece of dialogue in *The Lady Vanishes* seems to echo the original story. Mrs. Todhunter (Linden Travers) admonishes Todhunter (Cecil Parker) for his excessive concern about possible scandal: "You weren't so particular in Paris last autumn." "It was quite different then," he tells her; "the

Above: The film's three stars—Michael Redgrave, Margaret Lockwood, and Paul Lukas—pose for a publicity still.

The Spanish tie-in novelization of The Lady Vanishes.

like Robert in *Young and Innocent*? Incidentally, the business of Iris becoming irate because of loud dancing in the room above hers, caused by the man she will eventually love, was probably borrowed from *Top Hat* (1935).

Above all, Launder and Gilliat showed their form by creating that comic duo, Charters and Caldicott. There had been a golf-club bore played by Gordon Harker in Walter Forde's *Rome Express* (1932), and the two corset salesmen forever talking shop on the train in *The 39 Steps* are another likely influence. Also, Leslie Halliwell detects "more than a suggestion of Laurel and Hardy" in the scene where Charters and Caldicott must share a double-bed in the maid's room at the inn. Nonetheless, the duo are a pair of screen originals. Their function in the film is both to be comic figures and to caricature

always taught me never to desert a lady in trouble—he even carried that as far as marrying Mother." Hitchcock gave his screenwriters plenty of latitude. When Iris manages to have Gilbert thrown out of his attic room at the inn for making noise, it appears he was staying there in the first place because a German lady had paid his board. Is he, then, another gigolo figure

Margaret Lockwood listening to Hitch on the train set. Hitchcock won The New York Film Critics Award for Best Direction for his work on the film, although Roy William Neill had originally been assigned to the picture in 1936.

Exhibition was at its height." And she responds, "I realize that now. There's no need to rub it in."

Launder and Gilliat's dialogue is consistently splendid, and the script overall shows a considerable advance on their earlier train thriller, *Seven Sinners* (1936). The adulterous barrister Todhunter characterizes himself in a single line: "I was looking for a street called 'Straight.'" Gilbert has his own memorable lines, such as his remark to Iris, "My father

The climactic shoot-out, from outside and inside the train.

ming compared with his work in the theater. Educated at Cambridge, where he'd gained first-class honors, he felt that the cinema was a second-rate medium. He confessed afterwards, "I was nearly halfway through the picture before I started to try," and added, "you can see the join." Which may be true—such a join comes straight after the luggage-car scene. But as it corresponds to a transformation in Gilbert and Iris, Redgrave was probably mixing up the character and the performance. And he certainly threw himself into the part at the moment when Gilbert has to hit one of the foreign soldiers over the head with a chair. The soldier has just explained his command of English by saying politely, "I was at Oxford." Gilbert justifies his action by remarking, "Well, I was at Cambridge."

Margaret Lockwood competed with Lilli Palmer and Nova Pilbeam for the part of Iris. It's hard to imagine either of her competitors matching the several transformations that Iris undergoes, from the rather spoiled and jaded daughter of a jam manufacturer to resourceful and mature partner of Gilbert by the film's end. The character anticipates aspects of Melanie Daniels in *The Birds*. Iris's initial narcissism is signalled by the monogrammed scarf she wears in the first half of the film—it's discarded after the luggage-car scene, at which point she takes to wearing a sensible, English cardigan (until the final scene, when she's in a becoming suit). A similar transformation had happened in *Young and Innocent* to Erica, where the change was signalled by the loss of her beloved old car in the collapsed mineworks.

Distinguished careers lay ahead for

Above: *Miss Froy explains that she must be leaving.*

several of the qualities, good and bad, of their countrymen. In the opening scene, it's Charters and Caldicott who gallantly, if unthinkingly, open the inn door for Miss Froy to exit into a blizzard: an action that sums up the film. Miss Froy must get her coded message through to London at all costs, and the duo's indomitable spirit will help her do it. Both

men participate in the final shootout, and Caldicott helps Gilbert drive the train to neutral territory and safety. They are far from being merely the prize twits they're sometimes taken for.

On a cramped eighty-eight-foot-long sound stage at Gainsborough's Islington studio, a fine cast assembled. Initially Michael Redgrave saw his role as slum-

The cast of redoubtable English characters. Seated are Naunton Wayne and Basil Radford, who portrayed Charters and Caldicott. In 1940, the characters reappeared in Night Train to Munich, also written by Launder and Gilliat.

There's no denying the skill displayed in *The Lady Vanishes*, not least by its co-writers. Right at the start, as Charters and Caldicott talk of England being on the brink at a time of crisis, we imagine the duo want to flee the developing political situation around them. (The film was in fact put into general release at about the time of the Munich crisis.) Only after several minutes do we find out that all along they've really been talking about a cricket match in Manchester.

GAINSBOROUGH PICTURES

Basil Radford and Naunton Wayne in the 1948 Gainsborough picture It's Not Cricket.

many of those involved in *The Lady Vanishes*. Even elderly stage actress Dame May Whitty, who'd been made a Dame Commander of the British Empire in 1918 and had received an Oscar nomination for her part in *Night Must Fall* (1937), would return to settle in Hollywood and make several more excellent pictures, including *Suspicion* and George Cukor's *Gaslight* (1944). Likewise, the Hungarian Paul Lukas, a superbly urbane and gentlemanly villain for Hitchcock, would go back to Hollywood and eventually receive an Oscar for his starring role with Bette Davis in *Watch on the Rhine* (1943).

The film took just five weeks to shoot and was rushed out for its first public screening at London's Cambridge Theatre in August, 1938. Critical and popular acclaim was enormous. Sydney W. Carroll in the *Sunday Times* called it "the finest British thriller I can remember and one of the most vigorous I have ever seen." William Whitebait in the *New Statesman* noted that Hitchcock "has exploited to the full his particular sense of the sinister

and the bizarre and built up a tension by a masterly use of detail—the heavy panting, for example, of a powerful locomotive brought to a standstill on a side line." In America that year, the film won Hitchcock "Best Direction" in the New York Film Critics Awards.

In 1924, Michael Balcon formed a film company called Gainsborough—after the famous painter—with the promise of financial backing from Gaumont. Its studio was the one in Islington, north London, originally acquired by the American company Famous Players-Lasky. Hitchcock directed five features for Gainsborough in the 1920s, including two shot in Germany. The studio's biggest star at the time was Ivor Novello. He was followed in the 1930s by a number of music-hall figures—including Will Hay—and then such home-grown stars as James Mason and Margaret Lockwood. Hitchcock found himself back at Gainsborough in 1937, and made two more features there.

JAMAICA INN

First screening May 1939

**Production company:
Mayflower Pictures**

Duration 100 minutes

Black and white

In 1820, after the death of her mother in Ireland, Mary Yellan (Maureen O'Hara) comes to Cornwall to join her Aunt Patience (Marie Ney) and Uncle Joss (Leslie Banks) at their lonely Jamaica Inn. She soon learns that Joss leads a gang of wreckers and cutthroats; what she does not know is that the real organizer is the local magistrate, Sir Humphrey Pengallan (Charles Laughton). Mary saves the life of a gang member, Jem Trehearne (Robert Newton), whom the others think has been plundering their booty. Forced to flee, the pair go to Pengallan, who openly admires Mary's beauty. Jem reveals that he's a naval officer obtaining evidence against the wreckers. Pengallan, with the cunning of his approaching madness, pretends to send instructions for the militia to join the three of them at Jamaica Inn. In fact, he tips off Joss, who captures Jem. When a conscience-torn Patience frees Jem, Pengallan shoots her. Meanwhile, Joss dies from a wound inflicted by one of his gang, Harry (Emlyn Williams). Pengallan forces Mary to accompany him to the nearest port, with Jem close behind. Pengallan climbs a ship's rigging, then leaps defiantly to his death.

A main theme of *Jamaica Inn* is determinism. "People can't help being what they are," Aunt Patience says of Joss and herself. "He can't help himself," Mary cries at the climax as soldiers point their rifles at Sir Humphrey. Nonetheless, these same people must live—or die—as best they can. For once, a Hitchcock film struggles to give us a feeling of life being lived. The script falls back on a negative definition: Pengallan claims that one of his valuable china figurines is "more alive than half the people at this table." But such a definition, especially in such a visually nondescript film, isn't dramatic enough. In the end, *Jamaica Inn* is a rare Hitchcock failure.

The project struck trouble soon after Hitchcock had signed the contract with a new company, Mayflower Pictures. He knew both its leading figures: the German producer Erich Pommer, who had produced *The Blackguard* on which Hitchcock had worked in Berlin, and actor Charles Laughton, with whom he had lunched in the late 1920s and occasionally seen since. Laughton had talked Hitch into doing the film, and taking an advance of several thousand pounds, before the director had read the script. The initial idea had been that Laughton would play Joss, while the main villain, as in Daphne du Maurier's 1936 novel, would be an embittered albino parson who preaches Christianity by day and practices devil worship by night. Then someone realized that such a villain would cause distribution problems for the film in America, because the Hays Office would certainly object. So the villain

Above: *Sir Humphrey Pengallan (Charles Laughton), Joss (Leslie Banks) and Harry (Emlyn Williams). A year earlier, Hitchcock had written, "Usually I do not like historical subjects (for it is very difficult making characters in costumes behave credibly)."*

became Squire Pengallan. Laughton, who'd already thought of switching his role anyway, now wanted to play the Squire. Only at around this point did Hitch read the script by Clemence Dane. He immediately saw its basic flaw—with Laughton as the Squire, audiences would quickly guess that he was the evil mastermind figure.

As things turned out, Laughton did play Pengallan, but Hitch abandoned the whodunit approach and made other changes. He threw away the Clemence Dane script and had a new one written by Sidney Gilliat and Joan Harrison. Pengallan's part was expanded with additional dialogue by J. B. Priestley. On the production side, the film used many talented people. Photography was again in the charge of Bernard Knowles (who'd photographed most of Hitch's Gaumont thrillers), working with Harry Stradling (soon to photograph *Mr. and Mrs. Smith* and *Suspicion*). As well as Knowles, two

Above: *The shadow of Sir Humphrey hangs over Mary and naval officer Jem Trehearne (Robert Newton).*
Below: *Sir Humphrey entertains. "You can't direct a Laughton picture," claimed Hitchcock. "The best you can hope for is to referee."*

other future directors were employed: Robert Hamer as editor, Harry Watt for special effects. Art direction was by the admired Tom Morahan (whom David O. Selznick had his eye on), and music was composed by Eric Fenby, the man who'd been amanuensis to the blind Frederick Delius (1862–1934). Actually, the film's use of music is restricted to the opening scenes, so perhaps Fenby was chosen mainly to provide the folk tune that ironically accompanies the reference to "an old Cornish prayer."

The cast list was equally impressive, and included a find of Laughton's—a pretty colleen named Maureen O'Hara. Both she and Laughton would shortly leave for Hollywood to be re-teamed in *The Hunchback of Notre Dame* (1939). So what went wrong with Hitch's film, which he himself called "an absurd thing to undertake"? Laughton's performance sums the matter up: if boisterous, it's hardly searching. For the director's part, inasmuch as he was engaged with the film deeply at all, he said that he was mainly interested "in the Jekyll-Hyde mentality of the Squire." That may be true, but it was something that tended to be overwhelmed in performance by the various characters' endless comings and goings, posturings, and hiding behind doorways, rocks, and columns. *Film Weekly* noted about the incidents and clashes of character: "They are striking in themselves, but

have little value as part of accumulative suspense."

Pengallan lives in near isolation, and lacks stimulating company, especially the company of women. And he's constantly bawling for his manservant, "Chaaadwick!" It looks like Hitchcock had seen John Ford's *Wee Willie Winkie* (1937), set in a remote part of India, in which the garrison commander (C. Aubrey Smith) lacks for female company, and has become excessively rigid in man-

ner and outlook. Revealingly, he's forever bellowing for his adjutant, "Baaagsby!" But Ford's film has all the energy and extroverted action that *Jamaica Inn* lacks. In making the latter film more of a character study of a decaying and corrupted individual, Hitchcock became too negative. True, he attempted ingenious parallels with the wreckers themselves: for instance, one of the gang, known as "Salvation" (Wylie Watson), speaks of himself and Joss—and by extension the Squire—as "lost souls together." But it was all overly self-conscious. Indeed, Pengallan's aestheticism and some of his other characteristics suggest that these were too close to Hitchcock's own for the director to see his way clearly.

There were characteristic Hitchcock touches, however. Pengallan's obvious relish at being alone with his captive princess is disturbing, and the repeated business of pistols being cleaned and primed shows Hitchcock's care over matters of authentic detail. Despite a critical roasting, the film did excellent business when it opened at London's Regal Theatre (perhaps partially due to the elaborate exhibition of costumes, props, and sets from the film running in the department store Selfridges, which *Kinematograph Weekly* reported was "being seen by many thousands daily"). Meanwhile, the director himself was already far away—in America, preparing to work for Selznick on another adaptation of a du Maurier novel.

HOLLYWOOD
1940 — 1950

Hitchcock arrived in America with a film treatment for Daphne du Maurier's *Rebecca*, developed with Joan Harrison and Alma while aboard ship, but it was not at all well received by his new master, David O. Selznick. It was a rocky start to what proved a rocky eight-year relationship between two dynamic and power-hungry men. According to Selznick, Hitchcock had much to learn about American production methods. According to Hitchcock, Selznick had much to learn about staying out of a director's way. Yet as tense as their relationship was during this period, they never lost their fundamental respect for each other. And *Rebecca* did go on to win Selznick an Academy Award for Best Picture of 1940, although Hitch later felt he deserved to take it home.

In Hollywood, actors, writers, and directors worked under contract to studios or, as in Hitchcock's case, a strong producer. This made Hitch a commodity that Selznick could (and did) trade at a rate far greater than the salary he paid Hitchcock, and it was this aspect of their relationship that created the most tension between them. Hitch also resented Selznick and his films' stars taking home bigger weekly salaries than his own (no longer could Hitch pride himself as the

Above: The Hitchcocks at home.
Below: Rebecca, *Hitch's first Hollywood movie, won the 1940 Best Picture Oscar.*

country's highest paid director, as he reportedly once was back in Britain). At one point during his contract, Hitchcock staged a one-day walk out, exasperating Selznick. (It is with some irony that many years later a similar stunt by Kim Novak equally exasperated Hitch days before filming began on *Vertigo*.)

The Selznick years were as prolific for Hitchcock as his time in Britain had been. Between 1939 and the end of his contract in 1947, he directed ten films, including four which rank among his finest work: *Rebecca, Foreign Correspondent, Shadow of a Doubt,* and *Notorious*. The latter three are distinguished by the control Hitchcock was able to maintain over the production; two were made as loan outs to other producers (*Foreign Correspondent* for Walter Wanger, *Shadow of a Doubt* for Jack Skirball) and the third was produced at RKO when Selznick was busier with other projects (namely, *Duel in the Sun* [1946]). The remaining six movies are all high-quality studio product, which, with

the exception of *The Paradine Case*, his final film with Selznick, were all box-office successes. The eight-year period established Hitchcock's reputation as an accomplished director who knew his way around a Hollywood studio—and how to deal with the industry's strongest producer.

Privately, Hitchcock spent much of the time in anguish. Months after his arrival, war broke out in Europe. London filmmakers uniformly criticized the British Hollywood expatriate community for not returning home. Hitchcock in particular was singled out by former friend and producer Michael Balcon in a scathing attack published in newspapers in London and America. Hitch was stunned. Balcon wrote: "I had a plump young junior technician in my studio whom I promoted from department to department. Today he is one of our most famous directors and he is in Hollywood while we who are left behind short-handed are trying to harness the films to our great national effort." The reference was unmistakable

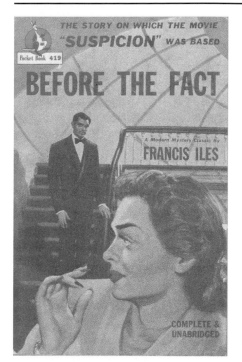

SPELLBOUND

Above left: *The tie-in reissue of* Before the Fact, *the novel on which* Suspicion *was based.*
Above right: *Teresa Wright, Joseph Cotton, and Henry Travers in* Shadow of a Doubt.
Right: *The sheet music for* Spellbound.

and Hitchcock did not mince words in his public response: "He's [Balcon] a permanent Donald Duck. We have all placed ourselves at the disposal of our government. By what authority does this man take this attitude? I can only regard it as his personal feeling. The British government has only to call upon me for my services. The manner in which I am helping my country is not Mr. Balcon's business and has nothing to do with patriotic ideals. Mr. Balcon apparently hates Hollywood. I can only put his remarks down as personal jealousy. How else could he be so unintelligent?"

Settling in to Hollywood life was not easy for the Hitchcocks, and also proved costly. The family took a three-bedroom residence at the Wilshire Palms Apartments, not far from Selznick's studio in Culver City, and later rented Carole Lombard's home in Bel Air. Their maid soon returned to England, and their cook also left. Help was provided by Alma who, according to Hitch, "memorized and executed my dishes to such a perfection that there's been no need to hire more than an understudy for the role." Their daughter, Patricia, enrolled at an exclusive Catholic school near Bel Air, quickly

adapting to American customs. And, despite Hitch's insistence otherwise, the family owned a car, in which the reluctant father would soon be giving driving instructions to his daughter.

The period also had its share of personal tragedy for Hitchcock. The director's mother passed away in September 1942 (during the production of *Shadow of a Doubt*), and the following January his brother William also died, in a suspected suicide. The stress over this personal turmoil mixed with anxiety about the war at home was perhaps tempered by

a return to London. In 1944, Hitch made a secret trip to direct two short propaganda films about the French Underground for the British Ministry of Information. Both were shot, in French, over two weeks at London's Welwyn Studios, and featured the Molière Players. Hitchcock thus made his contribution to the war effort, but the trip was also a convenient way to dodge Selznick, and also meet up with a friend, Sidney Bernstein, who had a business proposition.

Bernstein ran the successful Granada Theatre chain and was interested in mov-

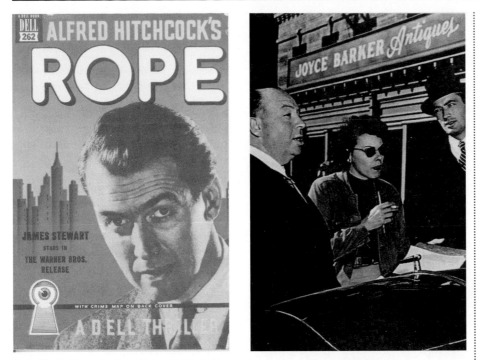

Left: *The tie-in novelization of* Rope, *Hitch's first production for his own Transatlantic Pictures.*
Right: *On the set of* The Paradine Case. *Gregory Peck can be seen on the far right.*

ing into film production. Hitchcock, tired of Selznick's domination, wanted to produce his own movies. The two laid the groundwork for forming an international production company after the war. However, Selznick was not oblivious to these events and it only served to increase his irritation with Hitchcock, whom he felt owed him everything.

Hitch longed for stability and independence, but the Selznick years provided him with neither. Since Selznick had limited studio space and, according to his biographer David Thomson, was always walking the financial tightrope, Hitchcock was bounced from one studio to another for his films. And the loan outs, while a break from Selznick (albeit limited, since he still found ways to interfere here as well), meant a somewhat vagabond life. Consider the films from these years: *Rebecca, Spellbound,* and *The Paradine Case* (all made for Selznick); *Mr. and Mrs. Smith, Suspicion,* and *Notorious* (for RKO); *Foreign Correspondent* (for Walter Wanger); *Lifeboat* (for 20th Century-Fox), and *Saboteur* and *Shadow of a Doubt* (for Universal Studios).

When the war ended, Hitchcock made his move. His final production for Selznick, *The Paradine Case,* was a project Hitch always maintained was forced on him. This is not entirely accurate. He

had problems with the source material, but was very much intrigued by the story. He was simply bristling at the continued and obsessive interference from the producer and, as earlier with *Jamaica Inn,* was already dreaming of the days ahead on his own.

Unfortunately, those days were far from heady or successful. Hitchcock and Bernstein formed Transatlantic Pictures in London in April 1946 and the company negotiated a production and distribution deal with Warner Brothers in the United States. Their first film, based on a successful stage play by Patrick Hamilton, was to be filmed in a revolutionary and cost-cutting method. Hitch convinced the businessman Bernstein that by shooting *Rope* in continuous, ten-minute takes—the length of a single reel of 35mm film—the picture could be completed in record time and thus reduce the budget.

During production at Warner Brothers' Burbank studios, filmmakers and actors dropped by to watch the Master at work on this ground-breaking process. But what they witnessed was a director and cast in panic, with frustration mounting and costs spiralling out of control. Early storm clouds formed when the first two weeks of filming had to be dumped and reshot after the Technicolor rushes came back with the background colors wrong. Then, the complicated camera movements, which also involved choreographed positioning of the set to enable the large Technicolor camera to roam through the New York apartment, resulted in many botched takes. Eight or nine minutes might be successfully completed before a mistake was made,

Hitch poses with the cast of Rope.

Alfred Hitchcock en train
de diriger Marlene Dietrich
et André Morell. Malgré
les exigences de l'actrice
de L'Ange bleu, il s'entendra
parfaitement avec elle.

Above: Hitch
directs Marlene
Dietrich and Hector
MacGregor in Stage
Fright.
Left: Hitch, Jane
Wyman, and
Michael Wilding in
London for Stage
Fright.

necessitating the entire ten-minute sequence to be reshot from the beginning. The process severely taxed the cast, to the extent that James Stewart vowed never to work with Hitchcock again. *Rope* was quite well received by both critics and audiences, but was hardly a runaway financial success.

At the end of the decade, Hitch returned triumphantly to London, with Hollywood star Ingrid Bergman on his arm. Both would be receiving healthy salaries on Transatlantic's second film, *Under Capricorn.* Unfortunately, this turned out to be a nightmarish production for Hitchcock, running way over budget, and letters from associates paint a picture of an anxious director. The story failed to evolve as he wanted, and during filming Hitchcock again insisted on experimenting with long takes. The experience was particularly trying on Bergman ("It's the only time I ever cried on the set," she told Donald Spoto years later).

The movie opened in September 1949 to devastating reviews and a tepid public reception. Transatlantic was finished. The remaining projects they had in development—*Stage Fright* and *I Confess*—were picked up by Warner Brothers, with whom Hitchcock signed a six-and-a-half year, four-picture production contract in January 1949. His attempt at true independence had failed.

Under Capricorn was a film Hitchcock always regretted, although it did introduce him to a young woman who handled continuity for the film—Peggy Singer. A decade later, Peggy Singer Robertson rejoined Hitch on *Vertigo* and thereafter remained at his side as a special assistant until his death in 1980. Robertson later recalled the difficulties of *Under Capricorn*'s production, in particular the long takes: "It was all very hard, especially as I was in charge of continuity. The camera was moving, the sets were flying out of the way, and the actors were trying to hit their marks and remember their lines. I remember sitting with Hitch watching the final cut and seeing with horror something I should have seen any number of times—a crew member standing in the background at the end of one of the long tracking shots. I told Hitch—it was too late to do anything, the sets had all been struck months ago—he just chuckled and said no one would notice. He pointed out that we had seen the film many times and had never seen it. An audience would only see the film once— so what was there to worry about?"

The humbled Hitchcock shot *Stage Fright* in London between June and September 1949, and then returned to the United States to continue work with Warner Brothers. *Stage Fright* was handled like all Hitchcock's films during a period of transition—with little real interest. As an aside, the director cast his daughter, Patricia, who had been training at the Royal Academy of Dramatic Art during her stay in London, in a small role.

After *Stage Fright*, Hitch's next project was to be *I Confess*, but the script refused to come together. Instead, he arranged an option on a new novel by Patricia Highsmith, a little thriller called *Strangers on a Train*.

Dan Auiler

REBECCA

First screening March 1940

Production company: Selznick International Pictures

Duration 130 minutes

Black and white

Maxim de Winter (Laurence Olivier), the master of "Manderley" in Cornwall, has his reasons for visiting Monte Carlo out of season. His beautiful wife Rebecca had drowned, and Maxim wants to "blot out the past." He meets a young woman, the future Mrs. de Winter (Joan Fontaine), who is currently employed as companion to the overbearing Mrs. Van Hopper (Florence Bates). Soon Maxim proposes, and the couple eventually go home to his mansion. But the housekeeper, Mrs. Danvers (Judith Anderson), was devoted to Rebecca and quickly shows her resentment of the new bride. She successfully humiliates her victim on the night of the Manderley ball. Then, following a storm at sea, a submerged boat is found, and in it is Rebecca's body. Maxim is suspected of murder. But the man who had been Rebecca's lover, her cousin Jack Favell (George Sanders), inadvertently helps clear Maxim. Favell's allegations prompt inquiries that uncover a Dr. Baker (Leo G. Carroll)—who reveals that Rebecca had been dying of cancer, giving a motive for suicide. Maxim tells his new wife that Rebecca had been totally evil. Mrs. Danvers goes mad and burns down Manderley, perishing in the flames.

The woman called Rebecca fascinates us—without our ever seeing her—but the logic of the film requires that she be repudiated. In fact, the film's position towards Rebecca matches that of John Buchan's 1912 novel *The Power House* towards its *Übermensch* villain, Julius Pavia. In a passage crucial to several forties Hitchcock films, the hero, Leithen, dismisses Pavia by telling him that despite his brilliance he's "a foe to society" who uses his superior brains for malevolent ends. Significantly, Maxim in

Above: "I" arrives at Manderley. Hitch was initially uncertain about casting Fontaine in the part.

Rebecca had once idolized his first wife for her "beauty, brains and breeding." Effectively, she was a female *Übermensch*—and at the same time a monster. The film does repudiate her, but not without ambiguity.

Everyone remembers *Rebecca*'s haunting opening sequence with the camera travelling up the twisting drive to the ruins of Manderley where Joan Fontaine's voice, soft yet urgent, begins to recall the events we are about to see. (Note: because the second Mrs. de Winter is never actu-

ally named in the film, it will be convenient to refer to her as "I"—the accepted term among du Maurier and Hitchcock aficionados.) The sequence came straight from the 1938 novel by Daphne du Maurier, who was still bitter at what Hitchcock had done to her *Jamaica Inn*. But David Selznick reassured her: "It is my intention to do *Rebecca* and not some botched up semi-original." That was pretty much how things turned out. Making *Rebecca* must have been a sometimes painful experience for its director. For a

Above: *The sinister Mrs. Danvers (Judith Anderson) clearly unsettles "I".*
Bottom: *"Marriage with Max is not exactly a bed of roses," observed Jack Favell (played by the splendid George Sanders). Sanders was also cast in Hitchcock's next film,* Foreign Correspondent.

work with her, and largely confined his comments to matters of her makeup and appearance.

Filming was scheduled to take five weeks, but in fact took nine. Then came such tasks as the laying in of the Franz Waxman score, rich in leitmotivs, and post-dubbing of new dialogue. An example of this, probably written by Selznick himself, can be detected in I's "Perfectly lovely!" exclamation at the end of the marriage bureau scene after Maxim buys her flowers. In addition, Selznick ordered thirty retakes, including one of the final close-up of flames engulfing the letter R on the pillow case in Rebecca's bedroom. After three months of testing at previews, and more trimming and re-recording of lines, *Rebecca* was finished at a cost of $1,280,000, some $513,000 over the original budget. Premièring at the Radio City Music Hall, New York, on March 28, 1940, the film was favorably reviewed by every newspaper in the city. Later, it won the Academy Award for Best Picture of 1940, with another Oscar going to cinematographer George Barnes. (Hitchcock received the first of his nominations for Best Director.)

Though Hitchcock seemed reluctant to fully acknowledge the fact, much of the power of *Rebecca* comes from the original novel. That power is expressed as an indefinable atmosphere—part ghostly,

start, Selznick threw out the film's first treatment, written by Philip MacDonald and Joan Harrison under Hitchcock's supervision. In one of Selznick's famous memos, he wrote: "Dear Hitch. It is my unfortunate and distressing task to tell you that I am shocked and disappointed beyond words by the [first treatment]. I regard it as a distorted and vulgarized version of a provenly successful work, in which, for no reason that I can discern, old-fashioned movie scenes have been substituted for the captivatingly charming du Maurier scenes." The treatment had begun by showing the characters on their way to the Riviera, including scenes of seasickness *à la Champagne* or perhaps Chaplin. Selznick thought these "cheap beyond words," and called for a total rewrite.

Hitchcock pressed on. Within three months, the final shooting script, dated September 7, 1939, was completed by distinguished playwright Robert Sherwood, and filming started the next day. From a hand-picked cast, Hitchcock drew uniformly excellent performances, with Selznick constantly checking on the rushes. (Script girl Lydia Schiller, who sat alongside Hitchcock on the set, was secretly instructed to tell Selznick if there was the slightest departure from the approved script. When Hitchcock found

out, he muttered obscenities at her under his breath for the rest of shooting.) Selznick thought that Olivier's lines weren't always delivered for optimum effect, but it was generally felt that Fontaine as the mousey heroine was very good. Selznick acknowledged Hitchcock's

LAURENCE OLIVIER
JOAN FONTAINE
in Alfred Hitchcock's
REBECCA
with George Sanders

Below:
Hitchcock in
discussion
with Laurence
Olivier and
Joan Fontaine.

part psychological—and arises from the mysterious domination over the present exercised by the dead woman. Hitchcock recreates and *sustains* that atmosphere brilliantly, but he could not have managed it without the character of the sinister housekeeper, Mrs. Danvers. She is seldom seen moving. Revealingly, Daphne du Maurier appears to have based the character on another, called Mrs. Unthank, found in the novel *The Great Impersonation* (1920) by espionage writer E. Phillips Oppenheim. Here's how Oppenheim introduces *his* malevolent housekeeper: "A woman whose advent had been unperceived, but who had evidently issued from one of the recesses of the hall, stood suddenly before them all. She was as thin as a lath, dressed in severe black . . ." And here for comparison is how du Maurier introduces Mrs.

Danvers: "Someone advanced from the sea of faces, someone tall and gaunt, dressed in deep black . . ."

In short, certain dramatic situations and devices are effective whoever employs them. (Just to underline the idea: the device of not humanizing a character by showing her moving was again used successfully in Richard Donner's 1976 film *The Omen*, to depict the creepy nanny called Mrs. Baylock, played by Billie Whitelaw!) In turn, the fascination exerted on readers and audiences by the absent Rebecca is something of an *archetypal* matter: as discussed below, Rebecca is a Great Mother figure, and Mrs. Danvers acts as a chilly high-priestess at her shrine. Hitchcock told Truffaut that "there was a whole school of feminine literature at the period," but that du Maurier's story lacked humor. Elsewhere, he criticized her

work in general for being "derivative." Altogether, on *Rebecca* he seems to have found himself more of a functionary than usual, and perhaps not wholly in sympathy with his material.

Hitch and Sherwood still had their work cut out for them. A major problem they faced was that Maxim in the novel is a murderer—goaded by Rebecca into shooting her. The novel ends with the crime undetected and, after Manderley is burned down, Maxim and I going away together. This isn't so far removed from the endings of *Blackmail* and *Sabotage*, and in England the filmmakers might have got away with showing a murderer who stays free. But the Production Code in America would not allow such a thing. Selznick lamented: "The whole story of *Rebecca* is the story of a man who has murdered his wife, and it now becomes the story of a man who buried a wife who was killed accidentally!" However, the final script used masterly sleight of hand. Though at the end of the film Maxim says explicitly that he did *not* murder Rebecca, the audience is left feeling that he could have. His behavior, and that of I, have been consistent with his guilt. Also, repeated reference has been made to Maxim's proneness to violent temper, prompting us to infer the often fine line between guilt and innocence.

What, then, is *Rebecca* about? In the novel of *Jamaica Inn*, du Maurier's villain had been a man out of sympathy with his age: a clergyman whose real allegiance is to paganism, to a time "when the rivers and the sea were one, and the old gods walked the hills." In *Rebecca*, what so shocks Maxim about his first wife is that she is both promiscuous and—apparently—bisexual. In effect, she is what Camille Paglia calls the Great Mother, "[t]he supreme symbol of fertility religion . . . a figure of double-sexed primal power." Maxim, by contrast, is an arch-conservative and patriarch; someone who firmly believes, he tells "I," in mastering an action by performing it "over and over again." When he learns the true nature of Rebecca, and afterwards (in the novel) kills her, he is virtually traumatized, and a pall descends on Manderley.

Maxim remarries on the rebound, as it were, and brings his new wife back to his ancestral home, hoping to make a fresh start. In the film, her first sight of Manderley is through the car windshield, and it isn't reassuring: it shows a mansion

"I" entertains Major Giles Lacey (Nigel Bruce). Bruce also appeared in Suspicion *and is best remembered as Dr. Watson opposite Basil Rathbone's Sherlock Holmes.*

THE USE OF MINIATURES IN *REBECCA*

Selznick production manager Ray Klune remembered how "the sets on *Gone With the Wind* were still up when we started on *Rebecca*... we couldn't wait to strike the Twelve Oaks hallway to make room for Manderley." Actually, most of the Manderley *exteriors* were either miniatures, of various sizes, or sections of the façade built full-scale. An example of the latter was the main entrance, with its ivy-surrounded double-doorway and wide steps leading up. The biggest miniature, which cost $25,000, "was just huge." It showed the front of the mansion in its entirety, and almost filled one of Selznick's unsound-proofed stages (a vestige of silent film-making). This exterior was used for close views, such as when, near the end of the film, a light is seen moving through the rooms. A second exterior model, of half the size, was built on another stage and used for the opening scene in which the camera tracks on concealed rails along a winding drive through a wood. The tracking motion and the use of a model seemed actually to enhance the dream-like effect required.

elderly.) Typical is a remark made about "Barmy" Ben (Leonard Carey), that he's "perfectly harmless." And the person who makes that remark is the estate-manager, Frank Crawley (Reginald Denny), a bachelor, whom Maxim calls "as fussy as an old mother hen." As for Maxim and I's marriage, it soon becomes one of mere companionship. A suppressed epilogue to the novel, not published until 1981, confirms this, revealing that the couple are still childless several years later.

In sum, *Rebecca* can be read as something of an allegory about the woes of civilization (cast in the form of a so-called woman's story). Rebecca herself may be "a foe to society," but the novel captures well the sort of subversive questioning that was quite commonplace in England between the wars, at least in the circles in which Daphne du Maurier moved. It's not clear, though, that Hitch ever saw things exactly that way. To Truffaut he simply said that the film "has stood up quite well over the years—I don't know why."

isolated, severely apart. That image perfectly captures the idea of a devastated place, one with a spell cast on it. Conveying the same idea is the fact that all of Manderley's menfolk seem to have become impotent and de-natured. (Even the younger Frith, at the lodge, seems

FOREIGN CORRESPONDENT

First screening August 1940

**Production company:
Walter Wanger/United Artists**

Duration 120 minutes

Black and white

On the eve of war, American newspaperman Johnnie Jones (Joel McCrea) is assigned to Europe under the name of "Huntley Haverstock." In London, he talks to elderly Dutch diplomat Mr. Van Meer (Albert Basserman), one of the few people who might yet prevent the war—but who will shortly be kidnapped and tortured while a double is assassinated in Amsterdam as a decoy. Johnnie attends a luncheon at the Savoy organized by the head of the Universal Peace Party, Stephen Fisher (Herbert Marshall), and meets Fisher's daughter Carol (Laraine Day). They meet again in Amsterdam. Returning by boat, Johnnie proposes to Carol and is accepted. Neither of them knows that her father is a renegade, and only after an attempt is made on Johnnie's life at Westminster Cathedral does he guess. When war comes, Fisher's job is done and he heads for America by clipper-plane, taking Carol—who has quarrelled with Johnnie—with him. But Johnnie is aboard, and when the clipper is shot down at sea by a German destroyer, not everyone survives. Fisher, now reconciled with his daughter, sacrifices himself. Johnnie and Carol return together to London, where Johnnie broadcasts to America: "hang on to your lights, they're the only lights left in the world."

Hitch directs Joel McCrea and Herbert Marshall. Ten years earlier, Marshall had starred in Murder!

For *Foreign Correspondent,* Hitchcock had hoped Gary Cooper and Barbara Stanwyck would play Johnnie and Carol. That way, Stanwyck could have fallen for the father in Cooper, which might have made all the difference. In the present film, there is no such nuance, and the two principals perform capably without being particularly convincing as lovers. Hitchcock would have to wait until *Notorious* before achieving an in-depth depiction of a traitor's daughter.

After *Rebecca,* Selznick chose to hire out Hitchcock's services to another independent producer, Walter Wanger. Selznick made a profit on the deal: charging Wanger $7,500 a week, he continued to pay Hitchcock his regular salary of $2,500 a week. Wanger was the producer of John Ford's *Stagecoach* (1939), but he specialized in topical films. For several years, he had held the screen rights to journalist Vincent Sheean's memoir *Personal History* (first published as *In Search of History* in 1935). After three previous attempts to get a workable script, he now assigned the project to Hitchcock and his screenwriter Charles Bennett. The thriller that resulted bears absolutely no relation to the book, apart from a wry reference in the latter to the "Richard Harding Davis tradition" of romantic adventure. In the opening scene of *Foreign Correspondent,* Johnnie

Jones's editor, Mr. Powers (Harry Davenport), notes that Davis was "one of our greatest war correspondents forty years ago."

Bennett had been working in Hollywood since *Young and Innocent.* He told an interviewer that Hitch summoned him back because he wanted "his best constructionist." The evidence for that is on the screen—few writers were more

adept at creating strong scenes, and giving them a plausible connection, than Bennett. In the same interview, the writer makes somewhat contradictory claims. He suggests that Hitch "loathed anybody [else] getting any credit whatsoever," yet also notes that Hitch asked for his secretary Joan Harrison to be given a screenplay credit when "[s]he had never come up with a solitary idea or a solitary

Top left: *Reporter Johnnie Jones (Joel McCrea) talks to Mr. Van Meer (Albert Basserman)—or actually his double—moments before he's assassinated (note the cameraman's hidden gun). Hitchcock had tried to get Gary Cooper for the lead role.*
Top right: *The famous assassination scene and the vast array of umbrellas.*
Above: *The real Mr. Van Meer is held hostage in an old windmill. Albert Basserman was nominated for a Best Supporting Actor Oscar for his performance.*

thought." (Bennett similarly discredits Alma Reville's contribution to the Gaumont films.)

This leads us on to *Foreign Correspondent*'s many brilliantly inventive set pieces: the famous assassination on the rain-swept steps of the Amsterdam Town Hall with a gun hidden in a camera; the sinister windmill whose sails turn against the wind as a signal; the death of Fisher's man Rowley (Edmund Gwenn), falling to his doom in an attempt to push Johnnie off Westminster Cathedral; the climactic clipper plane crash. In fact, all of these scenes (and several more) are derived from other sources!

Many of the film's most celebrated moments echo the Bulldog Drummond stories by "Sapper." Notably, the assassination of a man's double to conceal the fact that he has been kidnapped combines two separate incidents from *The Third Round* (1924), in which the kidnapped man is a Professor Scheidstrun, who has invented a formula for manufacturing cheap diamonds. There are also echoes in the film of John Buchan's *Mr. Standfast* (1919).

Foreign Correspondent is even more indebted to one of the most famous of all English spy stories, Erskine Childers's *The Riddle of the Sands* (1903). The film's Stephen Fisher is clearly based on Herr Dollman, a disgraced officer in Her Majesty's Navy who goes over to the Germans, taking his unsuspecting daughter, Clara, with him. Eventually, however, Clara marries the young Englishman, Davies, who has earlier alerted her to the truth about her father. The film's watery climax is a direct borrowing from Childers's novel. In both works, the renegade father apologizes to his daughter for his past actions, then quietly slips away and drowns. The episode, in chapter twenty-eight of the novel, concludes: "We cruised about for a time, but never found him."

In view of Hitchcock's remark about finding Daphne du Maurier "derivative" (see *Rebecca*), and of Bennett's concern that screenplay credit be fair, some of the above is doubtless ironic. Yet *Foreign Correspondent* contains many more borrowings than the literary ones above. Here's a partial list of films (including two produced by Wanger, and two from Gaumont-British) whose influence is detectable in Hitchcock's movie: *Frankenstein* (1931), *Die Dreigroschenoper*

(*The Threepenny Opera*, 1931), *A Night at the Opera* (1935), *Little Lord Fauntleroy* (1936), *Seven Sinners* (1936), *Non Stop New York* (1937), *The Life of Emile Zola* (1937), *History is Made at Night* (1937), *Trade Winds* (1938), *Espionage Agent* (1939).

What should we make of this? Perhaps no more than that Hitch was "running for cover" after the rarefied atmosphere of *Rebecca*, and felt the need on this occasion to be self-indulgent. No doubt, too, his collaborators were responsible for several of the borrowings: the windmill interiors would naturally have prompted the film's art designers to look at *Frankenstein*, for example. In any event, most audiences and critics loved the finished film (which ended up costing a staggering $1,484,167, taking ten weeks to shoot instead of the estimated six). Both *Rebecca* and *Foreign Correspondent* figured on the list of the ten best films of 1940 in the *Motion Picture Herald*.

Among the many original qualities of *Foreign Correspondent*, one might be singled out here: Hitchcock's close attention to matters of weather and atmosphere.

The plane, taking Carol and Johnnie to America, is forced down into the ocean. Joan Fontaine was not available to play the female lead, so Hitchcock settled for Laraine Day.

From the sunny interior of Mr. Powers's office high in the New York *Globe* building, to rainy Amsterdam, to the gritty streets of London, and finally a turbulent Atlantic, Hitchcock obviously strove for maximum realism. As both entertainment and propaganda, the film was a doubtless success.

MR. AND MRS. SMITH

First screening January 1941

**Production company:
RKO Radio Pictures Inc.**

Duration 95 minutes

Black and white

Lawyer David Smith (Robert Montgomery) and his wife Ann (Carole Lombard) live in a Park Avenue apartment and sometimes quarrel, as married couples will. So far they've always made up. One day, David learns that a technicality means that their marriage is not legal. Unknown to him, Ann also finds out. When, without saying why, he decides to romance her all over again, the plan backfires because Ann, insecure and fiery, resents being a potential "squeezed lemon." She throws him out. Now David really must court his wife—but she has tasted the thrill of independence. She takes a job as a sales clerk, though David soon has her fired. Also, she encourages the attentions of David's partner, Jefferson Custer (Gene Raymond). Custer's parents take their son's half-hearted romance seriously. They invite the couple to stay with them at the ski resort of Lake Placid, but David turns up, pretending to be suffering from pneumonia brought on by lovesick drinking. Ann can't help feeling concerned. Jefferson, rather wimpishly, doesn't intervene. David traps Ann in her skis, tips her over, and makes love to her. She reciprocates.

In 1938, J. B. Priestley wrote a farce called *When We Are Married* in which some stuffy Yorkshire bigwigs suddenly find that their marriages are invalid and they are living in sin. Perhaps coincidentally, American playwright Norman Krasna used a similar situation soon afterwards in his screenplay for a screwball comedy to be called *No for an Answer*, about a New York couple. It was this screenplay that RKO bought for Carole Lombard, and which was later filmed by Hitchcock as *Mr. and Mrs. Smith*. The film is hugely underrated, and belongs with Hitch's own brand of remarriage comedies (see *The Farmer's Wife*

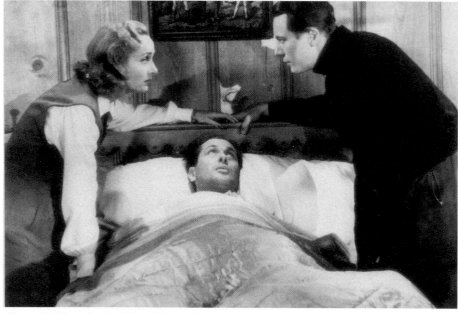

Above: *Ann (Carole Lombard), David (Robert Montgomery), and Jeff (Gene Raymond).*

and *Rich and Strange*). Carole Lombard is vivacious and sexy, yet once again a wife proves to be at least "half a mother."

The Hitchcocks were living at the time in a house rented from Lombard, who had married Clark Gable in 1939. When she asked Hitch to direct her in a screwball comedy as a favor because that's how her fans best remembered her (check out *My Man Godfrey* [1936], *Nothing Sacred* [1937]), he gladly accepted the challenge. RKO struck a two-picture deal with Selznick for Hitch's services, at a little over $100,000 for each picture. On the first, *Mr. and Mrs. Smith*, Lombard was the uncredited producer. During the

shoot, she took good-humored advantage of her position by insisting on directing Hitch's cameo appearance in the film, and ordering retake after retake. Hitch may well have thought back to the high-spirited times at Elstree when he was working with those other headstrong blondes, Betty Balfour and Anny Ondra.

The film wrapped in eight weeks, only slightly over schedule (and budget) compared with the overruns of *Rebecca* and *Foreign Correspondent*. Hitchcock told Truffaut that he didn't really understand the type of people portrayed, so he photographed the script as written. But as the film progresses, it attains a Hitchcockian

Above: Montgomery and Lombard. Having completed only one more film, Ernst Lubitsch's To Be or Not to Be *(1942), Hollywood lost one of its finest comediennes when Carole Lombard died in a plane crash.*
Below: Set design sketch for Mr. and Mrs. Smith.

look and feel. In a note on Krasna, critic Richard Corliss says: "As with so many delightful comedies, it is the writers who create the characters and establish a mood in the first half of the picture, and the director who develops both in the second half." In any case, the subject of *Mr. and Mrs. Smith* is the universal one of sexuality and marriage, about which Hitch had been making trenchant comments on film since the 1920s. The film played to sell-out crowds at Radio City, and became, if not a total smash, a solid commercial hit on its general release.

The critics, however, have never liked it. John Mosher's *New Yorker* review is typical: "As commonplace a film as one may find anywhere." A defense of *Mr. and Mrs. Smith* may start by noting that the film is *defining* the commonplace in marriage, and in a manner worthy of a philosopher (Kierkegaard, say). Thus it emphasizes the egotism of both David and Ann, and it implies that marriage, however inglorious, is the best medicine for that. For good measure, it shows that

the over-gentlemanly Jeff is inadequate. Near the end of the film, a defeated Jeff tells Ann it's possible that "as peculiar as David is, you couldn't be happy without him." Jeff promptly withdraws from the battle and seems almost glad.

One scene bears Hitchcock's indelible stamp. Ann and Jeff get stuck on a broken-down Ferris wheel at the New York World's Fair. Hours later, wet and bedraggled, they're finally brought down. The sign on the wheel reads, *Life*. Like the home movies scene in *Rebecca* when the film breaks in the projector, the Ferris wheel scene works as a metaphor for the woman's and the man's converging points of view. For the woman, there's a reminder of her imperilled marriage—Ann is left feeling literally uncomfortable, if not unbowed. For the man, there's a reminder that life is always forcing itself on us. Earlier, David's womanizing acquaintance Chuck Benson (Jack Carson), had given him some advice concerning his break-up with Ann: "As simple as staying in the world—ignore it." Staying in the world is indeed a simple matter, while what counts is how we deal with it.

The film's own take on all of this is ambiguous. At the climax, the name of Lake Placid belies what goes on there. Was Hitchcock perhaps remembering the ironic Lake Como sequence from *The Pleasure Garden*? The film's most placid character is the health-conscious Jeff, who is mocked. At the same time, the film leaves unclear whether Jeff would have been more virile if both he and Ann were really *free*. As things are, his concern for her is equated not with selflessness but with low libido. The crossed-skis last shot, signifying Ann and David's sexual reunion, thus seems inevitable. Perhaps Chuck Benson did indeed know something.

A perceptive article in *Film Quarterly* (Winter, 1946–47) remarked that "*Mr. and Mrs. Smith* has been insufficiently appreciated," and singled out for special praise the scene where David takes Ann back to Momma Lucy's, the restaurant of their first romantic meetings, now sadly run down. (The scene legitimately derives from one in King Vidor's 1938 vehicle for Robert Donat and Rosalind Russell, *The Citadel*.) Like that scene, much of the film is both humorous and touching, in a wry sort of way. Modern audiences who can see it for what it is will enjoy *Mr. and Mrs. Smith*.

SUSPICION

First screening September 1941

Production company: RKO Pictures Inc.

Duration 100 minutes

Black and white

A train enters a tunnel. In the dark, Johnnie Aysgarth (Cary Grant) brushes against the leg of a stranger, Lina McLaidlaw (Joan Fontaine). When he notices her dowdy appearance, he's discouraged. The next day he sees her at a local hunt, where she's altogether transformed, and on being introduced, he proceeds to sweep her off her feet. Though Lina's father (Sir Cedric Hardwicke) warns her of Johnnie's reputation for wildness, the pair marry and settle near the Sussex coast. In the ensuing months, Lina learns much about her husband that deeply disturbs her, including his capacity to lie, to embezzle, perhaps even to murder. Indeed, the strange death of Johnnie's dim chum Beaky (Nigel Bruce) makes Lina fear that she'll be next. She knows that after her father had died, Johnnie had secretly insured her life. One night, Johnnie brings her a glass of milk which she refuses to drink. In the morning, she packs to go to her mother (Dame May Whitty). But Johnnie insists on driving her himself. On the coast road, he frankly admits he's no good, though he's not a murderer, and is resigned to going to prison. The car makes a U-turn.

*S*uspicion works well as a teasing comedy-thriller, but Hitchcock would have preferred something more extreme. He had wanted Johnnie to be the wife-murderer of the source novel, in which he's also a philanderer and a mass poisoner. The character is based on one of the most audacious, and therefore fascinating, of real-life British criminals, William Palmer (1824–56). In fact, the lively Johnnie is the film's true hero—in the sense that a certain Tom Rakewell is the hero of Hogarth's famous series of engravings, *A Rake's Progress*. Hitchcock probably had such a resemblance in mind, for he has Johnnie stay at the Hogarth Club in London.

Principal photography on *Suspicion* commenced on February 10, 1941. RKO originally intended the part of Johnnie for Louis Hayward, then for Robert Montgomery or Laurence Olivier, but Cary Grant landed it, beginning his momentous association with fellow Englishman Hitchcock. At first, an apparent problem was Grant's chilliness towards co-star Joan Fontaine, whom he had last worked with on George Stevens' *Gunga Din* (1939). However, as the off-screen tension only helped the on-screen drama, Hitchcock didn't worry and Fontaine's acting eventually won her an Oscar. As for Grant's performance, in which he's debonair and charming one moment, and sinister the next, he made

Lina (Joan Fontaine), Johnnie (Cary Grant), and Beaky (Nigel Bruce), with a cheerful maid (Heather Angel).

the role distinctively his own (as opposed to life-like)—aided, naturally, by Harry Stradling's atmospheric lighting and photography, and Samson Raphaelson's dialogue. (Raphaelson wrote some of Ernst Lubitsch's best American films.) The original novel, *Before the Fact* (1932), by Francis Iles (A. B. Cox), was one of the first murder stories to be told from the victim's point of view. Hitchcock always

admired Cox's work, and almost certainly took the idea for the handcuffed hero and heroine of *The 39 Steps* from Cox's novel, *Mr. Priestley's Problem* (1927).

When *Suspicion* was released, immediately becoming a huge box-office success, *Time* noted that it "has a texture which can almost be touched," but added that unfortunately the film falls apart at the end. The ending had always been prob-

Left: *Is the glass of milk poisoned? Hitch had commented that "to have what is known as an unhappy ending is to commit the unforgivable Hollywood sin called 'being downbeat.'" A happy ending was forced on* Suspicion.
Below: *Lina and Johnnie.* Suspicion *was the first of four films Grant made for Hitch, the director having failed to land him for the lead in his previous* Mr. and Mrs. Smith.

to nothing. In the event, various other endings were hastily scripted and at least one tested on a preview audience. According to Hitchcock scholar Steven L. DeRosa, this ending began with Lina suspecting Johnnie's murderous intentions, and Johnnie, realizing the implications, leaving to join the Royal Air Force (RAF). Later, Lina learns that Johnnie is a hero, and has named his fighter with his pet name for her: Monkeyface. Apparently this ending was deemed not strong enough. Of course, the film's present ending also lacks punch, but it *is* consistent with what has gone before—that is, if one remembers Beaky's saying that Johnnie can lie his way out of *any* tight corner! In effect, the present ending is as ambiguous as that of *The Lodger*, a film it often resembles. Moreover, on the evidence, Johnnie really is lying. He tells Lina that he went to Liverpool to try to raise money on their insurance policy, but an earlier close-up of letters from Johnnie's insurers had shown that both had London addresses.

One can only speculate about how good a film *Suspicion* might have been with the ending Hitchcock wanted—the

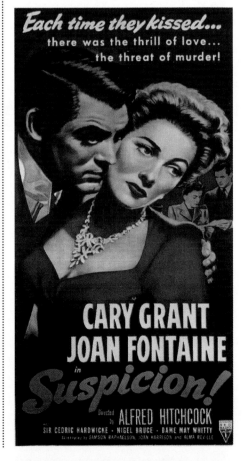

Each time they kissed... there was the thrill of love... the threat of murder!

**CARY GRANT
JOAN FONTAINE**
in
Suspicion!
Directed by **ALFRED HITCHCOCK**
SIR CEDRIC HARDWICKE · NIGEL BRUCE · DAME MAY WHITTY
Screenplay by SAMSON RAPHAELSON, JOAN HARRISON and ALMA REVILLE

lematic. From the outset, RKO forbade Hitchcock to portray Grant as a killer, but the director seems to have hoped they'd change their minds. The ending that he wanted involves Johnnie bringing Lina a glass of poisoned milk; just before she drinks it, she gives him a letter to mail to her mother. The letter names Johnnie as her murderer. It explains that though she desperately loves her husband, and is prepared to die, she believes that he should not be allowed to go free. During the film's shooting, Hitchcock artfully pre-

pared the audience for such an ending. In the opening scene on the train, Johnnie borrows a stamp from Lina; later, the camera repeatedly emphasizes the pillar box in the local village, and we even see Hitchcock himself posting a letter there. In other words, it seems likely that the director was employing the same cunning he'd used in shooting the silent version of *Blackmail*, where—without telling the producers—he'd made arrangements for a sound version to be filmed later.

This time, however, his strategy came

Cary Grant, Joan Fontaine and Hitch. Fontaine won the Oscar and the New York Film Critics Award for her performance.

dual-edged ending, at once romantic and anti-romantic, with Lina sacrificing her life to the man she loves, yet at the same time betraying him. Also, the implicit surrender to parental values, specifically the mother's, anticipates another film about a very conflicted person, namely *Psycho*. More broadly, the life-death struggle that runs through the film, and which is encapsulated in the early hillock scene (where Lina resists yet encourages Johnnie's advances), provides the basis for practically every Hitchcock film thereafter.

Certainly the film and its texture still fascinate. The main source of that fascination is Lina's emotional turmoil, always conveyed visually or via clever use of the soundtrack. One day, Lina returns home despondent from the coast, where she fears that Beaky has met with foul play. Suddenly, a sound and a slight shift of the camera tell us that Beaky is there with Johnnie. As Lina runs in relief towards her husband, the film's waltz motif swells and a cloud that's been hovering over the house moves away. As Hitchcock once said, "You play the audience like an organ."

FAMOUS LOCATIONS

Hitchcock notoriously delighted in "putting the audience through it." But in some respects he also liked to make things easy for the viewer—making sure, for example, that we know in just what country, or city, we're supposed to be right from the start of the film, so that we aren't looking out for landmarks, which might distract us from the story.

To this end, Hitchcock never shied away from using the most obvious national clichés, since they served as a rapid form of shorthand. "What do they have in Switzerland?" he asked himself when embarking on *Secret Agent*. "They have milk chocolate, they have the Alps, they have village dances, and they have lakes. All of these were woven into the picture."

Likewise, when we reach Holland in *Foreign Correspondent*, we naturally find windmills. In Montreal (*I Confess*), we see the city's best-known building, the Chateau Frontenac; in San Francisco (*Vertigo*), we obviously can't omit the Golden Gate Bridge; and when Hitchcock returned to London for *Frenzy*, he revisited the Thames Embankment that figured so prominently in *The Lodger*. Such reassuringly familiar sights also help anchor the story in a recognizable reality, making

us subconsciously feel that since these events, however far-fetched, are taking place somewhere we know to be real, they too must be real. *Psycho*, Hitchcock's weirdest and most disturbing film, even

starts with the pseudo-documentary authority of an onscreen title: "Phoenix, Arizona, Friday, December 11, 2:43 p.m."

But Hitchcock's teasing sense of humor is also evident in his use of well-known locations; he loves to make them serve deliberately inappropriate purposes. When, in *North by Northwest*, Cary Grant is framed for murder, the foyer of the United Nations building in Manhattan, an institution founded on the ideals of non-violence, provides a perfect setting. To have Grant, staring wildly round with a knife in his hand and an expiring diplomat at his feet, surrounded by all the pious trappings of international goodwill, makes the scene all the funnier and more piquant.

Likewise, when the Nazi spy played by Norman Lloyd plummets to his death in *Saboteur*, it's from the summit of the symbol of everything Nazism detested, the Statue of Liberty. In both versions of *The Man Who Knew Too Much*, the attempted assassination takes place in that temple of civilized culture, London's Royal Albert Hall. Similarly, Edmund Gwenn's decidedly un-Christian attempt to murder Joel McCrea in *Foreign Correspondent* is staged high on the bell tower of Westminster Cathedral. (Note that the Catholic Hitchcock chose London's premier Roman Catholic Church rather

Above: An early use of a well-known location: The British Museum as featured in Blackmail.
Below: The Royal Albert Hall is clearly visible in the poster for the remake of The Man Who Knew Too Much.

Above: San Francisco's Golden Gate Bridge seen in the background as James Stewart rescues Kim Novak in *Vertigo*.
Below: Cary Grant and Eva Marie Saint in *North by Northwest's* famous Mount Rushmore scene.

than the better known, but Anglican, Westminster Abbey.)

Saboteur and *Foreign Correspondent* furnish prime examples of Hitchcock's favorite use of famous landmarks: as spectacularly high places from which his characters could dangle or plunge. For Hitch wasn't only a master of psychological suspense—he also had a penchant for suspending in the literal meaning of the word. Wickedly skilled at tapping into our most basic fears, Hitchcock knew that almost all of us have a terror of heights (if not quite so acutely as James Stewart in *Vertigo*) and have suffered nightmares about falling. So what better way to bring an audience to the edge of its seat, gasping with terror, than to show somebody, whether hero or villain, perilously suspended over a yawning drop?

Of course, Hitchcock could have used any old cliff or building for this situation, and sometimes (as in *Suspicion* or *To Catch a Thief*) he did. But how much more effective to use some famous structure or monument that everyone would recognize—as if to emphasize that danger can strike even in broad daylight in the most public places. His earliest use of this device dates back to his first sound film, *Blackmail*, when the blackmailer (Donald Calthrop), fleeing from the police, climbs onto the dome of the Reading Room at the British Museum, only to meet his death when he falls through the glass. Once again there's sly humor in the unsuitability of the venue, with such violent events taking place in what's normally a haven of quiet scholarship.

Hitchcock's best-remembered use of a famous location, though, must surely be the Mount Rushmore sequence that cli-maxes *North by Northwest*. For years, apparently, Hitch had wanted to use the massive carved faces of the American presidents in a film, and this action-comedy offered the ideal opportunity. The hint of sacrilege, as Cary Grant and Eva Marie Saint, pursued by the sinister Martin Landau, scramble over the revered visages, must have appealed to Hitchcock's mischievous sense of humor. Indeed, he wanted to extend the joke and have the fugitives take refuge inside Abraham Lincoln's nostril, only for Grant to betray their hiding-place with a convulsive sneeze. Alas, the Mount Rushmore authorities prevailed upon Hitch to omit the gag. As it was, the production had to gain written permission from the U.S. Department of the Interior to film even with a mock-up Rushmore set in the studio, and then "on condition that only the shoulder, or below the chin-line" of the presidents' likenesses was used in close-up shots with the actors.

Finally, it's worth noting that some locations, little-known when Hitchcock chose them, have since become famous precisely because they appeared in his films. Both the small Californian town of Santa Rosa, setting for *Shadow of a Doubt*, and the quiet coastal resort of Bodega Bay, where much of *The Birds* takes place, still receive a steady influx of movie-buff tourists eager to see where the classic films were shot.

Philip Kemp

SABOTEUR

First screening April 1942

**Production company:
A Frank Lloyd Production
Inc./Universal Pictures, Inc.**

Duration 109 minutes

Black and white

A young worker in a government aircraft factory in California, Barry Kane (Robert Cummings), is a horrified witness to the death of a friend in a fire caused by sabotage. Barry guesses that a worker named Frank Fry (Norman Lloyd) is responsible, but Fry has disappeared. Barry himself comes under suspicion, so, remembering an address on an envelope dropped by Fry, he hitchhikes to a ranch owned by Charles Tobin (Otto Kruger). The truth is that Barry has stumbled onto a network of fifth columnists, and the genial-seeming Tobin is one of its leaders. Barry's suspicions become aroused. Eluding Tobin, he is joined by a girl, Patricia Martin (Priscilla Lane), and seeks out a ghost town called Soda City. There he encounters other saboteurs, tells them Tobin has sent him, and rides with them to New York. Pat, who works in the city, follows soon afterwards, but Tobin is onto the pair. They find themselves held prisoner, although both escape. Barry foils another sabotage attempt, then, alerted by Pat, catches up with Fry on the Statue of Liberty, from which Fry falls to his death. Only narrowly avoiding the same fate, Barry climbs back to Pat.

Actor Norman Lloyd has remarked that Hitchcock liked to leave audiences a bit puzzled, and *Saboteur* offers several teasers. Just why, for example, on the cross-country car trip, do a couple of the saboteurs sing "Tonight We Love" to the tune of Tchaikovsky's First Piano Concerto? For that matter, why has Barry earlier whistled a snatch of the "fate" passage from Beethoven's Fifth Symphony? (When the truck driver remarks on this, Barry says that he hadn't realized he *was* whistling.) The answer may be that most of the characters are themselves confused. As the film shows, they feel isolated and out of touch.

Above: Barry Kane (Robert Cummings) and Patricia Martin (Priscilla Lane). Selznick had originally considered Gene Kelly for the lead role, but sold the project to Frank Lloyd.

The original idea for *Saboteur* was Hitchcock's—a re-working of *The 39 Steps* set in America. Selznick assigned one of his stable of writers, twenty-one-year-old Peter Viertel, to work on the screenplay. John Houseman, the co-founder with Orson Welles of the Mercury Theatre, was asked to supervise and—ironically—to steer the director away from his "old-fashioned chase pic-tures." Viertel wrote a screenplay in two weeks. It wasn't very good, and was incomplete, but Selznick now had a package he could sell. Both Twentieth Century-Fox and RKO turned it down before Frank Lloyd (who had directed *Mutiny on the Bounty* [1935]) bought it for filming at Universal Studios.

For the lead roles, Hitchcock had to settle for Robert Cummings and Priscilla

Above: Hitch can be seen in the foreground on the set of Saboteur.

Left: The famous climax on the Statue of Liberty, as Barry tries to save Fry (Norman Lloyd). Lloyd later worked as associate producer and director on Alfred Hitchcock Presents.

Hitchcock was teasing his audience.

He'd have liked to tease them further by casting popular Western star Harry Carey as Tobin. Instead, he again ended up with an actor he thought unsuitable, this time Otto Kruger, a stock villain. Tobin is a crucial character. He's like Buchan's Julius Pavia (in the 1912 novel *The Power House*), someone who despises "the moron millions" and wants power. By contrast, Barry and Pat's adventures lead them to the symbol of democracy, the Statue of Liberty, with its inscription, "Give me your poor, your tired, your huddled masses..."

The Statue of Liberty scene is more than just the film's biggest tease. As noted, the early scenes tend to show a disunited country whose citizens are restless or lonely—an over-inquisitive neighbor, a bored truck driver, a hermit. And when we reach the scene in the home of New York hostess Mrs. Sutton (Alma Kruger), not much has changed. The people here whom Barry and Pat desperately appeal to for help reject the pair because they're not properly dressed or because they don't speak hep talk. But then comes the sequence that reverses all of this. Pat finds

herself imprisoned high up in the Rockefeller Building, and hits on the idea of tossing a *help* note out of the window. The message takes forever to reach the ground, but as it floats down we hear a broadcast describing the launching of a ship called *Alaska* at the Brooklyn Navy Yard. This, we know, is the ship the saboteurs have targeted. And it seems the whole city is listening in. Hitchcock cuts between several different locales where the broadcast is being received, including a taxi carrying Barry to the rescue . . .

In short, by means of melodrama, Hitchcock gives us a *sense* of disunity overcome. Further, we have constantly been reminded of the initial arson (remember Barry's line in Soda City, "the ground's burning up under my feet"), and who caused it. At Mrs. Sutton's, Barry and Pat manage to joke about chasing Fry over a glacier at the North Pole, an allusion to Frankenstein's monster. At the same time, the scene establishes a solid social milieu—Mrs. Sutton seems based on real-life socialite Countess Dorothy di Frasso, who was friendly with Mussolini, though in public she proclaimed the opposite.

Thus by the time the final sequence arrives, our attention is firmly focused. Under the very torch of liberty, citizen Barry Kane and arsonist Frank Fry meet to determine the destiny of America. After some initial music drawn from the studio library, evoking serials like *Don Winslow of the Navy* (1942), the scene plays in silence punctuated by wind noises and distant boat whistles. Hitchcock uses some trick cutting at the moment Fry appears on the torch parapet, and for a couple of close-ups of Fry's agonized face, he momentarily gives him fangs! (This anticipates the subliminal skull shots in *Psycho*.) The scene has the suspense intrinsic to a man's life literally hanging by a few threads, and Hitchcock films it straight—in all its gripping detail. He did, however, later note the scene's basic error: "If we'd had the hero instead of the villain hanging in mid-air, the audience's anguish would have been much greater."

The film, then, is far from perfect, and received mixed notices. The *Nation* reviewer called it "[w]ild without being exciting." In London's *Sunday Times*, Dilys Powell wrote astutely: "This is Hitchcock at his most Hitchcock, which doesn't necessarily mean at his best."

Lane, nominated by the studio when the production to which they'd previously been assigned fell through. Cummings lacked the expressive, Gary Cooper-type face Hitchcock wanted for his young all-American hero, but was a capable actor otherwise. The character's surname was changed from Ford to Kane at the last minute, possibly by the legendary Dorothy Parker, who was hired to do some script-doctoring, most noticeably on the scenes with the circus freaks. The thin man, "Bones" (Pedro de Cordoba), has a telling line, about normal people being "normally cold-hearted." Even here,

SHADOW OF A DOUBT

First screening January 1943

Production company: Universal/Skirball Productions

Duration 108 minutes

Black and white

Wealthy Charles Oakley (Joseph Cotten) travels by train to Santa Rosa, Northern California, to stay with his sister Emma Newton (Patricia Collinge) and her family. Emma's husband, Joe (Henry Travers), works in the local bank. His hobby is reading detective stories, which he discusses with next-door neighbor Herb Hawkins (Hume Cronyn). The Newtons' eldest child, the girl Charlie (Teresa Wright), feels that her family is in a rut, and hopes that Uncle Charlie, her namesake, can help them. But the teenager is in for a shock. Her uncle is the Merry Widow Murderer, so named by the press because his victims have all been rich widows. Two census takers visit the Newton household. They are really undercover detectives, and one of them, Jack Graham (MacDonald Carey), tells Charlie that her uncle may be a killer. She now sees that a ring given to her by Uncle Charlie is incriminating evidence. When her uncle makes attempts on her life, she uses the ring to force him to leave. As his train pulls out, he again tries to kill her, overbalances, and falls in front of an oncoming train. Jack reassures Charlie that the world just "needs a lot of watching."

Skirball Productions presents

TERESA **WRIGHT**

JOSEPH **COTTEN**

IN

ALFRED **HITCHCOCK'S**

Shadow of a Doubt

WITH

MACDONALD CAREY
PATRICIA COLLINGE
HENRY TRAVERS
WALLACE FORD

I n *Saboteur*, Hitchcock felt that he'd spread himself too thin and had literally tried to cover too much ground. *Shadow of a Doubt*, by contrast, combines a detailed picture of life in one small town with a brilliant study of adolescent psychology. Young Charlie's state of mind in the early part of the film resembles what the philosopher Kierkegaard called *dread*, a state of innocence or dreaming that awakens a thirst for the prodigious and the mysterious. Later, when Charlie learns the truth about her uncle in the public library scene, the camera's upward retreat evokes The Fall. There are echoes here of *The Ring*, but the degree of insight is much greater.

Hitchcock considered *Shadow of a Doubt* one of his best films. The idea of a fugitive murderer coming home to visit his family was suggested to the director by novelist Gordon McDonell, the husband of Selznick story supervisor Margaret McDonell. Hitchcock asked McDonell to write a short treatment, which he then showed to Jack Skirball, who had been associate producer on *Saboteur*. Skirball, a former rabbi, was keen to establish his own production company at Universal and to work with Hitchcock again. He purchased the treatment immediately.

Hitchcock could soon scarcely contain his excitement. Not only did he persuade Thornton Wilder to undertake his only writing for the screen (after flying to see the playwright in New York), but he started shooting the film even before casting was complete. He filmed a pursuit scene in some railway yards in Newark, New Jersey, several times, using extras of varying size: tall, medium, and short. When Joseph Cotten was cast, the shots

Above: Hitch on location in Santa Rosa. Principal photography ran from July 31 to October 28, 1942.

Top: Uncle Charlie (Joseph Cotten) comes to visit his sister's family.
Above: Charlie (Teresa Wright) grows closer to her namesake. The National Board of Review gave Wright their Best Actress Award for her performance.

featuring the tall man were selected. Sally Benson, author of the novel *Meet Me in St. Louis*, was hired to write the children's dialogue in the film. Alma Hitchcock then polished the script, making provision for Hitchcock's touches.

Both Teresa Wright and Patricia Collinge had appeared in William Wyler's *The Little Foxes* in 1941, and been nominated for Academy Awards. Several moments in *Shadow of a Doubt* echo ones in Wyler's film—when Collinge pops her head through a window to talk to someone outside, for example. Hitch invited Collinge to write the dialogue for the scene where young Charlie and Jack the detective speak of love and marriage. The actress remained a good friend of the Hitchcocks until her death in 1974.

The town of Santa Rosa was chosen for the film because it seemed delightfully average. Its population was then about 13,000. Cinematographer Joseph Valentine noted, "There was a public square, around which much of the city's life revolves. There was an indefinable blending of small town and city, and of old and new, which made . . . a much more typical background of an average American town than anything that could have been deliberately designed." Indeed, Hollywood kept coming back, to make such films as *Happy Land* (1943), a Kenneth MacGowan production, and *Peggy Sue Got Married* (1986), directed by Francis Ford Coppola. When Hitchcock was making *The Birds* at Bodega Bay in 1962, many of the cast and crew were accommodated in Santa Rosa.

According to Robert Boyle, art director on several Hitchcock films, the director liked to "tell his fairy tales against reality." If young Charlie in *Shadow of a Doubt* is perhaps Little Red Riding-Hood, her uncle is the wolf. Several elements came straight from real life, though, and some were less pleasant than others. Uncle Charlie's name, Charles Oakley, is a joking reference to a good friend of Hitch's who later wrote a history of the British film industry, *Where We Came In* (1964). The character himself, however, is based on serial murderer Earle Nelson, who travelled the United States in 1926 and 1927 killing people, mainly landladies; he claimed twenty-two victims in all, and wasn't caught until he crossed the border into Canada. When he was ten, Nelson was knocked down by a street car which rendered him unconscious for six days with concussion. Hitchcock's film cites that detail practically verbatim.

Nelson was also something of a religious fanatic, who thought his face was like Christ's. In *Frenzy*, Inspector Oxford says that "religious and sexual mania are often closely linked," but such matters in Hitchcock films go back to *The Lodger*, where the Ivor Novello character is shown with a cross shadow on his face. In many ways, *Shadow of a Doubt* is a remake of *The Lodger*. Uncle Charlie, however, scorns conventional religion (indeed, the film hints several times that he's the very

portrait of Mr. Newton. Joe and Herb's interest in detective stories matches Hitchcock's own. In essence, these two characters are perfectly ordinary—if harmless—bourgeoise. The clue this time is how they are modelled closely on two characters in one of Hitchcock's favorite plays, J. M. Barrie's *Mary Rose* (1925). Joe corresponds to Mary Rose's father, Mr. Moreland. By the end of the play, using the device of Mary Rose's supernatural comings and goings, Barrie has succeeded in showing the audience something beautiful and important about his average family, the Morelands. The effect is very similar to that achieved by Thornton Wilder's *Our Town* (1938).

On the other hand, all of Hitchcock's films are about the life force and sexuality—in effect, change. George Orwell has pointed out the typically "incestuous atmosphere" of happy endings in nineteenth century novels: such endings aren't to be found in Hitchcock. At the start of *Shadow of a Doubt*, young Charlie senses that her family is stagnating. Her parents are visibly aging (actor Henry Travers, who plays Joe, was sixty-eight when the film was made), while she herself is on the verge of womanhood. Accordingly, when she prays for "a miracle," and Uncle Charlie arrives, bearing gifts, the stage is set for some elaborate symbolism.

The ring that Uncle Charlie gives his niece, and which had belonged to one of his aging victims, has several meanings.

Joe (Henry Travers) is an avid reader of detective stories and smokes a Sherlock Holmes pipe when discussing them with Herb. Herb was played by Hume Cronyn, making his film debut.

Devil) and jokes about church to his niece: "Show's been running such a long time I thought attendance might be falling off." Ironically, she had seen him as the "one right person to save us."

Uncle Charlie is a complex figure. With his cape and knobbed stick, he's not only the Devil, he's also a dandy. In turn, his attitude to his sister Emma is at times less that of a brother than of a son. When he says, near the end of the film, "Emmy, you're a dream!" we think of the recurring shot of waltzing couples, the film's *most* dream-like—and nostalgic—image. But earlier, he'd chided his sister with the remark, "Emmy, women are fools! They

fall for anything!" Here the word *fall* seems significant. *The Lodger* again offers a clue. The Ivor Novello character appears to have killed his sister first, at her coming-out ball, then a succession of look-alikes. It's as if he considered her to have desecrated his ideal mother-image, and that all such persons must thereafter be punished.

Actually, Emma Newton in *Shadow of a Doubt* is depicted with great affection, for the character is in part a portrait of Hitchcock's own mother, who died in England while the film was being shot (on September 26, 1942). Scarcely less affectionate in its way is the gently satirical

Her family is concerned about Charlie's welfare. Joseph Cotten later starred in Under Capricorn.

His face when he presents it to her is eloquent—he invests the gift with great spiritual weight, associated with the dreamlike image of dancing couples. Young Charlie hadn't wanted a gift at all, but her own initial reaction likewise has a spiritual intensity. Eventually, though, the gift awakens in her a sexual instinct for which her earlier *dread* has prepared her. Her final rejection of her once-beloved uncle—but not of the ring itself, which she takes with her to Jack—may be seen as a repudiation of the "incestuous atmosphere" Uncle Charlie has stood for.

Consistent with young Charlie's decision to submit herself to the life force, rather than live in a kind of childish dream, is her ruthlessness. Hitchcock, who could be ruthless himself, acknowledged this quality in her. To critic Charles Thomas Samuels, he said: "She is ruthless. She comes down those stairs wearing that ring [as a sign to Uncle Charlie] and thus tells him that he must leave or be executed." Nonetheless, an undeniable spiritual bond has been established between these two people, who seemingly represent two aspects of one soul. One may think of *Wuthering Heights* and Catherine Earnshaw's fervent cry, "Nelly, I *am* Heathcliff." Young Charlie will always know that her uncle remains a part of herself.

Thus, Hitchcock's fairy tale ends on a characteristic note of ambiguity. Perhaps, in the larger scheme of things, Uncle Charlie really does save the Newtons. The reviewers concentrated on the film's thriller aspect. A perceptive writer in *Time* said that the film was similar to but much better than *Suspicion*, and singled out Teresa Wright's performance for special praise.

SHADOWS OF HITCHCOCK

Shadow of a Doubt has been remade three times. First, there was Harry Keller's *Step Down to Terror* (1958), which cast Charles Drake as the psychopathic killer hiding out in a small town. Colleen Miller played the girl, Josephine Hutchinson her mother, and Rod Taylor the detective. Writer Czenzi Ormonde (*Strangers on a Train*) helped in adapting the script. Then came Lee H. Katzin's *Strange Homecoming* (1974), a TV movie starring Robert Culp—now almost forgotten, perhaps because the plot was somewhat altered to make its debt to Hitchcock less apparent. The killer's sister (the girl's mother), so well played in the original by Patricia Collinge, became a brother who is also the local sheriff (Glen Campbell in his TV-movie debut). A third remake was filmed in 1991, directed for TV by Karen Arthur. It starred Mark Harmon, and had "Tippi" Hedren in a supporting role. Clearly *not* wanting to hide the Hitchcock connection, the filmmakers kept the original title and even included a carnival sequence straight out of *Strangers on a Train*. This third remake was the best, but none had the personal touch and human depth of Hitchcock's film.

LIFEBOAT

First screening January 1944

Production company:
Twentieth Century-Fox

Duration 96 minutes

Black and white

When a freighter is sunk by a U-boat in the mid-Atlantic, the U-boat is itself hit. Survivors from the freighter gather in an open lifeboat. They number eight: journalist Constance Porter (Tallulah Bankhead); ship's engineer Kovac (John Hodiak); radio operator Stanley Garrett (Hume Cronyn); army nurse Alice Mackenzie (Mary Anderson); rich industrialist Charles Rittenhouse (Henry Hull); an injured seaman Gus Smith (William Bendix); Negro steward Joe (Canada Lee); and a shell-shocked English woman Mrs. Iggley (Heather Angel), clutching her dead baby. Soon they are joined by the U-boat's sole survivor, its commander Willi (Walter Slezak). After a sea burial for the baby—whose mother drowns herself that night—the others must face their own prospects. They have a broken compass and limited rations, and hope they are heading for Bermuda. In fact Willi, who secretly has his own compass, is steering them towards a German supply ship. He also has hidden food and water supplies. One night, while the others are asleep, Gus catches Willi steering the boat in the wrong direction, but is tossed overboard and drowns. When the others discover Willi's treachery, they kill him. Subsequently, they are picked up by an Allied warship.

H itchcock's wartime allegory *Lifeboat* is about the War itself and the need of the Allies to settle their differences. But in the way of Hitchcock's films, it is also about the life force, as its title indicates. On this occasion, that force is very broad, akin to what philosophers call the world's *Will* (in German, *Wille*), symbolized chiefly in the film by the surrounding sea (as in another 1944 film, Lewis Allen's *The Uninvited*, in which the sea is called "a place of life and death and eternity, too.") It's fitting that when the would-be *Übermensch*-figure called Willi fails to share his secret water supply, what betrays him are the drops of salt water, sweat, on his forehead. Willi has tried to embody the Nietzschean notion of a will-to-power, but that notion was always perverted (as discussed later). Beyond the

individual's will, there's a universal Will, to which all individuals are finally subject.

The *Übermensch* notion was introduced into the film by Hitchcock. John Steinbeck's original treatment, a virtual novelette of 40,000 words, does not characterize the German as a superman—not even an "ersatz superman," as Constance ends up calling him in the film. The film came about when, in late 1942, the U.S. Merchant Marine contacted Darryl Zanuck of Twentieth Century-Fox to make a propaganda piece about the vital convoys that plied the North Atlantic in the face of U-boat attacks. Zanuck, whose studio had produced *The Grapes of Wrath* (1940), in turn asked Steinbeck to write a screenplay. Steinbeck agreed to do a treatment for which he would be paid only if the studio made use of it.

Left: Willi (Walter Slezak), Alice Mackenzie (Mary Anderson), Stanley Garrett (Hume Cronyn), Constance Porter (Tallulah Bankhead), Kovac (John Hodiak), Charles Rittenhouse (Henry Hull), Mrs. Iggley (Heather Angel), Smith (William Bendix), and Joe (Canada Lee).

Copies of the treatment exist in the Fox and Hitchcock archives, showing a highly realistic work that is at the same time an allegory. As in Steinbeck's novel *The Wayward Bus* (1947), the author isolates a group of representative individuals and has them interact. However, when the film came out, he claimed that it distorted

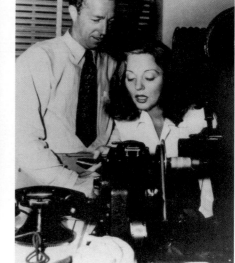

Left: *Charles Rittenhouse (Henry Hull) and Constance Porter (Tallulah Bankhead). The film earned Hitchcock another Oscar nomination.*
Right: *Tallulah Bankhead is given a preview of the film on a movieola by cutter Jerry Webb.*

his story, and tried to have his name taken off the credits.

Hitchcock, now loaned to Fox for a two-picture deal (though in the event only one film was made), asked Steinbeck to write the actual screenplay, but it didn't work out. In a private letter, the novelist later described Hitch as "one of those incredible English middle class snobs who really and truly despise working people." Fortunately for the director, he had another sympathetic producer, this time the film theorist and teacher Kenneth MacGowan—who told him to go ahead and choose another writer. Novelist MacKinlay Kantor lasted two weeks. It was Hollywood professional Jo(seph) Swerling who eventually turned Steinbeck's material into the final screenplay, adding most of the contemporary references to baseball, trumpeter Harry James, and the like. Besides making the German a superman figure, and calling him Willi, Swerling added the character of Stanley, or "Sparks," a radio operator from Greenwich, no doubt to stress the joint Anglo-American war effort. Finally, just before shooting, Hitch went through the script himself, tightening it and trying to give it dramatic cohesion.

John Russell Taylor praises Hitchcock's bold casting of Tallulah Bankhead, who had made few screen appearances in the preceding few years. Who, Hitch asked himself, would be the last person one would expect to meet, immaculately coiffured, adrift in a

lifeboat in the mid-Atlantic? However, Taylor finds the film preachy, and thinks it doesn't quite come off. Some reviewers agreed, though typically their main complaint was that the German appeared more competent and purposeful than any of the Allied representatives. In fact, the film was doing exactly what for centuries many morality plays had done, which was to give the Devil the best lines before delivering his comeuppance. *Time* called *Lifeboat* "one of the most ambitious films in years . . . remarkably intelligent."

Willi, played with suitable austerity by Walter Slezak, is another "Julius Pavia" figure. The title of the Buchan novel in which that character appears, *The Power House*, refers, of course, to Nietzsche's notion of a will-to-power. *Lifeboat*'s position apropos Willi is anticipated in the passage where Leithen tells Pavia: "You love power, hidden power. You flatter your vanity by despising mankind and making them your tools. You scorn the smattering of inaccuracies which passes

for human knowledge, and I will not venture to say that you are wrong. . . . Unfortunately, the life of millions is built on that smattering, so you are a foe to society."

Certainly *Lifeboat* is a key Hitchcock film. Its depiction of humanity adrift on a sea of contrasting moods, and its climactic scene where the Allies engage in what the script calls an "orgasm of murder" against the treacherous German, both conform closely to the view of Will set out by the philosopher Schopenhauer, who happened to be Nietzsche's predecessor. Schopenhauer saw Will as a life force that is also a death force, blindly pervading all of nature. He did *not* speak of a will-to-power in nature. That was a perversion introduced by Nietzsche. The Nazis then in turn perverted Nietzsche's concept by making "will-to-power" a dogma, a political imperative. Effectively, Hitchcock's film asks us to return to Schopenhauer's truer, if sometimes pessimistic, understanding. Not least, it asks us to be less cold-hearted. That is the implicit meaning of its last line, spoken by Constance, appealing to the lesson that the dead Mrs. Iggley and Gus would teach us.

BON VOYAGE

First screening 1944

Production company: Phoenix, for the British Ministry of Information (MOI)

Duration 26 minutes

Black and white

London, 1943. John Dougall (John Blythe), a Scottish airman escaped from a POW camp, tells a Free French colonel how he got out of occupied France. He'd been accompanied on the escape journey as far as Reims by a fellow prisoner, a Pole named Stefan Godowski. In Reims they had contacted the local Resistance and been taken to a farm run by a girl, Jeanne, and her father. A British plane, with one vacant place, had then landed nearby. After telling Jeanne that he hoped to see her again some day, John had boarded the plane; Stefan would follow later. The colonel now reveals to John how he had, in fact, been used. Godowski was a Gestapo agent, and the escape had been set up to penetrate the Resistance, some of whose members had died as a result. Among them was Jeanne.

The indirect basis of *Bon Voyage* may be Carol Reed's *Night Train to Munich* (1940), which hinges on an escape from a Nazi concentration camp by a professor's daughter accompanied by a "friend" who proves to be a Nazi plant. Officially, though, Hitchcock's film was adapted by J. O. C. Orton and Angus MacPhail from an original story by Arthur Calder Marshall, a novelist then working in the Ministry of Information. Hitch and MacPhail had known each other in the days of the Film Society, and were now brought back together by their mutual friend, Sidney Bernstein, head of the MOI's film division (MacPhail later worked on *Spellbound*, *The Man Who Knew Too Much* remake, and *The Wrong Man*). Bernstein had originally approached Selznick to borrow Hitch's services when on a visit to America in 1942, but it took Selznick a year to release him—and then grumblingly. Hitch's assignment in Britain was to make two short films lauding the French Resistance.

Both *Bon Voyage* and *Aventure Malgache* drew on a group of exiled French actors assembled under the name of the Molière Players. As many of the actors had relatives in France who were then active in the Resistance, performances by the Players were anonymous so as not to give possible clues to the occupying forces. The intention was to distribute both films in the liberated areas of France, but in the end *Aventure Malgache* was deemed not heroic enough, and was not released. Both were made in French, which Hitchcock spoke well. For his work as director he received a token

Above: Tense moments in Bon Voyage. The film was restored and released with new English subtitles in 1993.

£10 a week and a room at Claridge's (the hotel to which he always returned on subsequent visits to London).

There are foretastes of *Spellbound* in both films. The outcome of *Bon Voyage* anticipates the Green Manors scenes in which an unsuspected villain is finally unmasked. And Sergeant "Sandy" Dougall's sleepwalking through France anticipates John Ballyntine's amnesia.

Bon Voyage has a running gag involving Sandy's obsession with food, but it's more than that—it's also a sign that he's no mental giant. When he and Stefan find themselves in a cellar full of casks, he wonders aloud if it's a wine cellar. "Give the man a prize," says Stefan. The contrast is with the Free French officer in London. Twice Sandy asks him how he already knows so many details of what happened, and both times the colonel answers, "It's my intelligence that does it"—a telling play on words.

Also, there's a precedent for the cellar scenes in the windmill interiors of *Foreign Correspondent*. Visually, the correspondence isn't exact: cinematographer Günther Krampf (who had filmed Pabst's *Pandora's Box* [1928]) shrouds the cellar in menacing shadow with a few highlighted areas, such as the cellar steps, whereas Rudolph Maté gave the *Foreign Correspondent* windmill a suitably Dutch chiaroscuro. Nonetheless parallels remain, underlined by identical musical motifs and chords. Both scenes make use of a vibraphone to suggest dampness, dripping, a certain heaviness—and suspense.

The Hitchcock touch is most evident in *Bon Voyage* at its climax, when in a big close-up of Jeanne's face we see her lurch, and know that Stefan has shot her—this time anticipating a moment in *Topaz*. Altogether, it's a worthy film by Hitchcock, one whose running time and effective story-telling match the director's work for television a decade later.

AVENTURE MALGACHE

First screening 1993 (produced 1944)

Production company: Phoenix, for the British Ministry of Information (MOI)

Duration 31 minutes

Black and white

London, 1944. A company of refugee French actors have called themselves the Molière Players. In the actors' dressing room, someone says he's having trouble with his current role. Another actor, Clarousse, a former barrister, suggests he model himself on "my old friend . . . Jean Michel, the chief of police in Madagascar"—and tells him that he even looks like Michel. Then, in a series of flashbacks, Clarousse narrates his (reportedly) true story. Michel, far from being a friend, had sought to expose Clarousse as a Resistance leader on Madagascar after Pétain had ordered capitulation. When he's eventually found guilty and shipped off to a penal colony, Clarousse is miraculously saved by the intervention of a British warship. Later, when the British liberate Madagascar, Michel vainly tries to switch sides. After hearing Clarousse's account, the first actor takes offense at being likened to Michel. Tempers briefly flare, then subside.

The purpose of *Aventure Malgache*, an introductory title says, is to show how "the same spirit animated even the furthest colonies." To counterpoint its more pedestrian or political elements, the film is told with considerable comic gusto. Unfortunately its once topical references can spoil the film for today's audiences. But the general idea is the same as that of *Saboteur* or *Lifeboat*: to unite divided groups or factions. Hitchcock and Angus MacPhail devised the story after observing the bickering among the Free French who had worked with them on *Bon Voyage*.

Hitchcock's filmmaking intelligence is again displayed. Michel isn't made a heavy, just a rather weak and vainglorious man. He is intellectually no match for the barrister Clarousse, who in an early scene denounces him as corrupt. Later, the cross-cutting between an animated Clarousse broadcasting from offshore his anti-Vichy messages, and Michel listening dejectedly in his office, speaks volumes. Clarousse is presented as a humane and democratic man, who seems more than once to have Heaven on his side. Reprieved from a death sentence by the unlikely intervention of Pétain himself because Clarousse had served alongside him at Verdun in 1916, the barrister is told by a fellow actor in the dressing room, "Nice irony. Angel Gabriel please note." (That reference is taken up in *Spellbound*, where key events occur in Gabriel Valley.)

There are some delicious gags. As Michel visits the island's governor, the latter's personal secretary, named Monsieur Guyot, enters to report further escapes to the Resistance. Michel demands that a spy be set on Clarousse. In the next scene,

Aventure Malgache *was originally produced under the title* Madagascar Landing.

Guyot and Clarousse laughingly descend some stairs in a café where their Resistance comrades await them. The moment's saucy mood is perfectly caught by graffiti drawings of naked figures, including cherubs, on the nearby wall. In another scene, Michel comes into possession of coded messages supposedly representing commercial transactions sent by Clarousse. The camera gleefully records the police chief's hopeless attempt to render meaningful such instructions as, "Get stuffed. Where's the butter?" and, "The chestnuts will be ripe on 35th April."

A scene where the fiancée of one of the Resistance members betrays Clarousse has absurdly been called misogynistic. The film has taken pains to stress Clarousse's own weakness, his "sentimentality," in the preceding scene, where he consents to the fiancée's being told that

her young man is leaving immediately for overseas. Then, in a long scene in the fiancée's boudoir, she tells us of the near-intolerable pain of being parted from her lover, possibly for years. Hitchcock understands her pain, and her reaction, and simply records them as further facts of war.

Another recording function fell to Hitchcock in 1945, when he returned to England as treatment advisor on a German Special Film supervised by Sidney Bernstein, showing the horrors of the newly liberated concentration camps. Made for the Supreme Headquarters of the Allied Expeditionary Force, it was not released at the time. But in recent years, the footage has had limited showing under the title *Memory of the Camps*. It is devastating.

HITCHCOCK ON RADIO

It is not known exactly how many radio appearances Hitchcock made, but the following examples should give some idea of how frequently he could be heard over the airwaves.

The Royal Gelatin Hour was a variety program, hosted by Rudy Vallee, which presented music and drama for a full hour every Thursday evening. Many stars of stage and screen made their radio debut on the Vallee program. Hitch, who had recently arrived in America to begin filming *Rebecca*, was a guest on April 13, 1939, giving an exclusive interview to promote his first Hollywood movie.

The following year, Columbia Broadcasting System (CBS) launched *Forecast,* an hour-long pilot program aimed at gauging radio listeners' interests. The series premiered in the summer of 1940 and each episode showcased two half-hour presentations, both of which were potential new series. If they received a good response, the board at CBS would then consider developing the program sfurther. Popular series *Duffy's Tavern, Jubilee, The Country Lawyer, Hopalong Cassidy,* and *Mischa, the Magnificent* all started life on *Forecast.*

The largest success by far came from the second half-hour presentation on July 22, 1940, entitled *Suspense.* Alfred Hitchcock was asked to host a half-hour drama of his choice. He selected *The Lodger* and actors Herbert Marshall and Edmund Gwenn were cast in this suspenseful play, with Gwenn playing the same role that had been portrayed by his brother, Arthur Chesney, in Hitchcock's 1926 film version. Both Marshall and Gwenn could then be seen in Hitchcock's current release, *Foreign Correspondent.*

Interestingly, the end of the story was not dramatized. Instead, Hitchcock felt it better for the cast (especially Herbert Marshall) to debate the ending during the last few minutes of the broadcast. Even musician Wilbur Hatch got in on the act, also wanting to know whether The Lodger was caught or not. This trick apparently worked, as *Suspense* became one of CBS's longest running anthology series, lasting from 1942 until 1962.

"Malice Aforethought" was the short story dramatized for an ABC network pilot, with Hume Cronyn and Jessica Tandy as the (unbilled) lead stars. The program opened with church bells tolling twelve, followed by the announcer's opening monologue: "Suspense, shock, murder. All the makings of a spine-tingling mystery drama, in the hands of a past master of theatrical illusion, Alfred Hitchcock. We of the American Broadcasting Company believe this new series has the opportunity of becoming the most important and distinguished of its kind in radio."

Like most Hollywood personalities, Hitch was special guest on some of the popular comedy shows of the period, such as *The Texaco Star Theater,* which featured legendary radio wit Fred Allen. Hitch made his only appearance on this program on January 24, 1943. Later in the decade, he guested on *The Charlie McCarthy Show,* which starred popular ventriloquist Edgar Bergen with his wooden dummy Charlie McCarthy. Various Hollywood stars featured on the show, with a chance to perform a short humorous skit. Sadly, there is no recording known to exist of Hitch's March 21, 1948 broadcast.

Radio dramatizations of popular Hollywood movies were frequently heard on the radio, in shows such as *The Lux Radio Theatre* and *Screen Director's Playhouse.* The latter used the original film's director to introduce the drama and afterward to reminisce with the stars about the picture's production. Alfred Hitchcock featured on three occasions, the first, on January 30, 1949, when Robert Montgomery and Mary Jane Croft starred as "Mr. and Mrs. Smith."

His second involvement with the series came on November 16, 1950, when "Lifeboat" was broadcast. By this time the program had expanded from thirty minutes to an hour. For "Lifeboat," Tallulah Bankhead reprised her screen role, and Jeff Chandler and Sheldon Leonard played small supporting roles. Hitch's third and final contribution was with "Spellbound," which on January 25, 1951 starred Joseph Cotten as John Ballyntine and Mercedes McCambridge as Dr. Constance Peterson.

Martin Grams Jr.

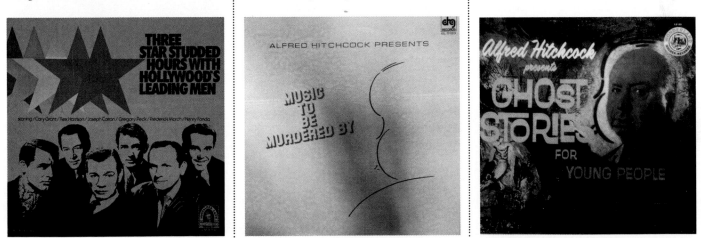

Left: *A three album box set of radio dramas, featuring Cary Grant in a version of* Suspicion *and Joseph Cotten in an adaptation of* Shadow of a Doubt.
Middle and right: *Hitchcock also lent his name to a number of records, including* Music to Be Murdered By *and* Ghost Stories for Young People.

SPELLBOUND

First screening October 1945

Production company: Selznick International

Duration 110 minutes

Black and white

"Green Manors," Vermont, a mental hospital, is headed by Dr. Murchison (Leo G. Carroll), who is about to retire. His young successor, "Dr. Edwardes" (Gregory Peck), arrives and promptly begins an affair with the brilliant but hitherto rather cold Dr. Constance Petersen (Ingrid Bergman). She soon detects that her lover, though he's a medical doctor, isn't Edwardes but an amnesiac, "J. B.," who may have killed Edwardes. When the police come, J. B. flees to New York City. Constance follows him, and together they go to Rochester to see Constance's mentor, old Dr. Alex Brulov (Michael Chekhov). Alex helps them analyze a dream of J. B.'s, which points them to a ski resort called Gabriel Valley. Here, J. B. remembers how he'd seen Edwardes plunge over a nearby precipice, a sight which had triggered his amnesia because of an unpleasant association to his childhood. The police find the body, discover a bullet hole in its back, and hold J. B., or John Ballyntine, on suspicion of murder. A forlorn Constance returns to Green Manors, where upon further analyzing Ballyntine's dream, she detects the real culprit, Dr. Murchison. Confronted, Murchison shoots himself, leaving Constance and Ballyntine free to marry.

*S*pellbound is an impressive Hitchcock film, full of bold effects. Near the end, everything hinges on a simple slip of the tongue—a Freudian slip?—made by Dr. Murchison. By repeating the line as if inside Constance's head, and by adding an echo effect and other elements of stylization, Hitchcock ensures that nobody misses the line's importance. Nonetheless, many ingredients of the film *do* elude conscious appreciation by audiences. A key to this complex film is Constance's remark, "We have the word 'white' on our side."

The film's basis is a novel, *The House of Dr. Edwardes* (1927), by John Leslie Palmer and Hilary Aidan St. George Saunders, writing as Francis Beeding. They are best known for their chilling detective story *Death Walks in Eastrepps* (1931). A first draft of a treatment for *Spellbound* was prepared by Angus MacPhail in January 1944, while Hitchcock was still in England making *Bon Voyage* and *Aventure Malgache*, and the final screenplay was completed in Hollywood by Ben Hecht in August 1944. Meanwhile, principal photography had already begun on July 10, and would take forty-eight days. The script underwent some last-minute changes. For example, the ski resort called Gabriel Valley had first been Lake Placid (as in *Mr. and Mrs. Smith*). Scenes with the inmates of Green Manors were considerably simplified from the original treatment, in which the inmates were depicted rehearsing William Congreve's comedy about frustrated marriage, *The Way of the World* (1700).

That expressive, or Expressionist, touch was typical of Hitchcock, and the final film still has many of them: the head of a mental institution who is himself insane, for example—an idea recalling the famous Erich Pommer production, *The Cabinet of Dr. Caligari* (1919). And instead of the inmates performing a play, Hitchcock now had them play cards—gambling was a common German Expressionist motif. When the action moves to New York, J. B. stays at the Empire State Hotel, in the world's tallest building at the time. In the lobby, a drunk (Wallace Ford) complains, "A fella could live and die in this town and couldn't meet nobody," (which anticipates *The Birds*, where Mitch calls San Francisco "an anthill at the foot of a bridge"). But using the hotel's guest registry, Constance manages to locate J. B.'s room number when a card headed "John Brown" seems to leap to her searching hand. In short, much about the film recalls a dream . . .

The heart of *Spellbound* is the actual dream sequence designed by Salvador Dali. Hitchcock said that he chose Dali "because of the architectural sharpness of his work" (and no doubt for his ability to render, in Jacques Dopagne's phrase, "the cosmic anguish of space-time"). Hitchcock didn't want any clichéd fuzzy-at-the-edges effects. But it seems that producer Selznick, for whom Hitch was again directly working, misunderstood, and thought that hiring Dali was just a publicity stunt. However, being back with Selznick had advantages for the director. For instance, it allowed him to cast Ingrid Bergman, who had taken over from Greta Garbo as the world's leading Swedish film actress. Intellectually, Bergman was said to be "like molasses." Years later, Hitch would murmur, "Ah, Ingrid. So beautiful, so *stupid . . .* " Yet her great gifts as a performer were tangible, and she gave *Spellbound* exactly the warmth it needed. The script capitalized on this. In an early scene, a bespectacled Constance rejects the advances of Dr. Fleurot (John Emery), as if she were Garbo in *Ninotchka* (1939): "You sense only your own desires and pulsations—I assure you mine in no way resemble them" (As in *Marnie*, where the heroine says, "I am not like other people"). Later, Constance begins to contact her real self. On the train to Gabriel Valley, she tells J. B. that she has resolved to henceforth wear the very feminine clothes she has always secretly loved.

Constance's mentor, Dr. Brulov, is a Russian, played by a perfectly cast Michael Chekhov, born in Petrograd and related to the famous Russian dramatist and writer Anton Chekhov (1860–1904).

A German magazine cover featuring the film.

Top: Hitchcock in discussion with Gregory Peck and Ingrid Bergman.
Above: "J. B." (Gregory Peck) visits the home of Dr. Alex Brulov (Michael Chekhov). Chekhov was nominated for that year's Best Supporting Actor Oscar.

Perhaps not by coincidence, composer Miklós Rózsa, a Hungarian, included a Russian instrument, the electronic theremin, in the film's score. It is first used in the credits sequence, to eerily suggest the wind that is blowing away the leaves on a tree; later, the same musical passage accompanies the onset of each of Ballyntine's anxiety attacks that begin soon after he meets Constance. This suggests the working of a force that's at once exotic and homely, a life force that is also a death force.

For the audience, such a force may be thought of as its collective libido. Freud had said that a basic cause of anxiety is frustration of the libidinal drive, and Hitchcock often built his suspense films on that principle (*The 39 Steps* for example). In *Lifeboat*, he'd specifically introduced Freudian symbolism when Stanley had untied the string holding up Alice's hair—an act that, according to the script, represents the Freudian symbol for being in love. Now, in *Spellbound*, Hitchcock and Hecht set out to make the first Hollywood film *about* psychoanalysis. Symbolism pervaded the script: the several references to J. B.'s having just one suitcase, for example, implying his amnesic condition. Most famous—or infamous—of all was the image of opening doors

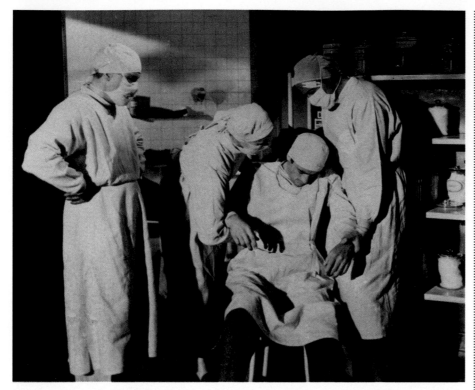

J. B. initially claims to be Dr. Edwardes. Peck received little direction from Hitchcock, which as a newcomer to the screen he felt he needed.

when the lovers first kiss. However, these things were just the film's manifest content.

Not everyone appreciated what else *Spellbound* had to offer. It's doubtful that Selznick fully understood what was being expressed in the dream sequence when he decided it didn't play, and, having trimmed the sequence overall by several minutes, then deleted an entire segment (see boxed feature). The film premiered on November 1, 1945, and proved a hit with audiences and most critics. Bosley Crowther, writing in *The New York Times*, said it was the first of Hitchcock's American films to achieve the excellence of his British thrillers. Later, in Britain, *Kinematograph Weekly* called it "[a]n exciting and mentally stimulating thriller," and praised George Barnes's cinematography. The film had cost $1,696,377; it made $7,000,000.

To begin to appreciate a deeper, more poetic *Spellbound*, one may start with the already mentioned "opening doors" shot. Hitch's own derisory comment was aimed at the music. "Unfortunately," he told Truffaut, "the violins began to play just then. That was terrible!" But the film is full of doors references (see *Marnie* again), so the metaphor for unblocking is central. Even more central is the radiant

whiteness behind the final door. That image is the film's symbol of freedom, based on time-honored associations found in poetry—such as Shelley's *Adonais*, with its "white radiance of Eternity." Earlier, it's true, Constance had mocked the idea of love as portrayed by poets. And the film's subsequent allusions to whiteness—an operating theater at Green Manors, white bathroom fixtures at Dr. Brulov's, a glass of milk—do in fact revert to more mundane imagery. But then comes the Gabriel Valley sequence. The novel calls the locale the "Gorge du Diable," which clearly didn't suit Hitchcock's purposes at all. The archangel Gabriel, whose name means "man of God," is traditionally seen as one of God's chief messengers. In *Paradise Lost*, Milton makes him "Chief of the angelic guards" placed over Paradise.

Basically, though, *Spellbound* is no different from several other Hitchcock films: they are all (or appear to be) *lost* paradise films. Freud can tell us why. Infancy, he says, is indeed a paradise, corresponding to the "unashamed period of childhood" which he defines as lasting until the end of the third year of life. This period might equally be called the pre-Oedipal period. In *Spellbound*, when J. B. and Constance ski across a snowfield which represents at

least a *potential* paradise—skiing, as in *Mr. and Mrs. Smith*, has sexual and connubial connotations—ironically they appear to be heading for an abyss and certain death, one more image of Ballyntine's recurring fear. However, they manage to avoid that extreme fate. What saves them is J. B. suddenly remembering an accident from his boyhood in which he had killed his brother. This doesn't mean (as the plot soon shows) that the pair are exactly out of difficulty. Freud taught that there is no such thing as an accident. In psychoanalytic terms, what happened to J. B. and his brother was a case of sibling rivalry manifesting itself as a realized wish.

Furthermore, sibling rivalry is related to a child's Oedipal desire to possess one or other parent exclusively—and can be very fierce. As far as John Ballyntine is concerned, he is both innocent *and* guilty of his brother's death. Thus Hitchcock finds in Freud one more metaphor of original sin. At some level, this explains Ballyntine's erratic behavior towards Constance throughout the film. Fortunately, in the final scene a prediction of Ballyntine's comes true, and it marks the typical Hitchcockian resolution. Ballyntine had told Constance that she was going to look wonderful wearing white and with orange blossoms in her hair. In a worldly sense, then, and perhaps rather more than that, the color white has indeed favored these two truth-seekers.

Another highlight of *Spellbound* besides the Gabriel Valley sequence is the Dali-designed dream, which has often been misunderstood. For example, one

DAVID O. SELZNICK presents
BERGMAN · PECK
in ALFRED HITCHCOCK'S
SPELLBOUND
A SELZNICK INTERNATIONAL PICTURE

huge phallic pair of scissors, which he uses to cut the eyes on the drapes (recalling the famous 1928 Dali/Buñuel film, *Un Chien Andalou*).

Hitchcock, if not Selznick, knew what was going on all right. Much of the imagery from *Spellbound* recurs in later films, especially *Psycho*.

Above: J. B. and Constance. Spellbound was the first of Bergman's three films for Hitchcock. Left: Constance and the real murderer, Dr. Murchison (Leo G. Carroll). On its initial release, a key gunshot sequence during the climax was shown with a few frames in color.

THE CUT BALLROOM SEGMENT

A cut segment of the Dali dream sequence.

The *Spellbound* dream sequence originally consisted of four segments, not three. The missing segment was scripted and filmed, and ran for perhaps fifty seconds, including a scene at the end where Constance turns into a statue. According to James Bigwood, in *American Cinematographer*, June 1991, Ingrid Bergman's claim that twenty minutes was cut from the dream at this point was exaggerated! On October 6, 1944, Selznick ordered that the segment be removed, despite its throwing light on Ballyntine's fears of marrying Constance. Here is the complete narration for the Ballroom Scene: "I don't know how I got there, but I was in a ballroom. The dancers were all dressed in white suits and pretending to dance, but not moving. There was an orchestra dressed in white fur hats. And Dr. Brulov was leading it. I was dancing with Constance, and she had a dance card and asked me to write my name on it. I refused, then grabbed her and we started dancing—rather wildly. We danced out of the ballroom and I kissed her. The dance card kept getting bigger. It was full of names and addresses. And Constance turned into a statue."

critic refers to a pair of phallic pliers that Selznick removed; but in fact the pliers are still visible, and are not so much phallic as castrating! This final part of the dream represents Ballyntine's Oedipal fear of what marriage to Constance may involve. (Fear of castration becomes a common fear in Hitchcock's heroes from *Spellbound* onwards.) Including the segment that was cut, the dream has four parts: the gambling segment; two men on a roof; the ballroom segment; and finally the downhill-uphill segment.

The first segment is the most elaborate, and is patently based on the idea that dreams are wish fulfillments. The gambling hall, which combines elements of Green Manors and the 21 Club (where Ballyntine had dined with Edwardes), might almost be a bordello, and is full of suggestive Dali symbolism: drapes that hang in folds, alluring eyes nestling between them; tables that have women's legs (against which the legs of the male card players rub); swaying metronomes also painted with eyes (suggesting copulation). In the background, a male figure wields what this time is very definitely a

NOTORIOUS

First screening July 1946

**Production company:
RKO Radio Pictures, Inc.**

Duration 100 minutes

Black and white

Miami, 1946. Alicia Huberman (Ingrid Bergman), the daughter of a convicted traitor, has a reputation for loose living. Government agent T. R. Devlin (Cary Grant) offers her an unspecified assignment in Brazil. She accepts, and they leave immediately for Rio. Settling in takes a few days, and during that time the pair fall in love. The idyll ends when Devlin's boss, Paul Prescott (Louis Calhern), briefs him: Alicia is to renew relations with a former suitor, and friend of her father's, Alexander Sebastian (Claude Rains), whose home shelters Nazi scientists and plotters. Both Devlin and Alicia are torn, but accede. Soon afterwards, when Alex proposes, Alicia marries him—to the displeasure of his viperish mother (Leopoldine Konstantin). Later, Devlin attends a party given by the Sebastians, and in the wine cellar finds uranium ore. But Alex sees that Alicia is a spy, and he and his mother begin to slowly poison her. Days pass. A worried Devlin goes to the house, and in front of Alex and his mother leads a weakened Alicia to safety. Also looking on, and speculating, have been Alex's Nazi colleagues. Alex will have some explaining to do.

The novelist E. M. Forster wrote: "If I had to choose between betraying my country or betraying a friend, I hope to God I would have the guts to betray my country." That controversial, not to say radical, idea is one that Hitchcock made the pivot of such films as *Notorious* and *North by Northwest*. Rather absurdly, critics often play favorites between Alicia and Devlin, and say that while her conduct in the film is admirable, his is reprehensible (until the end). In fact, the matter isn't so simple. Until Alex and his mother start poisoning her, Alicia is as free—or unfree—to call off the assignment as Devlin is. They both love each other, and much of the emotional standoff between them, which occupies the central part of the film, is the result of their legit-

Left: *Hitchcock and Bergman confer over the script.*

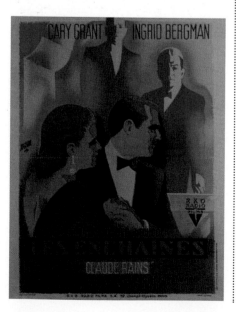

imately different outlooks and needs. *Notorious* is great film drama.

Early in 1945, Hitchcock and Ben Hecht completed a fifty-page first draft treatment for their film to follow *Spellbound*. The treatment was based, rather remotely, on John Taintor Foote's two-part story, "The Song of the Dragon," which had appeared in *The Saturday Evening Post* in 1921. The story is about Mary Brannigan, an eighteen-year-old actress who, appalled at the car-

nage being inflicted by the War on her country's young men, agrees to become a counter-spy and sleep with a foreign agent to get secret information. Later she becomes an Army entertainer, singing Irish songs, and falls in love with a young Captain. The boy's formidable mother is understandably suspicious, but finally, told the full facts, gives her blessing to her son's marriage.

Here was no more than the germ of the future *Notorious*, but it would have

Above: Devlin represents a certain American male of rather puritanical upbringing (here with Paul Prescott [Louis Calhern] and Alicia).

Below: Notorious is justly famous for the lengthy kiss between Alicia and Devlin on their balcony in Rio.

reminded Hitchcock of something else. Foote's story closely resembles a central episode in John Buchan's *Mr. Standfast* (1919), which is also set during the War, and in which hero Richard Hannay's future wife, the eighteen-year-old Mary Lamington, conceives of a bold move to undo a top German spy calling himself Moxon Ivery. The first half of the novel ends dramatically when Mary comes to Hannay and his intelligence boss, Macgillivray, and announces, "Last week Mr. Ivery asked me to marry him."

Hannay is nonplussed. Unofficially, the blonde Mary, half his age, is his adored girlfriend. However, she and several of their colleagues have been aware for some time of Ivery's activities, which have lately become even more threatening to the Allies. Mary therefore plans to entice Ivery into a trap. When Hannay, red-faced, protests that he won't let her go through with her "infernally degrading" scheme, a colleague reasons with him: "It isn't pretty, but war isn't pretty, and nothing we do is pretty." Mary herself then addresses Hannay affectionately, saying that she knows what she's doing. She notes that "women were always robuster than men," and asks Hannay to have faith in her. Contrite, he submits.

Buchan's novel has a startling climax. Ivery is captured, put into Allied uniform, and sent into the ranks—where he dies on the battlefield, shot by a German bullet. That irony matches the one at the end of *Notorious*. In fact, a comment of

Hannay's catches something of the film's brutality (in which Alicia can smile at Alex's likely fate): "I had no more pity for [Ivery] than I would have had for a black mamba that had killed my friend and was now caught to a cleft tree."

From the start, Hitchcock and Hecht's story concerned Nazis in Brazil. In the course of 1945, nine further drafts followed the initial treatment. Again and again, producer Selznick made criticisms and suggestions, many of them astute. The fact that *Notorious* is Hitchcock's best-constructed, least-flabby film must be attributed in large measure to Selznick's influence at the scripting stage, though the memo-happy producer undoubtedly tried Hitchcock and Hecht's patience. In May, he dictated such comments as "Madame Sebastian [behaves] like an idiot" and "Devlin just doesn't make sense to anybody but Ben Hecht;" criticized Alicia's character for being abrasive; and found grave fault with the dialogue for being both too much and too ordinary. He had also begun to have doubts about the film's MacGuffin, which had started out as a secret Nazi army being formed in Brazil, became chemicals and mechanisms for building a new German weapon, and

ended up as uranium ore concealed in wine bottles.

In fact, so uneasy did Selznick feel about building a whole film around a MacGuffin, especially one (uranium) he considered insignificant, that in July he sold the film as a package to RKO for $800,000 plus fifty percent of the net profits. (In August, the world heard about the dropping of the atom bomb on Japan, and of the part played by uranium in atomic fission.) Included in the package were costars Ingrid Bergman and Cary Grant. Both would give outstanding performances in *Notorious*. Of Bergman, Pauline Kael wrote in 1976 that she "is literally ravishing in what is probably her sexiest performance." Grant, though, is necessarily buttoned-up for much of the film. Recent Grant biographer Graham McCann sees Devlin as "a professional dissembler, secretive, deceitful, emotionally impotent and, beneath the cool exterior, acutely vulnerable." Rumor had it, says McCann, that Grant himself was like that; however, one can speculate that the description equally well (or badly) fits Hitchcock!

Another excellent performance was that of Claude Rains as the charmer Alex. Bosley Crowther in *The New York Times* called the English actor's playing "shrewd and tense" and "responsible for much of the anguish that the situation creates." A different aspect of the Sebastian household

CARY GRANT   INGRID BERGMAN
... ALFRED HITCHCOCK'S

Notorious!

Above: Mrs. Sebastian (Leopoldine Konstantin), Alicia, and Alex. The film earned Rains an Oscar nomination, although Clifton Webb had been Hitchcock's initial choice to fill the part.
Below: Is Alicia's drink drugged?

was seen in the "chilly arrogance" of Alex's mother, played by distinguished German actress Leopoldine Konstantin. The character merges traits of Mrs. Whittaker in *Easy Virtue* and the mother in "The Song of the Dragon."

Notorious cost $2,300,000 and grossed $7,100,000. Thus it proved a popular success and, on the whole, a critical one. (These days it is widely considered a masterpiece.) James Agee seems to have appreciated the film's lustrous perfection and endless nuances, but to have missed the careless excitement of some earlier Hitchcock. "*Notorious*," he wrote, "lacks many of the qualities which made the best of Alfred Hitchcock's movies so good, but it has more than enough good qualities of its own."

It is the most lucid of the director's films. For example, it allows that everyone has his reasons. There's great psychological acumen in the portrait of Alicia, working to redeem herself in her own eyes, but in desperate need of being told by her dream man that she is loved. In turn, what stops Devlin from speaking out until almost too late seems related to how he's a certain type of American male, of rather puritanical upbringing. (Consider the scene where he covers Alicia's bare midriff with his handker-

chief.) Agee noted a real-life agent who had much the same "cultivated, clipped puzzled-idealist brutality" as Devlin. That character's opposite number, in some respects, is Alex. He is extremely empathic, to the point of seeming at times almost

bisexual. When he first takes Alicia to lunch, he remarks on the presence of Prescott at a nearby table, "Rather handsome isn't he?" Of course, Alex is here imagining *Alicia's* feelings—rather like a good filmmaker must do when he enters into his various characters' states of mind. Hitchcock wants us to feel that Alex has qualities of sensitivity and charm that Devlin lacks, not just for reasons of dramatic light and shade but because those qualities are part of the total picture— which the film needs to establish if it is to work.

An underlying idea resembles that in *Saboteur*: each of the film's characters is, or feels, alienated from life, the total picture. The bemused drinking at the party in Miami, with its conversation about absent fish, is emblematic, even more so when Alicia remarks, "What this party needs is a little gland treatment." Soon love is posited as an obvious solution— and *Notorious* is one of the great films about love—but equally soon is (seemingly) thrust aside. More immediate issues arise, including what might be called a "friendship-versus-duty" matter. Clearly Alicia and Devlin approach it differently. We may guess, though, that he'll rescue her when the chips are finally down. "I've always been afraid of women," he has told her, "but I get over it." That is, he has what it takes to save her, to have her.

The invisible question is: when?

Alex, too, has it in him not to be a loser. The fact that he's a loser *this time* isn't because he's a Nazi, exactly, but more because he has happened to find himself on the wrong (i.e., defeated) side. (In the courtroom scene, Alicia's father starts to tell the judge that there *will* be a next time, but is hushed by his counsel.) Ideology isn't the issue in *Notorious*—people are. And there's a related matter:

all ideologies and their systems are ultimately indifferent to people. The CIA comes off no better in this film than in *North by Northwest*, where Thornhill gives the agency a stinging rebuke. Appropriately, the film's most crucial scene is the justly famous—because so warm and tender—first kissing scene between Alicia and Devlin on their balcony in Rio. In effect, the scene culminates in the film's final sequence at Alex's house, where Alicia again clings lovingly to Devlin as he escorts her down the stairs to freedom.

The entire final sequence deserves extended analysis. Ingrid Bergman was never photographed more beautifully than in the shots of her head cradled on a pillow—not, that is, until Hitchcock repeated the effect in color in *Under Capricorn*. Hitchcock's film is infinitely more dramatic about its Alicia/Devlin relationship than is *Mr. Standfast* about the Mary Lamington/Hannay relationship in similar circumstances. Even so, it's worth remembering that the film's underlying idea—something that Hitchcock always put great weight on—was in this case Buchan's: what would a man do and feel if the woman he loves elected to sleep with another man for noble motives? Devlin answers that when he finally declares his love: "I [acted like] a fatheaded guy full of pain."

WHAT'S A MACGUFFIN?

The term *MacGuffin* was coined by Hitchcock's Scottish friend, screenwriter Angus MacPhail, for something that sets the film's plot revolving around it. It's really just an excuse and a diversion. In a whimsical anecdote told by Hitchcock, he compared the MacGuffin to a mythical "apparatus for trapping lions in the Scottish Highlands." In other words, it could be anything—or nothing—at all. In *Notorious*, it's just a lot of fizz: uranium ore hidden in champagne bottles. In *North by Northwest*, it's government secrets, whatever they may be. (Hitchcock considered that this was his best MacGuffin, because it was virtually nonexistent.) Actually *North by Northwest* turns out to be one vast MacGuffin, being full of nothings like the "O" in Roger O. Thornhill's name, or the empty prairie, or the nonexistent agent named Kaplan. In effect, the function of a MacGuffin is like the meaning of a poem—which T. S. Eliot compared to the bone thrown by a burglar to distract the watchdog of the mind while the poem goes about its own, deeper business. Hitchcock's most prescient MacGuffin is in *Torn Curtain*, whose "Gamma Five" project, concerning an anti-missile missile, anticipated by more than a decade President Reagan's "Star Wars" project.

THE PARADINE CASE

First screening December 1947

Production company:
Selznick International/Vanguard
Films, Inc.

Duration 132 minutes

Black and white

In post-war London, the coldly beautiful Maddalena Paradine (Alida Valli) is charged with having poisoned her blind husband, Colonel Paradine. The family solicitor, Sir Simon Flaquer (Charles Coburn), engages a famous barrister, Anthony Keane (Gregory Peck), to defend her. Keane is happily married to Gay (Ann Todd), but from the moment he visits Mrs. Paradine in Holloway Prison he becomes infatuated with his client and convinced of her innocence. He goes to Cumberland to inspect Hindley Hall, the Paradine country residence. There he encounters the valet, André Latour (Louis Jourdan), who apparently worshipped his master but hated Mrs. Paradine. On Keane's return to London, he's clearly become obsessed. Gay realizes that, for the sake of their marriage, he must win the case, because otherwise Mrs. Paradine will become his great lost love. But the Old Bailey trial before Lord Horfield (Charles Laughton) goes badly for Keane. It emerges that Mrs. Paradine had indeed murdered the Colonel after falling in love with, and seducing, Latour. When word comes that Latour has committed suicide, Mrs. Paradine, in the dock, denounces Keane for his clumsy handling of the case. His career and illusions shattered, Keane returns to Gay.

At Hindley Hall, Mrs. Paradine's enigmatic portrait, set into the head of her bed, recalls the *Mona Lisa*. Equally, the portrait is a funerary one, like those on gravestones. Hitchcock is here evoking the Fatal Woman of Decadent literature. But the passionate, Italian-born Mrs. Paradine is also flesh and blood. At the end of the film, Lady Horfield (Ethel Barrymore) expresses great pity for her, though this doesn't impress Lord Horfield. He snorts that "the Paradine woman will be hanged within three clear Sundays"—and falls to picking his teeth with a gold toothpick. Much underrated, *The Paradine Case* is another intelligent, if cumbersome, drama by Hitchcock.

According to Leonard Leff, "Hitchcock freely selected *The Paradine Case*"—it wasn't forced on him by its producer and scriptwriter, Selznick. The film's basis was the 1933 novel by prolific author Robert Hichens, once an associate of Oscar Wilde. In turn, Hichens based the novel on two sensational English murder cases. The first was that of Madame Fahmy, an attractive Frenchwoman who in 1923 was acquitted by a British jury after she'd shot and killed her husband, an Egyptian prince, at London's Savoy Hotel. At the trial, it was suggested that the prince had been inti-

Gregory Peck and the courtroom set.

mate with his male secretary. The fact that Madame Fahmy herself seems to have been a woman of loose morals wasn't revealed to the jury—her famous advocate Edward Marshall Hall saw to that.

The other murder case was that of Florence Maybrick, a young American woman found guilty of poisoning her English husband at Liverpool in 1889. The Maybricks lived comfortably at "Battlecrease House." But the husband seems to have had a violent disposition, probably the result of his chronic hypochondria. It's also likely that he discovered that his wife

GREGORY **PECK** ANN **TODD** CHARLES **LAUGHTON** CHARLES **COBURN** ETHEL **BARRYMORE** *Valli* LOUIS **JOURDAN**

DAVID O. SELZNICK'S Production of ALFRED HITCHCOCK'S

THE **PARADINE** CASE

Der Fall Paradin

Gregory Peck   Ann Todd
Charles Laughton   Charles Coburn
Ethel Barrimore   Louis Jourdan   Alida Valli
REGIE ALFRED HITCHCOCK
Produktion David O.Selznick

was having an affair with a man named Brierly. Mrs. Maybrick eventually went to prison for fifteen years.

Further, Hichens based the novel's pivotal Keane/Horfield antagonism on a real-life clash of temperaments between Edward Marshall Hall and the most feared criminal judge of his time, Mr. Justice Avory. As Julian Symons notes, Marshall Hall was handsome and excitable, and said to be "at his best when able to identify himself strongly with his client's cause." In contrast, Mr. Justice Avory had been a merciless criminal prosecutor who "became an icy judge, one who disregarded all except purely legal considerations." He was known as a hanging judge, something that the novel's sadistic, as well as lecherous, Lord Horfield certainly is. So too is Horfield in the film, though the character has been bowdlerized.

In fact, just about all of these real-life details went into the film's script, and many reached the film itself. Smoothly handsome Louis Jourdan plays Latour as a woman-hater since being jilted on his wedding day. To emphasize the—supposedly—unlikely attraction this man of celibate lifestyle holds for the married Mrs. Paradine, Hitchcock wanted to cast a rougher type of actor such as Robert Newton: the director may have had in mind *Lady Chatterley's Lover*. Hitchcock was also unhappy with the casting of Gregory Peck, and would have preferred Laurence Olivier or Ronald Colman. Peck realized he looked too young for the part; after trying out various moustaches to suitably age himself, he settled for graying his temples. That the character is based

Upper left: Hitchcock with Ann Todd and Ethel Barrymore between takes. Barrymore was nominated for the Best Supporting Actress Oscar for her performance.
Above: Barrister, Anthony Keane (Gregory Peck), and his client, Maddalena Paradine (Alida Valli, billed simply as "Valli" in her American debut). Producer Selznick had long envisioned Garbo as Mrs. Paradine, but was unable to persuade her out of retirement.

on Marshall Hall is readily apparent from the script. At one point, Keane tells Mrs. Paradine, "Unless I can put my heart into this case, I shall lose it, and you're *deliberately* keeping me in the dark." That line was cut from the script at the last minute.

Hitchcock was happier with his actresses, especially the beautiful and accomplished Italian, Alida Valli. For the long trial scene, he used four cameras running simultaneously. This speeded things

up, and saved money, which was just as well since the film in any case cost an astronomical $4,000,000, and took ninety-two days to shoot. Hitchcock's rough-cut ran close to three hours, and Selznick reduced this to 132 minutes for the film's Los Angeles opening on December 31, 1947. (It was later cut for television by twenty minutes.) *Time* noted how the film has "high polish and intelligence," but the characters "are lifeless participants in a rigid, theatrical dance."

The film *is* top-heavy, but with interesting ideas. As in *Juno and the Paycock* and *Sabotage*, the men are the real destroyers, the women the ones who see more truly. The partial exception is obviously Mrs. Paradine, yet she has had great provocation. Latour, if not actually homosexual, has still come between her and her husband. Further, her *love* for Latour is very real, and surely owes much to the fact that she has been childless. Her instruction to Keane in her cell—"You are not to destroy him—if you do, I shall hate you as I've never hated a man"—is fierce with protectiveness. But Keane, not understanding, blunders on. The perceptive Judy Flaquer (Joan Tetzel) sees that he is jealous of Latour. The novel notes Keane's cruel streak, and also attributes cruelty to the Judge, to the Colonel, and to "the best of us."

The film ends with Keane and Gay getting back together, perhaps soon to have a child of their own. Gay's last line, "Incidentally, darling, you do need a shave," uses subjective camera angles to involve us in Hitchcock's conviction that the life force can put things right again—for a time.

R O P E

First screening August 1948

Production company: Transatlantic Pictures

Duration 80 minutes

Technicolor

One afternoon, in an elegant upstairs New York apartment, a Harvard undergraduate named David Kentley is strangled to death with a piece of rope by two killers scarcely older than he is. They are playboy-type Brandon (John Dall) and his partner, an aspiring concert pianist, Phillip (Farley Granger), both influenced by the Superman ideas of Nietzsche. They put the body in a chest. Then, to crown their demonstration of "superiority," they hold a party in the same room. Those attending include some of David's family and friends and the publisher Rupert Cadell (James Stewart), who had been Brandon and Phillip's housemaster at prep school. He knows the pair well, and has influenced their thinking. He soon feels that something is amiss, especially when at the end of the party he is handed the wrong hat and in it sees the initials D. K. Returning shortly afterwards, he confronts the pair. There is a struggle. Then Rupert flings open the chest. Horrified, and saying that his teachings have been tragically misunderstood, he steps to the window and fires three shots into the air. Soon a police siren is heard approaching.

Often in Hitchcock, one film complements another. In *The Paradine Case*, the barrister Keane, self-described as "the greatest realist in the country," falls victim to a Fatal Woman. In *Rope*, Brandon and Phillip are blinded by their intellectual theory that murder is "a privilege for the few." Both films are about hubris and its consequences. In *The Paradine Case*, serpentine camera movements associated with Mrs. Paradine suggest the way she deceives Keane. In *Rope*, the famous ten-minute take gives the impression that the film is one continuous shot—which becomes a metaphor for Brandon and Phillip's entrapment and lack of perspective. A related innovation in *Rope* was its fateful use of color, denoting the change in time of day from sunset to darkness. Altogether, it is one of Hitchcock's most remarkable films.

The idea to use the ten-minute take arose when Sidney Bernstein offered to form with Hitchcock a company called Transatlantic Pictures, for which Hitch would direct films in Britain or America, and Bernstein would be co-producer and handle the firm's business side. Hitch readily agreed, and suggested for their first film an old project of his, a version of Patrick Hamilton's 1929 play loosely based on the Leopold and Loeb murder case in Chicago, *Rope*. Being set

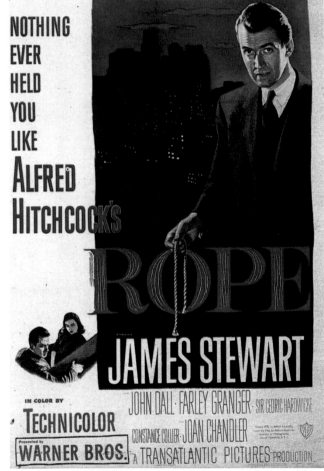

NOTHING EVER HELD YOU LIKE **ALFRED HITCHCOCK'S**

ROPE

JAMES STEWART

JOHN DALL · FARLEY GRANGER · SIR CEDRIC HARDWICKE

IN COLOR BY **TECHNICOLOR**

CONSTANCE COLLIER · JOAN CHANDLER

Presented by **WARNER BROS.** A TRANSATLANTIC PICTURES PRODUCTION

in one apartment, it could be shot quickly and inexpensively, especially if filming of each reel was continuous (i.e., without cuts). That's pretty much how it was done, though at three or four of the film's climaxes an undisguised cut is used for

dramatic emphasis. The film was shot in just eighteen days at the Warner Brothers Studios, Burbank, during May and June 1948.

Hitch worked on the adaptation with his actor friend Hume Cronyn, and the final screenplay was written by the American playwright, Arthur Laurents. The latter seems to have been chosen partly for his knowledge of the gay scene. A similar consideration influenced the casting of actors to play Brandon and Phillip, who are clearly lovers, though it's not explicitly stated. As far back as 1938, Hitchcock had written: "I like an actor to play a part for which his personal experience in life has raised him . . ." One of the qualities of *Rope*, in its play and film versions, is the study it offers not of gayness, exactly, but of how one partner dominates the other (creating a *folie à deux* situation). The screenplay is explicit here: it describes Brandon as "psychopathic" and Phillip as "neurotic . . . [someone who] wants to be and needs to be dominated."

The cost of the film eventually reached $1,500,000, a significant slice of which was James Stewart's $300,000 fee. Stewart follows the play in giving Rupert a limp, the result of a war wound. The play suggests that Rupert's war service makes him, too, a murderer, but the film doesn't go into this, perhaps

because Chaplin's *Monsieur Verdoux* (1947) had just stressed a similar irony. The screenplay merely observes that one cannot be sure whether "Rupert is essentially good or essentially evil." Rupert's former job of housemaster in a prep school seems apt: not too intellectually demanding, it would have let him use Nietzsche's ideas to show off his brilliance without having to be fastidious about how his words were understood (or misunderstood). A similar theme occurs in *To Catch a Thief*, where the Cary Grant character upbraids Grace Kelly: "To you, words are just playthings."

Also costly was the considerable preliminary testing needed to determine cloud and lighting effects, and the recording of these in Technicolor. The film has eight cloud changes during its nine reels, dropping from a sky full in reel one to one or two in reel nine. The film's finale, in which Rupert disarms the two youths and waits with them for the police to arrive, takes place while the room is flooded by red, green, and white light from a neon STORAGE sign just outside. Hitch likened this to a musical effect. He probably took it from the novel *Enter Sir John* (1929), on which *Murder!* was based, where the three colors evoke Harlequin. Its use in *Rope* may imply that the three characters are all merely players and that there's little essential difference between them—for all that Rupert tries to deny it.

Top: The cast, with Sir Cedric Hardwicke in the center. Hardwicke was later directed by Hitch in "Wet Saturday," an episode of Alfred Hitchcock Presents.
Above: Farley Granger, Hitchcock, James Stewart, and John Dall take a break from filming. Granger also appeared in the director's Strangers on a Train, before descending into lurid Italian fare like Confessions of a Sex Maniac (1972).
Right: The two murderers, Phillip (Farley Granger) and Brandon (John Dall), were based on the real-life killers Leopold and Loeb.

HIS MOST NERVE-STRETCHING THRILLER!

ALFRED HITCHCOCK'S

ROPE 'A'

starring JAMES STEWART

A Transatlantic Picture • TECHNICOLOR (R)

A Metro-Goldwyn-Mayer Release

Phillip and Brandon, with their old housemaster, Rupert Cadell (James Stewart). Stewart was making the first of four appearances for Hitchcock.

Even so, Rupert's denunciatory, "Did you think you were God, Brandon?" carries great weight. Phillip has repeatedly been heard playing the film's theme music—the gay composer Francis Poulenc's "Perpetual Movement No. 1" (1918)—on the piano, but *never right through*. Among other things, this suggests that both Phillip and Brandon are out of touch with the life force and *its* perpetual movement. In any case, if Brandon is "psychopathic," Phillip "neurotic," and Rupert "wounded"—i.e., if they're all flawed—then Rupert does, at last, seem to be speaking words to be heeded.

The film opened in New York in September 1948, and in London in November. Reviews were cautious. The *New Statesman* thought it as good a film as Hitchcock had made but that it fascinated "by an eel-like passage through actuality." Today, putting that actuality on the screen has become more acceptable, and another film on the original murder case, dwelling on its gay aspects—Tom Kalin's *Swoon* (1992)—has been widely shown.

HITCHCOCK AND FILM TECHNIQUE

"Of course, I'm a technician as well as a director," Hitchcock liked to point out, adding that before he directed his first film he had worked as scriptwriter, art director, and occasional cameraman. There's no record that he ever worked in the cutting room, but Hitchcock was famous for pre-editing his films before filming, leaving the bare minimum of spare footage. (This wasn't just for economy's sake; his "goddam jigsaw cutting," as a baffled David O. Selznick called it, meant that interfering producers, such as Selznick himself, couldn't recut the footage to their own taste.)

Given such expertise, it's not surprising that Hitchcock loved to try out new film techniques. Too much so, he sometimes admitted. "I played about with 'technique' in those early days," Hitchcock wrote in 1936, looking back on his work of the previous decade. "I tried crazy tricks with violent cuts, dissolves and wipes with everything in the room spinning round and standing on its head. . . . It never occurred to me that I was merely wasting footage with camera tricks and not getting on with the film. I have stopped all that today."

The no-nonsense Hitchcock of 1936 does his younger self a disservice. True, some of his early experiments, such as the expressionist montage sequences in *The Ring*, look more than a little self-conscious. But many of these devices work well in the service of the story. In *The Lodger*, the rapid montage that opens the film quickly and economically conveys the set-up—a serial killer on the loose in London—and the febrile atmosphere engendered by the killings. The angled, shadowy camerawork enhances the sinister mood, while the famous glass ceiling shot (as the host family gaze anxiously upwards at the sounds heard above, the ceiling seems to turn transparent, showing The Lodger in his room) not only reveals The Lodger's obsessive pacing but expresses the unhealthy fascination he holds for his hosts.

As for *Blackmail*, his first sound film, far from feeling inhibited by the new medium, Hitchcock seized the opportunity to explore subjective sound techniques well ahead of their time. The knife scene is deservedly celebrated: the heroine, who has stabbed a man to death, hears nothing of the gossipy neighbor's monologue except the recurring word *knife*, each time shriller and more intrusive, stabbing into her brain. (*Blackmail* also adopted the innovative Schüfftan process, an optical device combining foreground action with miniature sets, created for Fritz Lang's 1926 *Metropolis*, and previously used by Hitchcock in *The Ring*.) In *Murder!*, made the year after *Blackmail*, Hitchcock introduced possibly the cinema's first ever stream-of-consciousness soliloquy. Even at this early stage, he realized that sound and image need not slavishly duplicate each other; one could be used to enhance, counterpoint, or even contradict the other, and the film would be the richer for it.

Hitchcock, who had closely studied the Soviet art of montage, both through critical writings and in practice, often stated his preference for shooting "just the little bits of a scene that I really need" rather than long continuous takes. But when it served to build dramatic tension, he could use a long tracking or craning shot in masterly fashion. In *Young and Innocent* the heroine is scanning a bustling hotel lobby for the killer, whose identifying feature is a convulsively twitching eyelid. As she gazes around, the camera pulls back and up to the ceiling, passes though an invisible wall to the next-door ballroom, then swoops down

Left: Lifeboat *was shot within the confines of one set.*
Below: Dial M for Murder *saw Hitch experimenting with the recent craze in 3-D movies.*

Above: *Two impressive sets, from* Rear Window *and* Rope *(note Hitch's profile on the neon sign, far right).*

techniques. It is . . . a method of telling a story in which techniques, beauty, the virtuosity of the camera, everything must be sacrificed or compromised when it gets in the way of the story." But later in his career Hitchcock deviated from this austere principle, giving himself a series of technical challenges as if to prove his mastery. The first came in *Lifeboat*, where every shot (barring one brief underwater angle) is taken from within the bounds of the boat, as though the camera were one of the passengers. Similarly in *Rear Window* the camera, though not subjective (a technique Hitchcock disliked), observes all the action from the angle of the window where James Stewart sits immobilized, playing his voyeuristic games.

The most abstruse of Hitchcock's self-imposed technical challenges came in *Rope*, shot in a chain of unbroken ten-minute takes. (At the end of each reel the camera tracks into a dark surface and out again, camouflaging the cut.) This exercise required elaborate planning, with the camera gliding sinuously about the set on a mobile dolly while the crew silently rolled walls and furniture out of its path. From a technical angle it's fascinating to watch, but visual tedium soon sets in. Hitchcock, as he later acknowledged, had broken his own rule and put the story at the service of the technique. Though he also used long takes in his next film, *Under Capricorn*, he interspersed them with briefer shots.

Why did Hitchcock challenge himself? Perhaps out of curiosity, to see if it could be done; perhaps as a variant of the elaborate practical jokes he loved to play; or perhaps simply to stave off boredom. A skilled sketch artist, he meticulously storyboarded each film prior to production, planning every shot and camera movement in detail. Hitchcock described his films as "designed ahead of time—pre-cut," and added, "I wish I didn't have to shoot the picture. When I've gone through the script and created the piece on paper, for me the creative work is done and the rest is just a bore." Why then, someone once asked, didn't he delegate the shooting to someone else? "They might screw it up," responded Hitchcock laconically.

Philip Kemp

again through the circling dancers, past the blackface musicians to the drummer, and inexorably into a close-up of his eye—which suddenly twitches, as if faced down by the camera's accusing gaze. Hitchcock duplicated this virtuoso shot during the party scene in *Notorious*, when the camera glides smoothly down from a high gallery, through a crowded reception room, and pinpoints a crucial detail: a small key clutched in Ingrid Bergman's hand.

"I do not try to bend the plot to fit technique; I adapt technique to the plot," stated Hitchcock in 1939. "The motion picture is not an arena for a display of

UNDER CAPRICORN

First screening September 1949

Production company: Transatlantic Pictures

Duration 118 minutes

Technicolor

Australia, 1831. A new Governor (Cecil Parker) has arrived. With him is his nephew, the Honorable Charles Adare (Michael Wilding), who soon finds himself invited to dinner by Samson Flusky (Joseph Cotten), a prospering ex-convict. Flusky lives outside Sydney in a house called "Minyago Yugilla" ("Why Weepest Thou?") with his wife Lady Henrietta (Ingrid Bergman), who had been a friend of Charles's sister in Ireland. The house is aptly named: the Fluskys are childless and Henrietta is an alcoholic. The young housekeeper, Milly (Margaret Leighton), secretly loves Flusky, a fellow commoner, and maliciously encourages his wife's drinking. Charles undertakes to try and rehabilitate Henrietta, thus crossing Milly's designs. Emotions in the household flare. Flusky becomes jealous of Charles, accidentally shooting and seriously wounding him. To protect her husband, Henrietta reveals that she is guilty of the original crime for which Flusky had been transported. Milly makes a last-ditch attempt to gain Flusky for herself by trying to poison her rival, but Henrietta manages to summon help. Flusky finally understands Milly's scheming. Ironically, the now-recovered Charles, who has been so central to recent events, knows he must move on. Even Australia is "not quite big enough."

Under Capricorn is one of several Hitchcock films of the late 1940s and early 1950s that pleased few people at the time, but now seem full of interest. Scottish playwright James Bridie wrote the scenario, basing it less on the atmospheric novel by Helen Simpson (co-author of the novel that Hitchcock had filmed as *Murder!*) than on an unpublished dramatic version by Margaret Linden and John Colton. The result is a moody, stylized film where people talk endlessly while their real points stay unspoken. A key line is given to Flusky, who complains about the unfeeling legal process, which goes "on and on and on." The line is significant because beyond all the legality—and the talk—lies hope of something else, a return to a lost paradise. *Under Capricorn* may be Hitchcock's finest film to explore that theme.

Hitchcock, though, was never happy with the film, partly because of a series of events connected with its production and later its reception by the public. It was the second Transatlantic picture, this time filmed in England. Within days of Hitchcock's arrival to begin shooting at MGM's Elstree Studios, an electricians' strike halted proceedings. When shooting resumed, a general "hostile feeling" still lingered (as Ingrid Bergman told a friend). This was exacerbated by Hitchcock's use in several scenes of elaborate long takes, which tried everyone's nerves, much as *Rope*'s ten-minute takes had done.

Another blow came when Hitchcock returned to Hollywood to shoot exteriors.

Bad weather delayed filming for two weeks, by which time the Warner Brothers lot was booked for another production. Afterwards, the film was found to need considerable tightening. Urgent cables, with suggested cuts, flowed back and forth between Hitchcock and Sidney Bernstein in London. The final cost of the picture was a massive $2,500,000.

The film premiered at the Radio City Music Hall, New York, on September 8,

1949. Initial reviews were mixed. "At best, a florid, historical romance," *Time* called it; but several columnists gave plaudits to both Bergman and Michael Wilding. Then another setback occurred. The previous year, when *Under Capricorn* was being shot in England, Bergman had flown to Paris with her husband Petter Lindstrom to meet the Italian neo-realist director Roberto Rossellini. The meeting lasted two hours. There and then,

Another of Hitchcock's triangular relationships: Lady Henrietta stands between Flusky and Charles. This was Cotten's second appearance for Hitch, following Shadow of a Doubt.

Cotten succeed, against probability, in investing their stock characters with dignity and feeling. Miss Bergman, struggling not quite in vain, to translate her Swedish accent into a brogue, captures enough of the legendary glamour of the spirited Irish lady to make her humiliation genuinely touching. Mr. Cotten is authoritative enough to inspire respect as well as pity. Both are expert enough to make the passages in which each describes their early romance the most moving in the film.

However, the film soon closed, and was eventually reclaimed by the bank that had financed it. It proved to be Transatlantic's last picture. The fact that in the 1950s the critics of *Cahiers du Cinéma* voted it one of the ten greatest films ever made never changed Hitchcock's generally bad memories of it. He told Truffaut that he felt ashamed of having been literally intoxicated beforehand at the thought of the cameras and flashbulbs that would welcome him and Bergman at London airport. (Perhaps that explains a scene in the 1956 *The Man Who Knew Too Much*.) A certain general indifference to *Under Capricorn* has continued to the present day. Reportedly, not even the Hitchcock Estate now knows who, if anyone, owns the rights to the film, nor where the original negative is. If true, this is a sad state of affairs.

For *Under Capricorn* is more than a key Hitchcock film: it is one of his most lovely pictures. Its fluid design suggests life itself, sometimes wasting, sometimes

Top: The scheming Milly (Margaret Leighton, left) increases the tension in the household. Leighton and Michael Wilding married many years later.
Above: Hitchcock and Ingrid Bergman pose for a light-hearted behind the scenes publicity shot.

Bergman agreed to appear in Rossellini's next film, and joined him in Stromboli just before *Under Capricorn* was released. In fact, it was also a rendezvous of another kind. News of their affair and the scandal it caused spread quickly. Catholic organizations in America reacted by banning the Hitchcock film, and many cinema owners were sufficiently outraged to follow suit.

Hitchcock blamed Rossellini for what had happened and always remained bitter towards him. Nor was his temper improved by indifferent London reviews of the film. The assessment by *The Tatler* at least sought to be fair. After calling the film "ponderous," and professing shock at seeing "our most promising young screen leading lady, Margaret Leighton" cast as the serpent-like housekeeper, it commented:

But both Miss Bergman and Mr.

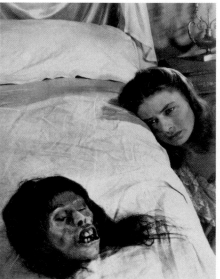

Lady Henrietta discovers a shrunken head in her bed.

being savored. Typical in this respect is the verandah scene between Charles and Lady Hattie that begins with a view of the house bathed in afternoon sunlight. Actually, the view is a painting, which proves appropriate. (The matching passage in the novel is also picturesque, describing Hattie's head "seen against red feathers of cloud" as she sits at a French window.) The scene has an audible stillness, and one almost *hears* sunset approaching. Meanwhile, the light is growing fiery. Hitchcock has caught a sub-tropical feel perfectly, doubtless reflecting his researches into light and cloud effects for *Rope*.

Everything in the scene is integral. First, its famous climax is the moment when Charles holds his jacket behind the window so as to make for Hattie what the novel calls "a mirror impromptu": irradiated by the sunset, her beauty proclaims that she may yet regain her kingdom. Charles, whose inspired gesture with the jacket bespeaks his own nobility, will later keep telling her that she's coming back.

Second, the fiery color is one of several reminders that Hell haunts this harsh land down under, this "infernal place" as the Governor calls it. Men and even animals are repeatedly described as having a bit of the devil in them. The contrast is with the Emerald Isle back home, a remembered paradise, associated most of all with Hattie. When Charles speaks of taking her boating on the bay (Sydney Harbor), or riding, as part of her rehabilitation, the phrasing recalls her beloved Galway Bay and how she used to ride

beside it. Flusky remembers that "she'd go at a fence as if it had the Kingdom of Heaven on the other side."

But Australia's very harshness has its own beauty. Some things, Flusky will tell his wife, are "all in your mind." Thirdly, then, the same fiery light that suggests the proximity of Hell is allowed, whenever it strikes Hattie's auburn hair (as in the verandah scene), to invoke a contrary condition. Several times during the film her hair is emphasized in this way, and each time we're invited to feel that Heaven may not be so distant after all. (One may think of William Blake's lines

about building "a Heaven in Hell's despair.")

Finally, the verandah scene marks Hattie's resumption of her embroidery. A note of self-help is being sounded, and a hint given of how art may activate inner healing. Then, in a brilliant transition, Charles's mirror gesture is followed by a cut to Hattie's smiling reflection the next

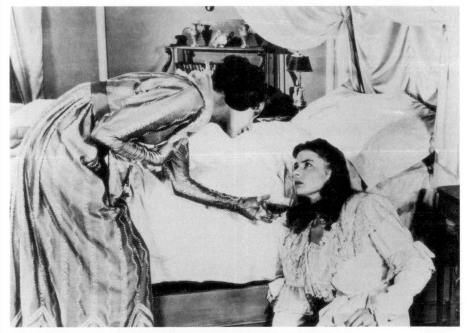

Milly and Lady Henrietta. Bergman was starring in her third and final Hitchcock movie.

Lady Henrietta, Samson, and the new Governor (Cecil Parker).

Both Helen Simpson (1897–1940), the author of the original novel, and the film's makers did their homework. Sydney-born Simpson took the *donné* of her book—a man's transportation to Australia for a crime committed by another—from one of Australia's nineteenth century classics: Marcus Clarke's *His Natural Life*. Her novel's theme of a quest for freedom found an appropriate corollary in the history of Australia under Governor Richard Bourke (1777–1855), portrayed in the film by Cecil Parker. Bourke, born of an Anglo-Irish family, originally trained as a barrister. A man of charm and humanity, he became during his six years in office perhaps the most popular Governor to that time, implementing several progressive reforms. The film's researchers gave special attention to visual matters. The design of Flusky's residence, "Minyago Yugilla," with its wide, turreted front, resembles work by ex-convict Francis Greenway (1777–1837), the most important architect in the young colony. The panoramic views of Sydney and its harbor seem based on oils by Conrad Martens (1801–78) done in the style of Claude Lorraine and Turner, painted soon after he arrived in the colony in 1835.

day in a real mirror—an image that resembles a painting. Much of the brilliance here is due to how the camera puts the audience in Hattie's position. Suitably, we hear Charles call her "the first work of art I've ever done;" then he allows himself to kiss her on the cheek.

This is the crux of the film. From this point on, Charles runs the risk of falling in love with another man's wife and losing control. His situation thus duplicates Milly's concerning Flusky, and in fact no Hitchcock film until *Psycho* may better illustrate its director's famous remark that

"everything's perverted in a different way." Implied is the existence of a basic life force (in which James Bridie believed), plus a whole set of attendant ambiguities. Charles is a nobleman and Milly is a commoner, and they end up taking opposed courses of action, but the film is lucid about the hard choices involved. Charles, luxuriating in his upper-class idleness, and Milly, prepared to work to the death for her master, both seemingly do what they are fated to do.

The final scene bears at least one similarity to *Rope*'s. Another of the film's motifs has been the recurring question, "Who gives the orders in Flusky's house?" which Charles gaily puts to the tune of "Here We Go Round the Mulberry Bush." At the end, as he prepares to sail for home, the soundtrack reprises the tune. But now it's clear that the question it asks is meant in general terms, and that none of the characters fits the bill: they are all merely players.

Cinematographer Jack Cardiff's work on *Under Capricorn* is thoroughly professional. Perhaps, though, his book *Magic Hour* (1996) misses the point when it suggests the film was "fatally inhibited" by its trundling camera and resulting loss of tempo. The film's theme of life's ebb and flow supports a case for technique drawing attention to itself in this way. There is fine work too from composer Richard Addinsell, whose evocative score suggests,

in its principal motif, the young Australian colony vigorously pressing on. Costumes were designed by Roger Furse, who also made an important contribution to the film's sense of style. An inspired touch was giving Hattie a tiara for the Governor's Ball where, for a few moments, she really does seem to have returned to her kingdom. Hitchcock had chosen his co-workers shrewdly. Laurence Olivier effectively complimented him a few years later by choosing the same triumvirate of Cardiff, Addinsell, and Furse to work on *The Prince and the Showgirl* (1957).

STAGE FRIGHT

First screening February 1950

**Production company:
Warner Brothers/First National**

Duration 110 minutes

Black and white

Eve Gill (Jane Wyman) is a student at London's Royal Academy of Dramatic Art. A friend, Jonathan Cooper (Richard Todd), a chorus dancer, asks her to shelter him from the police. It seems that his mistress, musical comedy star Charlotte Inwood (Marlene Dietrich), has killed her no-good husband, and Jonathan is suspected. Eve hides Jonathan in the home of her father, Commodore Gill (Alastair Sim), on the Essex marshes. Then, returning to London, she poses as a maid called "Doris Tinsdale" in order to gain employment with Charlotte and thus spy on her. As Eve, she meets Inspector Wilfred Smith (Michael Wilding), a Scotland Yard detective assigned to the case, who soon falls in love with her. Naturally this causes complications. At a theatrical benefit garden party, Smith finds out that Eve and Doris are the same person. Commodore Gill helps Eve explain, and suggests the next move: Doris will confront Charlotte while the police eavesdrop. Though the police agree, at the same time they bring Jonathan under arrest to the theater, where it emerges that he is the real killer. Jonathan then bolts, but is killed when the theater's safety curtain, suddenly lowered, pins him to the stage.

eality," Hitchcock told Huw Wheldon of the BBC, "is something that none of us can stand, at any time." *Stage Fright* explores that idea very cleverly, and again reminds us that we're all merely players. By means of its controversial lying flashback, the film makes us experience that what we took for reality is actually a falsehood. Because of the film's theatrical setting, Hitchcock saw fit to tease his audience even more than usual. Consequently, *Stage Fright* is amusing and insightful, but not really thrilling.

When a safety curtain rises at the start, it bears an image of Minerva, helmeted goddess of the arts, and that image resembles Marlene Dietrich. The glamorous,

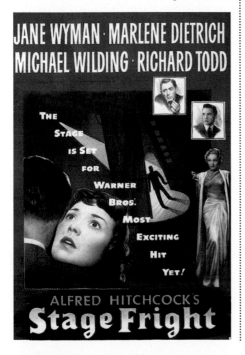

Above: *The cameras are trained on Jane Wyman and Richard Todd. Wyman was recently divorced from actor Ronald Reagan when she accepted a role in* Stage Fright.
Right: *Hitch with his daughter, Patricia.*

legendary Dietrich proved exactly the woman-of-the-theater the script required. Hitchcock invited her to contribute to the screenplay. She suggested her opening lines—"Johnnie, you do love me, don't you? Say that you love me!"—and the idea that the audience should hear her voice a fraction of a second before seeing her face. The note of melodrama was perfect. *Stage Fright*, like *Murder!*, is a film where life and theater constantly overlap.

The screenplay was written by

Left: "Marlene was a professional star," remarked Hitch. "She was also a professional cameraman, art director, editor, costume designer, hairdresser, makeup woman, composer, producer, and director."
Right: Jonathan Cooper (Richard Todd) and Charlotte Inwood (Marlene Dietrich).
Below: Jonathan Cooper.

playwrights James Bridie and Whitfield Cook, based on the 1948 novel *Outrun the Constable* (British title: *Man Running*) by Selwyn Jepson. The novel makes Charlotte Inwood a famous actress, always playing a part. Her current real-life role is that of a bereaved widow. But the film's scene where Charlotte tries on mourning clothes, and complains in her prima-donnaish way that they lack color, isn't from the novel: Hitchcock probably took it from Agatha Christie's *Lord Edgware Dies* (1933). A further complication is that Jepson based parts of the novel on the famous Thompson-Bywaters murder case of the 1920s. Charlotte, for example, appears to owe something to Mrs. Thompson, whose appearance and demeanor in the dock resembled that of a theatrical star.

Charlotte's nemesis is Eve, a drama student. In the novel, Eve is just a helper on her father's farm; but Hitchcock's

daughter, Patricia, was at the time a student at the Royal Academy of Dramatic Art, which may explain the change. (Pat appears briefly in the film as "Chubby.") The screenplay describes Eve as someone "apt to view everything in an overly dramatic light" but who learns "that adventure in the mind or behind the footlights is much easier than in actuality!" Recognizing the part's challenging aspects, Hitchcock cast thirty-five-year-old Jane Wyman, a recent Oscar-winner for her portrayal of a deaf-mute rape victim in Jean Negulesco's *Johnny Belinda* (1948).

Both Jonathan and Detective-Inspector Smith are described by the screenplay as boyish. But there the resemblance ends. Michael Wilding brings to the role of Smith all the lightweight charm he'd recently shown in a series of popular Mayfair comedies with Anna Neagle. Richard Todd as Jonathan also performs credibly, but his character is a psychopath. There's a note of self pity when Jonathan says in the novel, "I had a difficult war . . . rather more mental as well as physical strain . . . than some chaps had to take." The screenplay adds: "His handsome face seems immature . . . and a trifle weak."

Reviewers couldn't see the point of *Stage Fright*, calling it "second-rate" or "rambling." *Time* thought its main virtue was the performances. No one noticed how ingeniously Hitchcock had pursued his theatrical metaphor. The previously mentioned scene where Charlotte tries on mourning clothes (which are just one more costume) is typical. When Eve introduces herself as Doris Tinsdale, she receives the reprimand, "Not so loud, dear," as if she were back at the Academy, rehearsing. But Charlotte quickly finds

her a part, telling her to be ready to introduce the doctor when Charlotte gives her a cue by coughing. During this scene, Charlotte keeps forgetting her new maid's name, despite some prompting from Eve. And when, as bidden, Eve then goes into the next room to await the doctor, the ensuing action is photographed as if from the wings of a theater. There, Eve does seem for a moment to be suffering from stage fright—she doesn't want Smith to spot her—but eventually she manages to speak the lines she's been given.

Nor did anyone notice Hitchcock's other main metaphor, which was about the life force in post-War England. The film opens with a shot of St. Paul's Cathedral standing defiantly amidst a wasteland of rubble caused by the Blitz. Later, the film's most remarkable scene contains another reference to the War: the theatrical-benefit garden party is being held to raise money for war orphans. All the main characters turn up to help, with one significant exception—Jonathan. In addition, Hitchcock peoples the scene with a rich collection of English types, such as the cheery Joyce Grenfell and even the weak little man from the jury in *Murder!* Crucial to the scene's concept is the rain, which makes everyone bear up. (In 1987, Jane Wyman claimed that the filmmakers merely took advantage of some passing showers on the day of shooting, but an inspection of the screenplay shows that the rain was always scripted for the scene.)

In sum, *Stage Fright* tells us that life and theater overlap, but are decidedly not the same thing. The goddess-like Charlotte is finally revealed to be just one more vulnerable person like the rest of us. In a similar vein of showing it like it is (or was), even the film's slow pace has its point, inasmuch as it reflects the hesitancies of postwar England.

The turbulence in Hitchcock's professional and personal life during the forties gave way to prosperity in the fifties. With his return to the States and the box-office success of *Strangers on a Train*, Hitch began a fourteen-year winning streak. Just listing the extraordinary films of the period is enough to make one pause for thought: *Strangers on a Train, I Confess, Dial M for Murder, Rear Window, To Catch a Thief, The Trouble With Harry, The Man Who Knew Too Much, The Wrong Man, Vertigo, North by Northwest, Psycho, The Birds, Marnie*.

Of these thirteen films, eight are unquestionably considered American classics. There are three Hitchcock "experiments" in the crowd, but even these were hardly the box-office poison that earlier experiments had been. Nevertheless, Hitch ran for cover after each cinematic lab test. After the lackluster reception to *I Confess*, he made the fine *Dial M for Murder*; after the confused reaction to *The Trouble With Harry*, he returned with the wild commercial success of *The Man Who Knew Too Much*; and after the bemused response to *Vertigo*, he gave us *North by Northwest*.

To set the record straight, none of these films lost money for their studios. All turned a profit, the majority of them a considerable profit. The wisdom of the

Directing To Catch a Thief.

contracts written for Hitchcock under the shrewd negotiation of Lew Wasserman, his agent and the head of MCA talent agency, made Hitch one of the wealthiest directors in Hollywood, although the real financial fruit of these years only fully ripened towards the end of the sixties.

After the disastrous Transatlantic Pictures venture, things could only improve for Hitchcock. However, there must have been days during the production of *Strangers on a Train* that left him wondering. Hitch arranged for the rights to Patricia Highsmith's 1950 novel to be

bought for a miserly $2,000. Her agent thought it was probably the best offer she would receive, so Highsmith reluctantly accepted. With the rights secured and his own brief treatment completed, Hitch was still having problems finding a scriptwriter. Half a dozen turned him down before Raymond Chandler, the famed American novelist, accepted the challenge.

The relationship between the two men began promisingly, although their working styles were always at odds. Chandler preferred to write alone and with little

interference (except for a healthy amount of alcohol). He liked Hitch's personality, but considered his ideas and story conferences intrusive, and their relationship disintegrated, with Chandler making references to Hitchcock's weight in public. This was an unforgivable sin in Hitch's world.

Chandler's script was eventually sweetened by Ben Hecht's assistant, Czenzi Ormonde. The film's production also introduced Hitch to American cinematographer Robert Burks. Burks remained with the director for the next fifteen years, being instrumental in defining Hitchcock films' visual landscape. The two worked so comfortably together, and with such trust, that by the end of the decade Hitchcock had stopped viewing the rushes and dailies. Burks was also a master at filming scenes with process (or composite) shots, an expertise that was

stretched to its limits on their first film together. His ability was such that most of the process work is invisible.

Burks was just one member of a team of talented collaborators which Hitchcock began to build up around himself during the fifties. At its height during the Paramount years, the team would eventually include editor George Tomasini, assistant director (and later associate producer) Herbert Coleman, art director Henry Bumstead, costume designer Edith Head, title designer Saul Bass, personal assistant Peggy Robertson, and, perhaps most memorably, composer Bernard Herrmann.

After *Strangers on a Train*, Hitchcock finally filmed the troubled *I Confess*. He was never able to fully conquer the inevitable challenges of transferring the original play to the screen, not least in deciding on the ending. In the script's earliest drafts, written during the late forties, the priest is executed for a murder he did not commit, which would have been an impossible resolution for any studio. The film received a lukewarm reception, which must have made the seemingly sure-fire material already selected for his next film, the popular Frederick Knott play *Dial M for Murder*, appear even more appealing.

In 1953, Hitch wrote a series of

remarkable letters to his friend and now former business partner, Sidney Bernstein. They came at a unique time in Hollywood's history and were written on the eve of Hitchcock's portentous move to Paramount. In April, he admitted that *Dial M for Murder* would be his last picture for Warner Brothers, as it fulfilled his contract: "In any case, *Dial M* would be my last official picture for Warners, so I could make my own terms for the extra picture I'm giving them [this turned out to be *The Wrong Man* in 1956]. The Warner lot is the deadest that anyone can remember. They have just paid off Michael Curtiz [the prolific director of, among many other films, *Casablanca* (1942)] after twenty-six years, in addition to many actors. I think they have about six or seven contract players left."

Lew Wasserman was negotiating with Paramount, who were reluctant to sign Hitchcock to a long-term contract and ambivalent about *Rear Window* progressing without a major star attached. Wasserman was both Hitch's and James Stewart's agent, and had convinced Stewart to strike out on his own in the early fifties, negotiating one of the first back end deals (where the performer is not paid a salary but a percentage of the profits following the movie's release). However, Stewart was reluctant to work with Hitchcock again after his experience on *Rope*. He insisted on script approval, and only committed himself after Hitch

Above: *Hitchcock prepares Grace Kelly for a scene in* Rear Window.
Left: *Birthday celebrations with Cary Grant and Grace Kelly during the production of* To Catch a Thief.
Below: *Hitch caught by the camera during the making of* Strangers on a Train.

Above: Alfred Hitchcock Presents.
Below: The marketing of Hitchcock began in earnest in the fifties. Two examples of the board game Why.

had secured the services of Grace Kelly, the young actress who had lit up *Dial M for Murder.*

Wasserman had begun representing Hitchcock in 1946. His loyalty to Hitch and his shrewd negotiating skills increasingly served the director well. Wasserman was responsible for his timely contract with Warner Brothers and in 1953 began dealings with Paramount. Before *Rear Window* entered production, Hitchcock signed an extraordinary contract with the studio, giving him complete creative control. It was also agreed that ownership of the films his production company made would be returned to Hitchcock after eight years. In 1955, Hitchcock formally took up American citizenship (a move Alma had made a decade before). That same year, Wasserman talked him into creating a television show, in which the director himself would appear. Hitch was at first reluctant, but Wasserman persisted until he finally agreed. For this venture, he formed his own company, Shamley Productions, Inc., asked Joan Harrison (later joined by Norman Lloyd) to produce the series, and hired James Allardice to write his introductions and concluding remarks. Premiering on October 2, 1955, *Alfred Hitchcock Presents* was a huge hit and ran for the next ten years.

The Paramount years were surely Hitchcock's finest; *Rear Window, Vertigo,* and *Psycho* are among cinema's greatest films. The lesser Paramount movies hardly qualify as hack work: *The Trouble With Harry, To Catch a Thief,* and *The Man Who Knew Too Much* are all excel-

lent pictures and performed well at the box office. Hitchcock's television show, *Alfred Hitchcock Presents* (later *The Alfred Hitchcock Hour*), the wildly successful Hitchcock–branded short story anthologies, and the *Alfred Hitchcock Mystery Magazine* created a synergy for his films that previously had simply not existed. However, Hitch would soon find that the heightened profile this activity brought him resulted in a strictly defined public preconception of what he and his work represented: he was just a whimsical entertainer, the "Master of Suspense." It was a creative box that would be nearly impossible to escape.

At home, Hitch seemed the most content in his life. He was at his trimmest weight, and his films and investments brought continual success. Clouds did begin to form in 1957, when Hitchcock was in and out of the hospital during the first four months of the year for gall bladder and hernia surgeries. The following year, Alma was diagnosed with cancer, and although this was successfully treated, these were obvious signs of mortality for

the pair as they approached their sixties.

After completing *North by Northwest* for MGM in 1959, Hitch began *Psycho,* his last production for Paramount. Although the film was nothing less than a cultural event, Hitchcock now found himself without a studio. Several came courting, but he seemed destined to choose the one that his former agent and best friend Lew Wasserman now ran, MCA/Universal. Before his next film, *The Birds,* was completed, Hitch signed an exclusive contract with the studio that would see him through the remainder of his career.

For *The Birds,* Alma and Hitch had discovered the director's new contract player (his first had been Vera Miles in 1955) in a television commercial. "Tippi" Hedren—Hitchcock insisted on the quotation marks—was carefully trained and styled by the director for her role in the movie. Yet, despite all this effort, it is interesting to note that the actress was not Hitch's first choice for his next film, *Marnie.* He had dreamed of using Winston Graham's novel as Grace Kelly's comeback film, but when the citizens of

Above: *Doris Day and Hitch discuss the script for* The Man Who Knew Too Much.
Right: *Hitchcock, James Stewart, and Doris Day entertain the Prime Minister of Burma during filming of* The Man Who Knew Too Much.
Below: *Cary Grant starred in two of Hitchcock's biggest hits in the 1950s.*

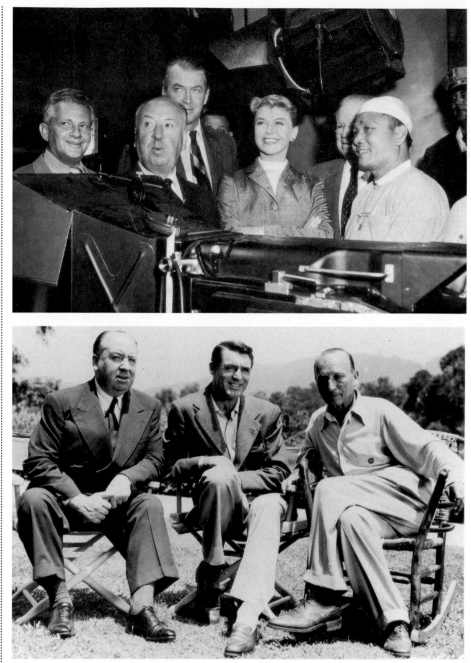

Monaco objected, he rethought the project as a challenge for Hedren.

Creatively, Hitchcock was now moving into difficult territory. He told the French director, François Truffaut, that he experienced a revelation during the filming of his avian nightmare. Unhappy with the way a scene was working, Hitchcock tore up the day's plans and improvised. To his surprise, he found the improvisation exciting; it actually turned out better than his original conception. What he did not articulate to Truffaut was that this improvisation was for him the light at the end of a long tunnel, a way out of the box that both his own marketing and his popular television series had put him in.

Truffaut had first met Hitchcock in France during the production of *To Catch a Thief* in 1955. In 1962, he proposed a series of taped interviews with Hitch, setting out to examine his entire career. These finally saw publication in 1966 (and were translated into English in 1967) as *Hitchcock/Truffaut*, which became the cornerstone of the growing Hitchcock scholarship, one that dared to take the director seriously. The French had been the first to take note in the mid-fifties, with Claude Chabrol and Eric Rohmer publishing their analysis of Hitchcock's first forty-four films in 1957. It would be over two decades before their book received an American publication, and then only after Truffaut's text had proved

that such a book could be popular.

Hitch was very much taken by this interest. After all, he had courted film critics shamelessly for years. However, while the French caught on to him as an auteur, the Americans and British still only saw in Hitchcock the aforementioned whimsical entertainer.

Meanwhile, *Marnie*'s production turned sour when the relationship between Hitch and Hedren disintegrated. Hedren maintains that during filming Hitchcock made untoward advances to her. The result was that, one afternoon on the set, the actress reproached him, com-

mitting the same unpardonable sin as Chandler had years earlier: she referred to his weight. Hitch walked off the soundstage and, despite returning the next day, he never really cared much for the film afterwards.

Marnie was a broken romantic cry from the director. It was poorly received at the time and has only lately gained some ground with film critics. It would also be Hitchcock's last romantic thriller. Only darkness and confusion lay ahead.

Dan Auiler

STRANGERS ON A TRAIN

First screening June 1951

Production company:
Warner Brothers/ First National

Duration 100 minutes

Black and white

Professional tennis player Guy Haines (Farley Granger) wants to divorce the tramp-ish Miriam (Laura Elliot) so that he can marry a senator's daughter, Anne Morton (Ruth Roman). On a train from Washington, D.C., Guy encounters Bruno Anthony (Robert Walker), a rich young eccentric. Bruno suggests they "swap murders": he'll kill Miriam if Guy will kill Bruno's hated father. Guy merely laughs, and alights. But Miriam again refuses to divorce him, and is later found strangled at a fair. Guy is unable to give the police a firm alibi for the time of the murder, and soon comes under pressure from Bruno, the real killer, to complete their so-called bargain. When Bruno invades a party at the senator's home and creates a scene, Guy confides to Anne what he knows. Both feel powerless. For his part, Bruno feels stalled, and decides to incriminate Guy by planting the tennis player's lighter at the scene of the crime. Guessing his intention, Guy hastens to win an important match, then confronts Bruno at the fairground. During a fight with Guy, Bruno is crushed to death in an accident with a merry-go-round. The police find evidence that shows Guy's innocence.

N ow back in Hollywood and faced with the fact that none of his past four pictures had been a hit with the public, Hitchcock read a novel by a new writer, Patricia Highsmith. The novel opens with a train journey, during which promising architect Guy Haines meets the alcoholic Charles Anthony Bruno and listens with a mixture of horror and fascination to Bruno's proposal that they exchange murders. Later there's a passage describing the two men: "Each was what the other had not chosen to be, the cast-off self, what he thought he hated but in reality loved." Recognizing the story's cinematic possibilities, akin to those of his fondly remembered *Shadow of a Doubt*, Hitchcock bought the film rights for a

The strangers on a train: Guy Haines (Farley Granger) and Bruno Anthony (Robert Walker).

WARNER BROS. PICTURES present
FARLEY · RUTH · ROBERT
GRANGER · ROMAN · WALKER
in ALFRED HITCHCOCK'S
" STRANGERS ON A TRAIN " (A)
with
LEO G. CARROLL
RELEASED BY WARNER-PATHE DISTRIBUTORS LIMITED

mere $2,000. Before long, he seemed a new person, even informing colleagues that his previous work didn't matter.

A treatment for *Strangers on a Train*, of some sixty-five pages, was written by Hitchcock and Whitfield Cook, and completed by June 1950. After a lengthy search for a writer who felt comfortable turning the material into a screenplay, the job went to distinguished author Raymond Chandler. He and Hitch didn't get on well, but, working from home, Chandler took only a few weeks to com-

plete a first draft. This ended with Bruno arrested for the murder of Miriam, committed to an asylum, and left writhing in a strait-jacket. Though *Psycho* a decade later would end in similar manner, it wasn't what Hitchcock now wanted. He called for changes. Then, just as he had in the case of *Shadow of a Doubt*, he began shooting footage even without a completed script or finalized casting details. He headed for Forest Hills to photograph the Davis Cup matches between America and Australia, intending to merge long shots

Top left: *Hitch's cameo, as Guy gets off the train at Metcalf.*

Top right: *Bruno threatens the happiness of Anne Morton (Ruth Roman) and Guy. Bruno provided Robert Walker with the best role of his career, unfortunately only a year before his death.*

Left: *Patricia Hitchcock checks up on the script.*

Above: *Bruno meets Anne's father, Senator Morton (Leo G. Carroll).*

and crowd scenes with closer shots of his actors, to be photographed later.

One of the first actors to be cast was Patricia Hitchcock. She'd appeared briefly in *Stage Fright* and now landed the plum part of Anne Morton's cheery sister, Babs. The character is outspoken and adventurous, but at the party has a moment of real terror when her resemblance to the mur-

dered Miriam stirs something inside Bruno. In effect, her character undergoes a growing-up experience like Eve's in *Stage Fright*. It's significant that, right after this encounter, she removes her glasses in an act of introspection as she tells Anne what had happened. Anne is played by Ruth Roman, who was Warner Brothers' rather staid leading lady at the

time. Hitchcock wasn't happy with the casting of either Roman or Farley Granger (instead of Granger he'd have preferred a stronger type like William Holden), but he took them in order to obtain Robert Walker from MGM. The sensitive-looking Walker had proved the perfect partner for Judy Garland in Vincente Minnelli's *The Clock* (1945), in which he played the shy soldier on leave in New York City. Walker's personal life deteriorated after his divorce from Jennifer Jones, but as Bruno in Hitchcock's film he showed real acting skill. He died the following year, at age thirty-three.

In the end, the screenplay was completed not by Chandler but by Czenzi Ormonde (standing in for her boss Ben Hecht, who was unavailable). In late October, Hitch took a final script with him on location, filming at Pennsylvania Station in New York City, at a railway station in Danbury, Connecticut, and in various parts of Washington, D.C. Danbury was chosen to represent the mythic Metcalf, no doubt because it had an annual fair—though the fairground scenes for the film were shot later in

Left: *Guy gets to grips with Miriam (Laura Elliot).*
Above: *Bruno demonstrates his strangling technique. Note Miriam's resemblance to Babs (Patricia Hitchcock, seen in the background of this picture).*

California. Thereby hangs a tale. As noted, Chandler's first draft screenplay ended in an asylum, but Hitchcock thought this too tame. Spotting a couple of passing references in the novel to a merry-go-round, the director suddenly saw what the film's finale must be. He was familiar with novels by English comedy-thriller writer Edmund Crispin whose real name was Robert Bruce Montgomery (1921–1978). Crispin's novels often had more than a touch of Hitchcockian bravura about them, and Hitch had already repaid the compliment by taking the safety curtain climax of *Stage Fright* straight from Crispin's *The Case of the*

Gilded Fly (1943). Now he instructed Warner Brothers to obtain Crispin's permission to use the runaway merry-go-round climax of the author's most famous novel, *The Moving Toyshop* (1946).

In fact, just as in *Foreign Correspondent* (another of Hitch's running-for-cover films), many of the celebrated moments in *Strangers on a Train* turn out to have been borrowed. The film's most famous gag is the shot of Bruno's lone stationary head in a tennis crowd where everyone else is intently following a rally. This is Hitch's variant on the gag in the British film *Quartet* (1948), based on four W. Somerset Maugham stories, in which Basil Radford and James Robertson Justice keep up an earnest conversation in a tennis crowd while swivelling their heads with the other spectators. Again, everyone admires the moment that signifies Guy's becoming complicit with Bruno's guilt, when he joins Bruno behind

a barred gate. The moment was taken in its entirety by Hitchcock from Robert Siodmak's *The File on Thelma Jordan* (1949).

What all this mainly reflects is the truth of Hitch's remark that he was always more interested in telling a story by means of pure film than in what the film contained. Walter Pater in the nineteenth century said that "all art tends to the condition of music," and there's a sense in which Hitchcock composed his films for their shape, rhythms, and counterpoint rather than for their content. Nonetheless, he knew that the latter is vital, and so he took care to give the films memorable touches. He could be absolutely systematic and cold-blooded about this. Donald Spoto describes how, during the last days of scripting, the director dictated to Czenzi Ormonde and associate Barbara Keon a long list of doubles images he wanted the film to contain. His

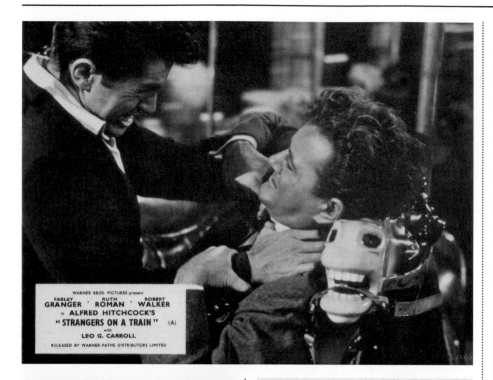

Hitchcock film, and together may be compared to the life force that Bruno in a wild moment speaks of harnessing. Hitchcock knew what he was doing when he included that line of Bruno's. In *Rope*, the perverted Brandon regrets his lack of creativity, and turns to murder instead, saying that "the power to kill can be as satisfying as the power to create." And in the novel of *Strangers on a Train*, Bruno, on his way to murder Miriam, is said to have seldom "felt more alive" (which puts him, in his eyes, on a par with the architect Guy). Hitchcock, a *true* creator, further knew that his film's very design, starting with the rail lines motif, was richly evocative: he remarked dryly to Truffaut that "[o]ne could study it forever."

THE TWO VERSIONS OF *STRANGERS ON A TRAIN*

The standard, American version of *Strangers on a Train* was slightly re-cut by Hitchcock after the film had a sneak preview in Los Angeles. Recently, a different print of the film was found in the Warner Brothers vaults. Because it was intended for British release, this print has been called for convenience the British version; it runs two minutes longer than the standard version. The opening scene on the train is extended, and the film's ending has been changed. On the train, Bruno coaxes Guy to have lunch with him in his compartment, ordering for himself lamb chops, french fries, and chocolate ice cream. Later, when the pair are alone, an obviously drunken Bruno expresses his view that murder is "not against the law of nature" and theorizes that "everybody is a potential murderer." Missing from the British version, however, is the delicious ending where Guy and Anne avoid the newest stranger on a train, a kindly minister who recognizes the tennis star. Instead, we conclude with a phone conversation between the couple that implies Guy is ready to quit tennis and get married.

Top: *The climactic fight between Guy and Bruno on the merry-go-round. Hitchcock told Truffaut, "... my hands still sweat when I think of that scene ..."*
Above: *Guy breaks into Bruno's house to confront him. Hitch had originally wanted to sign William Holden for the role.*

cameo, for example, would show him carrying an image of his own portly form—a double bass—and be carefully placed to fill an otherwise empty moment in the story.

By Christmas, principal photography was complete: Robert Burks's atmospheric images ensured him a regular place on the Hitchcock team thereafter. When *Strangers on a Train* opened in June 1951, it proved a huge success with audiences and most critics. The latter generally thought it "great fun," though Manny

Farber writing in *Nation* qualified this by adding, "... if you check your intelligence at the box office." He suggested that Hitchcock "has gone farther on fewer brains than any director since Griffith," which was an ironic comment in the circumstances, since Hitch had recently cited Griffith's *Way Down East* (1920) as his favorite chase film.

Is *Strangers on a Train* so brainless? Only, surely, if one discounts its highly professional blend of entertainment and energy (no empty moments!). Both those things are basic to practically any

I CONFESS

First screening February 1953

Production company: Warner Brothers/First National

Duration 95 minutes

Black and white

Found stealing, Otto Keller (O. E. Hasse), a church sexton in Quebec, one night murders a lawyer, Vilette. Wearing a priest's cassock, Keller hastens back to the rectory where he and his wife, Alma (Dolly Haas), have rooms. He enters via the adjacent church, and is seen by Father Michael Logan (Montgomery Clift), to whom he proceeds to make a formal confession. As it happens, Logan knows of Vilette, who had been attempting to blackmail Madame Ruth Grandfort (Anne Baxter) over a long-ago incident with Logan before he was ordained. When Police Inspector Larrue (Karl Malden) questions Logan, the priest can give no alibi for the time of the murder; nor, being bound by the rules of the confessional, can he disclose Keller's guilt. Subsequently, Logan himself goes on trial, where he arouses the jury's unwarranted suspicion about his conduct with the married Ruth. Though acquitted, he faces a hostile crowd. This proves too much for the watching Alma, who publicly accuses Keller. The latter shoots his wife, then flees into the nearby Château Frontenac hotel. Before dying from police bullets, Keller asks Logan's forgiveness.

Quebec City, site of several military battles, is located at the confluence of two rivers. As *I Confess* begins, the camera moves towards the city's silhouette dominated by the massive Château Frontenac, which resembles a castle in a fairy tale. Women's voices sing, siren-like. The same musical passage will later accompany Ruth Grandfort's description of her early love affair with Michael Logan. All of youth's ideals, and sense of what life offers, are implicit in the film's respective uses of that passage. But at the end the camera retreats back across the river, the city again wreathed in darkness. Though a city of churches, it has proved not to be the City of God.

Hitchcock discusses the script with Montgomery Clift. Hitch initially sounded out Samson Raphaelson, writer of Suspicion, *but he turned the job down.*

I Confess is another engrossing film on the lost paradise theme.

It is based on a 1902 play by Paul Anthelme, *Nos deux consciences* ("Our Two Consciences"), which Hitchcock discovered in the early 1930s. The play is a typical melodrama; stories about clerics or would-be clerics tempted by love were commonplace at the turn of the century. So, too, were stories about silent suffering, like that of "Madame X" in Alexandre Bisson's 1909 play, filmed many times. Anthelme's play combines both these motifs while cleverly employing the idea of a murderer's confession to a priest that so intrigued the Catholic Hitchcock. When Montgomery Clift

agreed to appear in the film version, early in 1951, the script had the priest being hanged at the end, then proven innocent. But Hitchcock bowed to pressure from ecclesiastical authorities, and the present ending was substituted during shooting, to its director's deep regret.

Clift's man-in-crisis performance is one of his finest. Fellow actor Karl Malden paid him tribute: "His ability to project mood and a held-back strength is quite extraordinary." The character's integrity is further suggested by his constant forward movement (and Dimitri Tiomkin's emphatic score), the antithesis of the non-movement of Mrs. Danvers in *Rebecca*. Anne Baxter was cast at the last

Top right: *Ruth Grandfort (Anne Baxter) and Father Michael Logan (Montgomery Clift). Clift spent a week living in a monastery, memorizing the Latin Mass and wearing priest's robes, for his part in the picture.*
Above: *Hitchcock directs Baxter and Clift in the flashback scene.*
Below: *Baxter and Clift pose for a misleading publicity still. Clift's method acting and drinking strained relations with Hitchcock.*

minute as Ruth Grandfort. Hitchcock had first hired Swedish actress Anita Bjork, following a recommendation by Sidney Bernstein, but Warner Brothers rejected her when she arrived in America pregnant and with an unmarried lover in tow. Baxter's playing in a demanding role is quietly effective. Madame Grandfort exists in a loveless marriage to the politi-cian Pierre (Roger Dann)—loveless on her side, at any rate, because she can't cease loving the no longer available Logan. She is selfish in the sense that all romantic love is selfish. Until the end of the film, when Logan is exonerated of murder, she secret-ly hopes that he is guilty because that would confirm her deepest fantasy that her love is reciprocated. As soon as Logan is cleared, she turns to her husband and says, "Take me home, Pierre." The char-acter resembles Yvonne, the fiancée of the dedicated young Resistance fighter named Pierre, in *Aventure Malgache*.

Hitchcock's reasons for locating the film in Quebec were complex, but basical-ly French Canada was as close as he could get to the play's original setting. Quebec in 1952 had an Old World quality, and was noted for its architecture of medieval flavor; also, the city was the only one in North America where priests still wore the cassock, a garment that suggests its wearer combines male and female quali-ties. With its sloping, narrow streets, and flights of steps and stairs, Quebec City prefigures the San Francisco of *Vertigo*. A memorable scene shows a radiant Ruth coming down a spiral staircase to greet her lover, Logan, outside her home. Here the staircase echoes the one in Elia Kazan's *A Streetcar Named Desire* (1951). Kazan's film is set in another French-American city, New Orleans, and Hitchcock astutely made a connection. Logan later descends a curving staircase of a different kind, in the courthouse, to face an angry mob who believe him a murderer. In fact, steps and stairs are everywhere in *I Confess*, like a secular version of the Stations of the Cross.

The film got mixed reviews, although it was generally well received in the Catholic Church. But it failed at the box office. John Russell Taylor, writing in 1978, thought it represented "another example of Hitch being ahead of his time," and he was surely right (despite the film's basis in turn-of-the-century melo-drama). *I Confess* is in various ways time-less. Its subject matter includes murder, blackmail, and human suffering. References to the Second World War, and earlier wars, are more potent here than in *Rope*, and make Keller's murder of Vilette seem part of a much larger scheme of things. Likewise, Vilette's piece of intend-ed blackmail finds its ironic equivalent at an official level: in court, the Crown Prosecutor (Brian Aherne) doesn't hesi-tate to force his friend's wife, Ruth, to answer painful questions about her mar-riage by threatening to quote from her signed testimony, which is of an even more intimate nature. And indications of human mortality are everywhere: the jury foreman combing his hair to hide his bald patch; a crippled girl passing in a street; black smoke drifting over the city; fre-quent references to eating and digestion. The film's open-ended pessimism (see *The Pleasure Garden*) accords with how philosophers tell us that the world's *Will*—a life force that is also a death force—has always worked like this. The film's medieval look is apt.

DIAL M FOR MURDER

First screening April 1954

**Production company:
Warner Brothers/First National**

Duration 105 minutes

Warnercolor/3-D

Tony Wendice (Ray Milland), who has played tennis at Wimbledon, lives with his wealthy wife Margot (Grace Kelly) in a small but well-appointed London flat. She has always financially supported his tennis career, now abandoned, but a year ago he felt foreboding when she began a friendship with an American mystery writer, Mark Halliday (Robert Cummings). To secure Margot's money for himself, Tony plans her murder. He has spotted at Victoria Station a rather shady acquaintance from his Cambridge days, C. A. Swann (Anthony Dawson), and on investigation finds him ripe for blackmail. Over drinks one evening, Tony outlines to Swann (currently calling himself Captain Lesgate) a murder plan for the following night: Swann will strangle Margot in the flat while Tony and Mark attend a stag party at a club. During the attack, Margot breaks free of Swann and kills him with a pair of scissors. Tony then cunningly tries to make the killing look like a murder by Margot. Police Inspector Hubbard (John Williams) is deceived, but eventually realizes the truth. He tricks Tony into showing his guilt and arrests him for what, on paper, had looked like the perfect crime.

Hitchcock's film makes few obvious changes to Frederick Knott's absorbing stage thriller. The director had profoundly understood the play's subject matter, and it shows. When Wendice speaks of suddenly realizing how much he had grown dependent on his wife, the remark could have come from, say, *Mr. and Mrs. Smith*. In its depiction of a marriage, *Dial M for Murder* is penetrating. If Wendice has become reliant on his wife, the reverse is also true. Margot has been subtly intimidated and bullied without ever quite realizing what has been happening. The film is finally about her liberation. Fittingly, when Grace Kelly returned in Hitchcock's next film, *Rear*

Tony Wendice (Ray Milland). Milland had appeared in a radio version of Strangers on a Train *in 1951.*

Window, she was never lovelier.

Hitchcock and Sidney Bernstein spent long evenings discussing Knott's play, which critic Stanley Richards has called "one of the theater's most adroit and ingenious tales of blackmail, murder, and sleuthing." Knott was an ex-Army major who trained as a screenwriter after World War II. He probably saw at this time the stage thriller *Dear Murderer* by St. John Legh Clowes, or its 1947 film version starring Eric Portman. In 1946, he would have read in the newspapers of the arrest and execution of ex-RAF officer Neville Heath for killing two women. The murderer in the Clowes play seems the predecessor of Wendice in *Dial M for Murder*,

while the latter's C. A. Swann is evidently loosely based on the real-life Heath. None of this detracts from the skill of Knott's play, which took eighteen months to complete. Its first public performance was on BBC television, on March 23, 1952, when it received rave reviews. Similar acclaim followed its opening in the West End in June, where it ran for 425 performances, and in New York in October, where it achieved a 552-performance run. Meanwhile, the film rights had been bought by Sir Alexander Korda for £1,000. When Hitchcock asked Warner Brothers to obtain the rights, they had to pay Korda exactly thirty times that amount.

WARNER BROS. PICTURES PRESENT
ALFRED HITCHCOCK'S
"DIAL M FOR MURDER" (A)
starring
RAY MILLAND GRACE KELLY
ROBERT CUMMINGS
RELEASED BY WARNER-PATHE DISTRIBUTORS LTD.

Above left: Mark Halliday (Robert Cummings), Tony, and his wife Margot (Grace Kelly). Hitch stuck closely to the original play: "I've seen so many stage plays go wrong through opening up," he claimed, "the tightness and tautness of the stage play is lost."
Above right: Swann (Anthony Dawson) tries to strangle Margot. Hitch considered Kelly "mousy" in High Noon, *but felt she "blossomed out for me splendidly."*
Left: Robert Cummings obviously enjoying working with Hitch. Cummings had previously starred in Saboteur.

By mid-1953, Hitchcock had a screenplay written by Knott himself, and had completed casting. To play Wendice he chose Welsh-born Ray Milland, now a Hollywood veteran. It's been said of Milland's characters that their ready smile was always insecure and even a little suspect, which certainly fits Wendice. For all his suavity, a part of him has never grown up: his manipulation of Margot resembles a spoiled child's of its mother. *Dial M for Murder* was the first of three films Grace Kelly made for Hitchcock. With her Catholic background and a sense of humor that kept her from being easily shocked, she had a temperament to match Hitchcock's. She became the perfect Hitchcock heroine, the embodiment of what he later called "sexual elegance." Though relatively subdued here, her

beauty is always expressive. After the killing, Margot leans over the desk, exhausted and trembling. Her bare back—she is wearing only a flimsy nightgown—makes her seem all the more vulnerable, especially as the raincoated Swann lies nearby with scissors embedded in *his* back.

Shooting of the film, in 3-D, took place largely on one set between July 30 and September 25, 1953. Even during filming, the actors knew that the picture was unlikely to be released in 3-D, as the process had rapidly lost its gimmick value with audiences. But Hitchcock was happy to experiment, especially early in the picture where his artful angles create striking effects. The latter are fairly moody and broad, for example when a foreground lamp separates Wendice and Swann as they converse on a sofa, subtly hinting at Wendice's designs on his listener. Later, the effects are more specific: for example, when Hubbard holds out to us the all-important key that's been hidden under the stair carpet. The same sort of narrowing-down is reflected in the film's use of color, which is warm and bright at

first, then becomes increasingly utilitarian and somber—though a glimpse of spring sunlight near the end when Margot enters through the garden window is invigorating.

As it happened, some cinemas did show the film in 3-D. In a generally positive review, *Time* wrote of how 3-D "brings alive the theater's intimacy and depth of involvement." However, the reviewer felt that new star Grace Kelly was wasted. Hitchcock's own punning verdict on the film was: "I could have phoned that one in." His direction, in fact, shows just how much he had learned over the years. For example, Wendice is another ruthless blackmailer, like Tracy in *Blackmail*, and the film makes him as audacious in his own polished way as his predecessor. Furthermore, as in Tracy's scenes, Hitchcock creates an intense crucible situation by effectively confining the action to one room. But there is now a greater sense by the director of what is at stake. When Wendice burns Swann's scarf—the failed murder weapon—as part of his hastily-improvised plan to incriminate his wife, Hitchcock shows us the flames on Wendice's face, a hint of diabolism. That much, one feels, the director of *Blackmail* could have achieved. But the cut-in of Margot slumped on her bed in the adjacent room—staring ahead, still shocked after what has happened—shows a much vaster sense of the nature of evil, and its consequences, that only Hitchcock's American films have.

The American films also display a profounder sense of the nature of cinema in all its aspects—as *Rear Window* would now demonstrate.

THE ICY BLONDES

Left: Hitch and Madeleine Carroll on the set of Secret Agent.
Below: Grace Kelly. Hitch professed a preference for "the ladylike blonde with the touch of elegance, whose sex must be discovered."
Bottom: Hitch and Kelly.

Hitchcock's ideal woman, at least in his films, was willowy, blonde, and cool. What intrigued him was the hint of uninhibited passion behind the cool façade; in his own words, "the drawing-room type, the real ladies, who become whores once they're in the bedroom . . . Sex should not be advertised. An English girl, looking like a schoolteacher, is apt to get into a cab with you and, to your surprise, she'll probably pull a man's pants open."

This revealing quote points to a recurrent (and some would say misogynistic) pattern in Hitchcock's treatment of his heroines. Time and again in the director's films one of these cool, *soignée* blonde women is reduced to a dishevelled, panic-stricken mess, or reveals unexpected depths of sexual ardor. This could be seen as the psycho-sexual equivalent of Hitchcock's love of showing us danger and terror lurking beneath the surface of seemingly everyday events and places, such as a children's party (*Young and Innocent*), an art auction (*North by Northwest*), a quiet London street (*The Man Who Knew Too Much*), or a sleepy small town (*Shadow of a Doubt*).

Like Hitchcock himself, the serial killer in *The Lodger* seems to have it in

for blondes: All the women he targets are fair-haired, and we see nervous blondes donning wigs or pulling down hats before braving the foggy streets, while their brunette colleagues laugh smugly. But the

Above left: *Hitch directs "Tippi" Hedren in* Marnie.
Above right: *Eva Marie Saint and Cary Grant pose for a publicity shot for* North by Northwest.
Left: *Kim Novak, female lead in* Vertigo, *had been groomed by Columbia boss Harry Cohn to replace Rita Hayworth.*

first of Hitchcock's ice maidens to be thoroughly disarrayed was Madeleine Carroll, who spent much of *The 39 Steps* handcuffed to Robert Donat, so that every time she moved her arm his hand stroked her thigh. Not only in the film, either. On the first day of rehearsal, when Donat and Carroll had only just met, Hitchcock handcuffed them together and then pretended for several hours to have lost the key.

Hitchcock's mischievous, semi-sadistic treatment of blondes hit its stride in Hollywood, perhaps provoked by the flawless glamour of its screen goddesses. Joan Fontaine, tormented by the sinister Judith Anderson in *Rebecca*, fears her husband is poisoning her in *Suspicion*. Her fears turn out to be illusory (though Hitchcock, if he'd been allowed, would have had it otherwise), but Ingrid Bergman really is being poisoned in *Notorious*, and again in *Under Capricorn*.

Bergman was the first of Hitchcock's actresses with whom he became obsessed, maintaining that she returned his passion. He became similarly fixated on Grace Kelly and "Tippi" Hedren. Kelly was put through it less than her counterparts, though in *Dial M for Murder* she was nearly strangled and then tried for murder; but more often she served to illustrate Hitchcock's taxi thesis (as outlined previously), revealing hidden fires behind her reserved, classic beauty. In *To Catch a Thief*, she makes bold physical advances toward Cary Grant, while in *Rear Window* she teases the immobilized James Stewart with a filmy negligé, purring about a "preview of coming attractions." In *North by Northwest* the alluring but lethal Eva Marie Saint, with her penchant for sex on trains, is equally ambivalent.

This view of the cool blonde as sexually schizoid is made explicit in *Vertigo* where Kim Novak, having seemingly died as the elegant, fair-haired Madeleine Elster, is resurrected as Judy Barton, a brunette dressed and made up to look as tarty as possible. But such overt carnality is rejected by James Stewart. Judy must dye her hair, change her clothes, and become Madeleine again before he'll make love to her. (The analogy with the

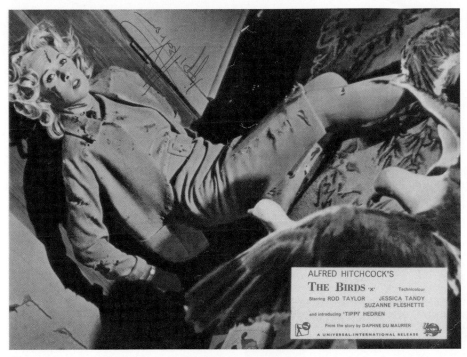

Above: *A bruised and bloodied Hedren in* The Birds.

director, avidly molding his female stars to fit his template, is inescapable.) To Hitchcock, only when a woman's sexuality is concealed is it truly erotic.

In the case of some actresses, it seems that the concealment was *too* thorough; Hitchcock could do little with the wholesomeness of Doris Day (in the remake of *The Man Who Knew Too Much*) or Julie Andrews (in *Torn Curtain*). Conversely, revealing all too early is dangerous: Janet Leigh, first seen in *Psycho* half-dressed on a bed with her lover, suffers a terrible fate for her lack of modesty.

The most problematic and extreme instance of Hitchcock's attitude toward his cool blondes was his treatment of "Tippi" Hedren. "I had always heard that his idea was to take a woman—usually a blonde—and break her apart, to see her shyness and reserve broken down," Hedren later recalled. "I thought this was only in the plots of his films." But the ordeal Hitchcock put her through in filming *The Birds* (where she was pecked and gouged by very real, panicky birds tied to her with threads) was matched by his obsessive personal pursuit of her offscreen. Hedren's rejection of his advances strained their relationship during the shooting of *Marnie*, where her icy blonde image is specifically linked with sexual frigidity.

Hitchcock liked to quote the nineteenth-century French playwright Victorien Sardou's advice, "Torture the women!"—adding provocatively, "The trouble today is we don't torture women enough." Hitchcock, at least, did his best to make up for the omission.

Philip Kemp

REAR WINDOW

First screening July 1954

Production company:
Paramount/Patron, Inc.

Duration 112 minutes

Technicolor

During a heat wave, normally itinerant news photographer L. B. Jefferies (James Stewart) finds himself confined by a broken leg to a wheelchair in his Greenwich Village apartment. Each day, and often into the night, he has little to do but gaze out of his rear window at the activities of his neighbors in the surrounding apartments. Jeff's main visitors are his fiancée Lisa Fremont (Grace Kelly), a high-fashion model, and Stella (Thelma Ritter), a wiry insurance company nurse. When Jeff says he suspects that his neighbor directly opposite, costume jewelery salesman Lars Thorwald (Raymond Burr), has murdered his wife, no one pays much attention at first. Lisa is mainly interested in overcoming Jeff's reluctance to get married. But Jeff intensifies his window-gazing, using binoculars and even a telephoto lens. After Lisa volunteers to cross the courtyard and obtain evidence against Thorwald, trouble erupts. Thorwald catches her in his apartment. Jeff frantically calls the police, who come and arrest Lisa. Meanwhile, having learned that Jeff has been spying on him, Thorwald decides to pay a visit. Only last-minute intervention by Jeff's detective friend Tom Doyle (Wendell Corey) saves him from the enraged killer.

Above: *Hitch is seated in front of the impressive* Rear Window *set.*
Right: *A rare signed still of James Stewart as news photographer L. B. Jefferies.* Rear Window *was Stewart's second film for Hitchcock.*

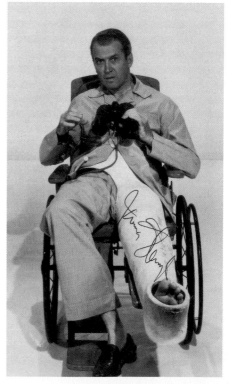

Rear Window takes place during a New York heat wave. More than a plot device explaining why everyone has their windows open, the heat intensifies a crisis for which it also serves as a metaphor. Photographer Jeff not only suddenly finds himself immobilized by a broken leg, but his beautiful fiancée Lisa wants to "immobilize" him in another way, by making him give up his top job with *Life* magazine and settle down with her. Thus the film, like *Notorious*, depicts a personality conflict between two people who love each other. The heat wave func-

tions like the sultry Rio climate in the earlier film, adding both realism and tone. *Rear Window* has tone aplenty, as well as classic suspense. Hitchcock noted modestly that his batteries were well charged when he was making it.

A key figure behind the film was Hitchcock's agent at MCA, Lew Wasserman. In the spring of 1953, Wasserman bought—at Hitchcock's request—a screen treatment of Cornell Woolrich's 1942 short story "Rear Window" (originally called "It Had To Be Murder"). The treatment was by leading

stage director Joshua Logan. Shortly afterwards, Wasserman arranged a deal with Paramount Pictures for Hitchcock to make a total of nine films. (He only made six of those.) The first of these was *Rear Window*, and Hitchcock had a screenwriter already lined up. A regular listener to radio shows like *Suspense*, the director had asked MCA if they knew of John Michael Hayes. Not only had Hayes adapted many of the *Suspense* shows, he had recently started writing film scripts, including one for the James Stewart picture *Thunder Bay* (1953). A delighted

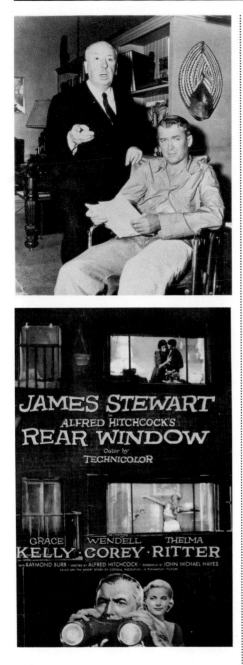

Above left: *Hitch and Stewart pose for the camera. The film was nominated for five Oscars, including one for Best Director.*
Above right: *Stella (Thelma Ritter), Lisa (Grace Kelly), and Jeff.*

MCA replied that Hayes was another of their clients.

Hitchcock and Hayes met together twice at Warner Brothers during production of *Dial M for Murder*. Woolrich's original story, Hitchcock noted, contained many good ideas, such as the moment when hero Hal Jeffries sends the suspected wife-killer Thorwald a note asking "What have you done with her?" and studies Thorwald's reaction through a spyglass. However, the story had no love interest. Logan's treatment overcame that basic problem by giving Jeffries an actress girlfriend named Trink, but Hitchcock wanted a part for Grace Kelly that would bring out the fire in her. He asked Hayes to write a new treatment. After spending a week with Kelly on the set of *Dial M for Murder*, and noting her sly humor and sexiness that hadn't been apparent in her previous pictures, Hayes obliged. It was on the basis of Hayes's treatment that James Stewart agreed to star in the picture.

When the present author interviewed Hayes in 1975, we spoke about what Hayes thought he had given Hitchcock. He singled out the quality of warmth. He had always felt that a film like *The Paradine Case* was too cold. For *Rear Window* he invented the down-to-earth character Stella, and as early as possible had her speak several comic lines. A related idea was to break down the unconscious hostility that members of an audience invariably feel toward both each other and the film. Stella's opening remark from the doorway, ticking off Jeff for being a Peeping Tom, rivets our attention. Moments later, she recalls the time she'd predicted the stock market crash of '29: "When General Motors has to go to the bathroom ten times a day, the whole country's ready to let go." That's the sort of line that makes an audience laugh out loud and prepare to enjoy themselves, Hayes said.

Hayes also noted that the part of Lisa was written as a combination of Grace Kelly and his own wife, who was a high-fashion photographer's model. Also drawn from the Hayes's own experience was the suggestive business with Lisa's Mark Cross overnight case that spills open revealing its fluffy and very feminine contents. Recently, Donald Spoto claimed that Lisa and Jeff's relationship was based by the filmmakers on the affair between Ingrid Bergman and photographer Robert Capa in 1946, but reportedly Hayes has never confirmed this.

The script of *Rear Window* does have real warmth. What's also clear is that Hitchcock responded in kind. Running through the film is a marvelous sensuousness, starting with the two initial pans around the courtyard, each coming to rest on Jeff's perspiring face as he sleeps beside his open window. The film was shot entirely on one gigantic set, the construction of which was supervised by Hitchcock personally. It comprised thirty-one apartments, a Manhattan skyline, gardens, trees, smoking chimneys, and an alley leading to a street complete with a bar, pedestrians, and moving traffic. The entire area was required to be lit for both day and night settings, and to be capable of withstanding a heavy rainstorm

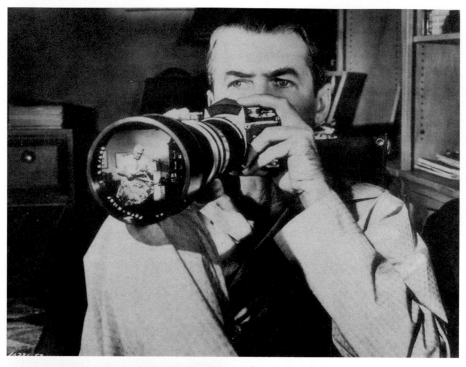

Above: Lars Thorwald (Raymond Burr) is caught in Jeff's lens.
Left: Rear Window *was a great hit, earning $5,300,000 in America alone, making it the fifth highest earner of 1954.*

(provided by special "rain birds" installed above the set). The rain scene is another sensuous highlight. When the rain comes in the early hours of the morning, it has a summery quality. It's heavy enough to drive the couple sleeping on their fire escape back indoors in an undignified scramble, yet gentle enough not to dissuade Thorwald from his several mysterious trips to and from his apartment, carrying a suitcase.

Principal photography was completed by January 1954, having taken approximately eight weeks. The overall budget scarcely exceeded $1,000,000. Following its world premiere at New York's Rivoli Theater on August 4, 1954, the film and its performances were hailed by critics and public alike. *Time* thought it "[p]ossibly the second most entertaining picture (after *The 39 Steps*) ever made by . . . Hitchcock." By May 1956, it had grossed $10,000,000.

Rear Window draws on subject matter related to the crime-thriller format with which Hitchcock would have felt fully at home. Three important literary influences would all have been on his shelves: E. T. A. Hoffmann's classic 1815 tale "The Sandman" (Hitchcock owned several editions of Hoffmann), H. G. Wells's 1894 short story "Through a Window" (Hitchcock owned a set of Wells's complete works), and Aldous Huxley's famous 1922 short story loosely based on the then-current Armstrong murder case, "The Gioconda Smile." The relevance of Hoffmann's tale may be seen from even a partial synopsis. The student Nathanael becomes fixated on a house opposite his own occupied by Professor Spallanzani and his beautiful "daughter" called

Olympia. Watching the house through binoculars, the student quite loses interest in his regular girlfriend, Klara. One day, he goes to the house and at last encounters Olympia—who turns out to be just a life-size doll.

This is of course the basis of the ballet *Coppelia* (1870). The tale is also the main subject of Freud's famous essay, "The Uncanny," in which he alludes to Spallanzani as a potentially castrating father-figure. As for Olympia, Freud writes: "She can be nothing else than a materialization of Nathanael's feminine attitude towards his father in infancy." Freud adds that Nathanael's "enslavement" to Olympia shows a purely narcissistic kind of love. In short, Nathanael has Oedipal problems—all of which recur, with variations, in *Rear Window*. For example, Jeff confined to his wheelchair feels himself infantilized and rendered impotent because of his broken leg, and is forced into a state of passive observation. (Hitchcock here implies a parallel with the cinema spectator, whose relative narcissism has been remarked on by critics Robert Stam and Roberta Pearson.) Over the way, he sees a quarrelling couple whose relationship reflects some of his own current feelings towards Lisa. And when the wife disappears, Jeff sends his note asking "What have you done with her?", whose wording represents the classic question of a child who observes the primal scene (the parents' love-making). Finally, Jeff confronts the father-figure himself, Thorwald, and engages with him in a life-death struggle.

Wells's *Through a Window* begins: "After his legs were set, they carried Bayley into the study and put him on a couch before the open window." The story patently influenced Woolrich's *Rear Window*, and ends in similar fashion with an outsider invading the apartment to attack the hero. In Bayley's case, he defends himself by throwing his medicine bottles at his assailant. The logic here recalls the film's, in which Jeff, a photographer, defends himself with flash bulbs which he fires at Thorwald. However, the film's symbolism is richer, for the assault on a person's eyes constitutes a further reference to castration (see *Spellbound*).

Castration is also implicit in Huxley's *The Gioconda Smile*, but this time it's castration by a woman. The story is about a man suspected of murdering his nagging wife, and about his mistress, whom he

James Stewart and Grace Kelly. Leading costume designer Edith Head claimed Kelly was "my personal favorite . . . [she] exhibited a rare combination of beauty, intelligence, and class that set her apart from other actresses of the period."

finally jilts. The latter becomes a Fatal Woman, much like the figure evoked in Walter Pater's celebrated essay on the *Mona Lisa*. Camille Paglia calls such a figure "the castrating and castrated moth-er," which Lisa fits neatly (at a certain level) in *Rear Window*. For example, the nagging Mrs. Thorwald, who even looks like Lisa, is certainly a castrating woman; and we're invited to draw parallels. (Hitchcock's own comment on Lisa, to Peter Bogdanovich, was that New York has many such active women, "more like men, some of them.") Equally, once Mrs. Thorwald disappears, Jeff's interest is piqued all the more: has her husband really killed her? That is, has she been castrated in her turn?

A turning point in Jeff's attitude toward Lisa comes when she makes him an offer he can't refuse: "I'll trade you—my feminine intuition for a bed for the night." (Here the soundtrack plays the hit song, "Mona Lisa.") Until now, feminine intuition has been faintly ridiculed, as when Stella claims that she'd predicted the crash of '29. Indeed, femininity itself has been mocked by would-be macho Jeff, feigning interest in what Slim Hayward wore at a cocktail party. But now the film takes both femininity and motherliness on board with a vengeance. When Lisa encounters danger by crossing the courtyard and entering Thorwald's apartment, Jeff finally becomes anxious for her. In Hitchcock's words, "the moth-er instinct comes out in him." And when Jeff himself is injured at the end, Lisa rushes to *cradle* his head in her lap. Her simple floral dress, one which isn't high-fashion, signals her own emerging femininity (see Constance in *Spellbound*), and Hitchcock lets the image fill the screen almost like a field of flowers.

Sure enough, we learn in a coda that Jeff has broken his other leg (i.e., he's now doubly castrated!). This is in line with Paglia's remark apropos Pater's "Mona Lisa" that the Great Mother—rather than anything done by men—ultimately prevails. (*To Catch a Thief* ends with a grim mother-in-law joke to similar effect.) But the film itself exists to perhaps contest that point, and in any case leaves just about any viewer more than satisfied.

REAR WINDOW ON NEIGHBORLINESS

Things like intuition and creativity—in effect, heightened life—can give us direct experience of freedom. This idea of the philosopher Henri Bergson (1859-1941) helps illuminate several Hitchcock films, including *Rear Window*. In the film's coda, as we listen to the song "Lisa," freedom seems almost palpable for a moment, though the song's lyrics hint that it may be just a dream. Significantly, the moment coincides with the meeting of Miss Lonely Hearts (Judith Evelyn) and The Composer (Ross Bagdasarian), the first time we've seen any such neighborly interaction. Earlier, for just two or three shots, the film had attempted to raise our consciousness in another way. The episode of the strangled dog provokes the dog's distraught owner to cry out to the other apartment dwellers, "You don't know the meaning of the word 'neighbor.'" Here, the camera momentarily frees itself from Jeff's apartment to show a wide view of the entire courtyard. Then, with separate close-ups, we get to meet Miss Torso (Georgine Darcy) and Miss Lonely Hearts—who suddenly are no longer just figures in Jeff's (and our) fantasies. Instead, they appear to be perfectly normal, even rather plain, *individuals*.

TO CATCH A THIEF

First screening July 1955

Production company: Paramount

Duration 97 minutes

Technicolor/VistaVision

American John Robie (Cary Grant), a retired cat burglar, has never married and now raises flowers and grapes on the French Riviera. He and other former prison inmates such as Bertani (Charles Vanel) had served in the Resistance, earning themselves paroles — but a recent outbreak of jewel robberies makes the police suspect Robie of breaking his. Seeking advice, he visits Bertani at his restaurant in Monte Carlo. Everyone there suspects him, but when the police arrive, they help him escape. A waiter's daughter, Danielle Foussard (Brigitte Auber), takes him by motor boat to Cannes. Bertani then arranges a meeting with Lloyds of London insurance agent H. H. Hughson (John Williams), who shows Robie a list of possible robbery candidates. Hughson hopes Robie will catch the real thief. Heading Hughson's list is Mrs. Jessie Stevens (Jessie Royce Landis), an American oil millionairess staying in Cannes with her daughter Francie (Grace Kelly). The Stevenses and Robie meet. Francie is initially reserved, but soon offers to become Robie's helper. Their deepening relationship climaxes one night during a spectacular fireworks display. Later, at a gala ball, Robie traps the jewel thief on a rooftop. It's Danielle, working for Bertani.

To *Catch a Thief* announces its subject matter at the start, where a sign says, "If you love life, you'll love France." But its hero is a paradox. A former thief, Robie now lives in a travel brochure heaven. When asked by Hughson what he did with the proceeds of his crimes, he cheerfully says that he "kept everything myself." Just as cheerfully, he admits that he killed seventy-two people during the War. To defend his present lifestyle, he resorts to casuistry, arguing that whenever Hughson cheats on his expense account, or takes an ashtray from a hotel, he's a thief too. But Robie is never censured by the film. Indeed, it implies that in a world subject to chance, where Mrs. Stevens can become a millionairess overnight while Robie's former comrades still "work like idiots for a loaf of bread" (as Danielle says), his attitude may even be commendable and life-enhancing. Three films later, *The Wrong Man* will put a more somber slant on these matters.

But after the rigors of *Rear Window*, Hitch felt like a diversion. Sidney Bernstein had bought for him the rights to a comedy-thriller novel by ex-accountant David Dodge, and the prospect of making it on location appealed. Dodge based *To Catch a Thief* on actual events involving a young cat burglar named Dario Sambucco. In turn, the housekeeper, Germaine, is a portrait of Dodge's own housekeeper, a good French peasant who disliked *flicks* on principle. (Reportedly, the real Germaine enjoyed the film so much that she saw it twenty-seven times!) The fact that the story's title is the same as one of the famous "Raffles" stories by

Hitchcock directs Cary Grant and Grace Kelly. Kelly was making her third and final film for Hitch. In 1956 she retired from the screen, becoming Princess of Monaco upon marrying Prince Rainier.

E. W. Hornung, to which it bears plot resemblances, may be just a coincidence.

Presumably it was also a coincidence that Cary Grant, like Robie, had engaged in dangerous wartime exploits against Germany. In their book on Grant, Charles Higham and Roy Moseley quote Grant's assistant, Ray Austin: "Cary went into Europe [probably Switzerland] under Nazi domination, and he could have been put away for it. He said . . . that he was rather like Raffles in the old book and movie about the safe cracker. He had to learn to crack safes, to get information."

Certainly, with both his stage background and his war service, Grant made the perfect Robie, who had been a trapeze artist before turning to burglary. To tempt Grant out of semi-retirement, Hitchcock simply told him the name of his co-star. Cary found Grace to be a fascinating person—beautiful, sensitive, and very professional. They became lifelong friends.

The French weather initially posed problems. Filming was due to start on May 1, 1954, in Cannes. But it rained for ten days, and the opening scene—a Mardi Gras parade—had to be changed. That

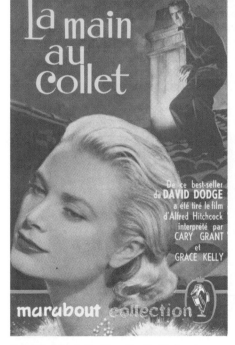

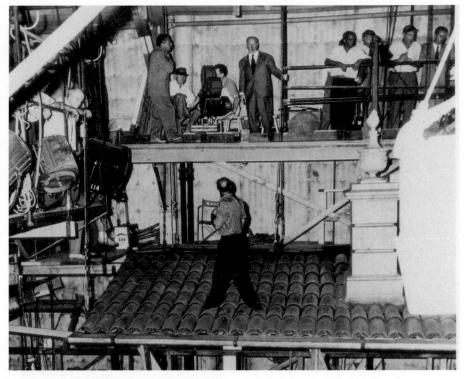

Top left: John Robie (Cary Grant) with Francie (Grace Kelly) at the fancy-dress ball. "I think I am prouder of the clothes in that film than those in any other picture on which I have worked," recalled costume designer Edith Head.
Top right: Hitch preparing to shoot on the rooftop set.
Above: The French tie-in edition of David Dodge's novel.

scene would have picked up on the reference to life in the title sequence, and signalled the film's theme of masquerade (check out the theme of fakery in *Family Plot*). Meanwhile, Hitch and Alma regularly dined out in the superb French restaurants, or enjoyed themselves at the local casinos. Filming eventually wrapped in September.

Everyone remembers and talks about the film's fireworks scene (even if its symbolism was anticipated by the 1948 Basil Dearden costume drama *Saraband for Dead Lovers*!). Less commented on is the scene that follows. Robie has returned to his room when suddenly Francie appears in the doorway with an anguished demand that he "give them back to me—Mother's jewels!" This incident, with *its* symbolism, echoes one in Wilkie Collins's famous mystery story about a jewel, *The Moonstone* (1868). Hitchcock, who would call Collins "quite brilliant," had lately had occasion to encounter that author's work when Patricia Hitchcock performed in a radio adaptation of *The Moonstone* on November 16, 1953. (Note that after Francie gets over the loss of her mother's jewels, she starts to grow up—though, rather ominously, she's still talking about Mother as the film ends!)

To Catch a Thief was much liked by audiences, though reviewers were lukewarm. *Variety*, for some reason, called it "pretentious." Hitchcock said that "[i]t wasn't meant to be taken seriously," but he didn't mean that the film lacked his usual attention to detail. For example, Robert Burks's VistaVision cinematography fully deserved the Academy Award it won; yet the aerial shots of the Côte d'Azur, whose villas cling intrepidly to ancient hills, do more than please the eye and create a certain visceral excitement. So do further shots featuring the region's architecture, some of it centuries old. What the philosopher Schopenhauer has called "temporal justice versus eternal justice" is felt—rather than stated—as a theme of *To Catch a Thief*, as it will be in *The Wrong Man* and *Vertigo*.

There's even a Kafkaesque edge. Robie has been given a parole, not a pardon—which effectively makes him an Everyman figure (we're all on parole), or, in Kafka's terms, still awaiting "definite acquittal." The film is insistent that a day of personal reckoning will come. Robie tells Hughson that one day he'll be sorry he took an ashtray from a hotel. At the film's climax, the police chief Lepic (René Blancard) sees Robie on the roof and remarks, "He's where I always knew he'd be some day." Of course, Lepic represents mere temporal justice. But the rooftop scene, with its eerie green limbo (shot with a filter), manages to imply that another tribunal may also be involved.

THE TROUBLE WITH HARRY

First screening October 1955

Production company: Paramount/Alfred Hitchcock Productions

Duration 99 minutes

Technicolor/VistaVision

One autumn day in Vermont, young Arnie (Jerry Mathers) plays in the woods. Suddenly three shots boom out and soon a man's voice cries, "Okay, I know how to handle your type." Then there's a thud. In a clearing, Arnie finds Harry Worp's body. It now appears that any of three local people might have killed Harry. One is his unlamenting widow, Arnie's mother Jennifer Rogers (Shirley MacLaine), while the others are the elderly Captain Wiles (Edmund Gwenn) and the middle-aged spinster Ivy Gravely (Mildred Natwick). For complicated reasons, they all conspire with artist Sam Marlowe (John Forsythe) to conceal Harry's death, though more than once Harry is first buried and then dug up again. The conspirators manage to arouse the suspicions of Deputy Sheriff Calvin Wiggs (Royal Dano), who lives next door to his widowed mother (Mildred Dunnock), the proprietress of the local general store. But after an eventful few hours, matters are resolved. Old Dr. Greenbow (Dwight Marfield) pronounces that Harry had, after all, died of natural causes, which frees Jennifer to marry Sam, and Ivy to wed the Captain.

The *Trouble With Harry* has great depth and charm. If Robie in *To Catch a Thief* was necessarily—given his past—a touch cynical, the characters in *The Trouble With Harry* are all without attitude, just pleasant and human. They're opportunists, of course, from the youngest upwards. (Arnie exchanges a dead rabbit for a live frog, then takes the rabbit back and trades it elsewhere for two blueberry muffins.) But this is Hitchcock's valid view of how people are. He balances it with some wise insights about the transforming power of love. Based closely on a much-translated book, *The Trouble With Harry* should delight any viewer who sees how well its comedy blends style and substance. As bonuses, it offers the film debut of Shirley MacLaine, a mellifluous and variegated score by Bernard Herrmann, and glorious autumn vistas photographed by Robert Burks.

As with *To Catch a Thief*, the biggest problem during filming proved to be the weather. The production was based at Vermont's ski capital, Stowe, where background plates were shot and a couple of scenes of Arnie running through the woods were filmed. According to scriptwriter John Michael Hayes (a native of nearby Worcester, Massachusetts), it was an absolutely spectacular fall. Then a storm hit, bringing with it the heaviest rain in eighty years. Afterwards, there wasn't a leaf left on the trees. Scouting around, the film makers found one small town that was in a hollow, and which still had some of its leaves. This became the village in the film where the Wiggs Emporium and Calvin's garage are situat-

Sam Marlowe (John Forsythe), Ivy Gravely (Mildred Natwick), Captain Wiles (Edmund Gwenn), and Jennifer Rogers (Shirley MacLaine). Forsythe later appeared in Topaz, as well as the Hitch-directed episode of The Alfred Hitchcock Hour.

ed. For some scenes, Hitchcock had leaves brought in by truck and tied to the trees. Other scenes had to be filmed back in Hollywood. All of the sequences of Harry's burying and unburying were shot there, using plastic trees with artificial leaves.

Nor was the weather friendly to Edmund Gwenn's arthritis. The seventy-nine-year-old actor, appearing in his fourth Hitchcock film, experienced considerable pain during shooting, and several scenes had to be edited to hide the fact. Another veteran in the cast (albeit

Gwenn's junior by more than thirty years) was Mildred Natwick, who had made several films for John Ford. Her comic skills are well showcased in *Harry*. But best of all was Shirley MacLaine. Critic Ken Wlaschin later wrote: "She was kookie before that word came into vogue, impish, off-beat, disconnected, and beautiful in her own way." The fourth of the film's conspirators was played by John Forsythe, who had both film and Broadway experience. Hitchcock later directed him for television and in *Topaz*.

Only a few reviewers at the time

Above left: The cast, with young Arnie (Jerry Mathers, center) and a very dead Harry. Mathers later became famous through the long-running television series Leave it to Beaver.
Above right: Robert Burks's splendid autumnal photography is seen here to good effect. "I wanted to take a nasty taste away by making the setting beautiful," Hitch explained.
Right: The French tie-in novel.

appreciated *Harry*, which also flopped at the box office (except in Paris, where it ran for six months). Yet critic Ed Sikov wrote in 1994: "*The Trouble With Harry* is a far richer, more complicated film than even Hitchcock's most ardent defenders have so far been willing to acknowledge." What has always told against it is its Englishness. The novel's author, Jack Trevor Story, who later wrote a series of rather scabrous novels featuring "Alfred Argyle," was suitably eccentric. For a while, he lived with a poodle in the Hertfordshire woods, where the novel of *Harry* is set. The novel's Sam Marlowe may be something of a self-portrait by the author. Sam first comes into view singing the song "Jerusalem": "And did those feet in ancient time/Walk upon England's mountains green…" These lines of artist-poet William Blake both establish a pastoral mood and imply an allegory about Christ. On the whole, though, the allegory is played down in favor of the mood.

The mood is itself English. A typically splendid passage beginning "The after-noon grew older and warmer . . ." might have come from a John Buchan novel like *John Macnab* (1925). In turn, for several decades English fiction had developed a tradition of just such idyllic passages, as shown recently in a study by Jackie Wullschlager, *Inventing Wonderland* (1995). To sum up: *The Trouble With Harry* represents a sort of throwback to a Lewis Carroll world—and therefore for many people is an acquired taste. Needless to add, not everyone acquires it.

Carroll's children's books are at the same time sophisticated works for delighted adult readers; and in making *Harry*, Hitchcock clearly had a similar effect in mind. The film's title sequence consists of sketches by Saul Steinberg done in the *faux naïf* style of Hitchcock's favorite painter, Paul Klee. In succession, we see birds, trees, a house and a body. The sketches are child-like, but the sequence's sting-in-the-tail (see Hitch's television shows) is something else. We're not being invited to laugh at death, exactly, because Harry isn't the film's villain, only its MacGuffin. Nonetheless, we *are* being put on alert.

Alerted, we may see that the film's villain is in fact Calvin Wiggs, with his puritanical outlook. His mother is very astute in describing the nature of Calvin's work. Referring to his interest in restoring antique cars, she calls them "mechanical antiques;" and she says that his other job as Deputy Sheriff involves "piece-work." In short, there's something non-organic and isolated about Calvin. The contrast is with the film's conspirators whose *combined* energies are marshalled by the artist Sam. As he cuts Ivy's hair, in a charming scene inside the Wiggs Emporium, Sam foresees that "the true Miss Gravely" will be "timeless with love and understanding." All of *Harry*'s "Bergsonian" thrust is in that remark. Ed Sikov rightly saw Sam as facilitating "the ongoing life force."

ALFRED HITCHCOCK PRESENTS

Hitchcock's television productions, which aired from 1955 to 1965, spanned one of the most creative periods of his career and resulted in hundreds of small screen films, still shown today throughout the world. Although Hitchcock only directed twenty television episodes, this handful of little "situation tragedies," as he called them, comprise a significant part of his authorship and show such a range of narrative techniques that we must not neglect them.

Hitchcock's television work comprises three series and a single hour-long show. The half-hour *Alfred Hitchcock Presents* was broadcast on a weekly basis from 1955 to 1962, helping establish Hitchcock as an international personality. In 1957, concurrent with this series, the short-lived but interesting *Suspicion* was launched. Ten well-made one-hour shows were produced by Hitchcock, of which he directed the premiere episode. In 1962, *Alfred Hitchcock Presents* was expanded to an hour and, retitled *The Alfred*

Hitchcock Hour, ran for another three years.

The wildly imaginative commentaries written by James Allardice for host Alfred Hitchcock were particularly important, both to the series's success and in establishing Hitchcock's public image. The

director's only guideline for Allardice was to have him view *The Trouble With Harry* and prepare something containing a similar kind of humor.

The structure of the *Alfred Hitchcock Presents* shows was as follows: Hitchcock's introduction or "lead-in," a commercial, the show with one commercial break, and Hitchcock's reprise or "lead-out," with a final commercial. Thus, each episode had a rigorous structure, and a plot twist at the end became the chief criterion for story selection.

At 9:30 p.m. on Sunday, October 2, 1955, Hitchcock fans eagerly awaited the series's debut. First there was the famous line-drawing profile, followed by Hitchcock's silhouette marching into it from the right to the strains of Gounod's "Funeral March of a Marionette." Next came the director himself: "Good evening, Ladies and Gentlemen . . ." and the first of his famous lead-ins began. Finally came those ominous Hitchcock title card musical chords leading into the first show. (In this premiere episode there was no other background score.)

"Revenge" was that show, directed (as are all the episodes discussed here) by Hitchcock himself. Ralph Meeker finds, to his dismay, that his mentally disturbed wife (Vera Miles) believes that every man

Above: "I shall not act in these stories but will only make appearances. Something in the nature of an accessory before and after the fact, to give the title to those of you who can't read and to tidy up afterwards for those who don't understand the endings."
Below left: The first episode. Ralph Meeker and Vera Miles in the Hitchcock-directed "Revenge."
Below right: Hitchcock and Jane Wyman in his reception room at CBS. Wyman was filming The Jane Wyman Show at the time.

DEAD LETTER OFFICE

"Breakdown" (1955), a *tour de force* for actor Joseph Cotten and Hitchcock, is told in a series of close-ups and point-of-view shots that most effectively put us into Cotten's shoes. Involved in a freak accident in a remote area, he is pinned and paralyzed behind his car's steering wheel. Now begins the suspense—how can he communicate that he is alive? Cotten's internal monologue acts as a counterpoint to the visual, rather than a supplement, making this show more successful than others using voice-over narration.

In "The Case of Mr. Pelham" (1955), the titular businessman (Tom Ewell) has a double, who gradually takes over his life. The universality and strangeness of the *doppelgänger* carries this episode rather than the direction, which is objective and without any of Hitchcock's stylistic flourishes.

"Back for Christmas" (1956) is stylistically perhaps the finest in the series. Superbly acted by two Hitchcock reliables, John Williams and Isabel Elsom, the episode is based on John Collier's variation of the Crippen case, which was one of Hitchcock's favorites: a man kills his wife, buries her in the cellar, and takes off for America. Hitchcock departs from the Collier story at several points—he changes the murder scene from the upstairs bath to the cellar—but preserves the central suspense idea. What is one to

Below: Father and daughter.

is the rapist who assaulted her—but only after he has clubbed the first man so identified (tastefully done off-screen). Nothing shows Hitchcock's narrative power more than the opening and closing of this gem. The opening takes us from far to near in a series of five shots that, in typical Hitchcock fashion, generates apprehension in the viewer, enhanced by the absence of an atmospheric score. The remarkable close illustrates the director's narrative economy: during the last scene in a car, he inserts a clip of a hotel maid announcing, "something terrible has happened . . . " This, together with the siren heard over the last close-up of Meeker, tells us everything. Finally, the penultimate shot is a close-up profile of Miles against the car's moving background—a beautiful Hitchcock signature shot, a variation of his famous "horizontal movement across a vertical line."

"Mr. Blanchard's Secret" (1956) is one of the least satisfying of the series. Imaginative mystery writer Mary Scott makes all sorts of inferences about her neighbors, none of which turn out to be true. We have Scott's soliloquys to carry the plot forward—very un-Hitchcockian—and more music than usual, perhaps necessary because of the lack of drama.

"One More Mile to Go" (1957) presents another bludgeoning. This time David Wayne bops his wife with a poker. The first half of the film is essentially without dialogue, providing many visual details about covering up the evidence and disposing of the body in the trunk of Wayne's car (anticipating images in *Psycho* three years later).

do when one is caught in the cellar, water is running upstairs and visitors walk into the house uninvited?

"Wet Saturday" (1956) is another excellent play, again featuring John Williams and a story by John Collier. Mr. Princey (Sir Cedric Hardwicke) presides over a rather weird family. As the play opens, unrequited love has led daughter Millicent (Tita Purdom, in a superb performance) to batter in the head of the local parson, a crime for which Hardwicke proceeds to frame Williams. While "Back for Christmas" has more open action and uses the moving camera with fewer close-ups, "Wet Saturday" shows Hitchcock's effectiveness with what is essentially a single-set dialogue piece.

"Four O'Clock" (1957) is the premiere episode of the hour-long *Suspicion* series. It is one of Hitchcock's best televisual efforts, rigorously done, without any atmospheric score, and climaxing in a stunning montage sequence. A watchmaker (E. G. Marshall) believes his wife (Nancy Kelly) is meeting her lover in the house at four o'clock, when Marshall will be at his shop. In their basement, Marshall wires a bomb to an alarm clock to explode at the appointed time. After he sets the mechanism, juvenile thieves break in to the house, and bind and gag him. He must now watch as the minute hand creeps inexorably towards four o'clock.

"The Perfect Crime" (1957) is one of the weaker shows, hindered by flashbacks, voice-over narration, and overbearing atmospheric music. A master detective (Vincent Price) throttles a defense attorney (James Gregory) who is about to reveal to the world that an innocent man was executed through the for-

mer's blunder. Surprisingly, since it is a preferred method of murder in Hitchcock's theatrical films, this is the first throttling in his television work. Hitchcock's lead-out for "The Perfect Crime" is particularly good and saves the show.

"Lamb to the Slaughter" (1958), a tale Hitchcock had been long eager to adapt, is the first of four Roald Dahl stories he directed. This time the bludgeoning is carried out with a frozen leg of lamb. The plot is simple: A policeman comes home, tells his pregnant wife (Barbara Bel Geddes) that he's leaving her, she bops him with a frozen leg of lamb, then pops it in the oven, and later serves it to her

husband's colleagues, who have spent several hours investigating the crime scene and searching for the weapon. "Probably right here on the premises, under our very noses," says one of the diners.

"Dip in the Pool" (1958) is also based on a Dahl story, but here the original has been enhanced. Mr. Botibol (Keenan Wynn), traveling on a liner, buys the low field in a betting pool on the distance that will be covered in the ship's daily run, and then tries to delay the journey by throwing himself overboard.

"Poison" (1958) was the third Dahl in succession directed by Hitchcock. For suspense, one can't go wrong with a snake lying asleep on a man's stomach

Above left: The hour show: James Mason and Sara Shane in "Captive Audience."
Top: "Tippi" Hedren appeared in the pilot of the eighties Alfred Hitchcock Presents.
Above: The first version of "Man From the South" starred Steve McQueen and Peter Lorre and was remade for the eighties pilot.
Left: The fifth Beatle.

under the bed covers. However, the original didn't really have an ending, so Hitchcock and his scriptwriter Casey Robinson added considerable tension between the main characters.

"Banquo's Chair" (1959) stars John Williams, in his third Hitchcock television film, as a retired Scotland Yard Inspector. He hopes to trap a murderer (Kenneth Haigh) by bringing on the victim's ghost during dinner on the anniversary of the crime. The show features one of the

series's most elaborate sets, and Hitchcock uses more moving cameras, seamless cutting, and deep focus than usual in his television films. The result is an elegantly directed and photographed period piece.

"Arthur" (1959) stars Laurence Harvey as a chicken rancher who disposes of his unwelcome girlfriend (Hazel Court) in a feed mixer. The feed produces especially plump birds, a pair of which he gives as a Christmas gift to the local police

(Robert Douglas and Patrick Macnee).

"The Crystal Trench" (1959) is one of the weaker episodes. A woman loses her beloved young husband in a mountaineering accident when he falls into a glacier's ravine. She spends her life waiting for his body to emerge from the ice, while the man who really loves her also waits. ("Our version of *The Iceman Cometh*," quipped Hitchcock.)

In 1960 Hitchcock made *Psycho*, his most famous and successful film. It was shot on a tight, television-style schedule, using his regular television director of photography, John L. Russell. The same year he also made his only television film to be photographed in color, "Incident at a Corner" (1960), produced for *Ford Startime*. A school crossing guard (Paul Hartman) is anonymously accused of molesting children. Vera Miles plays his granddaughter, and George Peppard her fiancé. Peppard heads up the family support, while Miles's role is largely passive, the major female part being played by Leora Dana.

"Mrs. Bixby and the Colonel's Coat" (1960), Hitchcock's fourth and final Dahl story, is an amusing tale of marital infidelity. Mrs. Bixby's (Audrey Meadows) dentist husband (Les Tremayne) does not know that for many years she's been seeing her wealthy lover, the "Colonel" (Stephen Chase), once a month on the pretext of paying her aunt in Baltimore an overnight visit. When the Colonel breaks off the relationship after giving her an expensive full-length mink coat, the suspense begins. How will she be able to take the coat home? Mrs. Bixby's dilemma is cleverly translated into visual terms, mostly in close-ups employing subtle touches which reward repeated viewings.

"The Horseplayer" (1961) focuses on a gambler (Ed Gardner) who tells the parish priest (Claude Rains) of his success in picking horses through prayer. The

The eighties remake of "Man from the South." Here John Huston (left) can be seen with Kim Novak (right).

priest also has a problem: his church needs a new roof. A final prayer leads to a happy conclusion in a surprising way. Hitchcock does a masterful job in the opening, showing in a montage of fourteen shots of how bad a leaky roof can be.

"Bang! You're Dead" (1961), Hitchcock's last directorial effort for the half-hour series, calls attention to the problem of firearms in the home. Six-year-old Jackie (Billy Mumy) finds a revolver with a box of cartridges in his uncle's (Steve Dunne) luggage and

believes it is a gift for him. He spins the cylinder and drops in a bullet. The suspense builds as he wanders around the neighborhood playing cowboy, dropping in more cartridges and filling the chamber. Everyday frustrations add to the agony: busy store clerks and managers who won't be interrupted, a spoiled child who insists on riding a mechanical pony. Fortunately, all ends well with a last minute rescue, but it's still a hand-wringer.

"I Saw the Whole Thing" (1962) completes the canon, and is the only show Hitchcock directed for *The Alfred Hitchcock Hour*. Although well constructed, it lacks stylistic interest. (The director was undoubtedly putting all his effort into *The Birds* at the time.) John Forsythe is accused of a felony hit-and-run after his car bumps a motorcyclist. Against the advice of his attorney, he defends himself. The most interesting sequence is the opening, in which the screech of car brakes interrupts the activities of five witnesses, who see the vehicle leave the scene. Hitchcock shows each person's reaction to this "sound event" in five little episodes, each ending with a freeze-frame shot. With the exception of *The Birds*, these are the only such shots found in Hitchcock's work. Interestingly, this opening is similar to that of "Incident at a Corner."

J. Lary Kuhns

THE MAN WHO KNEW TOO MUCH

First screening May 1956

**Production company:
Paramount/FilWite Productions**

Duration 120 minutes

Technicolor/VistaVision

Ben McKenna (James Stewart), a surgeon from Indianapolis, and wife Jo (Doris Day), a former musical comedy singer, holiday in Marrakesh with young son Hank (Christopher Olsen). On a bus, they meet Louis Bernard (Daniel Gélin), who is secretly working for the Deuxième Bureau. Later, the McKennas attend an Arab restaurant where an English couple, the Draytons (Bernard Miles and Brenda De Banzie), introduce themselves. The next day brings drama: Louis Bernard, wearing Arab robes, is knifed in the marketplace; dying, he whispers to Ben sketchy details of a planned assassination in London. Then, to silence Ben, Hank is kidnapped by the Draytons, whom the McKennas chase to London. The subsequent pursuit proceeds from a taxidermists' in Camden Town to a seedy chapel in Bayswater, and then to the Albert Hall, where Jo, almost inadvertently, foils the assassination attempt. Learning that Hank is being held in a nearby embassy, where the Prime Minister is the very man whose life Jo saved, the McKennas secure an invitation there. On arrival, Jo offers to sing. Upstairs, Hank hears her and whistles back. Ben now locates Hank and, after overpowering Drayton, returns the boy to his mother and safety.

The scene in which Ben McKenna sedates his wife before telling her of Hank's kidnapping recalls a rape. It's implied that relations between the couple have been strained, and that each feels some animosity. Jo indeed has just wondered out loud if they are about to have their monthly fight. But at the end of the film, in the Embassy, Jo sings "We'll Love Again." The note of happy family reconciliation links the second version of *The Man Who Knew Too Much* to the first, where a similar theme operated. Both versions have their special qualities, and their flaws. But the second version finally moves us more deeply.

For the difficult sedation scene, Hitchcock suggested to Doris Day that she and James Stewart try to achieve it in a single take. First, she and Stewart rehearsed their moves. Then, as Day describes it, "[a]fter lunch we assembled on the set and with no further preparation Hitch started the cameras and we did the scene in one take. Just like that." (The use of multiple cameras recalls *The Paradine Case*, or perhaps television.) Day, a fine actress, took away generally pleasant memories of the film, though Hitch's remoteness during shooting made her feel that she wasn't pleasing him—quite wrongly, as it turned out. She was also troubled when, on arriving in Marrakesh, she saw the poverty and starvation of the people and the animals. She refused to appear in any scene with animals, such as the one with the horse-drawn wagon, unless the creatures were properly fed.

Hitch on location in Marrakesh. He famously said of the two versions of The Man Who Knew Too Much, *"Let's say the first . . . is the work of a talented amateur and the second was made by a professional."*

Remaking *The Man Who Knew Too Much* had been on Hitchcock's mind since his Selznick days. He and John Houseman had tried to give the story an American setting, but couldn't make it happen. A sign of their efforts is a moment in *Saboteur* that anticipates the scene more than a decade later where Hank McKenna is smuggled into the Embassy through its kitchen—though, revealingly, both scenes derive from John

Buchan's novel *The Power House*. Like another great English story teller, Charles Dickens (1812–70), Hitchcock had always powerfully responded to London's back streets, courts, and alleyways. He had hoped to include these things in *The Paradine Case*. Now he seized his opportunity. The very contrast of hot, sprawling Marrakesh with the streets of London recalls Dickens's *Little Dorrit*, which opens in a sweltering Marseilles then

switches locale to "a Sunday evening in London, gloomy, close, and stale." (Such a contrast was intentional on Dickens's part, as it was on Hitchcock's.)

Likewise, Dickens's *Our Mutual Friend* has several episodes set in a taxidermy shop—based on an actual shop in London—crammed with stuffed animals, preserved babies, and articulated human skeletons. At one point, someone slams the street door, and the whole grisly population is shaken into momentary life ("paralytically animated," in Dickens's phrase). Hitchcock certainly had a similar effect in mind when filming the mêlée in Ambrose Chapell's taxidermy shop in Camden Town. Earlier, echoing footsteps in the nearby side street had provided another ambiguous life-death effect (though perhaps not as brilliant as the effect in Dickens's *A Tale of Two Cities*, where echoing footsteps in a London street foreshadow the coming French Revolution).

The Man Who Knew Too Much (1956) has its own brilliance. Jean-Luc Godard's positive review in *Cahiers du Cinéma* noted its documentary aspect. Full analysis would show that the film first systematically exhibits life (for example, different forms of religion, music, and social class), then in the Albert Hall and Embassy sequences achieves a deeply satisfying resolution. A crucial role is played by the "Storm Cloud Cantata," conducted in the film by Hitchcock's representative, Bernard Herrmann (in a cameo appearance). Besides building suspense, the performance effectively demonstrates a famous claim that music can evoke the world's *Will*. That claim was made by the philosopher Schopenhauer, who said in part that music "parallels the world"—

which is why the cantata does indeed sum up the film to this point.

In particular, the same philosopher (whose relevance to *Lifeboat* was noted earlier) said that the world is sometimes stormy and sometimes relatively calm, but always it manifests the life force. Furthermore, it's against the cantata's evocation of this *Will* that Jo wrestles with her terrible dilemma: should she intervene to save a statesman's life when doing so must jeopardize the life of her kidnapped son? In effect, the issue here is: *what is the will of an individual against that of the world itself?* In the end, Jo summons from her innermost depths a wordless scream that deflects the marksman's aim, a moment that is arguably Hitchcock's finest. It vividly expresses a universal predicament while being the valid response of the character.

Matters that can scarcely be articulated also affect Ben McKenna. A situation exists whereby he has sometimes put his job ahead of his marriage. In a line that Hitchcock cut from the film, Ben wonders how Jo can bear "sleeping with a man who always smells of ether." Much of Ben's rather bossy manner is attributable to his unease about this. But he is basically a good man. His opposite is Drayton. The script notes that, far from being bossy, Drayton has a "horrible servility" in the scene where he agrees to carry out the order of the Ambassador to dispose of Hank. So Drayton's defeat at the end, and the reunion of all the McKennas, now acting *in concert*, is very satisfying.

Above: "Que Sera, Sera" was a huge hit for Doris Day and won an Oscar. **Right:** Ben McKenna (James Stewart) tries to reassure his wife, Jo (Doris Day). In the original film, the characters were called Bob and Jill Lawrence, played by Leslie Banks and Edna Best.

THE WRONG MAN

First screening December 1956

Production company: Warner Brothers

Duration 105 minutes

Black and white

This really happened. Christopher Emmanuel Balestrero (Henry Fonda) plays the double-bass at the Stork Club. A family man, he lives in Jackson Heights with his wife Rose (Vera Miles) and their two boys. But on January 14, 1953, "Manny" is arrested on suspicion of having twice held up an insurance office and stolen $71. After witnesses identify him, he is arraigned; bail is set at $7,500. This is paid by Manny's brother-in-law, Gene Conforti (Nehemiah Persoff). Manny and Rose now hire a local barrister, Frank O'Connor (Anthony Quayle), who admits he's inexperienced in criminal cases. Nor is Manny's cause helped when potential alibi-witnesses prove to have either died or moved away. Rose breaks down and enters an institution. When the trial arrives, it's aborted after a juror protests at O'Connor's inept cross-questioning. Awaiting a retrial, a despairing Manny is told by his mother (Esther Minciotti) to "pray for strength." Shortly afterwards, the man who committed the earlier robberies, and who resembles Manny, is caught trying to hold up a delicatessen. Manny is cleared, but two years pass before Rose leaves the institution and the Balestreros start a new life in Florida.

In *To Catch a Thief*, Robie faces a personal Calvary on the rooftop at the end. "He's where I always knew he'd be some day," says the police chief. But if Robie is a Christ-figure, he's also an Everyman, symbolically guilty of original sin and granted a parole but not a pardon (like everyone else in this life). Eerily, the true story told in *The Wrong Man* contains similar elements. Manny is very much Everyman, as his nickname suggests, and the film stresses that he is indeed a simple family man. Yet his actual Christian names, Christopher and Emmanuel, the latter meaning "God with us," remind us of what he stands for. The film hinges on the moment when Manny prays to a picture of Christ, and shortly afterwards the real criminal is arrested.

Of course, neither Manny nor Robie *is* Christ, merely someone who endures great suffering (see Father Logan in *I Confess*). Afterwards, other burdens remain for Manny. Christians may give all of this a particular interpretation. Other viewers may regard the arrest of the real criminal as just the "ironic coincidence" that Hitchcock himself called it. The film is not without its Hitchcockian ambiguity.

The following events seem important in the genesis of *The Wrong Man*. The story of Manny Balestrero was written up by Herbert Brean as "A Case of Identity" and published in the June 29, 1953, issue of *Life*. The same year, NBC showed Paddy Chayefsky's *Marty*, the play that began a trend toward everyday realism (and featured Esther Minciotti as Marty's mother). In December, Robert Montgomery produced for NBC a teleplay about the Balestrero case, with Robert Ellenstein reportedly excellent as Manny. During Christmas 1954, CBS showed a television opera of Charles Dickens's ghost story, *A Christmas Carol*, which had lyrics by the renowned dramatist Maxwell Anderson and a score by

An image not seen in the final print: Hitch's cameo, which he later cut, fearing it might work against his documentary approach.

For the first time Alfred Hitchcock goes to real life for his thrills! It's all true and all suspense - - the all-'round biggest Hitchcock hit ever to hit the screen! Warner Bros. present HENRY FONDA and VERA MILES and the exciting city of New York in ALFRED HITCHCOCK'S **The Wrong Man**

Somewhere... somewhere... there must be the right man!

Bernard Herrmann. On October 2, 1955, the first episode of *Alfred Hitchcock Presents* aired on CBS, in which Hitchcock directed his newest protégée, New York model and actress Vera Miles. She played a wife who has suffered a nervous breakdown and finally proves to be totally deranged.

Hitchcock read "A Case of Identity" when it was first published, and now he decided to film it without fee for Warner Brothers, who held the screen rights. He hired both Angus MacPhail, his old friend, and Maxwell Anderson to work on a treatment and a screenplay. Anderson had written the famous play *Winterset* (1935), about false indictment and injustice in the Sacco/Vanzetti case.

Above left: Hitch and Fonda discuss the script in the study at Hitchcock's home.
Above right: Manny's wife Rose (Vera Miles, right) and distraught mother (Esther Minciotti). In January 1956, Hitchcock had signed Miles to an exclusive, five-year contract.
Below: Henry Fonda in a striking publicity still.

Another of his plays that Hitchcock admired was *High Tor* (1937), full of ghostly effects. Scripting of *The Wrong Man* proceeded in early 1956, with much careful factual research being done by MacPhail and Hitchcock in New York.

During the shooting—in stark black and white—Hitchcock often filmed at the authentic locations and used the real people from the case. Several of the original police detectives and the staff at the nursing home played themselves. Earlier, Henry Fonda and Vera Miles had spent several days talking to the Balestrero family in Florida. Curiously, when the film came out, it received contrary responses from the reviewers for *Time* and *Nation*. The former criticized it for its "completely literal rendering," while the latter, though liking the film overall, considered it could have been handled even more factually.

The truth is that *The Wrong Man* is both faithful to what happened and yet stylized in ways that prefigure *Vertigo*. Though loosely called Kafkaesque, it has the most in common with a great English novel about a seemingly interminable lawsuit, Dickens's *Bleak House* (1853)—which Kafka read, and which Hitchcock studied at school (it "seems to have engraved itself on Hitchcock's memory," notes Spoto). The hefty role of coincidence in the film is thoroughly Dickensian, being expressive of some-

thing the characters can't comprehend, that is more than fate, that concerns the whole time/space/causality nexus of our understanding. One such coincidence is the fact that all the alibi-witnesses have died or vanished.

It's as if the people concerned had been spirited away. In this connection, the film employs one of its stylizations, starting with the credits sequence. In a series of near-invisible dissolves, we watch as the patrons of the Stork Club dematerialize. The effect, as critic William Pechter noted, is positively eerie—and much facilitated by Bernard Herrmann's reedy modulations of the rumba score. The suggestion of death-in-life is soon extended to Manny's own home, and again the score contributes to the effect: the double-bass, Manny's own instrument, seems to stalk him down his hallway (see the use of the famous "Adagio" in Orson Welles's *The Trial* [1962]). But death is everywhere in Hitchcock's film. Pedestrians in Queens caught in car headlights look like wraiths.

Rose's breakdown, and even the mistrial, extend the impression of people and things dematerializing or dissolving. Before he prays to the religious picture, Manny seems headed the same way, having just told his mother, "You'd all be better off without me." But then the effect is reversed when an *emphatic* dissolve-in shows the real criminal. *The Wrong Man* posits an understanding of time and space that the bourgeois Manny simply can't grasp, though he has an inkling of it when he says that his arrest the day before "seems like a million years ago." The evidence for all of this is in the film, one of Hitchcock's most underrated.

VERTIGO

First screening May 1958

Production company:
Paramount/Alfred Hitchcock
Productions

Duration 128 minutes

Technicolor/VistaVision

When a colleague of policeman John "Scottie" Ferguson (James Stewart) plunges off a San Francisco rooftop, the acrophobic Scottie blames himself, and resigns. One day, an acquaintance, Gavin Elster (Tom Helmore), hires Scottie to shadow his wife, Madeleine (Kim Novak), whose behavior has become strange and potentially suicidal. After rescuing Madeleine from attempted drowning, Scottie falls in love with her. But because of his fear of heights, he later watches helplessly as she appears to plummet from a mission tower. He has a breakdown, followed by a lengthy convalescence, and is attended by ex-fiancée Midge Wood (Barbara Bel Geddes). Then, in a street, Scottie sees a shopgirl, Judy Barton (Kim Novak again), who resembles the dead Madeleine. He begins dating her. Eventually he asks her to dye her hair blonde, like Madeleine's, and they make love. But the truth is that Judy is the Madeleine he knew, having earlier helped trick Scottie into testifying that Madeleine Elster committed suicide. (In fact, Judy was an imposter: the real Madeleine had meanwhile been murdered by her husband.) Knowing he has been used, Scottie drives Judy back to the mission. This time he forces himself to ascend the tower, only to see the woman he still loves plummet from it.

Vertigo is a thriller whose subject is Romanticism. Madeleine awakens in Scottie the "transcendental pretense," the belief that the Self is everything. But when he finally confronts that Self, he finds it treacherous.

Hitchcock's most beautiful, and cruellest, film has its basis in a fine novel, *D'entre les Morts* (1954), by Pierre Boileau and Thomas Narcejac. The title means "From Among the Dead" or "Between Deaths," either translation equally fitting the story set in wartime France about a woman who seems possessed by a dead ancestor. Many of the film's key scenes are in the novel: for example, the episode of buying a gray suit for the Judy character, when Scottie's rough manner makes the shop assistant glance at him, startled. And a major theme of the film lurks in a passage that might have come from Poe, describing Scottie's guilt feelings after Madeleine's death: "It was will power he lacked. . . . He would have had to pour out far more vitality than he possessed to keep her in this world."

Dan Auiler's book on the making of *Vertigo* notes that Scottie is an Everyman figure, forcibly made aware of his own mortality. From the outset, Hitchcock chose James Stewart and Vera Miles for his stars. But Miles got pregnant, and was replaced by Kim Novak, whom Hitchcock had seen in George Sidney's *The Eddy Duchin Story* (1956). That film was written by playwright Samuel Taylor, who in January 1957 came onto the *Vertigo*

Kim Novak locked in discussion with Hitch.

project, replacing earlier writers Maxwell Anderson and Alec Coppel. The final screenplay is mainly Taylor's, though things like the dream sequence and the first tower scene are Coppel's work. Taylor invented the character of Midge, and considered that Barbara Bel Geddes should play her, because he recognized that she would provide a solid humanity which the story's extraordinary events and characters mainly lacked.

Principal photography began at the end of September 1957. Filming was in VistaVision, which Hitchcock had used three times already, on *To Catch a Thief*, *The Trouble With Harry*, and the remake of *The Man Who Knew Too Much*. The great merit of Paramount's widescreen process lay in its use of the width of two normal 35mm frames to give extra sharpness and size (aspect ratio) of screen image; during shooting, the film travelled

Above: *Kim Novak: "It was almost as if Hitchcock was Elster, the man who was telling me to play a role."*

Above right: *Hitch with his original choice for the female lead, Vera Miles. The pregnant Miles had to quit the production in March 1957.*

horizontally in the camera. According to Auiler, who quotes studio records, *Vertigo* was never actually shown in the horizontal mode, but only in reduced 35mm prints. Even then, the gain in image clarity was noticeable. For many of the film's day scenes, Robert Burks used fog filters of varying density. He also devised special diffusion filters to lend Madeleine a magical greenish glow for certain scenes. In both cases—and this was the film's rationale for the famous gray suit—Hitchcock wanted to suggest that Madeleine had materialized out of the San Francisco fog and that she might soon vanish again. (Throughout, she is constantly disappearing around corners and out of rooms.) He vividly remembered the production of J. M. Barrie's play *Mary Rose* he'd seen in 1920, with its green apparition accompanied by eerie music and a low moaning wind.

Samuel Taylor jokingly suggested that the film's title might be *To Lay a Ghost*. A famous scene shows Scottie and Judy kissing as the walls of her room appear to turn and change into the inside of the stable at the Mission San Juan Bautista, where Scottie had kissed Madeleine. The effect was achieved by first combining footage of the hotel room and the stable into one continuous panning shot, effectively

travelling 360 degrees. The shot was then projected behind the actors, who were placed on a turntable which rotated to follow the movement of the projected image.

For this scene, and the moments lead-

ing up to it, as Scottie waits for Judy to return from the hairdresser's, Bernard Herrmann paraphrased Wagner's "Liebestod" from *Tristan und Isolde* (1865). Herrmann's biographer, Steven C. Smith, has called the full sequence "perhaps cinema's most powerful evocation of romantic longing." Its music illustrates a famous notion of Schopenhauer's. "The effect of the *suspension*," Schopenhauer wrote, "[consists of] a dissonance delaying the final consonance that is with certainty awaited; in this way the longing for it is strengthened. . . . This is clearly an analog of the satisfaction of the [individual] will which is enhanced through delay." An analog of film, music, and the self (the character's, the viewer's) is integral to *Vertigo*. In one scene, Scottie tells Madeleine, "You see, there's an answer for everything," but the accompanying image of a car receding down a road immediately belies his words, as does the score's diminuendo.

Principal photography had finished by Christmas. When the film was released in May the following year, it proved too puzzling and downbeat to be generally popular, but has long since come to be regarded as one of the cinema's great works. A notable review was Jack Moffit's in the *Hollywood*

JAMES STEWART · KIM NOVAK

IN ALFRED HITCHCOCK'S 'VERTIGO'

BARBARA BEL GEDDES TOM HELMORE · HENRY JONES ALFRED HITCHCOCK · ALEC COPPEL & SAMUEL TAYLOR TECHNICOLOR®

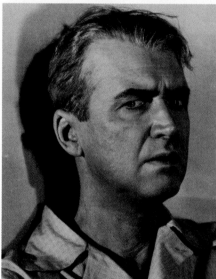

Above: *Madeleine and Judy (both Kim Novak), with Scottie (James Stewart). Novak and Stewart were teamed again the same year in* Bell, Book and Candle.

Left: *James Stewart, making the last of his four appearances for Hitch.*

Below: *Kim Novak: "I really identified with the story because to me it was saying . . . fall in love with me, not a fantasy."*

Reporter. After praising Stewart, Novak, and Bel Geddes for their performances, and suggesting "that an audience will buy any startling change in human behavior if you give it time (with montages and subtle buildups) to believe the transitions," Moffit called *Vertigo* "one of the most fascinating love stories ever filmed." His prescience was confirmed when the film was reissued in 1996, in a restored 70mm print. *Vertigo* was hailed around the world as a masterpiece.

As suggested above, the film is about Romanticism. The term "transcendental pretense" refers to an attitude that dominated Western thinking after Rousseau (1712–78). That attitude was based, somewhat wilfully, on the assumption that the Self is a microcosm of humanity and that everything needful to know can

be found there. Out of such an attitude came Romanticism, which Goethe (1749–1832) called a "disease." In *Vertigo*, Scottie catches that disease.

Or, rather, he's had it all along. Midge seems to have sensed it when she broke off their engagement back in college days,

which is when Gavin Elster also first knew Scottie. Accordingly, Gavin now sends Madeleine to awaken in the "hard-headed Scot" his *alter ego*: all part of a plan to take advantage of his weakness. Gavin subtly tempts Scottie, talking of "color, excitement, power, freedom" (i.e., heightened life). The plan is set in motion in the scenes where Madeleine leads Scottie around San Francisco.

With its missions, forts, shops, and art galleries, the city represents perennial human concerns—in the film it's a city seen *sub specie aeternitatis* (strictly, "under the appearance of eternity"). The scene at the Mission Dolores—originally the Mission San Francisco de Asis—is particularly telling in this respect. The mission was founded in the same year, 1776, as the city to which it eventually gave its name. Further, both here and in the other places Madeleine visits, time and worldly matters seem suspended. Madeleine thus comes to represent for Scottie the *eternal feminine*, defined by Carl Jung apropos Goethe's *Faust* as a figure who "embodies an experience . . . far older than that of the individual."

Again, these early scenes establish the film's main pattern: alternating lightness and darkness. The dream that Madeleine reports, in which she is walking down a corridor into darkness, is the key here. Darkness threatens constantly to descend, as in the bookstore scene. (At one point, too, the film quotes from Eugene

Madeleine. Startled, she steps back and falls to her death. But to Scottie, the nun is one more of Hitchcock's forbidding mother-figures. Camille Paglia has a brilliant comment on *Faust*, about what happens when Faust tries to materialize the spirit of his lost Helen, and it seems to apply to *Vertigo*. Paglia notes that Faust retains a repressed feminine side. Accordingly, when he journeys to the supernatural realm of "the Mothers," they frustrate his attempts. In Paglia's words, "The male struggles through his sexual stages, returning to the mother even when he thinks himself most free of her." And *Vertigo*'s nun, or mother-superior, is the Great Mother who has the final say yet again.

THE MCKITTRICK HOTEL EPISODE

This often puzzles people. Hitchcock appears to have remembered an episode from Curtis Bernhardt's *Conflict* (1945), starring Humphrey Bogart. In both films, the landlady is helping to hoodwink the main character. In Scottie's case, Gavin Elster stages Madeleine's disappearance from her room, and pays the landlady (Ellen Corby) to play dumb. Elster presumably wants to increase Scottie's *obsession* with the mysterious Madeleine. More broadly, the scene works like the wild baggage-car scene in *The Lady Vanishes* to mystify and tease the audience. The scene's visual centerpiece is a magnificent chandelier, evoking what the film calls "the gay old Bohemian days." The chandelier, with its crystal pendants, is one of several hanging objects, and references to *suspension*, that the film uses to echo the situation of the opening scene; there are other hanging lamps, less ornate, in Elster's club and at San Juan Bautista. (Surrealist painter Paul Delvaux [1897–1994] often depicted such lamps.) The film uses gravity as a metaphor for death: it can only be defied for so long, mainly by beautiful things, though also by the "ever-green, always living" sequoias. Functionally, of course, the chandelier simply gives Scottie something to look at while the landlady goes upstairs.

Left: *Scottie Ferguson, suffering from vertigo, a universal fear evoked in many Hitchcock films. "It's a powerful thing to be almost engulfed by that kind of fear," said Stewart later.*
Right: *Scottie with Judy during the film's climax.*

O'Neill's play, *Long Day's Journey Into Night* [1956].) Yet Madeleine seems to offer Scottie transcendence, signalled by her first, incredibly beautiful, profile shot at Ernie's Restaurant where the light rises as she approaches the camera.

Paradoxically, Madeleine appears to need saving from herself and from the dark Wagnerian (or Schopenhauerian) sea into which she plunges. Never was a basically good man, as Scottie is, so trapped! At any rate, not since Faust! Goethe's great drama does seem pertinent to *Vertigo*, not least because the way in which Gavin Elster traps Scottie is positively Mephistophelean. Played by English actor Tom Helmore, Elster effectively represents the film's true mastermind, Hitchcock. Also, on this reading of

the film, Madeleine is the eternal-feminine figure, Helen of Troy, while Midge is the abused Margaret/Gretchen.

The final scene brings all of these elements together. The (superimposed) tower at San Juan Bautista is much more than one of the film's phallic images, though it is that too. All of the film's accrued meanings now pertain, and something like Coleridge's "dread watchtower of the absolute self" seems meant. If Scottie had more vitality, he might perhaps yet keep his beloved Judy, though she's an accessory to murder. But by this stage of the film he is desolate, and, besides, the supposedly knowable Self never stops playing its tricks. This explains the sudden apparition of a nun at the top of the tower. To Judy, the nun is like the ghost of the dead

THE HOLLYWOOD LEADING MEN

worked as an acrobat before making his film debut in *This Is the Night* (1932). He remained a top box-office star for more than thirty years until his retirement in 1966, equally at home in comedy, adventure films, or light drama. But Grant also had a rarely exploited darker side, expertly tapped in his films with Hitchcock, which hinted at a selfishness and ruthlessness that lay beneath the serene surface. This could result in characters like the charming Johnnie, who may really be a killer in *Suspicion*, or the manipulative Devlin in *Notorious*.

In over three decades at the top, Grant appeared in a stream of classic movies, starring in five for director Howard Hawks (including *Bringing Up Baby* [1938] and *His Girl Friday* [1940]). He received Oscar nominations for both *Penny Serenade* (1941) and *None But the Lonely Heart* (1944), but was only acknowledged by the Academy

Above left: James Stewart (with Farley Granger and John Dall) in his first Hitchcock movie, Rope. The actor found filming the lengthy takes a trying experience.

Below: Cary Grant (with Joan Fontaine) in Suspicion, *his first picture with Hitch and one that explored the darker side of the sophisticated star's screen persona.*

When, in 1939, Hitchcock left the British film industry behind for Hollywood, he was relishing using "the best cinema equipment in the world," and part of that equipment would obviously include America's biggest stars. Hitchcock certainly understood the power of the star system. Not only was he aware of the financial benefits a top box-office draw could bring, but he also saw the artistic advantages as well. A film headlined by a charismatic actor often gave him the freedom to take greater risks than normal with his material. Hitchcock was also interested in playing with a star's screen persona, and thus manipulating the viewers' expectations, enabling his characters to occasionally perform unsavory acts (James Stewart's voyeurism in *Rear Window* or Cary Grant's suspected murderous intentions in *Suspicion*, for example) and yet still retain the audience's sympathy. In fact, Hitchcock's only real complaint came when certain performers were forced on him, sometimes shoehorned into unsuitable roles (as happened when Selznick's preference for Louis Jourdan in *The Paradine Case* won out over Hitchcock's own choice of the more earthy Robert Newton).

Hitch's preferred male lead was an actor like Gary Cooper (who turned down the lead role in *Foreign Correspondent*), someone with, according to the director, "that rare faculty of being able to rivet the attention of an audience while he does nothing." An actor who undoubtedly fits that description is Cary Grant (1904–1986), the archetypal Hitchcock star. He appeared in *Suspicion*, *Notorious*, *To Catch a Thief*, and *North by Northwest*, and was also the original choice for both *Mr. and Mrs. Smith* (for the Robert Montgomery role), and *Rope* (in the part that eventually went to James Stewart). Grant's inimitable style was summed up by co-star Irene Dunne, who admired the "excellence of his timing—the naturalness, the ease, the charm." Grant was born Archibald Leach in Bristol, England, and

in 1969, with a special Oscar awarded for "his unique mastery of the art of screen acting."

Almost as indelibly associated with Hitchcock is the incomparable James Stewart (1908–1997), star of *Rope*, *Rear Window*, *The Man Who Knew Too Much*, and *Vertigo*. Stewart frequently portrayed slightly diffident, shy, yet determined and decent characters (perhaps best realized in *Mr. Smith Goes to Washington* [1939]). Equally adept at comedies, thrillers, and Westerns, he was held in great affection by the public throughout his long career.

Stewart was born in Indiana, Pennsylvania, and worked in the theater (including a stint alongside Henry Fonda) before making his Hollywood debut in *The Murder Man* (1935). A string of classic movies followed (including *The Philadelphia Story* [1940] with Cary Grant), before Stewart's acting career was interrupted by his distinguished war service with the Air Force. After World War II, Stewart gradually took on more complex roles, beginning with perhaps his best loved performance, as George Bailey in Frank Capra's *It's a Wonderful Life* (1946), and culminating in *Vertigo*.

As the fifties progressed, Stewart's characters became more troubled, embittered, and isolated, particularly in the classic Westerns he made with Anthony Mann. "I look for a man . . . it is an effort to get along with in life," the actor once said about his choice of roles, "whose judgment is not always too good and who

Top left: *Cary Grant in* To Catch a Thief.
Top: *Henry Fonda in his only Hitchcock film,* The Wrong Man *(seen here with Vera Miles).*J
Above: *ames Stewart and Doris Day in the remake of* The Man Who Knew Too Much.

makes mistakes." Stewart received Oscar nominations for *Mr. Smith*, *It's a Wonderful Life*, *Harvey* (1950), and *Anatomy of a Murder* (1959), receiving the statuette for best actor for *The Philadelphia Story* and a special Oscar in 1985 for fifty years of memorable performances and "for his high ideals both on and off the screen."

Two other stars fitting the classic Hitchcock mold are Gregory Peck (1916–) and Henry Fonda (1905–1982). Screenwriter Casey Robinson recalled his first impressions of Peck: "He was over six feet tall and darkly handsome, with a physical presence of a young Abe Lincoln. He had a deep, resonant, and quietly compelling voice—an actor with charisma." Peck made his debut as the lead in *Days of Glory* (1944) and the following year starred in Hitchcock's *Spellbound*. He only made one other appearance for Hitch, in *The Paradine Case*, where the director felt him miscast ("I don't think that Gregory Peck can play an English lawyer," he complained). Peck effortlessly epitomized basic decency and integrity, but it was frequently accompanied by a slight sense of stolidness (for example in *The Man in the Gray*

Gregory Peck starred in two Hitchcock movies.

Flannel Suit [1956]). Although he starred in many well-loved films (including his Oscar-winning performance in *To Kill a Mockingbird* [1962]), Peck never formed an ongoing relationship with one director in the manner of Grant (Hitchcock and

Hawks), Stewart (Hitchcock, Capra, and Mann), and Fonda (Ford). His career seemed to suffer because of it.

Henry Fonda similarly typified honesty, being Hollywood's finest representative of solid intelligence and basic decency. However, even Fonda claimed, "I ain't really Henry Fonda. Nobody could have that much integrity." This also made him, again like Peck, slightly too stiff for comedy roles. He made only one film for Hitchcock, but was perfectly cast as the confused, falsely accused Christopher Emmanuel Balestrero in *The Wrong Man*. Fonda's reputation was established in seven movies with director John Ford (including *The Grapes of Wrath* [1940] and *My Darling Clementine* [1946]), although perhaps his best-known role is as the juror with conscience in Sidney Lumet's *12 Angry Men* (1957).

Hitchcock never formed really close relationships with his male leads, and in interviews always seemed happier talking about his actresses. Nevertheless, all of his leading actors admired the director, and working with Hitch undoubtedly enhanced each one of their careers.

NORTH BY NORTHWEST

First screening July 1959

**Production company:
Metro-Goldwyn-Mayer**

Duration 136 minutes

Technicolor/VistaVision

When foreign agents mistake Madison Avenue man Roger Thornhill (Cary Grant) for "George Kaplan"—a non-existent decoy agent—they forcibly take him to a Long Island mansion, where Philip Vandamm (James Mason) orders him killed. Managing to escape, Thornhill seeks information at the United Nations from a delegate who is promptly knifed, for which he is blamed. Thornhill next heads for Chicago. On the train, he meets an obliging platinum blonde, Eve Kendall (Eva Marie Saint), who, unknown to Thornhill, is both Vandamm's mistress and an American counteragent. Later, at a remote prairie crossroads, Thornhill survives an attempt on his life when a biplane strafes him before crashing. A counter-intelligence boss, the Professor (Leo G. Carroll), now tells Thornhill that Eve, who loves him, is staying near Mount Rushmore, South Dakota, where Vandamm is preparing to fly out of the country. The Professor takes Thornhill there. The next day, Vandamm learns Eve's true identity, and plans to kill her. But Thornhill warns her, and they run to the top of the mountain. Pursuing them, Vandamm's secretary, Leonard (Martin Landau), plunges to his death, though Thornhill and Eve survive to see Vandamm arrested—and then they get married.

In a celebrated sequence, Thornhill jokes about being lured to his doom on the Twentieth-Century Limited by (a woman named) Eve. *North by Northwest* is one vast free-association on that line, "the Hitchcock picture to end all Hitchcock pictures" as its screenwriter Ernest Lehman called it. Naturally it's a chase thriller, and very properly Cary Grant is in every scene.

That is to say, it's not really a James Stewart-type picture, though Hitchcock apparently gave that actor the impression that he might be starring in it. When it became clear that the part better suited the urbane Grant, Hitchcock simply stalled until Stewart had to start work on *Bell, Book, and Candle* (1958). At one stage, Sophia Loren's name was mentioned as the film's co-star, but "contractual problems" stopped her. Co-starring was Eva Marie Saint, the Academy Award-winning actress from Elia Kazan's *On the Waterfront* (1954).

It's well known that Hitchcock personally chose Saint's wardrobe for her, after expressing dissatisfaction with the MGM costumers' designs, by taking her to Bergdorf Goodman in New York and selecting items off the rack. Less well known is that he did the same for Martin Landau! According to Charles Higham and Roy Moseley, Hitch wanted Landau to be better dressed than Grant, if that were possible. He therefore took Landau to Quintino, Grant's tailor in Beverly Hills, where he ordered several suits to be made for him. Hitch's intention was that

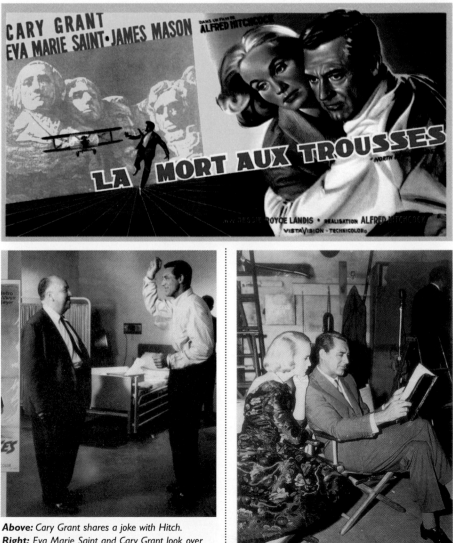

Above: Cary Grant shares a joke with Hitch.
Right: Eva Marie Saint and Cary Grant look over the script

interest was genuine is obvious from his attempts around this time to buy the rights to Graham Greene's comedy-thriller, *Our Man in Havana* (1958; about a spy's phony reports from Cuba), but he was turned down by Greene himself. Then he remembered a conversation with a New York newspaperman who had offered him the idea of the CIA inventing a fake decoy agent in a spy plot.

John Michael Hayes said that Hitch invited him to script *North by Northwest* well before Lehman was given the job. The reason that Lehman was finally chosen to write the script—apart from his impressive credentials, which included such films as *Executive Suite* (1954) and *Sweet Smell of Success* (1957)—was MCA's negotiation for Hitchcock of a one-picture deal with MGM, where Lehman happened to be under contract. The two began work, calling their project *In a North-westerly direction*, a title later changed at the suggestion of MGM itself to *North by Northwest*. (Any allusion to Hamlet's madness, notes John Russell Taylor, was entirely accidental.)

Lehman wasn't greatly familiar with the adventure-chase genre, whose roots are in such English novels as *King Solomon's Mines* (1885) and *Kim* (1901), though both those stories had been filmed by MGM as recently as 1950. But Hitchcock certainly was. Presumably, then, the director's input accounts for how two big scenes in *North by Northwest* echo the Bulldog Drummond adventure novel, *The Final Count* (1926). Firstly, the "Sapper" novel has a scene

Above: *"I take the loneliest, emptiest spot I can so that there is no place to run for cover." The justly famous cropduster scene.*
Right: *Roger Thornhill (Cary Grant) and Eve Kendall (Eva Marie Saint). Hitchcock claimed he "supervised the choice of [Eva Marie Saint's] wardrobe in every detail—just like Stewart did with Novak in Vertigo."*

Landau's character, the homosexual Leonard, be menacing and dominant.

Hitchcock had long wanted to film a chase across the presidential faces sculpted into Mount Rushmore. He also had an idea for a film that would begin at the United Nations in New York and end in the wastes of Alaska. Another idea that intrigued the director was for a story involving a non-existent character or event (as in Buchan's *John Macnab* [1925] and Ronald Neame's 1955 film *The Man Who Never Was*). That Hitch's

THE ALFRED HITCHCOCK STORY

Above: *The film's sheet music. Herrmann later claimed, "Hitchcock is very sensitive; he leaves me alone! (Fortunately, because if Hitchcock were left by himself, he would play 'In a Monastery Garden' behind all his pictures!)"*

where spies take over an absent person's house and install a phony female owner to divert police suspicions. Later, the novel climaxes at the spies' remote hideaway built on a rocky cliff where they wait for their aircraft—a dirigible—to come and fly them to Russia. Nor did the film pass up Graham Greene as a "source." The scene where Thornhill disguises himself from the police by lathering his face and using a lady's razor comes straight from Greene's *The Confidential Agent* (1939). Of course, Lehman's stamp is everywhere on the picture, especially its crackling and sophisticated dialogue, but the basic format, a very English one, might almost be called Hitchcock's secret inspiration.

Filming began on August 27, 1958, in the lobby of New York's Plaza Hotel. Conveniently, Grant was living there at the time. Hitchcock gave him the usual minimum of direction, and, such was

their mutual trust and respect, encouraged Grant to make suggestions about the script and the camera. Production went fairly smoothly, despite some complicated process-work on several scenes. Near the start of filming and near the end of final editing, Hitchcock took time off to direct two of his television shows ("Poison" and "Banquo's Chair"). Grant several times introduced personal touches into the dialogue, such as his favorite motto, "Think thin." Shooting wrapped on December 24, 1958, and was followed by months of editing, scoring, and retakes. Then, on August 6, 1959, the film premiered at the Radio City Music Hall. The public's response was favorable, and most critics were enthusiastic. *Time* thought the film "[s]moothly trowelled and thoroughly entertaining," though Stanley Kauffmann's review in *The New Republic* spoke of "the decline of Alfred Hitchcock" and called the prairie cross-

roads scene "probably the low point of Hitchcock's career."

Today, *North by Northwest* stands out as a classic thriller, whose subject (insofar as it can be pinned down) might be described as "surviving" in the twentieth century. Thornhill's/Grant's resilience is of the film's essence, and Hitchcock does whatever he can to make an audience *live* the experience. In its sumptuousness and wit, the film illustrates a remark of the Surrealists: "Fear, the incongruous, and the fascinations of luxury are emotional factors to which we never appeal in vain." But everything keeps coming back to Thornhill. As in *Vertigo*, a correlation is implied between the character and the film—and thus also the spectator. At the Chicago airport, Thornhill is told by the Professor that Eve is a government agent. As he realizes her peril, Thornhill gasps; simultaneously, the image pales as if in empathy. Here, emotion is conveyed to

Above: Mount Rushmore had to be recreated in the studio. "I wanted Cary Grant to slide down Lincoln's nose and hide in the nostril. Then Grant has a sneezing fit ..." One of the film's original titles was allegedly The Man on Lincoln's Nose.
Below: Philip Vandamm (James Mason), Eve, Valerian (Adam Williams), and Leonard (Martin Landau)

the spectator not just by Grant's performance but by an actual change in the film. Hitchcock had used an identical tactic in *Vertigo*, paling the image at the moment when Scottie had looked down from Midge's footstool.

In fact, a whole scene, or the entire film, may work like this. The prairie scene is one of the most exciting—and nonsensical—set pieces that Hitchcock ever dreamed up. Significantly, he called *North by Northwest* a "fantasy of the absurd," and added that he had no idea who is in the plane that tries to kill Thornhill. Yet the prairie scene is literally pivotal: it occurs at the film's midpoint and involves a vast emptiness. One may think of how, on the train, Thornhill had told Eve that his middle initial was "O" and that it stood for nothing. In other words, perhaps the whole film is a *portrait* of Thornhill, and now, at a turning point in his story, he encounters his own hollowness, finding it deadly.

In turn, it seems legitimate to recall other twentieth-century depictions of

"hollow men" (like T. S. Eliot's) and their "metaphysical voids" (as painted by an artist whose work Hitchcock admired, Giorgio di Chirico). Equally, the laconic exchange at the prairie crossroads between Thornhill and a farmer (Malcolm Atterbury) suggests a scene out of *Waiting for Godot* (1952). Samuel Beckett's play, described as being about "the meaninglessness of life," was already

widely held to epitomize the Theatre of the Absurd.

Certainly *North by Northwest* is full of references to art and modernity, and these constitute one of its most striking features. The New York scenes highlight two notable glass buildings: the newly-opened Seagram Building, designed by the gifted Ludwig Mies van der Rohe (1886–1969), and the United Nations Headquarters, whose architect was Wallace K. Harrison (1895–1981). The glassiness here seems fully in keeping with the film's emphasis on *surface*. But there are other associations. In a film where religion is hardly mentioned (versus, say, *The Wrong Man* and *Vertigo*), the New York skyscrapers are basically monuments to Mammon. That nuance is retained for the auction-gallery scene in Chicago, with its reminder that art in the twentieth century is a valuable *commodity*. The emphasis is only slightly different at Mount Rushmore, which features another monument. From the adjacent observation deck, casually-dressed tourists inspect through binoculars Gutzon Borglum's (1871–1941) sculpted faces of the Presidents—carved into a mountain sacred to the dispossessed Sioux. While the film doesn't dwell on that particular irony, it does add one of its own. Adjoining the top of this "Shrine of Democracy," Russian spies live in a comfortable Frank Lloyd Wright house and

Above: "I wanted Cary Grant to slide down Lincoln's nose and hide in the nostril. Then Grant has a sneezing fit..." One of the film's original titles was allegedly The Man on Lincoln's Nose.
Right: The climax, just before the train disappears into a tunnel.

operate a private airfield. Wright (1869–1959) died shortly before Hitchcock's film was released. Just two years earlier, on American television, he'd proclaimed himself the greatest architect who ever lived, and immortal. No doubt he and Borglum were two of a kind.

So a brief interpretation of *North by Northwest* may go like this. Vandamm is associated with art as represented by his house and the pre-Columbian statuette he uses to smuggle microfilm (another debasement). He's cultured and considerate ("God bless you, sir," says his housekeeper [Nora Marlowe]), yet ruthless. He was prepared to leave Eve behind, which may imply that he has a wife or another mistress elsewhere. That he concerns himself not at all with immortality, except through his taste in beautiful things, seems likely. The essential point is that his opposite number, Thornhill, cares less about art than "the art of survival"—and in the end the life force favors the American (see *Notorious*). Once

THE SAUL BASS TITLE SEQUENCE

The credits unfold against successive backgrounds, the first an unnatural green. This soon dissolves to a tall building recalling one of Mondrian's New York paintings. The façade reflects in distorted and even eerie fashion a street at rush hour, filled with yellow taxis. Next the image becomes a ground-level view, showing office workers pouring out of buildings and down subways *en masse*, like a collective tidal wave. Finally, as Bernard Herrmann's fandango ends, Alfred Hitchcock misses a bus. The office workers recall those at the start of *Rich and Strange*, but the sequence is much closer to a passage in T. S. Eliot's "The Waste Land" (1922)—whose "Unreal City" is inhabited by ghosts. Images of mortality are everywhere in *North by Northwest* (for example, the prairie). But late in the film, in the pine forest, Thornhill says, "I never felt more alive." He grows increasingly *real*. That is the point, ultimately, of Vandamm's remark about the police's use of "real bullets." Thornhill is on the side of *life*.

Thornhill quits the city where he has been stagnating, the film indeed shows him coming alive. The turning point for him is the prairie scene, which is appropriately gritty and physical. Finally, by the time he reaches Mount Rushmore, Thornhill has become real (see *The Saul Bass Title Sequence*). However, despite the phallic symbol at the end, his return to New York with Eve is ambiguous. Perhaps the only lesson of *North by Northwest* is: Anything can happen.

PSYCHO

First screening June 1960

Production company:
Paramount/Shamley Productions

Duration 109 minutes

Black and white

In Phoenix, Arizona, Marion Crane (Janet Leigh) steals $40,000 from her boss, then drives towards Fairvale, California. She just wants to marry Sam Loomis (John Gavin), but her mad act of theft will prove fatal. Exhausted from driving, she stops at a lonely motel run by the youthful Norman Bates (Anthony Perkins). As she eats supper, he tells her that he lives with his mother, an invalid, in the brooding old house behind the motel. Later, as Marion takes a shower before retiring, she is stabbed to death by "Mother." When Norman realizes what has happened, he puts the body and Marion's luggage in her car and sinks it in a nearby swamp. The following week, an insurance investigator, Milton Arbogast (Martin Balsam), calls, inquiring if Marion has been there. He, too, is knifed, and again an appalled Norman tidies up. Finally, Marion's sister Lila (Vera Miles), accompanied by Sam, comes looking for both Marion and Arbogast. When Lila attempts to search the house, she is confronted by a knife-wielding Norman dressed as Mother, but is saved by Sam. All along, it now appears, Norman has been inclined to "go a little mad sometimes."

novel was based on the shocking Ed Gein murders at Plainfield, Wisconsin, about 50 miles from where Bloch lived. When Paramount bosses heard that Hitch intended filming it, they tried to dissuade him. He responded by offering to finance the film himself, with the studio acting solely as distributor. A deal was struck.

To keep costs down, Hitchcock decided to shoot in black and white at MCA's Revue Studios on the Universal lot, using

Left: *The famous* Psycho *house, now a leading tourist attraction for Universal Studios.*
Below: *Vera Miles, John Gavin, and Janet Leigh pose for a publicity still.*

At the least, *Psycho* is a great horror film, with a dark vision. Its first forty minutes are brilliant, detailing Marion's flight from Phoenix, her brutal murder at the Bates Motel, and the clean-up by Norman afterwards. More problematic is the next hour, basically the Fairvale scenes. What these have going for them are a bleak expressionism and the character of Arbogast, but they're largely plot-driven. Finally, the last ten minutes rise to fresh heights of terror and poetry, interrupted by the psychiatrist's explanation (normality has its claims, too). On balance, the film is a lesser work than either *Rebecca* or *Vertigo*. The for-

mer has a richer texture overall, and *Vertigo* is more profound. But this hardly matters. Behind all three films is the figure of the Great Mother, and *Psycho* is Hitchcock's ultimate statement about that particular lady.

Hitchcock had noticed that cheaply-made horror films from companies like American International Pictures and Hammer Film Productions were netting their producers big money. Could he, he wondered, do as well or better, but with a quality product? He decided to buy the rights to Robert Bloch's novel *Psycho*, which Anthony Boucher in the *New York Times* had called "icily terrifying." The

Above: One of Hitch's double images: Marion Crane (Janet Leigh) and the stolen money.
Left: Mother.
Below: Janet Leigh is readied for a scene.

possibilities. "What if we get a big-name actress to play the girl? Nobody will expect to see her die!" He mentioned someone really big whom Stefano thought unsuitable. But when Janet Leigh's name was mentioned, it was a different matter. Both men had recently seen that actress in Orson Welles's *Touch of Evil* (1958), and knew that she was pretty, talented, and suitably warm and alive. Also, noted Stefano, she had no association with horror movies, which was just what they sought. A new screenplay was quickly written. Stefano fought Hitch on certain things, such as the inclusion of a shot from the house showing Lila Crane approaching the front door. The director objected that this would necessitate building a further wall to the motel grounds, but soon conceded its importance. (In the film, Lila stands and literally *confronts* the house.) The screenplay was finished in November. Filming was completed with impressive speed by early January 1960, and *Psycho* came in on budget, which was a low $800,000.

Psycho premiered in New York on June 16, 1960, at the DeMille and Baronet Theaters, soon followed by summer openings around the country. The film received a middling-to-hostile reaction from the New York critics, notes Rebello, but the response of the public was something else again. Rebello calls it "a firestorm." "[N]o one," he writes, "could have predicted how powerfully *Psycho* tapped into the American subconscious. Faintings.

headed man in his forties—but Hitch mollified him with a single question: "How would you feel if Norman were played by Anthony Perkins?" Stefano recalled, "I suddenly saw a tender, vulnerable young man you could feel incredibly sorry for. Then I suggested starting the movie with the girl instead of Norman."

Here Hitchcock was quick to spot the

his regular television crew, including cameraman John L. Russell. (He insisted, however, on using his veteran editor George Tomasini.) The first writer hired, on June 8, 1959, was MCA client James P. Cavanagh, who had scripted several episodes of *Alfred Hitchcock Presents.* Stephen Rebello's excellent book on the making of *Psycho* indicates that the resulting screenplay was a dispirited affair. Cavanagh was replaced by another MCA client, former lyricist/composer Joseph Stefano. He and Hitch hit it off straight away. Stefano had been somewhat dismayed by the novel, especially the character of Norman—a pudgy, red-

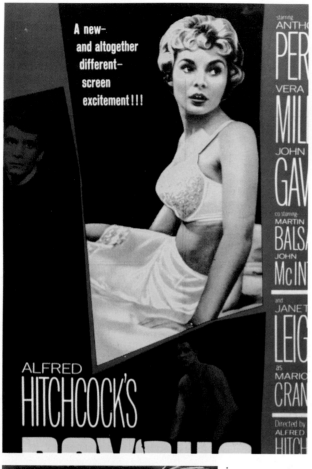

ALFRED
HITCHCOCK'S

A new-
and altogether
different-
screen
excitement!!!

starring
ANTHO
PER
VERA
MIL
JOHN
GAV
co starring
MARTIN
BALS
JOHN
McIN
and
JANET
LEIG
as
MARIO
CRAN
Directed by
ALFRED
HITC

Above: *Anthony Perkins and one of his stuffed birds. "Obviously [Norman Bates] is interested in taxidermy since he'd filled his own mother with sawdust," noted Hitchcock.*
Right: *Filming the Psycho trailer.*

Walk-outs. Repeat visits. Boycotts. Angry phone calls and letters. Talk of banning the film rang from church pulpits and psychiatrists' offices. Never before had any director so worked the audience like stops on an organ console." Within weeks Hitchcock had personally made $2,000,000 from the film. Yet he had feared that it might be a disaster, and was at a loss to explain the public's overwhelming response. "I've always been able to predict the audience's reaction," he confided to Tony Perkins. "Here, I haven't been able to."

To explain *Psycho*'s excellence as a horror film, as well as its vision, is something that commentators have been attempting since the 1960s, with varying degrees of success. (Essays from Robin Wood and Raymond Durgnat from that early period remain among the best.) One thing that does seem crucial is Hitchcock's continuing experiment in taking a film right up to, and inside, the spectator. In this, he was helped immeasurably by Bernard Herrmann's score. Well, maybe *not* immeasurably—Hitchcock himself reportedly said that "thirty-three percent of the effect of *Psycho* was due to the music." A famous German Expressionist play, Georg Kaiser's *From Morn till Midnight* (1912), which at times *Psycho* resembles, begins with the words, "This morning I went out in search of the unknown. Something was driving me on . . . " Effectively, Herrmann's main-title music makes a similar statement, and after hearing it, the audience knows that something terrible is going to happen.

Throughout *Psycho*'s shooting, Hitchcock insisted that a 50mm lens be used so as to approximate the normal field of human vision. Script supervisor Marshall Schlom explained: "He wanted the camera, *being* the audience all the time, to see as if . . . with their own eyes." Clearly, then, that's *our* eye that peers at Marion through a hole in the wall of

9401-2325

9401-2312

9401-2326

9401-2328

Hitch and Janet Leigh working on the shower scene. "It was, of course, very grueling to stand in a shower getting drenched for a week," recalled Leigh.

Norman's office. Equally, those are our own hands that mop and towel away all last flecks of blood in the bathroom after Marion's death. And, at the end, emanating from deep within us, that's surely our own voice that "condemns" Norman—the voice of "Mother." What is happening?

When Marion, whom Hitchcock called "a perfectly ordinary bourgeoisie," steals the $40,000 at the start, she is seeking more life—like Fred and Emily in *Rich and Strange*. In the manner of Expressionism, Marion wants a more authentic existence, though in her case this simply means marrying Sam and having a child by him. Here, she is like Patsy in *The Pleasure Garden*, whom we see at Lake Como gaze wistfully at several mothers with their babies. A photo of a baby is on the wall of Marion's room as she packs to run away (presumably the photo is of Marion herself); the stolen money had been intended by Cassidy (Frank Albertson) as a wedding present for his baby daughter. Thus the maternal instinct, even when travestied, is basic to *Psycho*.

So, too, is the mother's voice generally, which Dr. Margaret Mead's influential book *Male and Female* (1949) had linked to toilet-training, a universal growing-up experience. Here's Mead: "The clean white-tiled restaurant and the clean white-tiled bathroom are both parts of the [subsequent] ritual, with the mother's voice standing by, saying: 'If every rule of health is complied with, then you can enjoy life.'" Another suggestive fact about

Psycho is that Norman's relation to Mother is like that of Mrs. Danvers in *Rebecca* to her dead mistress. Hitchcock obviously sensed this when, during *Psycho*'s pre-production, he tweaked the press by announcing that Mother might be played by Judith Anderson. In effect, then, the mythical Great Mother is again behind the film, much as the Bates house dominates the motel. Significantly, Camille Paglia has written that the Great Mother's traditional main disciple is her son and lover, indicating an incestuous relationship between them. In Stefano's original script for *Psycho*, Mother refers to Norman as "ever the sweetheart."

All of those shots in which we see or hear *ourselves* are thus reminders of our own internal compulsions, and of the fact that the life force (Will) is also a death force; and that the most deathly figure of all is the Great Mother, though she is more chimerical than real. "The myth of matriarchy," Paglia reminds us, "may have originated in our universal experience of mother power in infancy." That *Psycho* seeks to *involve* its audience in these essentially psychological matters is consistent with its aim of shocking us, but also with a general tenet of

The final result—one of cinema's most famous scenes. "Psycho is probably one of the most cinematic pictures I've ever made."

Expressionism. Typically, Expressionism sought to show people their inauthentic existence, and to this end to involve them in the act of creativity itself.

Something very like this is in *Psycho*. Reference is made to Beethoven's Eroica Symphony much as *The Wrong Man* alludes to the genius of Mozart, and *North by Northwest* to the "immortal" Frank Lloyd Wright, et al. In each case, Hitchcock is outflanking us, introducing a fundamental (and therefore probably healthy) perspective—just as he does in a different way in *The Birds*, reminding us that "birds have been on this planet since archaeopteryx." But there is an even more telling allusion in *Psycho*. When Marion says, "They also pay who meet in hotel rooms," she is effectively invoking the famous last line of Milton's sonnet known as "On His Blindness." That last line is, of course, "They also serve who only stand and wait." It refers to the privileged order of angels who attend on God, patiently waiting to do His bidding.

"Patience doesn't run in my family," Lila Crane says. There is the irony. Creativity requires a special kind of patience, and it takes an artist (perhaps an artist of genius, as Milton knew himself to be) to stand firm and capture a vision of what the world is really like. Such a vision is in *Psycho*, and Hitchcock shares it with us. Both Marion and her sister are depicted as of the lower order of angels, not least at the moment when Marion dies beneath a shower nozzle that is like a nimbus, in a gleaming white bathroom that recalls similar imagery in *Spellbound*. (Earlier, in Norman's parlor, we'd seen a picture of angels ascending towards Heaven, a picture literally overshadowed by a black bird with a knife-like beak.) For her part, in Sam's hardware store, Lila is consistently photographed against an effulgence of garden rakes. Curiously, the film's allusions to angels, light that is "spent," "this dark world," patience, waiting, and especially *blindness*, are all echoes of Milton's own imagery. Coincidence? Or a homage by one great Cockney artist to another?

REMAKES, SEQUELS, AND HOMAGES

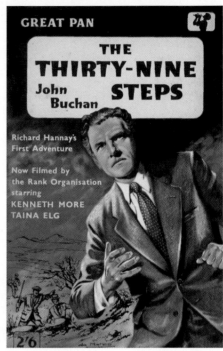

Above: Emily Taylor (Gwyneth Paltrow) and her husband, Steven (Michael Douglas), in A Perfect Murder, *a remake of* Dial M for Murder.
Above right: John Buchan's The Thirty-Nine Steps, *reissued to tie-in with the Rank movie directed by Ralph Thomas in 1959.*
Below: Norman Bates (Anthony Perkins) and the infamous Psycho *house.*

Only a handful of Hitchcock's films were remade during his lifetime, and then it was frequently a case of fellow filmmakers using the same source material to create their own movies. Obvious examples would include the three versions of Mrs. Belloc Lowndes's *The Lodger* that appeared in 1932 (which again starred Hitchcock's lead, Ivor Novello), 1944 (with Laird Cregar well cast in the title role), and 1953 (featuring Jack Palance and retitled *The Man in the Attic*). A similar reworking of shared source material can be found in *The Farmer's Wife* (1940; based on the Eden Phillpotts play) and *The 39 Steps* (1959; from John Buchan's novel), while Hitch's own versions of *The Manxman*, *The Skin Game*, and *Number Seventeen* were based on works (Sir Hall Caine's novel, John Galsworthy's play, and J. Jefferson Farjeon's play, respectively) that had already received at least one previous cinematic treatment.

Also worth mention are the numerous variations of the same real-life murder cases that inspired *The Lodger* (there are far too many films based on Jack the Ripper to list here), *Rope* (based on the famous Leopold and Loeb case, as were *Compulsion* [1959] and *Swoon* [1992]) and *Psycho* (loosely inspired by the crimes of Ed Gein, better known as the basis for Tobe Hooper's *The Texas Chain Saw Massacre* [1974]).

The first bona fide remake came from Hitchcock himself, with his second version of *The Man Who Knew Too Much*, which was released in 1956. The only other remakes over the following two decades are both minor movies: *Step Down to Terror* (1958), a reworking of *Shadow of a Doubt*, and *Once You Kiss a Stranger* (1969), a vacuous remake of *Strangers on a Train*. No doubt other directors felt too daunted to follow in the master's footsteps, and it wasn't until the late seventies that a change was perceptible. In 1978 a new version of *The 39 Steps* was released, followed in 1979 by Hammer Films' remake of *The Lady Vanishes*. The former, which returned to the original novel rather than Hitchcock's movie for inspiration, was by far the more successful and ten years later a television spin-off series followed, with Robert Powell recreating the title role in *Hannay* (1988–89). Earlier, in 1985, Robin Bailey and Michael Aldridge had starred in the television series *Charters and Caldicott*,

Mel Brooks's High Anxiety, here spoofing Vertigo.

portraying the characters made famous by Basil Radford and Naunton Wayne in the original *The Lady Vanishes* (and played by Arthur Lowe and Ian Carmichael in the remake).

In fact, television producers generally seemed more willing to adapt or rework Hitch's movies. The eighties saw largely dull versions of *Dial M for Murder* (1981), *Under Capricorn* (1982), *Jamaica Inn* (1985), and *Suspicion* (1987). In the cinema, there were also two sequels to the classic *Psycho*, both based around Anthony Perkins's career-making performance as Norman Bates. Perkins even directed *Psycho 3* himself. *Psycho* also found a home on television, with the failed pilot *Bates Motel* (1987; which even Perkins declined to appear in) and *Psycho IV: The Beginning* (1990), which boasted a script by *Psycho* screenwriter Joseph Stefano.

Filmmakers seem to have felt a little more secure plundering Hitchcock's back catalogue during the past decade, although largely to little effect. However, it is worth mentioning that *Lifepod* (1993) was a fairly ingenious science fiction reworking of *Lifeboat* by Ron Silver, making his directorial debut. Decidedly less necessary were television versions of *Shadow of a Doubt* (1991), *Notorious* (1992), and *Rear Window* (1998), or the big screen remakes of *Psycho* (1998; directed by Gus Van Sant as an almost shot-for-shot recreation of the original) and *Dial M for Murder* (filmed as *A Perfect Murder* in 1998). There were also further versions of *Sabotage* (1996; released under the original novel's title, *The Secret Agent*) and *Rebecca* (as a 1997 television mini-series; there had also been a television version as early as 1947). The bottom of the barrel was finally scraped with *The Birds* sequel, *The Birds II: Land's End* (1994), which featured "Tippi" Hedren in a minor role as a shopkeeper. Director Rick Rosenthal replaced his name in the credits with the Directors' Guild pseudonym Alan Smithee.

Generally more interesting than the straight remakes were those films that drew on Hitchcock's legacy. As well as the aforementioned *Lifepod*, there was also Danny DeVito's comedy *Throw Momma From the Train* (1987; obviously inspired by *Strangers on a Train*) and Robert

Lepage's *Le Confessional* (1995), set in Quebec during the filming of *I Confess* and featuring a supporting role for Ron Burrage as Alfred Hitchcock.

Perhaps most telling is John Frankenheimer's oft-repeated quote that "any American director who says he hasn't been influenced by him is out of his mind." The notion of the Hitchcockian thriller has long been commonplace, with examples ranging from thirties films, such as *Seven Sinners* (1936) and *They Drive by Night* (1938), to more recent efforts, such as Arthur Hiller's *Silver Streak* (1976), Jonathan Demme's *Last Embrace* (1979), and Curtis Hanson's *The Bedroom Window* (1987). Numerous offerings from Claude Chabrol, Brian de Palma, and Dario Argento also owe a debt to Hitchcock's work.

Psycho and *The Birds* were both hugely influential. The box-office success of *Psycho* led to a number of similarly titled movies, like William Castle's *Homicidal* (1961) and Hammer's *Paranoiac* (1963). However, these films' plots were frequently inspired as much by Clouzot's *Les Diaboliques* (1954) as they were by Hitchcock's movie. Nevertheless, in crude terms *Psycho* could be viewed as a precursor to the "body count" slasher movies that proliferated on cinema screens in the late seventies and early eighties, following the success of *Halloween* (1978) and *Friday the 13th* (1980). During this period, no horror film seemed complete without a pointlessly jokey reference to *Psycho*'s famous shower scene. *The Birds* was also much ahead of its time, practically setting the pattern for the plethora of "nature-fights-back" movies that followed the release of *Jaws* in 1975.

But the most blatant Hitchcock tribute has to be Mel Brooks's affectionate if rather wayward spoof, *High Anxiety* (1977). Director Brooks also takes the lead role, as a psychiatrist who arrives as the new head of a sanatorium and soon finds himself involved in murder. Crammed in to the ninety-four-minute running time are gags based on *Spellbound*, *Vertigo*, *North by Northwest*, *Psycho*, and *The Birds* among others. Hitchcock took all this in good spirits, reportedly even sending Brooks a good-luck bottle of champagne during production.

THE BIRDS

First screening March 1963

Production company: Universal/Alfred Hitchcock Productions

Duration 120 minutes

Technicolor

Melanie Daniels ("Tippi" Hedren), a wealthy, shallow playgirl, meets Mitch Brenner (Rod Taylor), a young lawyer, in a San Francisco pet shop. Stung by his sarcasm, she tracks him down to Bodega Bay, bearing a pair of lovebirds as a gift for his little sister, Cathy (Veronica Cartwright). After a diving seagull gashes Melanie's forehead, she stays overnight with the local schoolteacher, Annie Hayworth (Suzanne Pleshette). Annie speaks of how Mitch's widowed mother, Lydia (Jessica Tandy), fears being abandoned when her son marries. Next day, Melanie attends Cathy's outdoor birthday party, where seagulls swoop down on the children. This is the first of many mass bird attacks, which come in waves, soon devastating the area. During one of them, Annie is killed by crows. In a nearby restaurant, an hysterical mother (Doreen Lang) accuses Melanie of somehow causing the birds' bizarre behavior. Now staying with the Brenners, Melanie's second night with them is one of terror as birds besiege the house. Melanie is attacked in a room upstairs, but is dragged free by Mitch, who realizes that she needs hospital care. Mitch orders the house evacuated, and, at dawn, birds watch from all sides as the car drives away.

"D oesn't this make you feel awful . . . keeping birds in cages?" Mitch asks Melanie in the pet shop. "We can't just let them fly around the shop," she replies, missing (or evading) his point. That point proves an important one. Both the film and its trailer remind us that birds have been caged, shot at, eaten, and otherwise abused by humans throughout recorded history. All of which illustrates the working of the world's Will, typified by human egoism and rapaciousness. Understandably, Schopenhauer (who coined the term) considered Will to be a cruel joke, best turned against itself, notably with the help of art or music. *The Birds* is an almost literal enactment of that thought. As Mitch leaves the pet shop, he says that it's time Melanie found herself "on the other end of a gag." He gets his wish—writ large. But the film's ending has little to do with misogyny and much more to do with the need for a true sympathy.

Daphne du Maurier's "The Birds" had appeared in a 1952 collection of her short stories. It wasn't the first story to describe birds turning against humans: precedents were Frank Baker's "The Birds" (1935) and Philip MacDonald's "Our Feathered Friends" (1945). But as so often with Hitchcock, the story was only a departure point. From du Maurier, the film took its vaguely apocalyptic tone (see John Wyndham's *The Day of the Triffids*

[1951]) and a few details: a remote seaside setting, the death of a neighboring farmer in his house, an explosion that starts a fire. Early on, Hitch decided to shoot the film in California rather than in du Maurier's Cornwall. He had first gotten to know the fishing village called Bodega Bay, north of San Francisco, when he was making *Shadow of a Doubt* in nearby Santa Rosa.

Novelist Evan Hunter began work on the screenplay in September 1961. Hunter's best-known novel is *Blackboard Jungle* (1954), for which he drew on his own teaching experiences; as Ed McBain,

he has written many popular detective novels. Recently, Hunter maintained that *The Birds* would have been improved if Hitchcock had allowed him to add a murder mystery. If that sounds an unlikely idea, too much of an "Americanism" imposed on an almost decorous English genre, one may note that Hitch had some unlikely ideas of his own: apparently, he wanted Cary Grant to play Mitch. And another Americanism of Hunter's was one that Hitchcock jumped at: the idea to begin the story as a screwball comedy that gradually turns into stark terror.

This, of course, was right in line with

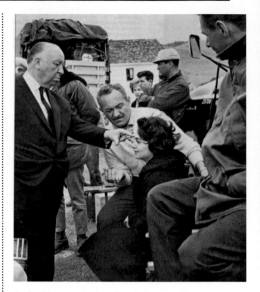

Left: *Filming in Bodega Bay. Scriptwriter Evan Hunter can be seen on the far left.*
Above: *Hitch and makeup artist Howard Smit examine Suzanne Pleshette.*
Below left: *"Tippi" Hedren's makeup tests, showing her before and after the bird attacks.*

Hitchcock's own thoughts about the dramatic curve, and story situations that get turned around. He'd begun the essentially lightweight *Young and Innocent* with a scene of high melodrama: a marital quarrel during a raging storm. Now he and Hunter mirrored that film. Ironically, neither was happy with how the story finally worked out. To *Cinefantastique* magazine, Hitchcock admitted: "I wasn't too keen on the girl's [Melanie's] story . . . But I didn't worry about it too much, because I had devised the basic shape of the film far in advance—making the birds gradu-

ally increase in number." He did more than that. Like, say, Josef von Sternberg designing *The Saga of Anatahan* (1953), he rigorously planned not just the film's overall structure but the rise and fall of each sequence, and the alternations of dialogue with action. All of this was plotted as a series of graphs on Hitchcock's office walls, to which he constantly referred.

In December, the director and his long-time collaborator Bernard Herrmann spent several weeks in West Berlin consulting with electronic sound experts

Remi Gassman and Oskar Sala. The result would be a film in which there is no conventional music score, but rather one in which natural sounds and silence are stylized to give great resonance and power. For a scene of crows waiting to attack schoolchildren, a bird's low caw sounds like a golf ball dropped on a concrete slab.

Location filming took place in Bodega Bay during March and April 1962, followed by four months in the studio. For a film of such enormous technical complexity, the shooting went very smoothly. *The Birds* contains some 1,400 shots, about twice as many as the average Hitchcock film, of which 371 were trick shots of one sort or another. Famously, the final image consists of thirty-two different pieces of film. But trick shots *weren't* used in the scene in the upstairs room—the so-called attic sequence—in which Melanie bears the full brunt of the birds' savage fury. Hitchcock's new discovery, model "Tippi" Hedren, had to endure a week of live seagulls being thrown at her from off-camera, and of being pecked at by live birds, many of which were fastened to her arms and legs with elastic bands and nylon threads. Such a drawn-out and dangerous ordeal by an actress for a movie may have had no precedent since D.W. Griffith spent weeks shooting the ice-floe

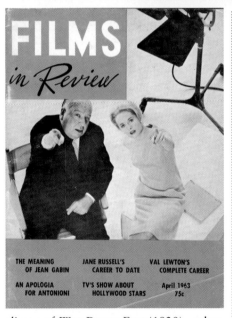

Above: Hitch and friends pose for a publicity still.
Below: Mitch (Rod Taylor) fights off the birds which are attacking the house.

Generally, though, reviewers found the film's plot nothing more than a pretext for the bird attacks, and stinted their praise even for those, feeling that the birds weren't "doing their stuff." Poor "Tippi" Hedren had to endure a fresh ordeal at the critics' hands, mainly because she wasn't Grace Kelly à la *Rear Window*. They tended to forget that Grace's early film appearances were undistinguished.

The fact is that *The Birds*, though structured rather like *North by Northwest*, has much less tractable material with which to appease an impatient viewer at the outset. In both films, a shallow person departs the city and gradually changes for the better. In Melanie's case, though, practically all that the film can do in the early scenes is score some easy points, either at her expense or at ours. (Storekeeper, doubtfully: "Did you ever *handle* an outboard boat?" Melanie, smugly: "Of course.") Hitchcock himself seems to have been unhappy with these scenes. But then something significant happened. Reportedly, as shooting progressed, Hitch began to enter into the characters in a way he'd never done before, becoming far more subjective than he had originally intended. The great scene in which the Brenners and Melanie are besieged at home by the birds was totally re-thought by him. He became more empathic—or sympathetic—towards the characters, especially

climax of *Way Down East* (1920)—when Lillian Gish was forced to request a stand-in and the latter came away with permanent injuries to one hand from frostbite.

The Birds was given a multi-million dollar publicity campaign and did reasonably well at box offices around the world. It immediately had its supporters, such as Peter Bogdanovich—who arranged for it to be screened as part of a full Hitchcock retrospective he was mounting for the Museum of Modern Art in New York. In *Film Culture*, he called the film "indescribable" and pleaded for recognition of Hitchcock as a "consummate artist."

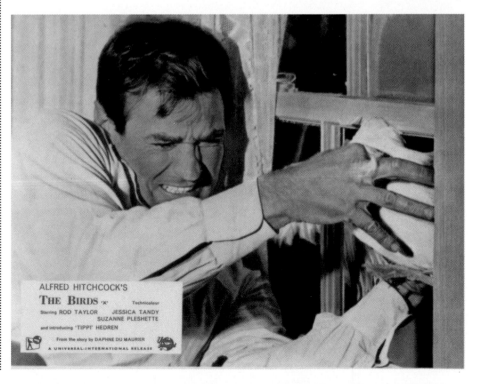

ROD TAYLOR
JESSICA TANDY
SUZANNE PLESHETTE
and introducing
'TIPPI' HEDREN
A Fascinating New Personality

Screenplay by EVAN HUNTER
Directed by ALFRED HITCHCOCK
Based on Daphne Du Maurier's
classic suspense story
A Universal Release

TECHNICOLOR

Copyright © 1963 by Universal Pictures Co., Inc.   Printed in U.S.A.

ALFRED HITCHCOCK'S
THE BIRDS 'X'   Technicolour
Starring ROD TAYLOR   JESSICA TANDY
              SUZANNE PLESHETTE
and introducing 'TIPPI' HEDREN

From the story by DAPHNE DU MAURIER
A UNIVERSAL-INTERNATIONAL RELEASE

Top: Melanie ("Tippi" Hedren) is trapped in the attic. Live birds were used for this scene, which took a week to shoot, causing Hedren considerable discomfort.
Above: The attack on the school children.
Left: Bird masks were given away to theater-goers.

Melanie. It was as if Hitch had arrived at a more profound understanding, where beyond individual problems, but incorporating them, is seen a *universal* condition. Hitchcock's favorite painter, Paul Klee (1879–1940), had called such an understanding "that Romanticism which is one with the universe."

Actually, there *are* precedents in Hitchcock's films for this sort of understanding. To the extent that it involves a recognition of universal suffering, its most apt statement is *Vertigo*. (The Mission Dolores is particularly well-named in such a context: see the house called "Minyago Yugilla" "Why weepest thou?" in *Under Capricorn*.) However, in *The Birds*, Hitchcock effectively confronts us with the Will that causes the suffering. Schopenhauer characterized the Will as ultimate reality, not finally knowable, and the *blind* cause of suffering in the world. Allusions to blindness are everywhere in *The Birds* (e.g., the game of blindman's buff at the children's party; the farmer whose eyes are pecked out), and this is doubly appropriate, given both our own inability to know ultimate reality and the blind way in which that reality, Will, operates. The birds effectively symbolize the Will.

Naturally, as in *Vertigo*, there is a phallic aspect to the film's symbolism (the bird attacks begin when Melanie and Mitch first approach each other near the Tides Bar), but other associations soon accrue. Thus Lydia's initial hostility towards Melanie, as well as her fear of being abandoned, are both also represented by the bird attacks. Yet *all* of these meanings are subsumed in the notion of *Will*. This is one of the film's great insights. Crudely stated, the truth of the matter is that "it's all One," and to those who can grasp it (the Hindus speak of penetrating the veil of *maya* or illusion), a bond of common sympathy is possible. It is no accident that we hear Lydia say of Melanie at the end, "Poor thing!" (Midge says the same phrase in *Vertigo* after hearing the sad story of Carlotta Valdes.) Nor is it likely that the title of Hitchcock's next-but-one film, *Torn Curtain*, refers to just political matters . . .

To sum up: Hitchcock's statement about *The Birds*, that it shows how "catastrophe surrounds us all," is something that Schopenhauer taught as basic. The latter, still the only major philosopher to combine Western and Eastern outlooks,

The birds is coming!

further taught that catastrophe and suffering are the result of the working of Will. He defined situations of suffering very broadly—as everything from natural disasters to boredom—and developed an "ethics of sympathy" to oppose their terrible consequences. The only positive result of suffering may be the lesson it teaches about our common humanity, a lesson strongly emphasized in *The Birds*, which is a film far more profound in this respect than, say, *Saboteur*, if not *Lifeboat*. (Melanie Daniels is like a composite of *Lifeboat*'s Constance Porter and Iris Henderson from *The Lady Vanishes*, two other chastened heroines.) The sheer business of living may make us complacent about our true situation, and we may become indifferent and cruel. But at such times art can come to our rescue, and a film like *The Birds* is a masterly example of a work that offers to do that.

THE CHILDREN'S SONG

As Melanie smokes a cigarette in the school yard while waiting to collect Cathy, crows gather like a storm cloud on the climbing frame behind her. Meanwhile, the children sing a roundelay-type song whose words are at once sad and a warning: "She combed her hair but once a year/Ristle-tee, rostle-tee, now, now, now./With every stroke she shed a tear." The effect recalls the "Storm Cloud Cantata" scene in *The Man Who Knew Too Much* (either version), in which a musical *divertissement* threatens to dissolve at any moment into terror. Teasingly, it keeps sounding as if about to end, then continues. The song in *The Birds* was chosen by Evan Hunter, whose own children were fond of singing it. Its role in the film anticipates *Marnie*'s use of a children's skipping rhyme about illness. Essentially, the scene is one of Nature versus Art, or atavism versus civilization. The song's note of sadness is underlined by the scene's chill wind that buffets Melanie as she smokes. The same chill wind blows through all of Hitchcock's films from *Psycho* to *Torn Curtain*.

MARNIE

First Screening June 1964

Production company:
Universal/Geoffrey Stanley, Inc.

Duration 130 minutes

Technicolor

Marnie Edgar ("Tippi" Hedren) is a fly-by-night thief and a loner. As "Mary Taylor" she obtains clerical work with a Philadelphia publishing company owned by Mark Rutland (Sean Connery), a young widower. Sensing a resemblance between this auburn-haired woman and a brunette who had earlier robbed the company's accountant, Sidney Strutt (Martin Gabel), he keeps an interested eye on her. When Marnie empties the Rutland safe and disappears, he tracks her to a riding stables in Maryland, then virtually blackmails her into marrying him. But the resulting shipboard honeymoon proves disastrous as Marnie is both deeply disturbed and frigid; she attempts suicide. Later, back in Philadelphia, Mark's sister-in-law Lil Mainwaring (Diane Baker) does some snooping, informing Mark that Marnie's mother is still alive, and lives in Baltimore. After Marnie's beloved horse, Forio, is killed in a fall, Marnie is desolate. She again attempts to rob the Rutland safe, but is powerless. Mark now takes her to her mother's. Bernice Edgar (Louise Latham) reveals that as a young child Marnie had killed a sailor (Bruce Dern) to protect Bernice, a prostitute. All of Marnie's strange behavior, and criminality, have stemmed from this forgotten incident.

The fox hunt scene in *Marnie* is a *tour de force* of integrated music and camerawork (including a stunning helicopter shot), but it also serves as both a symbol of the ambivalent life force and a metaphor of Marnie's life so far. At another level, the scene works in complex ways towards bringing about Marnie's "cure." Thus it typifies a film that is richer and more innovative than many commentators have allowed. Importantly, *Marnie* continues the subjectivity of *The Birds*, and reveals depths of sympathy that make it a worthy successor to that film.

Sympathy, though, has its dangers, and Hitchcock reportedly didn't manage to avoid some of them when making *Marnie*. The project, an adaptation of Winston Graham's 1961 novel set in the

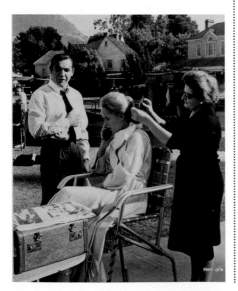

Above: *Mark (Sean Connery) confronts Marnie ("Tippi" Hedren).*
Left: *Connery and Hedren on location. "I wasn't convinced Sean Connery was a Philadelphian gentleman . . . you need . . . a more elegant man than what we had," Hitch later told Truffaut.*

English midlands, was one with which the director had hoped to tempt Grace Kelly out of retirement. Now he reactivated it as a vehicle for "Tippi" Hedren, and first asked Evan Hunter to write the screenplay. However, in April 1963, the two men fell out over the honeymoon sequence in which Marnie is raped by Mark, to which Hunter had objected. So Hitchcock sacked him and recruited Jay

Presson Allen, who had recently adapted for the stage Muriel Spark's remarkable *The Prime of Miss Jean Brodie* (1961), about a blinkered Edinburgh schoolteacher. This astute piece of writer-casting by Hitchcock should have worked out even more successfully than it did.

What happened was that the director had himself become blinkered: at age sixty-four, he was infatuated with "Tippi"

Above: Hitchcock in discussion with Hedren, as Diane Baker and Sean Connery look on. Conversation between director and star later stopped altogether.
Below: Marnie, disguised in her black wig.

would speak to the other, and they communicated by means of third parties: "Would you ask Miss Hedren to . . . ?" "Would you tell Mr. Hitchcock . . . ?"

Spoto also reports that hereafter "Hitchcock seemed to want *Marnie* to fail," and that many of the film's more visually jarring moments show "the director's cavalier disinterest in the final product." But this claim, too, needs to be considered in context. The screenplay of the film *already* contained deliberately jarring elements, like the sudden flooding of the screen with red, or Mark's no-nonsense line, "Let's back up and turn that Mount Everest of manure into a few facts." (Likewise, Bernard Herrmann's score, added after the film's shooting, is full of wild leaps and falls.) Also, some of the things that Spoto mentions, like the oppressively looming ship at the end of Mrs. Edgar's street early in the film, *are* clearly expressionistic, badly painted or not. The whole film is a portrait of Marnie, as discussed below. Hitchcock's very moodiness during production reflects the extreme subjectivity involved, even perhaps to the extent that he developed a "death wish" (in the Freudian sense) like that of Marnie during much of the film.

What is undeniable is that the film flopped with audiences and most reviewers. A lone New York journalist wrote that *Marnie* has "a human warmth and sympathy that makes it Hitchcock's most appealing film since *Rear Window*," and

Hedren. To cinematographer Robert Burks (tragically killed in a house fire shortly after the film's completion), he gave instructions to photograph a kiss between Hedren and Connery in an extreme close-up which has been called "virtually pornographic"—though zoological might be fairer, given a theme of the film. Then, in late February 1964, after the day's work was over, Hedren and Hitchcock were briefly alone together in the actress's caravan; here, according to Donald Spoto, the director propositioned her. For the rest of the picture, neither

called it "an altogether superior film." His view was not widely shared. "With this film," notes Spoto, "Alfred Hitchcock fell from public grace."

But if the passing of years has shown *Vertigo* to be a masterpiece, then *Marnie* may yet receive comparable acclaim (and there are signs that it is starting to happen): the two films mirror each other in all kinds of ways, but basically both are perfect projections of their respective subjects. *Vertigo*, of course, has a *formal* perfection, befitting its heroine who represents the eternal female, a sort of Platonic ideal of womanhood. But the heroine of *Marnie* represents, on the contrary, all that patriarchal society is afraid of and finds unacceptable in womanhood—what Julia Kristeva famously calls "the abject"—and the form of the film is accordingly jarring and, at times, confronting. It's no accident that Strutt speaks of Marnie as a witch, the epitome of hated womanhood in history. And here's just one example of how *Marnie* has been misunderstood. Bernard Herrmann's biographer, Steven C. Smith, in an otherwise fine book, criticizes the *Marnie* score's excessive repetition of its main theme, associated with Marnie herself. But Marnie, remember, has been banished to the realm of the abject, and feels imprisoned there—riding Forio is her one release. So the repetitive score, like Marnie's recurring nightmares, is *perfectly* in keeping.

At one point in the film, Mark half-quotes a line about duty from one of Emerson's "Voluntaries" (much as Marion in *Psycho* half-quotes a line from Milton's "On His Blindness"). Lil is quick to tell him that he has in fact misquoted. The full passage in Emerson is famous because of these lines: "So nigh is grandeur to our dust,/ So near is God to man." A viewer of *Marnie* who has been moved by its heroine's afflictions, and by its haunting extreme long shots (balancing the extreme close-ups), may feel that Hitchcock is trying to tell us something here. The film is one of Hitchcock's strangest, but also (for its admirers) one of his most special.

By the mid-sixties, MCA/Universal, with whom Hitchcock had signed his most exclusive contract, was beginning to interfere in an annoying, corporate way. Hitch began to be second-guessed, as what were once suggestions from Lew Wasserman now became instructions carried out by his second and third level executives.

Hitchcock had conceived the story for his fiftieth solo feature film, *Torn Curtain*, from which Brian Moore wrote a good script. In fact, reading the screenplay, it is easy to understand how Peggy Robertson could enthuse to Bernard Herrmann that *Torn Curtain* would be Hitch's finest film. But "they" (as Hitch would refer to the MCA/Universal executives) wanted both stars and a pop, jazzy film score. Hitchcock lost the battle over the former, rather uncomfortably taking on Paul Newman and Julie Andrews. However, he fought to retain the services of his friend Herrmann, promising that the composer could write a more contemporary score. Although Herrmann agreed to this, it was not what he delivered. Hitchcock fired him on the spot, apologizing to the very executives against whom he had previously backed Herrmann.

Film critics and audiences alike universally disliked the film that was intended as a celebratory fiftieth classic. The failure of *Marnie* and *Torn Curtain* placed the once powerful director in an awkward position with the studio. Associates described Hitchcock as desperate. Each project that Hitch developed fell apart. After MCA/Universal rejected *Frenzy*, which

Here's to the next half-century, Hitch!

Technicolor®

TECHNICOLOR LIMITED, BATH ROAD, HARMONDSWORTH, WEST DRAYTON, MIDDX   SKYPORT 0422

Above: *Technicolor celebrates Hitch's fiftieth picture,* Torn Curtain.
Left: *Princess Margaret visits Paul Newman and Hitchcock on the set of* Torn Curtain.

Hitch had nurtured through 1967 and into the winter of 1968, he eventually let Wasserman suggest something for him to work on.

Universal had acquired *Topaz*, Leon Uris's bestselling novel based on a real-life spy scandal, and the studio's contract with the author allowed him to write his own first draft. With the production schedule already pressing, Hitch realized that much of what Uris had penned was unusable. In a panic, he brought in Samuel Taylor (who had written *Vertigo*)

Top left: Hitchcock poses for the cameras while filming Frenzy.
Top center and right: Hitch in the sixties.
Above: Back in London shooting Frenzy, with the River Thames in the background.
Left: Sheet music for the disappointing Torn Curtain.

to work on the screenplay, but this was completed only after production had commenced, a situation the director loathed.

There were problems with *Topaz*'s ending and the audience at the first preview, which Hitchcock attended, hated the film. The effect was devastating, with studio insiders claiming it was the worst preview reaction to a film they could remember. In truth, the preview cards are not that disastrous, but the audience nevertheless found the film tedious, the actors lackluster and the whole enterprise curiously lacking in anything Hitchcockian.

Some cards identified the few excellent elements—the Harlem hotel sequence and the Cuban scenes—but most gave the same reaction as the critics and the public did upon release: *Topaz* was Hitchcock at his worst. The director couldn't agree more.

From 1968 until 1971, Hitchcock came the closest in his career to semi-retirement. In 1968 he sold the *Psycho* rights to MCA/Universal, which, along with an earlier sale of his television series to the company, gave him a significant share of their stock. Some estimates calculated Hitch to be the third largest stock-

holder at the time, and the transaction ensured that he had considerably more clout, particularly useful after the box-office decline which commenced with *Marnie*.

In 1968, the Academy of Motion Picture Arts and Sciences presented Hitchcock with an honorary Oscar, the Irving G. Thalberg Award for "the most consistent high level of production achievement by an individual producer." He had been nominated for the Best Direction Oscar five times before, without ever winning. Considering the turmoil in his professional life, Hitch may have felt

Above left: *Hitchcock (seen here with Jeanne Moreau) received many awrds and tributes toward the end of his life.*
Above right: *Ever the self-publicist, Hitch poses with his dog, Sarah.*
Far left: *With admirer, interviewer, and fellow director François Truffaut.*
Left: *Hitch celebrates his birthday with Alma.*

that the award was timed with bitter irony. He gave the shortest Oscar acceptance speech in history. He slowly walked to the microphone, looked out at the audience, said, "Thank you," and left the stage.

Although it is perhaps Hitchcock's darkest film, and certainly his darkest comedy, *Frenzy* was something of a comeback for the director. Its release in 1972 was heralded as such, and suddenly critics and film organizations began to wake up to the Master. For instance, he received honorary degrees from the University of California and Columbia University, and in 1974 the Film Society of Lincoln Center in New York honored him with a star-studded tribute.

Hitch's own health was now requiring constant maintenance. A pacemaker was installed, which the director loved to show off to visiting journalists. The tiny machine inside such a large man was routinely put in sync via the telephone by his doctors. In his mid-seventies, Hitch was finally slowing down.

Hitchcock settled on an adaptation of Victor Canning's 1972 novel *The Rainbird Pattern* for his next project. Compared with *Frenzy*, *Family Plot* was a charmer, although many critics could sense the end (and indeed, the film has not held up well over the years). Hitchcock had been right in an assertion he had made back in 1967—the cinematic world had moved beyond his kind of filmmaking. After completing *Family Plot*, Hitch continued to show up at his office to work on projects. The screenplay which occupied most of his time, entitled *The Short Night*, was based on the story of the British spy George Blake.

Another tribute, this time the Life Achievement Award from the American Film Institute, had the air of a farewell party, which it in fact turned out to be. Cary Grant, Ingrid Bergman, James Stewart, and many of the remaining great stars from Hitchcock's career attended. But Hitch seemed frail, and Alma appeared even more so (she had recently suffered a second stroke). The world had seen a snapshot of what friends and

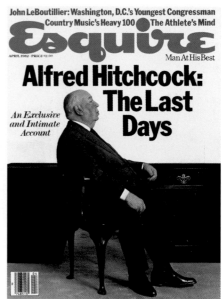

Above: *Publicity for his final film,* Family Plot.
Above right: Esquire *commemorates the end of a filmmaking era. The issue featured an in-depth article by David Freeman, who worked with Hitchcock on* The Short Night.

co-workers knew: Hitch was on the wane, and there would never be another Hitchcock film.

Following the death in May 1979 of longtime friend and associate Victor Saville, a fellow director whom he had known since his earliest days in the film industry, Hitchcock decided it was time to officially close his production office at Universal. He returned occasionally to work with temporary secretaries on personal correspondence and some script revisions, but by the winter of 1979 Hitch

remained at his home on Bellagio Road in Bel Air.

At the start of 1980, the announcement came that Hitchcock was to receive a knighthood from Queen Elizabeth II. With Hitch unable to make the trip back to London for the occasion, the ceremony was conducted by a British emissary on a Universal soundstage in a mock office. It was the final recognition and fittingly came from his home country, the source of all that made Hitchcock unique.

On April 28, 1980, the director grew

weaker and doctors were summoned. Then, just after nine the next morning, the great director died quietly in his sleep. The inevitable front-page news stories followed, with banner headlines announcing the end of the "Master of Suspense." Film historians and select filmmakers knew that his death was actually the end of something more vital than just the man. Jean-Luc Godard proclaimed that with Hitchcock, cinema as we knew it had died. Alma Reville Hitchcock died two years later, on July 6, 1982.

Since 1980, Hitchcock's fame has remained undiminished. John Russell Taylor's and Donald Spoto's biographies are still in print, along with numerous academic works and popular celebrations. Critical work on his films exploded, and in 1984 the core Paramount films, now owned by the Hitchcock estate and distributed by Universal Studios, were rereleased, increasing public and critical interest in his movies still further.

In 1996, the film once trounced by *Time* magazine as just another "Hitchcock and bull story" was restored and rereleased to an even larger and more appreciative audience. Indeed, the acceptance of *Vertigo* as Hitchcock's masterpiece (as Saul Bass's poster design had promised in 1958) is symbolic of the entire reassessment of Hitch's career since his death. His position in cinema history is now unassailable.

Dan Auiler

TORN CURTAIN

First Screening July 1966

Production company Universal

Duration 128 minutes

Technicolor

American nuclear scientist Professor Michael Armstrong (Paul Newman) travels with his assistant and fiancée Sarah Sherman (Julie Andrews) to a physics congress in Copenhagen, then flies to East Germany where he announces that he is defecting to the Communists. A stunned Sarah loyally follows him, but Michael withholds from her that he is actually working for the Americans and that he intends picking the brain of a fellow scientist, Professor Lindt (Ludwig Donath), in Leipzig. Meanwhile, when his East German "minder," Herrmann Gromek (Wolfgang Kieling), detects Michael contacting an American underground group known as "Pi" at a farm outside Berlin, Michael is forced to kill him. In Leipzig, Michael finally tells Sarah the true situation, then tricks the elderly Lindt into revealing the crucial formula. As the security police, alerted to Gromek's death, prepare to arrest Michael, he and Sarah flee back to East Berlin on a bus run by Pi. A chance encounter in the street with a Countess Kuchinska (Lila Kedrova) then puts Michael and Sarah in touch with other Pi workers, who arrange for the pair to be smuggled out of Germany by boat in costume baskets belonging to a Czech ballet company bound for Sweden.

Hitchcock's sympathy for suffering humanity is most pronounced in the group of films from *The Birds* to *Topaz*, and is basic to *Torn Curtain*. In that film in particular the sympathy is analyzed, not taken for granted. The character of the vain, egotistical ballerina (Tamara Toumanova) represents an aspect of Michael himself, who undergoes a learning experience during the film. If *Torn Curtain* disappoints as a thriller, much else about it is admirable.

Hitchcock, of course, knew Berlin from his UFA days, and had been back there several times. Nonetheless, early in the preparation of *Torn Curtain*, he made a point of visiting all of the locales that would be seen in the film. From Copenhagen he took a Rumanian plane to East Berlin, then travelled to Leipzig, returned to East Berlin, and finally took a boat to Trelleborg in Sweden. He'd originally thought of setting the film in Poland. A sign of that intention is the film's scatterbrained Polish countess, dispossessed of her property, who helps Michael and Sarah in East Berlin by taking them to the Friedrichstrasse post office. In Richard Wormser's novel of the film, based on Brian Moore's screenplay, the Countess says, "I am an old woman. But there is *la vie* left in me. Lots of *la vie*." The film suggests as much by giving her a colorful scarf. By contrast, the East Berlin scenes are generally drab, with just occasional ironic touches of color. To further ensure a degree of authenticity in the film's settings, Hitchcock employed German production designer Hein Heckroth, whose

Hitch with Paul Newman. The director found Newman's method acting difficult to get along with.

most famous work, interestingly enough, had been done in England on Powell and Pressburger's *The Red Shoes* (1948).

There's an actual echo of *The Red Shoes* in the scene where the ballerina several times freezes in mid-pirouette and glares into the auditorium. Her vindictiveness towards Michael and Sarah, whom she sees there, parodies the political hostility that is the film's basis— and effectively mocks it. Hitchcock originally had every intention of giving *Torn Curtain* a downbeat note. He saw, like Carl Jung writing in 1964,

Top left: *Jacobi (David Opatoshu), Sarah (Julie Andrews), and Michael (Paul Newman). Hitch was searching for "a photographic style that would help us tell the story in a more realistic, not so 'glossy' way."*
Top right: *Hitch with Julie Andrews.*
Above: *The* Torn Curtain *press book.*
Above right: *The lengthy death scene, as Michael and the farmer's wife (Carolyn Conwell) kill Gromek (Wolfgang Kieling). "I thought it was time to show that it was very difficult, very painful, and it takes a very long time to kill a man."*

that the world had become "dissociated like a neurotic, with the Iron Curtain marking the symbolic line of division," and that the human cost was high. Accordingly, he had wanted to end the film with a scene where Michael, having arrived in Trelleborg, burns Lindt's formula in the fire. But finally he bowed to commercial pressures. The film, which cost $6,000,000, was one he later described as "filled with compromises."

Filming began in November 1965, of a screenplay only marginally tightened after Hitchcock had brought in Keith Waterhouse and Willis Hall—the English playwrights and screenwriters of *Billy Liar* (filmed in 1963)—to polish the dialogue. Nor, this time, or ever again, would

a Hitchcock film have a score by Bernard Herrmann. The famous break-up of the director and his best composer occurred at the end of March 1966, precisely because Herrmann had *not* compromised and given Hitchcock what he had asked for, a more popular score. Herrmann was promptly replaced by John Addison (Academy Award-winner for *Tom Jones* [1963]), who did an excellent job in the circumstances. The film received mixed reviews. A fair assessment came from veteran British reviewer Richard Mallett in *Punch*: "The film as a whole may be a bit diffuse . . . but it has some brilliant scenes, it's pleasing to the eye, and it is *continuously* entertaining." At the box office, *Torn Curtain* did well. It generated more

American rental income (approximately $7,000,000) for its distributor, MCA/Universal, than any of Hitchcock's other post-*Psycho* films.

What Mallett calls diffuse about the film seems to have been at least partly intentional. Scene after scene is built on a *stretching* of time, a deliberate drawing-out, sometimes accompanied by actual straining and striving by the characters. (However, for the bus sequence, Hitchcock was forced to *compress* events while still trying "to create the illusion of a long journey," as he told Truffaut). When, over drinks, Michael poses Lindt a leading question about his work, the German seems to take an eternity before finally answering with a chuckle. But that is nothing compared to the scene at a faculty interrogation in which Sarah is asked to answer questions about Michael's research. The camera holds on her for fully thirty seconds before she responds, "I have nothing to say." Likewise, the film's most famous scene, at the farm, was said by Hitchcock to show that "it takes a very long time to kill a man."

All of this seems related to the idea that people are basically alike, one human community. The film begins with what may be the best title sequence in all of Hitchcock. It defies short analysis, but essentially what we see is a flame burning fiercely on the left of screen, representing the sun, the life force. Meanwhile, on the right, a succession of people struggle to avoid being smothered by a swirling gray mist. Two hours later, the film ends with a *wholly* grey screen. The image is that of the blanket behind which Michael and Sarah huddle for warmth after their escape. But the general message is clearly pessimistic, and will be elaborated in *Topaz.*

THE SHORT STORY ANTHOLOGIES

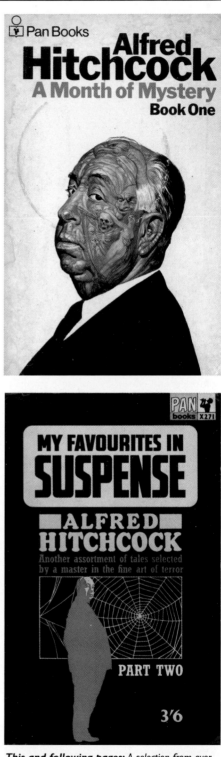

In 1957, publishers Simon and Schuster approached Hitch, an avid reader of horror and suspense tales, about compiling a book of short stories to be "branded" with the title of his popular television series, *Alfred Hitchcock Presents*. Their proposal was accepted, and over 100 "Hitchcock titles" followed during the next forty years.

The deal with Simon and Schuster followed a similar arrangement that Hitch had made in 1955 with businessman Richard E. Decker, for the *Alfred Hitchcock Mystery Magazine* (still running into the 1990s!). The first book was a collection of twenty-five short stories, entitled *Alfred Hitchcock Presents: Stories They Wouldn't Let Me Do on TV*. Published in hardcover, it was a tremendous success. The collection featured short stories by Robert S. Hichens ("How Love Came to Professor Guildea"), Ray Bradbury ("The October Game"), Richard Connell ("The Most Dangerous Game") and M. R. James ("Casting the Runes"). Surprisingly, two of the stories *were* later dramatized for his television series: A. M. Burrage's "The Waxwork" and Robert Arthur's "The Jokester."

Alfred Hitchcock himself wrote the introduction. "Being what is probably one of the most obtrusive producers on television has spoiled me. I cannot conceive of giving people stories without adding my own comments. The publishers of this book, being far wiser than my television sponsors, have limited my interference to this short preface . . . This particular selection of tales is primarily aimed at those of you who find television too bland. You may not care for some of these stories because you think them too shocking, macabre, or grotesque, but I am confident that you will not find any of them bland or dull. The reason why some of these stories cannot be produced on the home screen will be obvious on reading."

The success of *Stories They Wouldn't Let Me Do on TV* attracted interest from other publishers and both Random House and Dell acquired the rights to Hitchcock's name. Contrary to popular

This and following pages: A selection from over 100 books featuring Hitchcock's name, including a condensed reprint of the first title, Stories They Wouldn't Let Me Do on TV.

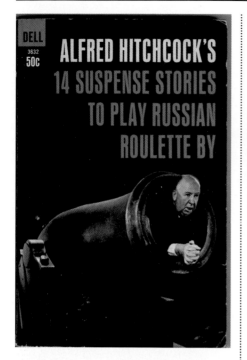

belief, the majority of these titles were compiled and edited by in-house publishing staff, who also wrote the introductions. Only a handful of books featured introductions actually supplied by Hitch, although he was always credited—and would duly receive the royalty checks. As an interesting aside, for one collection, an editor at Dell made the mistake of mentioning how Hitchcock was driving down the road one day and came upon a queer sort of situation. Of course, Hitch pub-

licly claimed to never drive a vehicle, because of his fear of being stopped by the police!

Among the titles resulting from the Random House/Dell deal was *Alfred Hitchcock Presents: Stories For Late at Night*, which was first published, as a light blue hardcover, in 1961, with Hitchcock once again choosing the stories. These proved popular enough for the title to be reprinted a number of times over the years (going through at least nine more editions), sometimes containing as few as half of the same stories, reissued either in a smaller format or in paperback rather than hardcover. The stories selected for this volume include: "It's a Good Life" by Jerome Bixby, "The Whole Town's Sleeping" by Ray Bradbury, "Evening Primrose" by John Collier, "The Fly" by George Langelaan (previously filmed in 1958 with Vincent Price), and "The Man Who Liked Dickens" by Evelyn Waugh.

In January 1962, after his anthologies had proven successful, Dell asked Hitchcock to compile and edit another book. "A collection of stories of suspense which I edited for Dell Books having proved a success," Hitchcock recalled, "the publishers asked me to bring together a group of tales which I admire because of their skilful handling of the element of terror." This second Dell title was *Alfred*

Hitchcock Presents: Bar the Doors. Selling on the bookstands for fifty cents, this 192-page collection featured thirteen tales, including "Pollock and the Porroh Man" by H. G. Wells, "Moonlight Sonata" by Alexander Woollcott, "The Damned Thing" by Ambrose Bierce, and "The Corpse at the Table" by Samuel Hopkins Adams.

By the mid-sixties, Dell had become the primary publisher of Hitchcock

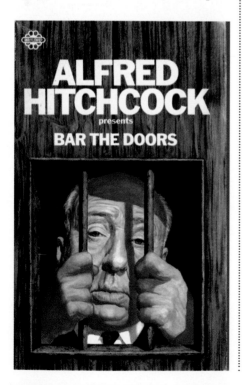

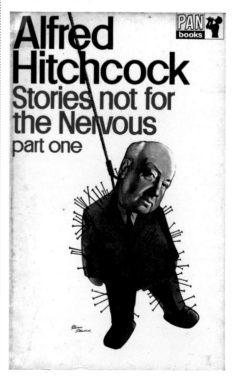

anthologies, with Random House occasionally putting out a hardcover edition. In fact, Dell's sixty-five to seventy-five-cent paperbacks were compiled and released at the rate of one per month for many years! Soon after the end of the television series, "Alfred Hitchcock Presents" was dropped from the books' titles and they simply became "Alfred Hitchcock's . . . "

Hitchcock's appeal was such that his anthologies were not just limited to adults. Calmer tales were compiled for children, with Random House publishing a number of large hardcover anthologies, including *Alfred Hitchcock's Monster Museum*, *Alfred Hitchcock's Haunted Houseful*, *Alfred Hitchcock's Sinister Spies*, *Alfred Hitchcock's Ghostly Gallery*, and so on. *Boy's Life Magazine* excitedly reviewed *Ghostly Gallery* as "These are cool creepies from the master of the wacky ghastly. . . . Some of the greatest storytellers present their best ghosts in this volume: Robert Louis Stevenson, H. G. Wells, Lord Dunsany."

In 1963, *Alfred Hitchcock's Solve-Them-Yourself Mysteries* appeared on the bookshelves, featuring five short mysteries which allowed the reader to figure out the solutions before the last page. A couple of years later, another line of children's books using the Hitchcock name was launched—*Alfred Hitchcock and the Three Investigators*. First published by Random House at the rate of two per year, all in hardcover, there were eventually as many as eighteen books in this series. Each had its own subtitle, for example *The Secret of Skeleton Island*, *The Mystery of the Screaming Clock*, and *The Secret of Terror Castle*. The *Three Investigators* adventures have since gone through numerous printings by various publishers, both in hardcover and paperback. Winward Silverback Editions began a paperback printing in October 1972, and Scholastic Publishers reprinted the series during the early 1980s.

There are now over 100 editions of these Hitchcock-related titles, many of which have become valuable collectors' items. Even Hitchcock's death didn't stop new books being published; for example, *Alfred Hitchcock's Tales to Make Your Hair Stand on End* appeared from Davis Publications in 1981, complete with an introduction "written by Alfred Hitchcock."
Martin Grams Jr.

THE SHORT STORY ANTHOLOGIES

From over 100 editions, here is an A–Z selection of some of the memorable titles published:

Alfred Hitchcock and the Three Investigators (series)
Alfred Hitchcock: I Want My Mummy
Alfred Hitchcock: Murders I Fell in Love With
Alfred Hitchcock Presents: A Hangman's Dozen
Alfred Hitchcock Presents: Bar the Doors
Alfred Hitchcock Presents: Death Can Be Beautiful
Alfred Hitchcock Presents: Don't Look a Gift Shark in the Mouth
Alfred Hitchcock Presents: Games Killers Play
Alfred Hitchcock Presents: I Am Curious, Bloody
Alfred Hitchcock Presents: More of My Favorites in Suspense
Alfred Hitchcock Presents: More Stories My Mother Never Told Me
Alfred Hitchcock Presents: More Stories Not for the Nervous
Alfred Hitchcock Presents: More Stories to be Read with the Lights On
Alfred Hitchcock Presents: My Favorites in Suspense
Alfred Hitchcock Presents: Rolling Gravestones
Alfred Hitchcock Presents: Scream Along With Me
Alfred Hitchcock Presents: Sixteen Skeletons From My Closet
Alfred Hitchcock Presents: Stories for Late at Night
Alfred Hitchcock Presents: Stories My Mother Never Told Me
Alfred Hitchcock Presents: Stories Not for the Nervous
Alfred Hitchcock Presents: Stories They Wouldn't Let Me Do on TV
Alfred Hitchcock Presents: Stories to Be Read With the Door Locked
Alfred Hitchcock Presents: Stories to Be Read With the Lights On
Alfred Hitchcock Presents: Terror Time
Alfred Hitchcock Presents: The Master's Choice
Alfred Hitchcock Presents: This One Will Kill You
Alfred Hitchcock Presents: 12 Stories for Late at Night
Alfred Hitchcock's A Baker's Dozen of Suspense Stories
Alfred Hitchcock's A Hearse of a Different Color

Alfred Hitchcock's A Month of Mystery
Alfred Hitchcock's Anti–Social Register
Alfred Hitchcock's Bleeding Hearts
Alfred Hitchcock's Boys and Ghouls Together
Alfred Hitchcock's Breaking the Scream Barrier
Alfred Hitchcock's Dates With Death
Alfred Hitchcock's Death Bag
Alfred Hitchcock's Death-Mate
Alfred Hitchcock's Down by the Old Bloodstream
Alfred Hitchcock's 14 Suspense Stories to Play Russian Roulette By
Alfred Hitchcock's Get Me to the Wake on Time
Alfred Hitchcock's Ghostly Gallery
Alfred Hitchcock's Happiness Is a Warm Corpse
Alfred Hitchcock's Happy Deathday
Alfred Hitchcock's Hard Day at the Scaffold
Alfred Hitchcock's Haunted Houseful
Alfred Hitchcock's Having a Wonderful Crime
Alfred Hitchcock's Let It All Bleed Out
Alfred Hitchcock's Monster Museum
Alfred Hitchcock's More Stories to Stay Awake By
Alfred Hitchcock's Murder Racquet
Alfred Hitchcock's Murderer's Row
Alfred Hitchcock's Murder-Go-Round
Alfred Hitchcock's Murders on the Half-Skull
Alfred Hitchcock's Noose Report
Alfred Hitchcock's Once Upon a Dreadful Time
Alfred Hitchcock's Sinister Spies
Alfred Hitchcock's Skull Session
Alfred Hitchcock's Slay Ride
Alfred Hitchcock's Solve-Them-Yourself Mysteries (series)
Alfred Hitchcock's Speak of the Devil
Alfred Hitchcock's Stories to Stay Awake By
Alfred Hitchcock's Tales to Be Read With Caution
Alfred Hitchcock's Tales to Make Your Hair Stand on End
Alfred Hitchcock's The Best of Friends
Alfred Hitchcock's Witches' Brew

(Anthology information compiled by Martin Grams Jr., author of the forthcoming *The Alfred Hitchcock Presents Companion*.)

T O P A Z

First screening December 1969

Production company: Universal

Duration 126 minutes

Technicolor

In Copenhagen, just months before the Cuban missile crisis, a high Russian official, Boris Kusenov (Per-Axel Arosenius), defects with his family to the Americans. In Washington, D.C., intelligence expert Michael Nordstrom (John Forsythe), concerned at Kusenov's reports, asks local French agent André Devereaux (Frederick Stafford) to question some Cubans as a favor. André ends up going to Cuba himself. His wife Nicole (Dany Robin) is upset, not least because she knows that his contact there is actually his mistress, Juanita de Cordoba (Karin Dor), widow of a hero of Castro's revolution. Though André obtains the required information, it costs several lives, including that of Juanita, shot by the Cuban military leader Rico Parra (John Vernon). Back in Washington, André finds that Nicole has returned to Paris. He himself receives instructions to go to Paris to explain his recent actions. Michael cautions him: according to Kusenov, Russian spies, collectively called "Topaz," have infiltrated top levels of the French government. In Paris, André unmasks the master spy, Jacques Granville (Michel Piccoli), an old family friend—and currently Nicole's lover. Granville shoots himself.

Hitch surrounded by the cast: Claude Jade, John Forsythe, Frederick Stafford, and Dany Robin.

Topaz was written and filmed in haste, and parts do look more like a work-in-progress. But it is deeply intelligent. Its most ironic line may be Michael's expression of thanks to André after the latter's return from Cuba. "What you found out," Michael says, "confirms our information from other sources, including the U-2 photos." In its emphasis on the human cost of divisive politics, *Topaz* is a follow-up to *Torn Curtain*. In some ways it is more down-to-earth and penetrating than the earlier film.

After Leon Uris published his novel called *Topaz* in 1967—the same year that "Kim" Philby told in detail how he had spied for Russia from within British intelligence—a reviewer in *Life* magazine asked what Mr. Uris had been smoking when he wrote it. Just weeks later, the same magazine featured a story by Phillippe de Vosjoli, former chief of French intelligence in America, that effectively showed the novel was based on fact. The article concerned the penetration of De Gaulle's government by Russian spies as described by a top KGB official who had defected to America in 1961. Universal bought the film rights to the novel and hired its author to write the screenplay. They then asked Hitchcock to direct. But Hitchcock at the last minute threw out the Uris screenplay, and urgently summoned Samuel Taylor, who had written *Vertigo*, to produce a rewrite from scratch.

By this time the director was already in London picking his European locations and beginning casting. Many of the cast were French, including leading lady Dany Robin, who had begun her film career in René Clair's *Le Silence est d'Or* (1947). Hitchcock seems to have compared her character to the neglected wife played by Ann Todd in *The Paradine Case*, providing her with some identical mannerisms. One of *Topaz*'s definitive performances is given by Swedish actor Per-Axel Arosenius as the irritable Boris Kusenov. If Kusenov defects out of conscience, as an introductory title says, he still finds it

Top: In discussion with Herbert Coleman. Despite being unhappy with the finished film, Hitchcock won the National Board of Review Award for Best Director with Topaz.
Above: Cuban military leader Rico Parra (John Vernon, center) with his mistress, Juanita de Cordoba (Karin Dor, right).
Left: Hitch's preferred ending, featuring a duel, was cut after pressure from studio executives (at least two other endings were also filmed).

hard to discard his official Russian point of view—and in this he reflects the "unfree" thinking of the other characters. For contrast—emotionally, at any rate—the film has the beautiful Juanita, who keeps an open bed for both Rico Parra and André. Top German star Karin Dor, who earlier had a small role in the James Bond film *You Only Live Twice* (1967), was cast in the part at the last minute.

A degree of tragedy surrounds the ending of *Topaz* that was released. Hitchcock and Samuel Taylor devised a sequence that was fully in keeping with the film's ironic tone: André and Jacques meet to fight a pistol duel at dawn in a Paris soc-cer stadium. Then, before they can fire their weapons, Jacques is killed by a distant sniper, obviously sent by the Russians who have no further use for their agent code-named "Columbine." The film's research showed that a duel had actually been fought in Paris only five years before. According to Hitchcock scholar Richard Franklin (the director of *Psycho II* [1983]), Hitch lavished more care on this sequence than any other in the picture. But studio executives successfully pressured the seventy-year-old director to remove it, telling him that a couple of preview screenings of the unscored print in Los Angeles and London had shown that audiences found the sequence confusing. Another ending, in which André and Jacques simply bid farewell to each other at the airport, and go their separate ways, was filmed but not used. The released ending shows Jacques's implied suicide after he appears to enter his house and a shot is heard. (In fact, the figure who goes through the door is the character played by Philippe Noiret from an earlier scene.)

So *Topaz* was another "terrible compromise" (in Hitchcock's words), and was generally set upon by the reviewers. However, Andrew Sarris in *The Village Voice* sought to make a more balanced judgment. "[W]ith all its blemishes and drawbacks," he wrote, "*Topaz* is a haunting experience, both inspired and intelligent, convulsive and controlled, passionate and pessimistic."

Indeed it is. The Cuban scenes suggest the lost paradise of earlier Hitchcock films: the garden that is invaded by cutthroats and hooligans (who, though, represent no less than the life force). Juanita's villa is its centerpiece: tastefully filled with paintings, flowers, lead-light windows, a fountain. Juanita herself is like a beneficent mistress/mother, her surreal death literally shocking. As she dies, she sinks onto the black and white tiled marble floor, and her purple dress spreads like a rich stain. Perhaps, though, at this moment we may think of "Venus Asleep," as in Paul Delvaux's famous painting, which uses similar imagery.

Imagery and sound provide keys to *Topaz*. In several ways, the inverse of Juanita's death is represented by the meticulously composed shot of Kusenov's daughter, Tamara (Tina Hedstrom), happily playing a sonata in the safe house outside Washington. The image invokes Vermeer ("The Music Lesson," say). Then, as the sonata continues over the scene of Kusenov's interrogation—in which "Topaz" is first mentioned—the scene "becomes a lament for harmonious existence" (in the excellent phrase of critic Joseph McBride). Later, Kusenov remarks to André that the Americans "will give you a new life," then excuses himself to take "a walk in the garden before the sun goes down." But in his case, he hardly seems a happy person. More like a lost soul.

F R E N Z Y

First screening May 1972

Production company: Universal

Duration 116 minutes

Eastmancolor (filmed in Technicolor)

London is gripped by a series of "necktie murders." Richard Blaney (Jon Finch), his RAF career and his ten-year marriage to Brenda (Barbara Leigh-Hunt) both over, finds himself unemployed and broke. He tells Brenda the news, and she is sympathetic despite his ill temper. So, too, are his girlfriend, barmaid "Babs" Milligan (Anna Massey), and his pal Bob Rusk (Barry Foster), a Covent Garden wholesale fruit merchant. Unbeknownst to Blaney, Rusk is the necktie strangler. His very next victim is Brenda, whom he visits at her matrimonial agency, where he rapes and kills her. The police, led by Inspector Oxford (Alec McCowen), immediately suspect Blaney. Knowing this, Rusk kills Babs too, then dumps her body in a potato truck. He has a nasty moment when he has to retrieve his tiepin, clutched by the corpse, from the now moving truck. Later, back in Covent Garden, Rusk frames Blaney, who is arrested and jailed. Blaney vows vengeance. Throwing himself down some stairs, he gets himself transferred to a hospital, from which he escapes. Heading straight for Rusk's flat, he finds that Rusk has just killed another victim. Oxford arrives and arrests the right man this time.

Much of Hitchcock's inspiration when making *Frenzy* came from Covent Garden's marketplace and the immediate vicinity. In the 1920s, he had visited playwright Winifred Ashton (who wrote as Clemence Dane) in her Henrietta Street flat situated over a publishing office. This gave him the idea to have murderer Bob Rusk live on the same street, above the well-known publisher Duckworth and Co. Another of Hitchcock's notions was that Rusk should work at the market. This effectively fixed the film's theme as the corrupted garden, which had been a major theme of Hitchcock's work since *The Pleasure Garden*. Also, given the market's

daily bustle and clamor, the director was surely right to tell a journalist that *Frenzy* was full of *life*.

Equally, the film is full of death. The rather cynical novel by Arthur La Bern, *Goodbye Piccadilly, Farewell Leicester Square*, was first published in 1966. What particularly attracted Hitchcock was its in every sense *earthy* potato truck scene. (This and the rape–murder of Brenda were both filmed practically *verbatim* by Hitch.) Several prominent British murder cases were drawn on by La Bern: those involving Gordon Cummins, Neville Heath, John Christie (and Timothy Evans), and the recent "Jack the Stripper" case, in which a succession of naked women's bodies had been pulled from the Thames near Hammersmith. For six weeks, Hitchcock and his writer Anthony Shaffer, whose play *Sleuth* was proving a smash in London and New York, researched these and other matters, and visited possible locations.

Above all, *Frenzy* marked something of a homecoming for Hitchcock. Appropriately, it begins with a helicopter shot of the Thames and Tower Bridge, recalling the similar shot that opens Sidney Gilliat's *London Belongs To Me* (1948). *Frenzy* shows Hitchcock in reminiscing, if impish, mood. For the scenes in which Inspector Oxford's wife (Vivien Merchant) plies her husband with meals prepared from gourmet cookbooks, Hitchcock recalled the often unsuccessful culinary experiments of Cary Grant's wife, actress Betsy Drake. To play the straight-laced Gladys, the receptionist at the Coburg Hotel, Bayswater, he cast

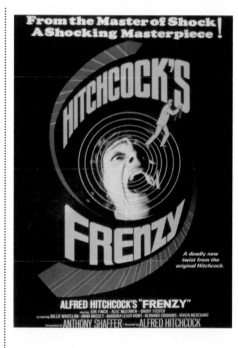

Never one to let a good publicity shot pass him by, Hitch cradles the head of his mannequin, seen floating down the Thames in Frenzy's *trailer.*

Elsie Randolph who, forty years earlier, had pleased him with her portrayal of the spinster in *Rich and Strange*. And when Blaney mocks Gladys by signing the register for himself and Babs as "Mr. and Mrs. Oscar Wilde," the moment recalls both the real-life case of murderer Neville Heath, who took a hotel room in Bournemouth under the name of the famous poet Rupert Brooke, and the inn scene in *The 39 Steps*, where Hannay and Pamela sign in with a flourish as "Mr. and Mrs. Henry Hopkinson, The Hollyhocks, Hammersmith." Though the jokes in *Frenzy* often have a private aspect, they invariably make a point—even if some English reviewers understandably noted

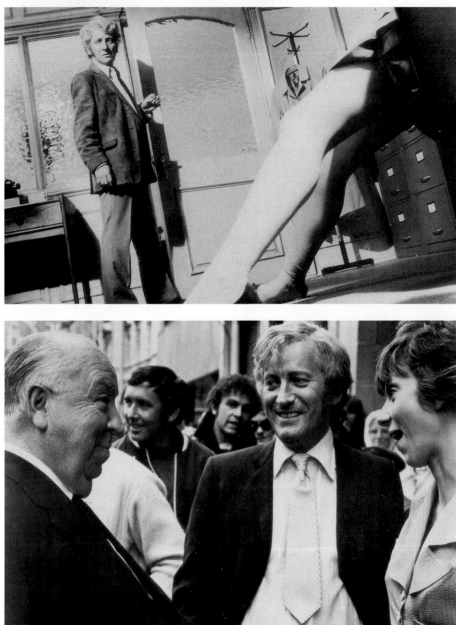

Left: Bob (Barry Foster), retrieving his tiepin. "It was quite disturbing to act the rape and the potato truck sequences," Foster recalled.
Below: Bob visits the matrimonial office.
Bottom: Hitch talks to Barry Foster and Anna Massey. Foster was cast after Hitchcock had seen him in the Boulting brothers' Twisted Nerve (1968).

like, so all the actors are getting together to work out something reasonable," said Finch. If the English reviewers (and, in private, Shaffer and the cast) still picked holes in the finished film, the reviewers in America lauded it. Paul Zimmerman in *Newsweek* called *Frenzy* "a psychological thriller that ranks among [Hitchcock's] very best." And Jay Cocks in *Time* was only slightly less keen: "It is not at the level of his greatest work, but it is smooth and shrewd and dextrous." The film cost $2,000,000 and soon grossed $16,000,000.

Frenzy is a perfect illustration of Hitchcock's (and Schopenhauer's) idea that "everything's perverted in a different way," and that ultimately all is One. The film's imagery, like Dickens's depiction of London in *Our Mutual Friend* (1865), reminds us that everything comes to dust. Explaining what it was about the potatoes in La Bern's story that attracted him, Hitchcock said: "I liked the fact that the story was set in a produce market— Covent Garden—and that . . . the murderer is apprehended because of potato dust on his clothes." The film draws a clear analogy between potatoes, bodies in rivers, effluent of all kinds, and Mrs. Oxford's *soupe de poisson*—the latter a virtual cesspool of marine carnage. In turn, the lesson taught by *The Birds* (and again by Schopenhauer), that "catastrophe surrounds us all," is very much what *Frenzy* implies. The film is far less superficial than *The 39 Steps*, even if it isn't necessarily profound. Moreover, Donald Spoto's criticism that *Frenzy* is "devoid of any positive human feeling" is misleading.

Marnie had hinted that dust and grandeur are contiguous. *Frenzy* opens with grandeur. The effect is only incidentally, and jokingly, that of Hitchcock hailing his own homecoming. The scene's symbolism, with the camera appearing to sweep under the upraised arches of Tower Bridge, is joyously sexual, certainly an echo of the end of *North by Northwest*. At one level, Hitchcock is announcing his love affair with London. At another, he is reminding us that, in spite of all the loveless liaisons and hatred that the film proceeds to display (and Blaney is as guilty as anyone of such failings), the means to resist and overcome them lie close at hand. *Family Plot* will take up that idea.

how anachronistic the Coburg Hotel sequence was.

During the film's shooting, which took fifty-five days from August to October in 1971, actor Jon Finch (fresh from Roman Polanski's *Macbeth* [1971]) told the press that while the cast had great respect for Hitchcock's visual expertise, they found some of the dialogue unbelievable. "He has told us to change anything we don't

FAMILY PLOT

First Screening March 1976

Production company: Universal

Duration 120 minutes

Eastmancolor (but filmed in

Technicolor)

Slightly kooky Blanche Tyler (Barbara Harris) is a professional medium in California; her boyfriend George Lumley (Bruce Dern) is an actor turned cab driver. An elderly client, Julia Rainbird (Cathleen Nesbitt), offers Blanche $10,000 to locate the illegitimate son of her sister, given away at birth to a couple named Shoebridge forty years ago. But he turns out to have changed his name. Jewel merchant Arthur Adamson (William Devane) and his pleasure-loving girlfriend Fran (Karen Black) have lately taken to kidnapping prominent public figures for ransom. Accordingly, Adamson feels annoyed when told by an old acquaintance, garage owner Joseph Maloney (Ed Lauter), that someone is seeking him as Eddie Shoebridge. Remembering how Maloney had once helped him incinerate his foster parents, Adamson orders Maloney to turn his murderous attention to Blanche and George. Maloney's plan misfires, and he dies when his car plunges off a steep road and burns up. Later, Blanche stumbles on Adamson and Fran just as they are smuggling a kidnapped bishop (William Prince) from their home. She finds herself drugged and locked in a secret room, until George arrives and they turn the tables on the kidnappers.

renzy had a central character for whom love had gone absent, and in the subjective nature of Hitchcock's films, the whole of London was shown as blighted. The central couple of *Family Plot* do love each other, and, despite obstacles, they muddle through. Indeed, when they finally get to "move as one," at the end, they are unstoppable. The film is a joy because it knows exactly what it's about and never overreaches. Its serenity is a quality in itself; fittingly, the film often seems close in spirit to *Young and Innocent* and *The Trouble With Harry*.

Hitchcock read *The Rainbird Pattern* by Victor Canning in the spring of 1973. Canning was an Englishman who had begun writing suspense and spy fiction after World War II; *Reader's Digest* once called him one of the six finest thriller writers in the world. What may have attracted Hitch to Canning's latest novel was its episode in which the Archbishop of Canterbury is "bundled up like a sack of potatoes" and kidnapped while on a solitary country walk. Also, Hitch saw similarities between the medium Madame Blanche and Noël Coward's Madame Arcati (based on Clemence Dane) in *Blithe Spirit*. In November, he began story conferences with Ernest Lehman, the screenwriter of *North by Northwest*. Eighteen months later, on May 12, 1975, the cameras finally rolled.

An unusual amount of preparation—even by Hitchcock's standards—went into *Family Plot*, and whole sequences were elaborately storyboarded to the director's instructions by artist Tom Wright. Typical of Hitch's attention to detail was his

Hitch with the cast: William Devane, Karen Black, Barbara Harris, and Bruce Dern. Universal had been keen to use a cast with more clout at the box office.

request to Edith Head concerning costume design. Head was asked to design four levels of costume. Adamson and Fran were to be seen as figures of fashion, George and Blanche as workaday, wealthy Julia Rainbird as fastidious, and a figure like Blanche's client Ida Cookson (Louise Lorimer) as dowdy. In the film, the various levels increasingly interact, and reveal a hidden pattern, much like in a nineteenth-century novel by, say, Dickens. It's significant, for example, that Ida Cookson is a friend of Miss Rainbird, and that both are clients of Blanche (who, the film's trailer implies, is herself something of a surrogate for Hitchcock).

The present author watched the shoot-

ing of the scene where Fran, disguised in a blonde wig, collects a ransom diamond from the Police Aviation Academy. Filming started after sunset on a Universal backlot. An airport office, with three or four steps leading up to it, had been built beside a strip of asphalt representing the edge of the tarmac. Only the front part of the ground floor was in place: the rest of the building as seen in the film is a matte painting by Albert Whitlock. Hitch that night seemed mentally as alert as ever. It was he who noticed that a defusing scrim on one of the lights had come loose and was casting almost imperceptible shadows on the tarmac. An assistant was sent up a ladder to hold the scrim during

There's no body in the family plot.

From the devious mind of Alfred Hitchcock, a diabolically entertaining motion picture.

ALFRED HITCHCOCK'S
FAMILY PLOT A
You must see it twice!
starring
KAREN BLACK · BRUCE DERN
BARBARA HARRIS · WILLIAM DEVANE
Music by JOHN WILLIAMS · Screenplay by ERNEST LEHMAN
From the novel "THE RAINBIRD PATTERN" by VICTOR CANNING
Directed by ALFRED HITCHCOCK A UNIVERSAL PICTURE · TECHNICOLOR®
DISTRIBUTED BY CIC

Above and right: The film's two main couples: Arthur (William Devane) and Fran (Karen Black) on the left; George (Bruce Dern) and Blanche (Barbara Harris) on the right. Roy Thinnes was originally cast in Devane's role, but Hitch was unhappy with his performance.

shooting. Karen Black asked why the establishing shot of the office door was needed: "Why not just go directly inside the building?" To which the director answered in his lugubrious drawl: "You see, Karen, it's like the trombones in the orchestra. We can't just let them blare out in-dis-crim-in-ate-ly, can we?"

This was in May. After a total of seventy-one shooting days, including location filming in San Francisco and Los Angeles, the film wrapped on August 18. Still to be done were some process shots and the recording of the deft and imaginative score by John Williams. (Sur-

prisingly, Williams wasn't even brought onto the film until after shooting was complete.) The film premiered at the Los Angeles International Film Festival on March 21, 1976, where everyone was delighted by it. Later, Charles Champlin reviewed it for the *Los Angeles Times*. *Family Plot*, he wrote, "is atmospheric, characterful, precisely paced, intricately plotted, exciting and suspenseful, beautifully acted, and, perhaps more than anything else, amusing."

The characters of Blanche and George

are at the center of the film. They're superb comic creations, with many shadings—which critic John Simon was unkind enough to call "mugging." Sadly, he was one of a number of reviewers who just couldn't accept the film for what it was, and viewed it askance. A piece by Al Auster in *Cineaste* twice referred to moments involving Blanche and George—such as when they come home from doing the shopping together, or when in the kitchen he ogles her "great little behind"—as beside the point or superfluous. It should be obvious, though, that *Family Plot* can't be separated from its details, and especially not from its California ambience (which, obliquely at any rate, recalls Raymond Chandler). Those homely details matter. Besides, Hitch is drawing parallels with the film's other main couple, and suggesting that love will win out: Adamson's purely sexual phrase, "move as one," will return to haunt him.

Memorably, *Family Plot* has its coda, designed by Hitchcock himself, that culminates with Blanche's thrilling final wink at the camera. The most important thing here is not whether she's psychic, nor even what her further intentions for the evening may be, but rather the charm with which Hitch acknowledges firstly us, his life-long collaborators in crime, and secondly his own sense of fun. It seems only appropriate to say: Thanks, Hitch!

UNREALIZED PROJECTS

Above left: *Cary Grant, proposed star of* Hamlet.
Above right: *Audrey Hepburn was to have starred in* No Bail for the Judge.

In a career that spanned over fifty years, Hitchcock developed remarkably few projects that failed to make it to the screen. And of these, even fewer were anything more than mere pipe dreams.

Hitchcock was always on the lookout for ideas, and would therefore list all sorts of possibilities—but an entry on a list was often as far as they went. For example, after the war he sent an excited telegram to his business partner Sidney Bernstein outlining "Hitchcock's *Hamlet*" with Cary Grant as the doomed Dane. The idea was to modernize the language and

treat it stylistically as a Hitchcock film. As it turned out, the cost of the telegram was the sum total spent on serious development. He did talk up the "new project" with a few journalists, and the resulting stories then caught the attention of an American scholar who threatened to sue Hitchcock because *he* had already written the modern language *Hamlet*. But by then, Hitch had long moved on to other ideas.

Hitchcock toyed more seriously during his career with John Buchan's *The Three Hostages* (1924) and David Duncan's

One-time Hitchcock project The Mary Deare *was filmed by Michael Anderson in 1959 as* The Wreck of the Mary Deare, *starring Charlton Heston and Gary Cooper. Featured actors Michael Redgrave, Emlyn Williams, and Cecil Parker had all previously appeared in a Hitchcock movie.*

Bramble Bush (1952), both novels that appear to be more appropriately Hitchcockian. He also considered filming H. G. Wells's *The Food of the Gods* (1904) and Robert Louis Stevenson's *The Strange Case of Dr. Jekyll and Mr. Hyde* (1886), had discussions with Ernest Lehman about adapting Hammond Innes's *The Mary Deare* (1956; ultimately filmed for MGM by Michael Anderson in 1959), and acquired the rights to Elmore Leonard's *Unknown Man #89* (1977).

However, there were only four projects which were truly "crashed" films (in that they got as far as extensive screenplay and preproduction work). The first real experience of turnaround for Hitchcock was an adaptation of Judge Henry Cecil Leon's novel *No Bail for the Judge* (1952), which was set to go before the cameras in the late fifties. The screenplay had been written by Samuel Taylor, and preproduction was well underway when the project was abruptly halted by the film's star, Audrey Hepburn, pulling out. Hitchcock could have recast, but chose instead to let it drop. Much later, at the end of his career, script and even preproduction work was completed on a film about the escaped spy George Blake, *The Short Night*, but progress was curtailed by age's infirmities and ultimately Hitchcock's death.

Hitchcock had one project that he held particularly close to his heart, yet never fully realized. As a young man he had been mesmerized by J. M. Barrie's haunting *Mary Rose* (1925) on the London stage. Throughout his career, Hitch considered directing a screen version, and his estate even owned the film rights until long after his death. Parts of the play were actually used as inspiration for *Vertigo*—and, indeed, many critics consider the film to be Hitchcock's variation on *Mary Rose*.

In the sixties and seventies, Hitchcock told journalists that it was the one film that his contract with MCA/Universal strictly forbid him from doing. American film critic Andrew Sarris relates how, having lunch with the Hitchcocks in the mid-seventies, Alma turned to him and asked, "Why won't they let Hitch do *Mary Rose*?" All of this is curious, as there appears to be no evidence in Hitchcock's files of any serious effort to realize the film. Hitchcock's contracts with Universal are not available in the massive collection, but the only time the project seemed viable was during his MCA/Universal

The fight scene in *The Lady Vanishes*—which Hitchcock admits disappointed him

Hitchcock discusses the script of *The Lady Vanishes* with Dame May Whitty

ALFRED HITCHCOCK discusses his work and plans—and his clashes with censorship—in this interview with J. Danvers Williams.

THE CENSOR
wouldn't PASS IT

says ALFRED HITCHCOCK

Guardsmen at the Sydney Street siege in 1911. The censor wouldn't let Hitchcock put them in his picture

Armoured cars in London during the general strike of 1926. Another subject that Hitchcock wasn't allowed to make in his own way

A 1938 magazine article, in which Hitchcock outlines how the censor prevented him from restaging the Siege of Sydney Street in The Man Who Knew Too Much, and barred him from making a film about the 1926 General Strike. The article also contains pictures from Hitchcock's then current release, The Lady Vanishes.

period. After *Marnie*, Hitch did have Jay Presson Allen write a script based on the play, but there are no notes or memos in relation to the film, and no discussion in letters or transcripts about a possible *Mary Rose* production. Despite the lost project's legendary status, the Hitchcock files are strangely silent on *Mary Rose*.

The lost project which does loom large in the Hitchcock archive is the ill-fated 1967 *Frenzy* (which was mischievously entitled *Kaleidoscope* in the files). The film consumed more than a year of his career, with nearly a dozen screenplay drafts and elaborate preproduction work. The plot of this first *Frenzy* (unrelated to the 1972 film) was based on the true story of Neville Heath, a sadistic twenty-eight-year-old RAF officer hanged in 1946 for the sexual assault and savage murder of two young women.

Hitchcock first brought over Benn Levy from England, although he had not worked with Levy since the early thirties (when Hitch had produced his *Lord Camber's Ladies*). Levy outlined the story and then wrote just over half of the first screenplay in the spring of 1967, returning to England in May. Hitchcock took it upon himself to finish the script, and the June 1967 draft bears his name as the author. He then began preproduction in earnest, having photographers shoot detailed storyboards for the film, resulting in hundreds of slides featuring models and unknown actors.

Hitchcock also had preliminary 35mm film reels shot in New York. After editing, there was about ten minutes of screen time. The first scene presents a nude model in her apartment; the second, set in an artist's studio, shows the young killer meeting the model. In a break with tradition, Hitchcock proposed using unknown actors for his new production.

As 1967 progressed, Hitchcock had Howard Fast write a draft of the screenplay, followed by Hugh Wheeler in early 1968. But nothing would satisfy MCA/Universal, and despite an in-depth proposal using the slides and test sequences, the studio killed the project. Hitchcock was stunned, according to assistant Peggy Robertson, and took *Topaz* only at Lew Wasserman's insistence. The sad irony is that the studio was willing to go ahead with a screenplay that was far from ready, containing a story structure that would never be satisfactorily repaired, yet would not trust Hitchcock with a project he had developed (and which, compared to *Topaz*, had few script problems). It was an irony certainly not lost on Hitchcock, who later appeared disenchanted with Universal. Hitchcock was never afraid to drop projects that didn't meet his requirements—the fact that he held on so long to the 1967 *Frenzy* only serves to tantalize. How would his career have developed after such a revolutionary film?

Dan Auiler

HITCHCOCK FILMOGRAPHY

A–Z Index of Film Entries

Below is an alphabetical list of the Hitchcock-directed films which have an entry in the book, followed by the entry's page reference.

This filmography endeavors to list all the film projects with which Alfred Hitchcock was involved during his career (except those which did not progress past preproduction). In addition to consulting film prints, scripts, and press books where available, the compiler has drawn from, and is indebted to, the work of Sloan, Spoto, and Truffaut.

The films are noted thus: Title (Hitchcock's key direction credits have titles in bold); American title in parentheses where applicable; year of first screening; approximate duration of exhibition print; film stock/screen ratio (see also the Author's Note); silent/sound (where applicable); production company; cast (with character names in brackets); selected technical/production credits where available for costume design/wardrobe [Cd], art direction [Art dir], supervising editor [Sup ed], editor [Ed], Makeup, special effects [Spfx], music [M], assistant director [Asst dir], director of photography [Dp], screenplay [Scrp], based on/source of script [Bo], executive producer [Exec prod], associate producer [Assoc prod], producer [Prod], director [Dir]. Alfred Hitchcock is abbreviated to **AH**. Certain other noteworthy credits are given in full (excepting the word design/designer, which is abbreviated to des (e.g. Inter-titles design [Inter-titles des]). In the selected awards information, AA denotes Academy Award and AAN denotes Academy Award Nomination.

THE CALL OF YOUTH
1920. B&w. Silent. Famous Players-Lasky.
Inter-titles des: **AH**. Dir: Hugh Ford.

THE GREAT DAY
1920. B&w. Silent. Famous Players-Lasky.
Inter-titles des: **AH**. Dir: Hugh Ford.

APPEARANCES
1921. B&w. Silent. Famous Players-Lasky.
Inter-titles des: **AH**. Dir: Donald Crisp.

BESIDE THE BONNIE BRIER BUSH
1921. B&w. Silent. Famous Players-Lasky.
Inter-titles des: **AH**. Dir: Donald Crisp.

DANGEROUS LIES
1921. B&w. Silent. Famous Players-Lasky.
Inter-titles des: **AH**. Dir: Paul Powell.

THE MYSTERY ROAD
1921. B&w. Silent. Famous Players-Lasky.
Inter-titles des: **AH**. Dir: Paul Powell.

THE PRINCESS OF NEW YORK
1921. B&w. Silent. Famous Players-Lasky.
Inter-titles des: **AH**. Dir: Donald Crisp.

THE MAN FROM HOME
1922. B&w. Silent. Famous Players-Lasky.
Inter-titles des: **AH**. Dir: George Fitzmaurice.

NUMBER 13
1922. B&w. Silent. Famous Players-Lasky.
Cast: Clare Greet, Ernest Thesiger.
Selected Credits: Dp: Rosenthal. Scrp: Anita Ross. Prod/Dir: **AH**. Note: This is an unfinished two-reeler.

PERPETUA
1922. B&w. Silent. Famous Players-Lasky.
Inter-titles des: **AH**. Dir: John S. Robertson, Tom Geraghty.

SPANISH JADE
1922. B&w. Silent. Famous Players-Lasky.
Inter-titles des: **AH**. Dir: John S. Robertson, Tom Geraghty.

TELL YOUR CHILDREN
1922. B&w. Silent. International Artists (Gaumont).
Inter-titles des: **AH**. Dir: Donald Crisp.

THREE LIVE GHOSTS
1922. B&w. Silent. Famous Players-
Lasky.
Inter-titles des: **AH**. Dir: George
Fitzmaurice.

ALWAYS TELL YOUR WIFE
1923. B&w. Silent. Seymour Hicks
Productions.
Dir: Hugh Croise.
Note: **AH** finished directing the film,
with producer Seymour Hicks, when
Croise was removed from the picture.

THE WHITE SHADOW
1923. B&w. Silent. Balcon-Saville-
Freedman.
Scrp: Michael Morton, **AH**. Set
dir/Ed/Asst dir: **AH**. Dir: Graham
Cutts.

WOMAN TO WOMAN
1923. B&w. Silent. Balcon-Saville-
Freedman.
Scrp: Graham Cutts, **AH**. Art dir/Asst
dir: **AH**. Dir: Graham Cutts.

THE PASSIONATE ADVENTURE
1924. B&w. Silent. Gainsborough.
Scrp: Michael Morton, **AH**. Art dir/Asst
dir: **AH**. Dir: Graham Cutts.

THE PRUDE'S FALL
(American title: Dangerous Virtue)
1924. B&w. Silent. Balcon-Saville-
Freedman.
Scrp/Art dir/Asst dir: **AH**. Dir: Graham
Cutts.

THE BLACKGUARD
1925. B&w. Silent. UFA/Gainsborough.
Scrp/Art dir/Asst dir: **AH**. Dir: Graham
Cutts.

THE PLEASURE GARDEN
1926. Approx. 85 mins. B&w. Silent.
Gainsborough/Emelka GBA.
Cast: Virginia Valli (Patsy Brand),
Carmelita Geraghty (Jill Cheyne),
John Stuart (Hugh Fielding), Miles
Mander (Levett), Nita Naldi (Native
girl), C. Falkenburg (Prince Ivan),
Frederick Martini (the patron),
Florence Helminger (the patron's
wife), George Snell (Oscar Hamilton).
Selected credits: Dp: Baron Giovanni
Ventigmilia. Scrp: Eliot Stannard. Bo:
novel by Mrs. Oliver Sandys. Prod:
Michael Balcon. Dir: **AH**.

THE MOUNTAIN EAGLE
1926. Approx. 89 mins. B&w. Silent.
Gainsborough/Emelka GBA.
Cast: Bernard Goetzke (Pettigrew), Nita
Naldi (Beatrice), Malcolm Keen
(Fearogod), John Hamilton (Edward
Pettigrew).
Selected credits: Dp: Baron Giovanni
Ventigmilia. Scrp: Eliot Stannard.
Prod: Michael Balcon. Dir: **AH**.

THE LODGER, A STORY OF THE
LONDON FOG
1926. Approx. 100 mins. B&w. Silent.
Gainsborough.
Cast: Ivor Novello (The Lodger), "June"
[June Tripp] (Daisy Bunting), Marie
Ault (Mrs. Bunting), Arthur Chesney
(Mr. Bunting), Malcolm Keen (Joe
Betts).
Selected credits: Art dir: C. W. Arnold,
Bertram Evans. Inter-titles des: E.
McKnight Kauffer. Ed/captions: Ivor
Montagu. Asst dir: Alma Reville. Dp:
Baron Giovanni Ventigmilia. Scrp:
Eliot Stannard. Bo: novel *The Lodger*
by Mrs. Belloc Lowndes. Prod:
Michael Balcon. Dir: **AH**.

WHEN BOYS LEAVE HOME
(British title: **Downhill**)
1927. Approx. 105 mins. B&w. Silent.
Gainsborough.
Cast: Ivor Novello (Roddy Berwick),
Robin Irvine (Tim Wakely), Lillian
Braithwaite (Lady Berwick), Isabel
Jeans (Julia), Ian Hunter (Archie),
Norman McKinnel (Sir Thomas

Berwick), Sybil Rhoda (Sybil Wakely),
Hannah Jones (the dressmaker),
Violet Farebrother (the poet), Ben
Webster (Dr. Dawson), Jerrold
Robertshaw (Rev. Henry Wakeley),
Annette Benson (Mabel), Barbara
Gott (Mrs. Michet), Alfred Goddard
(the Swede), J. Nelson (Hibbert).
Selected credits: Art dir: Bert Evans. Ed:
Lionel Rich. Dp: Claude McDonnell.
Bo: play by "David L' Estrange" (Ivor
Novello and Constance Collier). Prod:
Michael Balcon. Dir: **AH**.

EASY VIRTUE
1927. Approx. 105 mins. B&w. Silent.
Gainsborough.
Cast: Isabel Jeans (Larita Filton),
Franklyn Dyall (Mr. Filton), Eric
Bransby Williams (Claude Robson),
Robin Irvine (John Whittaker), Ian
Hunter (Counsel for the plaintiff),
Violet Farebrother (Mrs. Whittaker),
Enid Stamp Taylor (Sarah), Frank
Elliot (Mr. Whittaker), Darcia Deane
(his older sister), Dorothy Boyd (his
younger sister), Benita Hume.
Selected credits: Art dir: Clifford Pember.
Ed: Ivor Montagu. Dp: Claude
McDonnell. Scrp: Eliot Stannard. Bo:
play by Nöel Coward. Prod: Michael
Balcon, C. M. Woolf. Dir: **AH**.

THE RING
1927. Approx. 110 mins. B&w. Silent.
British International Pictures.
Cast: Carl Brisson (Jack Sander), Lilian
Hall-Davis (Mabel), Ian Hunter (Bob

Corby), Forrester Harvey (James Ware, the promoter), Gordon Harker (the trainer), Harry Terry (Showman), Billy Wells (a boxer), Clare Greet (Gypsy), Tom Helmore, Charles Farrell.

Selected credits: Art dir: C. W. Arnold. Asst dir: Frank Mills. Dp: John [Jack] J. Cox. Scrp: **AH**. Prod: John Maxwell. Dir: **AH**.

THE MANXMAN
1928. Approx. 100 mins. B&w. Silent. British International Pictures.

Cast: Carl Brisson (Pete Quilliam), Malcolm Keen (Philip Christian), Anny Ondra (Kate Cregeen), Randle Ayrton (Caesar, Mr. Cregeen), Clare Greet (Mrs. Cregeen).

Selected credits: Stills photographer: Michael Powell. Art dir: C. W. Arnold. Ed: Emile de Ruelle. Asst dir: Frank Mills. Dp: John [Jack] J. Cox. Scrp: Eliot Stannard. Bo: novel by Sir Hall Caine. Prod: John Maxwell. Dir: **AH**.

THE FARMER'S WIFE
1928. Approx. 100 mins. B&w. Silent. British International Pictures.

Cast: Jameson Thomas (Samuel Sweetland), Lilian Hall-Davis (Araminta Dench), Gordon Harker (Churdles Ash), Maud Gill (Thirza Tapper), Louise Pounds (Louisa Windeatt), Olga Slade (Mary Hearn), Antonia Borough (Mercy Bassett), Ruth Maitland Hayward Watts, Gibb McLaughlin.

Selected credits: Art dir: C. W. Arnold. Ed: Alfred Booth. Asst dir: Frank Mills. Dp: John [Jack] J. Cox. Scrp: **AH**. Bo: play by Eden Phillpotts, based on his novel *Widdicombe Fair*. Prod: John Maxwell. Dir: **AH**.

CHAMPAGNE
1928. Approx. 104 mins. B&w. Silent. British International Pictures.

Cast: Betty Balfour (The Girl), Jean Bradin (The Boy), Theo von Alten (The Man), Gordon Harker (The Father), Marcel Vibert (Maitre d'Hotel), Clifford Heatherly (the manager), Balliol and Merton (the dancers), Claude Hulbert, Jack Trevor, Hannah Jones.

Selected credits: Art dir: C. W. Arnold. Asst dir: Frank Mills. Dp: John [Jack] J. Cox. Adaptation: **AH**. Scrp: Eliot

Stannard. Bo: story by Walter C. Mycroft. Prod: John Maxwell. Dir: **AH**.

Note: Reportedly, a German version was directed by Géza von Bovary in 1929.

BLACKMAIL
1929 Approx. 80 mins. B&w. Silent/Sound. British International Pictures.

Cast: Anny Ondra (Alice White), John Longden (Frank Webber), Sara Allgood (Mrs. White), Charles Paton (Mr. White), Donald Calthrop (Tracy), Cyril Ritchard (Crewe, the artist), Phyllis Monkman (the neighbor), Hannah Jones (the landlady), Harvey Braban (Chief Inspector, sound version), Sam Livesay (Chief Inspector, silent version), Ex-detective Sergeant Bishop (the Detective Sergeant), Joan Barry (voice of Alice White).

Selected credits: Camera asst: Michael Powell, Derick Williams, Ronald Neame. Set dir: C. W. Arnold, Norman Arnold. Ed: Emile de Ruelle. M: Campbell and Connelly, Henry Stafford. Asst dir: Frank Mills. Dp: John [Jack] J. Cox. Adaptation: **AH**. Scrp: Benn W. Levy. Bo: play by Charles Bennett. Prod: John Maxwell. Dir: **AH**.

JUNO AND THE PAYCOCK
1929. 85 mins. B&w. British International Pictures.

Cast: Sara Allgood (Juno Boyle), Edward Chapman ("Captain" Jack Boyle), Sidney Morgan (Joxer Daly), Maire O'Neil (Mrs. Madigan), Kathleen O'Regan (Mary Boyle), John Laurie (Johnny Boyle), John Longden (Charles Bentham), Denis Wyndham (the Mobilizer), Barry Fitzgerald (the Orator), Dave Morris (Jerry Devine), Fred Schwartz (Mr. Kelly).

Selected credits: Art dir: J. Marchant. Ed: Emile de Ruelle. Dp: John [Jack] J. Cox. Scrp: **AH**, Alma Reville. Bo: play by Sean O'Casey. Prod: John Maxwell. Dir: **AH**.

ELSTREE CALLING
1930. 86 mins. B&w/Pathécolour. British International Pictures.

Cast: Tommy Handley, Cicely Courtneidge, Jack Hulbert, Helen Burnell, Gordon Harker, Hannah Jones, Anna May Wong, Jameson Thomas, Donald Calthrop, Lily

Morris, Will Fyffe, The Berkoffs, Bobby Comber, Lawrence Green, Ivor McLaren, John Longden, The Charlot Girls.

Selected credits: M: Reg Casson, Vivian Ellis, Chic Endor. Lyrics: Ivor Novello, Jack Strachey Parsons. Dp: Claude Freise Greene. Scrp: Val Valentine. Exec prod: John Maxwell. Dir: **AH**, André Charlot, Jack Hulbert, Paul Murray. Sup dir: Adrian Brunel.

MURDER!
1930. 100 mins. B&w. British International Pictures.

Cast: Norah Baring (Diana Baring), Herbert Marshall (Sir John Menier), Miles Mander (Gordon Druce), Esmé Percy (Handel Fane), Edward Chapman (Ted Markham), Phyllis Konstam (Doucie Markham), Donald Calthrop (Ion Stewart), Hannah Jones (Mrs. Didsome), Amy Brandon-Thomas (lawyer for Diana Baring), Joynson Powell (the Judge), Esmé V. Chaplin (Prosecutor), Marie Wright (Mrs. Mitcham), S. J. Warmington (Bennett), Una O'Connor (Mrs. Gogram), R. E. Jeffrey (Jury Foreman), Alan Stainer, Kenneth Kove, Guy Pelham Boulton, Violet Farebrother, Ross Jefferson, Clare Greet, Drusilla Wills, Robert Easton, William Fazan, George Smythson, Picton Roxborough (Jury Members).

Selected credits: Art dir: J. F. Mead. Sup ed: Emile de Ruelle. Ed: Rene Marrison. M: John Reynders. Asst dir: Frank Mills. Dp: John [Jack] J. Cox. Scrp: **AH**, Walter Mycroft, Alma Reville. Bo: novel *Enter Sir John* by Clemence Dane (Winifred Ashton) and Helen Simpson. Prod: John Maxwell. Dir: **AH**.

MARY
(German version of **Murder!**)
1930. B&w. Sud Film A. G.

Cast: Alfred Abel, Olga Tschechowa, Paul Graetz, Lotte Stein, Ekkehard Arendt, Jack Mylong-Münz, Louis Ralph, Hermine Sterler, Fritz Alberti, Hertha von Walter, Else Schünzel, Julius Brandt, Rudolph Meinhardt-Jünger, Fritz Grossmann, Lucic Euler, Harry Hardt, H. Gotho, Eugen Burg.

Selected credits: Art dir: J. F. Mead. Sup ed: Emile de Ruelle. Ed: Rene Marrison. M: John Reynders. Dp:

Jack Cox. Scrp: Alma Reville, Herbert Juttke, Dr. Georg C. Klaren. Bo: novel *Enter Sir John* by Clemence Dane (Winifred Ashton) and Helen Simpson. Prod: John Maxwell. Dir: **AH**.

THE SKIN GAME
1931. 89 mins. B&w. British International Pictures.
Cast: Edmund Gwenn (Mr. Hornblower), Jill Esmond (Jill Hillcrist), John Longden (Charles Hornblower), C. V. France (Mr. Hillcrist), Helen Haye (Mrs. Hillcrist), Phyllis Konstam (Chloe Hornblower), Frank Lawton (Rolf Hornblower), Herbert Ross (Mr. Jackman), Dora Gregory (Mrs. Jackman), Edward Chapman (Dawker), R. E. Jeffrey (first stranger), George Bancroft (second stranger), Ronald Frankau (Auctioneer).
Selected credits: Art dir: J. B. Maxwell. Ed: Rene Marrison, A. Gobett. Asst dir: Frank Mills. Dp: John [Jack] J. Cox, Charles Martin. Scrp: **AH**, Alma Reville. Bo: play by John Galsworthy. Prod: John Maxwell. Dir: **AH**.

NUMBER SEVENTEEN
1932. 65 mins. B&w. British International Pictures.
Cast: Leon M. Lion (Ben), Anne Grey (Nora), John Stuart (Gilbert Allardyce/Barton), Donald Calthrop (Brant), Ann Casson (Rose Ackroyd), Henry Caine (Mr. Ackroyd), Barry Jones (Henry Doyle), Garry Marsh (Sheldrake), Herbert Langley (Guard).
Selected credits: Art dir: C. W. Arnold. Ed: A. C. Hammond. M: A. Hallis. Asst dir: Frank Mills. Dp: John [Jack] J. Cox, Bryan Langley. Scrp: Alma Reville, **AH**, Rodney Ackland. Bo: play *JoyoUSMelodrama* by J. Jefferson Farjeon. Prod: John Maxwell, Leon M. Lion. Dir: **AH**.

RICH AND STRANGE
(American title: **East of Shanghai**)
1932. 87 mins. B&w. British International Pictures.
Cast: Henry Kendall (Fred Hill), Joan Barry (Emily Hill), Betty Amann (the princess), Percy Marmont (Commander Gordon), Elsie Randolph (Miss Imery), Hannah Jones.
Selected credits: Art dir: C. W. Arnold. Ed: Rene Marrison, Winifred Cooper. M: Hal Dolphe. Asst dir: Frank Mills. Dp: John [Jack] J. Cox, Charles Martin. Scrp: **AH**, Alma Reville, Val Valentine. Bo: story by Dale Collins. Prod: John Maxwell. Dir: **AH**.

LORD CAMBER'S LADIES
1932. 80 mins. B&w. British International Pictures.
Cast: Gertrude Lawrence (Lady Camber), Sir Gerald du Maurier (Lord Camber), Benita Hume, Nigel Bruce, Clare Greet, A. Bromley Davenport.

Selected credits: Scrp: Benn W. Levy, Edwin Greenwood, Gilbert Wakefield. Bo: novel *The Case of Lady Camber* by Horace Annesley Vachell. Prod: **AH**. Dir: Benn W. Levy.

WALTZES FROM VIENNA
(American title: **Strauss's Great Waltz**)
1934. 80 mins. B&w. A Tom Arnold Production.
Cast: Jessie Matthews (Rasi), Esmond Knight (Chani Strauss), Frank Vosper (the Prince), Fay Compton (the Countess), Edmund Gwenn (Johann Strauss, Sr.), Robert Hale (Ebezedar), Hindle Edgar (Leopold), MarcUSBarron (Drexler), Charles Heslop (Valet), Sybil Grove (Mme. Fouchet), Bill Shine Jr. (Carl), Bertram Dench (Engine Driver), B. M. Lewis (Domeyer), Cyril Smith (Secretary), Betty Huntley Wright (Lady's Maid), Berinoff and Charlot.
Selected credits: Set dir: Peter Proud. Art dir: Alfred Junge, Oscar Werndorff. Ed: Charles Frend. M: Johann Strauss, Sr. and Jr. Asst dir: Richard Beville. Dp: Glen McWilliams. Scrp: Alma Reville, Guy Bolton. Bo: play by Guy Bolton. Prod: Tom Arnold. Dir: **AH**.

THE MAN WHO KNEW TOO MUCH
1934. 85 mins. B&w. Gaumont-British
Cast: Leslie Banks (Bob Lawrence), Edna Best (Jill Lawrence), Peter Lorre (Abbott), Frank Vosper (Ramon Levine), Hugh Wakefield (Clive), Nova Pilbeam (Betty Lawrence), Pierre Fresnay (Louis Bernard), Cicely Oates (Nurse Agnes), D. A. Clarke Smith (Inspector Binstead), George Curzon (Gibson).
Selected credits: Set dir: Peter Proud. Art dir: Alfred Junge. Ed: H. St. C. Stewart. M: Arthur Benjamin. Dp: Curt Courant. Scrp: Edwin Greenwood, A. R. Rawlinson. Additional dialogue: Emlyn Williams. Bo: story by Charles Bennett and D. B. Wyndham Lewis. Assoc prod: Ivor Montagu. Prod: Michael Balcon. Dir: **AH**.
Selected awards: *New York Times* Ten Best Films list, 1935. National Board of Review Awards: Best Foreign Films list.

PUBLIC ENEMY NO.1 OF ALL THE WORLD··

NOVA PILBEAM
PETER LORRE
LESLIE BANKS
EDNA BEST

THE MAN WHO KNEW TOO MUCH

A GB PRODUCTION

Directed by ALFRED HITCHCOCK

THE 39 STEPS

1935. 81 mins. B&w. Gaumont-British.

Cast: Robert Donat (Richard Hannay), Madeleine Carroll (Pamela), Lucie Mannheim (Annabella Smith), Godfrey Tearle (Professor Jordan), John Laurie (John), Peggy Ashcroft (Margaret), Helen Haye (Mrs. Jordan), Frank Cellier (the Sheriff), Wylie Watson (Mr. Memory), Peggy Simpson (Maid), GUSMcNaughton, Jerry Verno (Travellers), Hilda Trevelyn (Innkeeper's Wife), John Turnball (Inspector).

Selected credits: Cd: J. Strassner, Marianne. Set dir: Albert Jullion. Art dir: O. Werndorff. Ed: Derek N. Twist. M: Louis Levy. Dp: Bernard Knowles. Scrp: Charles Bennett. Dialogue: Ian Hay. Bo: novel *The Thirty-Nine Steps* by John Buchan. Assoc prod: Ivor Montagu. Prod: Michael Balcon. Dir: **AH**.

SECRET AGENT

1936. 83 mins. B&w. Gaumont-British.

Cast: Madeleine Carroll (Elsa Carrington), John Gielgud (Richard Ashenden), Peter Lorre (the General), Robert Young (Robert Marvin), Percy Marmont (Mr. Caypor), Charles Carson (R), Florence Kahn (Mrs. Caypor), Michel Saint-Denis (Coachdriver), Tom Helmore (R's Adjutant), Lilli Palmer, Michael Redgrave.

Selected credits: Cd: J. Strassner. Set dir: Albert Jullion. Art dir: O. Werndorff. Ed: Charles Frend. M: Louis Levy. Dp: Bernard Knowles. Scrp: Charles Bennett. Dialogue: Ian Hay, Jesse Lasky Jr. Bo: play *Ashenden* by Campbell Dixon, "Ashenden" stories by Somerset Maugham. Assoc prod: Ivor Montagu. Prod: Michael Balcon. Dir: **AH**.

Selected awards: National Board of Review Awards: Best Foreign Films list.

SABOTAGE

(American title: **The Woman Alone**)
1936. 76 mins. B&w. Gaumont-British.

Cast: Sylvia Sidney (Winnie Verloc), Oscar Homolka (Mr. Verloc), Desmond Tester (Stevie), John Loder (Ted), Joyce Barbour (Renée), Matthew Boulton (Superintendent Talbot), William Dewhurst (The Professor), Martita Hunt (The Professor's daughter), S. J. Warmington (Hollingshead), Peter Bull, Torin Thatcher, Austin Trevor, Clare Greet, Sam Wilkinson, Sara Allgood, Pamela Bevan.

Selected credits: Cd: J. Strassner, Marianne. Set dir: Albert Jullion. Art dir: O. Werndorff. Ed: Charles Frend. M: Louis Levy. Dp: Bernard Knowles. Adaptation: Alma Reville. Scrp: Charles Bennett. Dialogue: Ian Hay, Helen Simpson, E. V. H. Emmett. Bo: novel *The Secret Agent* by Joseph Conrad. Assoc prod: Ivor Montagu. Prod: Michael Balcon. Dir: **AH**.

YOUNG AND INNOCENT

(American title: **The Girl Was Young**)
1937. 80 mins. B&w. Gainsborough.

Cast: Derrick de Marney (Robert Tisdall), Nova Pilbeam (Erica Burgoyne), Percy Marmont (Colonel Burgoyne), Edward Rigby (Old Will),

Mary Clare (Erica's Aunt), John Longden (Inspector Kent), George Curzon (Guy), Basil Radford (Erica's Uncle), Pamela Carme (Christine), George Merritt (Sergeant Miller), J. H. Roberts (Solicitor), Jerry Verno (Lorry Driver), H. F. Maltby (Police sergeant), John Miller (Police Constable), Torin Thatcher, Peggy Simpson, Anna Konstam, Beatrice Varley, William Fazan, Frank Atkinson, Fred O'Donovan, Albert Chevalier, Richard George, Jack Vyvian, Clive Baxter, Pamela Bevan, Humberston Wright, Gerry Fitzgerald, Syd Crossley.

Selected credits: Cd: Marianne. Art dir: Alfred Junge. Ed: Charles Frend. M: Louis Levy. Dp: Bernard Knowles. Adaptation: Alma Reville. Scrp: Charles Bennett, Edwin Greenwood, Anthony Armstrong. Dialogue: Gerald Savory. Bo: novel *A Shilling for Candles* by Josephine Tey. Prod: Edward Black. Dir: **AH**.

THE LADY VANISHES

1938. 97 mins. B&w. Gainsborough.

Cast: Margaret Lockwood (Iris Henderson), Michael Redgrave (Gilbert), Paul Lukas (Dr. Hartz), Dame May Whitty (Miss Froy), Googie Withers (Blanche), Cecil Parker (Mr. Todhunter), Linden Travers (Mrs. Todhunter), Mary Clare (Baroness), Naunton Wayne (Caldicott), Basil Radford (Charters), Philip Leaver (Signor Doppo), Emil Boreo (Hotel Manager), Zelma Vas Dias (Signora Doppo), Sally Stewart (Julie), Catherine Lacey (the Nun), Josephine Wilson (Madame Kummer), Charles Oliver (the Officer), Kathleen Tremaine (Anna).

Selected credits: Set dir: Alec Vetchinsky, Maurice Cater, Albert Jullion. Ed: R. E. Dearing, Alfred Roome. M: Louis Levy. Dp: John [Jack] J. Cox. Adaptation: Alma Reville. Scrp: Sidney Gilliat, Frank Launder. Bo: novel *The Wheel Spins* by Ethel Lina White. Prod: Edward Black. Dir: **AH**.

Selected awards: *New York Times* Ten Best Films list, 1938. The New York Film Critics Awards: Best Direction.

JAMAICA INN

1939. 100 mins. B&w. Mayflower Pictures.

Cast: Charles Laughton (Sir Humphrey

Pengallan), Maureen O'Hara (Mary Yellan), Leslie Banks (Joss Merlyn), Marie Ney (Patience Merlyn), Robert Newton (Jem Trehearne), Emlyn Williams (Harry the Pedlar), Wylie Watson (Salvation Watkins), Horace Hodges (Pengallan's Butler [Chadwick]), Hay Petrie (Pengallan's Groom), Frederick Piper (Pengallan's Broker), Morland Graham (Sea Lawyer Sydney), Edwin Greenwood (Dandy), Stephen Haggard (the Boy), Mervyn Johns (Thomas), Herbert Lomas, Clare Greet, William Delvin (Pengallan's Tenants), Jeanne de Casalis, A. Bromley Davenport, Mabel Terry Lewis, George Curzon, Basil Radford (Pengallan's Friends).

Selected credits: Cd: Molly McArthur. Art dir: Tom Morahan. Ed: Robert Hamer. Makeup: Ern Westmore. Spfx: Harry Watt. M: Eric Fenby. Dp: Bernard Knowles, Harry Stradling. Scrp: Sidney Gilliat, Joan Harrison. Additional dialogue: J. B. Priestley. Bo: novel by Daphne du Maurier. Prod: Erich Pommer, Charles Laughton. Dir: **AH**.

REBECCA
1940. 130 mins. B&w. Selznick International.

Cast: Laurence Olivier (Maxim de Winter), Joan Fontaine (Mrs. de Winter), George Sanders (Jack Favell), Judith Anderson (Mrs. Danvers), Nigel Bruce (Major Giles Lacey), C. Aubrey Smith (Colonel Julyan), Florence Bates (Mrs. Van Hopper), Leo G. Carroll (Dr. Baker), Leonard Carey (Ben), Reginald Denny (Frank Crawley), Gladys Cooper (Beatrice Lacey), Philip Winter, Edward Fielding, Forrester Harvey, Lumsden Hare, Edith Sharpe, Melville Cooper.

Selected credits: Set dir: Joseph B. Platt, Herbert Bristol. Art dir: Lyle Wheeler. Ed: Hal Kern, James E. Newcom. Spfx: Jack Cosgrove. M: Franz Waxman. Asst dir: Edmond F. Bernoudy. Dp: George Barnes. Adaptation: Philip MacDonald, Michael Hogan. Scrp: Robert E. Sherwood, Joan Harrison. Bo: novel by Daphne du Maurier. Prod: David O. Selznick. Dir: AH.

Selected awards: AA: Best Picture; Black and White Cinematography (George Barnes). AAN: Best Director; Best Actor (Laurence Olivier); Best Actress (Joan Fontaine); Best Supporting Actress (Judith Anderson); Writing: Screenplay (Robert E. Sherwood, Joan Harrison); Interior Decoration (Lyle Wheeler); Best Score (Franz Waxman); Film Editing (Hal Kern), Special Effects (Jack Cosgrove). *New York Times* Ten Best Films list, 1940. National Board of Review Awards: Best American Films list; Joan Fontaine, George Sanders on Best Acting list.

THE HOUSE ACROSS THE BAY
1940. 88 mins. B&w. Walter Wanger/United Artists.

Selected Cast: Joan Bennett, George Raft, Lloyd Nolan, Walter Pidgeon, Gladys George, June Knight.

Selected credits: Dp: Merritt Gerstad. Scrp: Kathryn Scola. Prod: Walter Wanger. Dir: Archie Mayo, AH (uncredited).

(Note: When director Mayo fell ill, Hitchcock shot some retakes involving Pidgeon, Nolan, and Bennett in a plane.)

FOREIGN CORRESPONDENT
1940. 120 mins. B&w. Walter Wanger/United Artists.

Cast: Joel McCrea (Johnnie Jones/Huntley Haverstock), Laraine Day (Carol Fisher), Herbert Marshall (Stephen Fisher), George Sanders (Ffolliott), Albert Bassermann (Van Meer), Robert Benchley (Stebbins), Eduardo Ciannelli (Krug), Edmund Gwenn (Rowley), Harry Davenport (Mr. Powers), Martin Kosleck, Eddie Conrad, Gertrude W. Hoffman, Jane Novak, Ken Christy, Crawford Kent, Joan Brodel-Leslie, Louis Borell, Eily Malyon, E. E. Clive, Frances Carson, Emory Parnell, Ian Wolfe.

Selected credits: Cd: I. Magnin & Co. Set dir: Julia Heron. Art dir: Alexander Golitzen, Richard Irvine. Ed: Otto Lovering, Dorothy Spencer. Spfx: Paul Eagler, Lee Zavitz. Special production effects: William Cameron Menzies. M: Alfred Newman. Asst dir: Edmond F. Bernoudy. Dp: Rudolph Maté. Scrp: Charles Bennett, Joan Harrison, Ben Hecht (uncredited). Dialogue: James Hilton, Robert Benchley. Prod: Walter Wanger. Dir: AH.

Selected awards: AAN: Best Picture; Best Supporting Actor (Albert Basserman); Writing: Original Screenplay (Charles Bennett, Joan Harrison); Black and White Cinematography (Rudolph Maté); Interior Decoration (Alexander Golitzen); Special Effects (Paul Eagler, Lee Zavitz).

MR. AND MRS. SMITH
1941. 95 mins. B&w. RKO.

Cast: Carole Lombard (Ann Krausheimer/Smith), Robert Montgomery (David Smith), Gene Raymond (Jeff Custer), Jack Carson (Chuck Benson), Philip Merivale (Mr. Custer), Lucile Watson (Mrs. Custer), William Tracy (Sammy), Charles Halton (Mr. Deaver), Esther Dale (Mrs. Krausheimer), Emma Dunn (Martha), Betty Compson (Gertie), Patricia Farr (Gloria), Williams Edmunds (Proprietor of Lucy's), Adele Pearce (Lily), Murray Alper, D. Johnson, James Flavin, Sam Harris.

Selected credits: Cd: Irene. Set dir: Darrell Silvera. Art dir: Van Nest Polglase, L. P. Williams. Ed: William Hamilton. Spfx: Vernon L. Walker. M: Edward Ward. Asst dir: Dewey

Starkey. Dp: Harry Stradling. Scrp: Norman Krasna. Exec prod: Harry E. Edington. Prod: Carole Lombard (uncredited). Dir: AH.

SUSPICION
1941. 100 mins. B&w. RKO.

Cast: Cary Grant (Johnnie Aysgarth), Joan Fontaine (Lina McLaidlaw), Sir Cedric Hardwicke (General McLaidlaw), Nigel Bruce (Beaky), Dame May Whitty (Mrs. McLaidlaw), Isabel Jeans (Mrs. Newsham), Heather Angel (Ethel), Auriol Lee (Isobel Sedbusk), Reginald Sheffield (Reggie Wetherby), Leo G. Carroll (Captain Melbeck).

Selected credits: Cd: Edward Stevenson. Set dir: Darrell Silvera. Art dir: Van Nest Polglase. Ed: William Hamilton, Carroll Clark. Spfx: Vernon L. Walker. M: Franz Waxman. Asst dir: Dewey Starkey. Dp: Harry Stradling. Scrp: Samson Raphaelson, Joan Harrison, Alma Reville. Bo: novel *Before the Fact* by Francis Iles (Anthony Berkeley Cox). Prod: Harry E. Edington. Dir: AH.

Selected awards: AA: Best Actress (Joan Fontaine). AAN: Best Picture; Scoring of a Dramatic Picture (Franz Waxman). National Board of Review Awards: Joan Fontaine on Best Acting list. New York Film Critics Awards: Best Actress (Joan Fontaine).

MEN OF THE LIGHTSHIP
1941. B&w. British Ministry of Information.

Wartime documentary.

Sup ed (U.S. version): AH (uncredited). Dir: David MacDonald.

TARGET FOR TONIGHT
1941. 48 mins. B&w. The Crown Film Unit.

Wartime documentary.

Sup ed (U.S. version): AH (uncredited). Dir: Harry Watt.

Selected awards: Winner of Special Academy Award.

SABOTEUR
1942. 109 mins. B&w. Frank Lloyd/Universal.

Cast: Robert Cummings (Barry Kane), Priscilla Lane (Patricia Martin), Otto Kruger (Charles Tobin), Norman Lloyd (Frank Fry), Alan Baxter (Mr. Freeman), Alma Kruger (Mrs. Sutton),

Vaughan Glazer (Mr. Miller), Dorothy Peterson (Mrs. Mason), Ian Wolfe (Robert), Pedro de Cordoba (Bones), Anita Bolster (Lorelei), Jeanne and Lynn Romer (Siamese Twins), Oliver Blake, Anita Le Deaux (Fat Woman), Kathryn Adams (Young Mother), Murray Alper (Truck Driver), Frances Carson (Society Woman), Billy Curtis (Midget).

Selected credits: Set dir: R. A. Gausman. Art dir: Jack Otterson, Robert Boyle. Ed: Otto Ludwig. M: Frank Skinner, Charles Prévin. Asst dir: Fred Frank. Dp: Joseph Valentine. Scrp: Peter Viertel, Joan Harrison, Dorothy Parker. Bo: original subject by **AH**. Assoc prod: Jack H. Skirball. Prod: Frank Lloyd. Dir: **AH**.

FOREVER AND A DAY
1943. 104 mins. B&w. RKO.
Selected cast: Ida Lupino, Ray Milland, Claude Rains, Cedric Hardwicke, Buster Keaton.
Selected credits: Scrp: 21 credited co-writers, including Charles Bennett. Dir: René Clair, Edmund Goulding, Cedric Hardwicke, Frank Lloyd, Victor Saville, Robert Stevenson, Herbert Wilcox.
(Note: **AH** prepared the sequence featuring Ida Lupino, but his schedule prevented him from shooting it. It was ultimately directed by René Clair, working from Hitchcock's script.)

SHADOW OF A DOUBT
1943. 108 mins. B&w. Universal/Skirball Productions.
Cast: Joseph Cotten (Uncle Charlie Oakley), Teresa Wright (Charlie Newton), Macdonald Carey (Jack Graham), Patricia Collinge (Emma Newton), Henry Travers (Joe Newton), Hume Cronyn (Herb Hawkins), Wallace Ford (Fred Saunders), Janet Shaw (Louise), Estelle Jewell (Catherine), Clarence Muse (Pullman Porter), Charles Bates (Roger Newton), Edna May Wonacott (Ann Newton), Irving Bacon (Station Master), Eily Malyon, Ethel Griffies, Frances Carson.
Selected credits: Cd: Adrian, Vera West. Set dir: R. A. Gausman, E. R. Robinson. Art dir: John B. Goodman, Robert Boyle. Ed: Milton Carruth. M: Dimitri Tiomkin. Asst dir: William Tummell. Dp: Joseph Valentine. Scrp:

Thornton Wilder, Sally Benson, Alma Reville. Bo: original treatment by Gordon McDonell. Prod: Jack H. Skirball. Dir: **AH**.
Selected awards: AAN: Writing: Original Story (Gordon McDonell). National Board of Review Awards: Best Actress (Teresa Wright).

LIFEBOAT
1944. 96 mins. B&w. 20th Century-Fox.
Cast: Tallulah Bankhead (Constance Porter), William Bendix (Gus Smith), Walter Slezak (Willi), Mary Anderson (Alice Mackenzie), John Hodiak (Kovac), Henry Hull (Charles Rittenhouse), Heather Angel (Mrs. Iggley), Hume Cronyn (Stanley Garrett), Canada Lee (Joe).
Selected credits: Cd: Rene Hubert. Set dir: Thomas Little, Frank E. Hughes. Art dir: James Basevi, Maurice Ransford. Ed: Dorothy Spencer. Makeup: Guy Pearce. Spfx: Fred Sersen. M: Hugo W. Friedhofer. Dp: Glen MacWilliams. Scrp: Jo Swerling, Ben Hecht (uncredited). Bo: original treatment by John Steinbeck. Prod: Kenneth MacGowan. Dir: **AH**.
Selected awards: AAN: Best Director; Writing: Original Story (John Steinbeck); Black and White Cinematography (Glen MacWilliams). National Board of Review Awards: Best English-Language Films list.

New York Film Critics Awards: Best Actress (Tallulah Bankhead).

BON VOYAGE
1944. 26 mins. B&w. Phoenix, for the British Ministry of Information.
Cast: John Blythe (John Dougall), The Molière Players.
Selected credits: Set dir: Charles Gilbert. Dp: Günther Krampf. Scrp: J. O. C. Orton, Angus MacPhail. Bo: original story by Arthur Calder Marshall. Dir: **AH**.

AVENTURE MALGACHE
1944 (released 1993). 31 mins. B&w. Phoenix, for the British Ministry of Information.
Cast: The Molière Players.
Selected credits: Set dir: Charles Gilbert. Dp: Günther Krampf. Dir: **AH**.

MEMORY OF THE CAMPS
Documentary footage of the Nazi concentration camps.
Selected credits: Ed: Stewart McAllister, Peter Tanner. Treatment advisor: **AH**. Treatments: Colin Wills, Richard Grossman. Scrp: Colin Wills. Exec prod: Sidney Bernstein. Prod: Sergi Nolbandov. (For Frontline: Ed/prod: Stephanie Tapper. Exec prod: David Fanning. Narrated by: Trevor Howard.)

John Emery (Dr. Fleurot), Leo G. Carroll (Dr. Murchison), Michael Chekhov (Dr. Alex Brulov), Norman Lloyd (Garmes), Steven Geray, Paul Harvey, Erskine Sandford, Janet Scott, Victor Kilian, Bill Goodwin, Art Baker, Wallace Ford, Regis Toomey, Teddy Infuhr, Addison Richards, Dave Willock, George Meader, Matt Moore, Harry Brown, Clarence Straight, Joel Davis, Edward Fielding, Richard Bartell.

Selected credits: Cd: Howard Greer. Set dir: Emile Kuri. Art dir: James Basevi, John Ewing. Dream sequence des: Salvador Dali. Sup ed: Hal Kern. Ed: William Ziegler. Spfx: Jack Cosgrove. M: Miklós Rózsa. Asst dir: Lowell J. Farrell. Dp: George Barnes. Adaptation: AngUSMacPhail. Scrp: Ben Hecht. Bo: novel *The House of Dr. Edwardes* by Francis Beeding (Hilary Aidan St George Saunders and John Leslie Palmer). Prod: David O. Selznick. Dir: **AH**.

Selected awards: AA: Best Score of a Dramatic or Comedy Picture (Miklós Rózsa). AAN: Best Picture; Best Director; Best Supporting Actor (Michael Chekhov); Black and White Cinematography (George Barnes); Special Effects (Jack Cosgrove). *New York Times* Ten Best Films list, 1945. New York Film Critics Awards: Best Actress (Ingrid Bergman).

NOTORIOUS
1946. 100 mins. B&w. RKO.

Cast: Ingrid Bergman (Alicia Huberman), Cary Grant (Devlin), Claude Rains (Alexander Sebastian), Louis Calhern (Paul Prescott), Leopoldine Konstantin (Mme. Sebastian), Reinhold Schunzel (Dr. Anderson), Moroni Olsen (Walter Beardsley), Ivan Triesault (Eric Mathis), Alexis Minotis (Joseph), Eberhard Krumschmidt (Hupka), Fay Baker (Ethel), Ricardo Costa (Dr. Barbosa), Sir Charles Mendl (Commodore), Wally Brown (Mr. Hopkins), Lenore Ulric, Ramon Nomar, Peter von Zerneck.

Selected credits: Cd: Edith Head. Set dir: Darrell Silvera, Claude Carpenter. Art dir: Albert S. D'Agostino, Carroll Clark. Ed: Theron Warth. Spfx: Vernon L. Walker, Paul Eagler. M: Roy Webb. Asst dir: William Dorfman. Dp: Ted Tetzlaff.

WATCHTOWER OVER TOMORROW
1945. 15 mins. Produced for the Department of State and the OWI (Office of War Information) by the War Activities Committee, Motion Picture Industry.
Documentary concerning the formation of the United Nations.
Cast: Secretary of State Edward Stettinius Jr. (gives introductory remarks), Jon Nesbitt (Narrator), Grant Mitchell, Jonathan Hale, Miles Mander, George Zucco.

Selected credits: Dp: Lester White. Scrp: Ben Hecht, Karl Lamb. Dir: John Cromwell, Harold Kress, **AH** (uncredited), Elia Kazan (uncredited).

SPELLBOUND
1945. 110 mins. B&w. Selznick International.
Cast: Ingrid Bergman (Dr. Constance Petersen), Gregory Peck (John Ballyntine), Jean Acker (the Directress), Rhonda Fleming (Mary Carmichael), Donald Curtis (Harry),

Scrp: Ben Hecht. Bo: a subject by **AH**.
Assoc prod: Barbara Keon. Prod/Dir:
AH.

Selected Awards: AAN: Best Supporting
Actor (Claude Rains), Writing:
Original Screenplay (Ben Hecht).

THE PARADINE CASE
1947. 132 mins. B&w. Selznick
International/Vanguard.

Cast: Gregory Peck (Anthony Keane),
Ann Todd (Gay Keane), [Alida] Valli
(Mrs. Paradine), Charles Laughton
(Lord Horfield), Ethel Barrymore
(Lady Sophie Horfield), Charles
Coburn (Sir Simon Flaquer), Louis
Jourdan (André Latour), Leo G.
Carroll (Sir Joseph Farrell), Joan
Tetzel (Judy Flaquer) John
Goldsworthy, Isobel Elsom, Lester
Matthews, Pat Aherne, Colin Hunter,
John Williams.

Selected credits: Cd: Travis Banton.
Production des: Joseph MacMillan
Johnson. Set dir: Joseph B. Platt,
Emile Kuri. Art dir: Tom Morahan.
Ed: Hal Kern, John Faure. Spfx:
Clarence Slifer. M: Franz Waxman.
Asst dir: Lowell J. Farrell. Dp: Lee
Garmes. Adaptation: Alma Reville.
Scrp: David O. Selznick, Ben Hecht
(uncredited). Bo: novel by Robert
Hichens. Prod: David O. Selznick.
Dir: **AH**.

Selected awards: AAN: Best Supporting
Actress (Ethel Barrymore).

ROPE
1948. 80 mins. Technicolor.
Transatlantic.

Cast: James Stewart (Rupert Cadell),
John Dall (Brandon), Farley Granger
(Philip), Joan Chandler (Janet), Sir
Cedric Hardwicke (Mr. Kentley),
Constance Collier (Mrs. Atwater),
Edith Evanson (Mrs. Wilson),
Douglas Dick (Kenneth), Dick Hogan
(David Kentley).

Selected credits: Cd: Adrian. Set dir:
Emile Kuri, Howard Bristol. Art dir:
Perry Ferguson. Ed: William Ziegler.
Makeup: Perc Westmore. M: Leo F.
Forbstein, based on "Perpetual
Movement No. 1" by Francis
Poulenc. Asst dir: Lowell J. Farrell.
Dp: Joseph Valentine, William V.
Skall. Adaptation: Hume Cronyn.
Scrp: Arthur Laurents. Bo: play by
Patrick Hamilton. Prod: **AH**, Sidney
Bernstein. Dir: **AH**.

UNDER CAPRICORN
1949. 118 mins. Technicolor.
Transatlantic.

Cast: Ingrid Bergman (Lady Henrietta
Flusky), Joseph Cotten (Sam Flusky),
Michael Wilding (Charles Adare),
Margaret Leighton (Milly), Jack
Watling (Winter), Cecil Parker
(Governor) Denis O'Dea (Corrigan),
Olive Sloan (Sal), John Ruddock (Mr.
Potter), Ronald Adam (Mr. Riggs), G.
H. Mulcaster (Dr. McAllister),
Maureen Delaney (Flo), Francis de
Wolff (Major Wilkins), Bill Shine,
Victor Lucas, Julia Lang, Betty
McDermot, Roderick Lovell.

Selected credits: Cd: Roger Furse.
Production des: Tom Morahan. Set
dir: Philip Stockford. Ed: A. S. Bates.
Makeup: Charles Parker. M: Richard
Addinsell. Asst dir: C. Foster Kemp.
Dp: Jack Cardiff. Adaptation: Hume
Cronyn. Scrp: James Bridie. Bo: novel
by Helen Simpson. Managing prod:
John Palmer, Fred Ahern. Prod: **AH**,
Sidney Bernstein. Dir: **AH**.

STAGE FRIGHT
1950. 110 mins. B&w. Warner
Brothers/First National.

Cast: Marlene Dietrich (Charlotte
Inwood), Jane Wyman (Eve Gill),
Michael Wilding (Inspector Wilfred
Smith), Richard Todd (Jonathan
Cooper), Alastair Sim (Commodore
Gill), Dame Sybil Thorndike (Mrs.
Gill), Patricia Hitchcock (Chubby
Banister), Kay Walsh (Nellie Goode),
Miles Malleson (Mr. Fortesque),
André Morell (Inspector Byard),
Hector MacGregor (Freddie
Williams), Joyce Grenfell (Lovely
Ducks), Ballard Berkeley (Sergeant
Mellish).

Selected credits: Set dir: Terence Verity Jr.
Ed: E. B. Jarvis. Makeup: Colin
Garde. M: Leighton Lucas. Dp:
Wilkie Cooper. Adaptation: Alma
Reville. Scrp: Whitfield Cook.
Additional dialogue: James Bridie. Bo:
novel *Man Running* by Selwyn
Jepson. Prod: **AH**, Fred Aherne. Dir:
AH.

Cinematography (Robert Burks). National Board of Review Awards: Best American Films list. Directors Guild of America Quarterly Award.

I CONFESS

1953. 95 mins. B&w. Warner Brothers/First National.

Cast: Montgomery Clift (Father Michael Logan), Anne Baxter (Ruth Grandfort), Karl Malden (Inspector Larrue), Brian Aherne ([Crown Prosecutor] Willy Robertson), O. E. Hasse (Otto Keller), Dolly Haas (Alma Keller), Roger Dann (Pierre Grandfort), Charles André (Father Millais), Judson Pratt (Murphy), Ovila Legare (Vilette), Gilles Pelletier (Father Benoit).

Selected credits: Cd: Orry-Kelly. Set dir: George James Hopkins. Art dir: Edward S. Haworth. Ed: Rudi Fehr. Makeup: Gordon Bau. M: Dimitri Tiomkin. Asst dir: Don Page. Dp: Robert Burks. Scrp: George Tabori, William Archibald. Bo: play *Nos deux consciences* by Paul Anthelme. Prod/Dir: **AH**.

DIAL M FOR MURDER

1954. 105 mins. Warnercolor/3-D. Warner Brothers/First National.

Cast: Ray Milland (Tom Wendice), Grace Kelly (Margot Wendice), Robert Cummings (Mark Halliday), John Williams (Chief Inspector Hubbard), Anthony Dawson (Captain Lesgate/Swann), Leo Britt (the Narrator), Patrick Allen (Pearson), George Leigh (William), George Alderson (Detective), Robin Hughes (Police Sergeant).

Selected credits: Cd: Moss Mabry. Set dir: George James Hopkins. Art dir: Edward Carrere. Ed: Rudi Fehr. Makeup: Gordon Bau. M: Dimitri Tiomkin. Asst dir: Mel Dellar. Dp: Robert Burks. Scrp: Frederick Knott. Bo: play by Frederick Knott. Prod/Dir: **AH**.

Selected awards: National Board of Review Awards: Best Actress (Grace Kelly). New York Film Critics Awards: Best Actress (Grace Kelly).

REAR WINDOW

1954. 112 mins. Technicolor. Paramount/Patron, Inc.

Cast: James Stewart (L. B. Jefferies), Grace Kelly (Lisa Fremont), Wendell

Selected awards: National Board of Review Awards: Best American Films list.

STRANGERS ON A TRAIN

1951. 100 mins. B&w. Warner Brothers/First National.

Cast: Farley Granger (Guy Haines), Robert Walker (Bruno Anthony), Ruth Roman (Anne Morton), Leo G. Carroll (Senator Morton), Patricia Hitchcock (Barbara Morton), Laura Elliot (Miriam Haines), Marion Lorne (Mrs. Anthony), Jonathan Hale (Mr. Anthony), Howard St John, John Brown, Norma Varden, Robert Gist, John Doucette, Charles Meredith, Murray Alper, Robert B. Williams, Roy Engel.

Selected credits: Cd: Leah Rhodes. Set dir: George James Hopkins. Art dir: Edward S. Haworth. Ed: William Ziegler. Spfx: H. F. Koenekamp. M: Dimitiri Tiomkin. Dp: Robert Burks. Adaptation: Whitfield Cook. Scrp: Raymond Chandler, Czenzi Ormonde. Bo: novel by Patricia Highsmith. Prod/Dir: **AH**.

Selected awards: AAN: Black and White

Corey (Tom Doyle), Thelma Ritter (Stella), Raymond Burr (Lars Thorwald), Judith Evelyn (Miss Lonely Hearts), Ross Bagdasarian (The Composer), Georgine Darcy (Miss Torso), Jesslyn Fax (Miss Sculptress), Rand Harper (Honeymooner), Irene Winston (Mrs. Thorwald), Denny Bartlett, Len Hendry, Mike Mahoney, Alan Lee, Anthony Ward, Harry Landers, Dick Simmons, Fred Graham, Edwin Parker, M. English, Kathryn Grandstaff, Havis Davenport, Iphigénie Castiglioni, Sara Berner, Frank Cady.

Selected credits: Cd: Edith Head. Set dir: Sam Comer, Ray Moyer. Art dir: Hal Pereira, Joseph MacMillan Johnson. Ed: George Tomasini. Spfx: John P. Fulton. M: Franz Waxman. Asst dir: Herbert Coleman. Dp: Robert Burks. Scrp: John Michael Hayes. Bo: story by Cornell Woolrich. Prod/Dir: **AH**.

Selected awards: AAN: Best Director; Writing: Screenplay (John Michael Hayes), Color Cinematography (Robert Burks), Sound Recording (Harry Lindgren, John Cape). National Board of Review Awards: Best Actress (Grace Kelly). New York Film Critics Awards: Best Actress (Grace Kelly). Directors Guild of America Awards: Outstanding Directorial Achievement.

TO CATCH A THIEF
1955. 97 mins. Technicolor/VistaVision. Paramount.

Cast: Cary Grant (John Robie), Grace Kelly (Francie Stevens), Charles Vanel (Bertani), Jessie Royce Landis (Mrs. Jessie Stevens), Brigitte Auber (Danielle Foussard), René Blancard (Commissioner Lepic), John Williams (H. H. Hughson), Georgette Anys, Roland Lesaffre, Jean Hebey, Dominique Davray, Russel Gaige, Marie Stoddard, Frank Chellano, Otto F. Schulze, Guy de Vestel, Bela Kovacs, John Alderson, Don McGowan, W. Willie Davis, Edward Manouk, Jean Martinelli, Martha Bamattre, Aimee Torriani, Paul "Tiny" Newlan, Lewis Charles, Gerard Buhr.

Selected credits: Cd: Edith Head. Set dir: Sam Comer, Arthur Krams. Art dir: Hal Pereira, Joseph MacMillan Johnson. Ed: George Tomasini.

Makeup: Wally Westmore. Spfx: John P. Fulton. M: Lyn Murray. Asst dir: Daniel McCauley. 2nd unit dir: Herbert Coleman. Dp: Robert Burks. Scrp: John Michael Hayes. Bo: novel by David Dodge. Prod/Dir: **AH**.

Selected awards: AA: Color Cinematography (Robert Burks). AAN: Color Art Direction/Set Direction (Hal Pereira, Joseph MacMillan Johnson); Color Costume Design (Edith Head).

THE TROUBLE WITH HARRY
1955. 99 mins. Technicolor/VistaVision. Paramount/Alfred Hitchcock Productions.

Cast: Edmund Gwenn (Captain Albert Wiles), John Forsythe (Sam Marlowe), Shirley MacLaine (Jennifer Rogers), Mildred Natwick (Miss Gravely), Jerry Mathers (Arnie Rogers), Mildred Dunnock (Mrs. Wiggs), Royal Dano (Calvin Wiggs), Philip Truex (Harry), Parker Fennelly (Millionaire), Dwight Marfield (Dr. Greenbow), Barry Macollum, Leslie Wolff, Ernest Curt Bach.

Selected credits: Cd: Edith Head. Set dir: Sam Comer, Emile Kuri. Art dir: Hal Pereira, John Goodman. Ed: Alma Macrorie. Spfx: John P. Fulton. M: Bernard Herrmann. Asst dir: Howard Joslin. Dp: Robert Burks. Scrp: John Michael Hayes. Bo: novel by Jack Trevor Story. Assoc prod: Herbert Coleman. Prod/Dir: **AH**.

THE MAN WHO KNEW TOO MUCH
1956. 120 mins. Technicolor/VistaVision. Paramount/FilWite Productions.

Cast: James Stewart (Dr. Ben McKenna), Doris Day (Jo McKenna), Daniel Gélin (Louis Bernard), Brenda de Banzie (Mrs. Drayton), Bernard Miles (Mr. Drayton), Ralph Truman (Inspector Buchanan), Mogens Wieth (the Ambassador), Alan Mowbray (Val Parnell), Hilary Brooke (Jan Peterson), Christopher Olsen (Hank McKenna), Reggie Nalder (Rien, the assassin), Yves Brainville, Richard Wattis, Alix Talton, Noel Willman, Carolyn Jones, Leo Gordon, Abdelhaq Chraibi, Betty Baskomb, Patrick Aherne, Louis Mercier, Anthony Warde, Lewis Martin, Richard Wordsworth.

Selected credits: Cd: Edith Head. Set dir: Sam Comer, Arthur Krams. Art dir: Hal Pereira, Henry Bumstead. Ed: George Tomasini. Spfx: John P. Fulton. M: Bernard Herrmann. Asst dir: Howard Joslin. Dp: Robert Burks. Scrp: John Michael Hayes, AngUSMacPhail. Bo: story by Charles Bennett and D. B. Wyndham Lewis. Assoc prod: Herbert Coleman. Prod/Dir: **AH**.

Selected awards: AA: Best Song ("Whatever Will Be, Will Be," by Jay Livingston and Ray Evans).

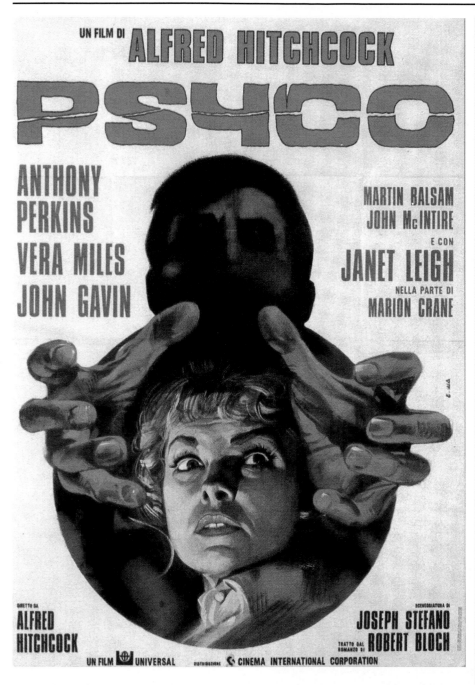

UN FILM DI ALFRED HITCHCOCK
PSYCO

ANTHONY PERKINS
VERA MILES
JOHN GAVIN

MARTIN BALSAM
JOHN McINTIRE
E CON
JANET LEIGH
NELLA PARTE DI
MARION CRANE

DIRETTO DA
ALFRED HITCHCOCK

SCENEGGIATURA DI
JOSEPH STEFANO
TRATTO DAL ROMANZO DI
ROBERT BLOCH

UN FILM UNIVERSAL   DISTRIBUZIONE CINEMA INTERNATIONAL CORPORATION

VERTIGO

1958. 128 mins. Technicolor/VistaVision. Paramount/Alfred Hitchcock Productions.

Cast: James Stewart (John "Scottie" Ferguson), Kim Novak ("Madeleine Elster"/Judy Barton), Barbara Bel Geddes (Midge Wood), Henry Jones (Coroner), Tom Helmore (Gavin Elster), Raymond Bailey (the doctor), Konstantin Shayne (Pop Liebl), Ellen Corby (Hotel McKittrick landlady), Lee Patrick.

Selected credits: Cd: Edith Head. Set dir: Sam Comer, Frank McKelvey. Art dir: Hal Pereira, Henry Bumstead. Ed: George Tomasini. Makeup: Wally Westmore. Spfx: John P. Fulton. Titles des: Saul Bass. M: Bernard Herrmann. Asst dir: Daniel J. McCauley. Dp: Robert Burks. Scrp: Alec Coppel, Samuel Taylor. Bo: novel *D'entre les Morts* by Pierre Boileau and Thomas Narcejac. Assoc prod: Herbert Coleman. Prod/Dir: **AH**.

Selected awards: AAN: Art Direction/Set Direction (Hal Pereira, Henry Bumstead); Sound (Harold Lewis, Winston Leverett).

NORTH BY NORTHWEST

1959. 136 mins. Technicolor/VistaVision. MGM.

Cast: Cary Grant (Roger O. Thornhill), Eva Marie Saint (Eve Kendall), James Mason (Philip Vandamm), Jessie Royce Landis (Clara Thornhill), Leo G. Carroll (the Professor), Philip Ober (Lester Townsend), Josephine Hutchinson (Mrs. Townsend, the housekeeper), Martin Landau (Leonard), Adam Williams (Valerian), Robert Ellenstein (Licht), Malcolm Atterbury (Farmer at crossroads), Edward C. Platt (Victor Larrabee), Philip Coolidge (Dr. Cross), Edward Binns (Captain Junket), Les Tremayne (Auctioneer), Pat McVey, Ken Lynch (Chicago policemen), Doreen Lang, Nora Marlowe, Carleton Young, Robert B. Williams, Larry Dobkin, Ned Glass, John Berardino.

Selected credits: Production des: Robert Boyle. Set dir: Henry Grace, Frank McKelvey. Art dir: William A. Horning, Merrill Pye. Ed: George Tomasini. Makeup: William Tuttle. Spfx: Arnold Gillespie, Lee LeBlanc. Titles des: Saul Bass. M: Bernard Herrmann. Asst dir: Robert Saunders.

THE WRONG MAN

1956. 105 mins. B&w. Warner Brothers.

Cast: Henry Fonda (Christopher Emmanuel Balestrero), Vera Miles (Rose Balestrero), Anthony Quayle (Frank O'Connor), Harold J. Stone (Lieutenant Bowers) Charles Cooper (Detective Matthews), John Heldabrand (Tomasini), Richard Robbins (Daniell), Esther Minciotti (Mrs. Balestrero), Doreen Lang (Mrs. James), Laurinda Barrett (Constance Willis), Norma Connolly (Betty Todd), Nehemiah Persoff (Gene Conforti), Lola D'Annunzio (Olga Conforti), Kippy Campbell (Robert Balestrero), Robert Essen (Gregory Balestrero), Dayton Lummis (Judge), Peggy Webber (Miss Dennerly), Frances Reid.

Selected credits: Set dir: William L. Kuehl. Art dir: Paul Sylbert. Ed: George Tomasini. Makeup: Gordon Bau. M: Bernard Herrmann. Asst dir: Daniel J. McCauley. Dp: Robert Burks. Scrp: Maxwell Anderson, AngUSMacPhail. Bo: *Life* article "A Case of Identity" by Herbert Brean. Assoc prod: Herbert Coleman. Prod/Dir: **AH**.

Dp: Robert Burks. Scrp: Ernest Lehman. Assoc prod: Herbert Coleman. Prod/Dir: **AH.**

Selected awards: AAN: Best Story and Screenplay Written Directly For the Screen (Ernest Lehman); Color Art Direction/Set Direction (Robert Boyle, William A. Horning, Merrill Pye); Film Editing (George Tomasini). *New York Times* Ten Best Films list, 1959. National Board of Review Awards: Best American Films list.

PSYCHO

1960. 109 mins. B&w.
Paramount/Shamley Productions.

Cast: Anthony Perkins (Norman Bates), Janet Leigh (Marion Crane), Vera Miles (Lila Crane), John Gavin (Sam Loomis), Martin Balsam (Milton Arbogast), John McIntire (Al Chambers), Simon Oakland (Psychiatrist), Frank Albertson (Cassidy), Patricia Hitchcock (Caroline), Vaughn Taylor (Mr. Lowery), Lurene Tuttle (Mrs. Chambers), John Anderson ("California Charlie"), Mort Mills (Highway patrolman), Helen Wallace (Customer at hardware store).

Selected credits: Cd: Helen Colvig. Set dir: George Milo. Art dir: Joseph Hurley, Robert Clatworthy. Ed: George Tomasini. Spfx: Clarence Champagne. Titles des: Saul Bass. M: Bernard Herrmann. Asst dir: Hilton A. Green. Dp: John L. Russell. Scrp: Joseph Stefano. Bo: novel by Robert Bloch. Prod/Dir: **AH.**

Selected awards: AAN: Best Director; Best Supporting Actress (Janet Leigh); Black and White Cinematography (John L. Russell); Black and White Art Direction/Set Direction (Joseph Hurley, Robert Clatworthy). *New York Times* Ten Best Films list, 1960. Golden Globe: Best Supporting Actress (Janet Leigh).

THE BIRDS

1963. 120 mins. Technicolor.
Universal/Alfred Hitchcock Productions.

Cast: Rod Taylor (Mitch Brenner), "Tippi" Hedren (Melanie Daniels), Jessica Tandy (Lydia Brenner), Suzanne Pleshette (Annie Hayworth), Veronica Cartwright (Cathy Brenner), Ethel Griffies (Mrs. Bundy), Charles McGraw (Sebastian Sholes), Ruth

"It could be the most terrifying motion picture I have ever made!"— *Alfred Hitchcock*

"...and remember, the next scream you hear may be your own!"

ALFRED HITCHCOCK'S "The Birds"
TECHNICOLOR®

STARRING
ROD TAYLOR · JESSICA TANDY
SUZANNE PLESHETTE *and Introducing* 'TIPPI' HEDREN
Based on Daphne Du Maurier's Classic Suspense Story!

A Fascinating New Personality

Screenplay by EVAN HUNTER · Directed by ALFRED HITCHCOCK

McDevitt (Mrs. MacCruder), Joe Mantell (Travelling salesman), Malcolm Atterbury (Al Malone), Karl Swenson (Drunk), Elizabeth Wilson (Helen Carter), Lonny Chapman (Deke Carter), Doodles Weaver (Fisherman), John McGovern (Postal clerk), Richard Deacon (Man in elevator), Doreen Lang (Mother in Tides Café), Bill Quinn.

Selected credits: Cd: Edith Head. Production des: Norman Deming. Set dir: George Milo. Art dir: Robert Boyle. Ed: George Tomasini. Makeup: Howard Smit. Spfx: Lawrence A. Hampton, Robert Hoag, L. B. Abbott, Linwood Dunn. Special photographic adviser: Ub Iwerks. Electronic sound production and composition: Remi Gassmann, Oskar Sala. Titles des: James S. Pollak. Sound consultant: Bernard Herrmann. Asst dir: James H. Brown. Dp: Robert Burks. Scrp: Evan Hunter. Bo: story by Daphne du Maurier. Prod/Dir: **AH.**

Selected awards: AAN: Special Effects (Lawrence A. Hampton, Robert Hoag, L. B. Abbott, Linwood Dunn)

MARNIE
1964. 130 mins. Technicolor. Universal/Geoffrey Stanley, Inc.
Cast: "Tippi" Hedren (Margaret [Marnie] Edgar), Sean Connery (Mark Rutland), Diane Baker (Lil Mainwaring), Martin Gabel (Sidney Strutt), Louise Latham (Bernice Edgar), Bob Sweeney (Cousin Bob), Alan Napier (Mr. Rutland), S. John Launer (Sam Ward), Mariette Hartley (Susan Clabon), Bruce Dern (Sailor), Edith Evanson (Rita), Meg Wyllie (Mrs. Turpin), Henry Beckman (First Detective), Milton Selzer.
Selected credits: Cd: Edith Head, Vincent Dee, Rita Tiggs, James Linn. Set dir: George Milo. Art dir: Robert Boyle. Ed: George Tomasini. Makeup: Jack Barron, Howard Smit, Robert Dawn. M: Bernard Herrmann. Asst dir: James H. Brown. Dp: Robert Burks. Scrp: Jay Presson Allen. Bo: novel by Winston Graham. Prod/Dir: **AH**.

TORN CURTAIN
1966. 128 mins. Technicolor. Universal.
Cast: Paul Newman (Michael Armstrong), Julie Andrews (Sarah Sherman), Lila Kedrova (Countess Kuchinska), Hansjoerg Felmy (Heinrich Gerhard), Tamara Toumanova (Ballerina), Wolfgang Kieling (Hermann Gromek), Günter Strack (Professor Karl Manfred), Ludwig Donath (Professor Lindt), David Opatoshu (Jacobi), Gisela Fischer (Dr. Koska), Mort Mills (Farmer), Carolyn Conwell (Farmer's wife), Arthur Gould-Porter (Freddy), Gloria Gorvin (Fraulein Mann).
Selected credits: Cd: Edith Head, Grady Hunt. Production des: Hein Heckroth. Set dir: George Milo. Art dir: Frank Arrigo. Ed: Bud Hoffman. Makeup: Jack Barron. M: John Addison. Asst dir: Donald Baer. Dp: John F. Warren. Scrp: Brian Moore. Prod/Dir: **AH**.

TOPAZ
1969. 126 mins. Technicolor. Universal.
Cast: Frederick Stafford (André Devereaux), Dany Robin (Nicole Devereaux), John Vernon (Rico Parra), Karin Dor (Juanita de Cordoba), Michel Piccoli (Jacques Granville), Philippe Noiret (Henri Jarre), Claude Jade (Michele Picard), Michel Subor (François Picard), Roscoe Lee Browne (Philippe Dubois), Per-Axel Arosenius (Boris Kusenov), John Forsythe (Michael Nordstrom), Edmond Ryan (McKittreck), Sonja Kolthoff (Mrs. Kusenov), Tina Hedstrom (Tamara Kusenov), John Van Dreelen (Claude Martin), Don Randolph (Luis Uribe), Roberto Contreras (Munoz), Carlos Rivas (Hernandez), Lewis Charles (Mr. Mendoza), Anna Navarro (Mrs. Mendoza), John Roper (Thomas), George Skaff (René d'Arcy), Roger Til (Jean Chabrier), Sandor Szabo (Emile Redon), Lew Brown (American official).
Selected credits: Cd: Edith Head, Peter Saldutti, Pierre Balmain. Set dir: John Austin. Art dir: Henry Bumstead. Ed: William Ziegler. Makeup: Bud Westmore, Leonard Engelman. Spfx: Albert Whitlock. M: Maurice Jarre. Asst dir: Douglas Green, James Westman. Dp: Jack Hildyard. Scrp: Samuel Taylor. Bo: novel by Leon Uris. Assoc prod: Herbert Coleman. Prod/Dir: **AH**.
Selected awards: *New York Times* Ten Best Films list, 1969. National Board of Review Awards: Best Director; Best Supporting Actor (Philippe Noiret); Best English Language Films list.

FRENZY
1972. 116 mins. Eastmancolor. Universal.
Cast: Jon Finch (Richard Blaney), Barry Foster (Robert Rusk), Barbara Leigh-Hunt (Brenda Blaney), Alec McCowen (Chief Inspector Oxford), Anna Massey (Barbara "Babs" Milligan), Vivien Merchant (Mrs. Oxford), Bernard Cribbins (Felix Forsythe), Billie Whitelaw (Hetty Porter), Elsie Randolph (Gladys), Rita Webb (Mrs. Rusk), Clive Swift (Johnny Porter), Jean Marsh (Monica

Barling), Madge Ryan (Mrs. Davison), George Tovey (Mr. Salt), John Boxer (Sir George), Noel Johnson (Man at bar), Gerald Sim (Man at bar), June Ellis (Barmaid), Bunny May (Barman), Robert Keegan (Hospital patient), Jimmy Gardner (Hotel porter), Michael Bates (Sergeant Spearman), Michael Sheard.
Selected credits: Cd: Dulcie Midwinter. Production des: Syd Cain. Set dir: Simon Wakefield. Art dir: Bob Laing. Ed: John Jympson. Makeup: Harry Frampton. Spfx: Albert Whitlock. M: Ron Goodwin. Asst dir: Colin M. Brewer. Dp: Gil Taylor. Scrp: Anthony Shaffer. Bo: novel *Goodbye Piccadilly, Farewell Leicester Square* by Arthur La Bern. Assoc prod: William Hill. Prod/Dir: **AH**.
Selected awards: *New York Times* Ten Best Films list, 1972. National Board of Review Awards: Best English Language Films list.

FAMILY PLOT
1976. 120 mins. Eastmancolor. Universal.
Cast: Karen Black (Fran), Bruce Dern (George Lumley), Barbara Harris (Blanche Tyler), William Devane (Arthur Adamson), Cathleen Nesbitt (Julia Rainbird), Ed Lauter (Joseph Maloney), Katherine Helmond (Mrs. Maloney), Warren J. Kemmerling (Grandison), Edith Atwater (Mrs. Clay), William Prince (Bishop Wood), Nicolas Colasanto (Constantine), Marge Redmond (Vera Hannagan), John Lehne (Andy Bush), Charles Tyner (Wheeler), Alexander Lockwood (Parson), Martin West (Sanger), Louise Lorimer (Ida Cookson).
Selected credits: Cd: Edith Head. Set dir: James W. Payne. Art dir: Henry Bumstead. Ed: J. Terry Williams. Makeup: Jack Barron. Spfx: Albert Whitlock. M: John Williams. Asst dir: Howard G. Kazanjian, Wayne A. Farlow. Dp: Leonard South. Scrp: Ernest Lehman. Bo: novel *The Rainbird Pattern* by Victor Canning. Prod/Dir: **AH**.
Selected awards: National Board of Review Awards: Best English Language Films list.

Entries for each of the twenty Hitchcock–directed television films are given. Episodes are given in transmission order, and are all from *Alfred Hitchcock Presents* unless otherwise stated. Following this is a full episode listing for *Alfred Hitchcock Presents*, *The Alfred Hitchcock Hour*, *Suspicion*, and the 1980s *Alfred Hitchcock Presents* revival series. (See also pages 130–135.)

Revenge
Broadcast 10/2/55 (ep. 1).
25 mins. B&w. Shamley Productions.
Selected cast: Ralph Meeker, Vera Miles, Frances Bavier, Ray Montgomery, Ray Teal.
Selected credits: Scrp: Francis Cockrell, A. I. Bezzerides. Bo: story by Samuel Blas. Prod/Dir: **AH**.

Breakdown
Broadcast 11/13/55 (ep. 7).
25 mins. B&w. Shamley Productions.
Selected cast: Joseph Cotten, Raymond Bailey, Forrest Stanley, Lane Chandler, Aaron Spelling.
Selected credits: Scrp: Francis Cockrell, Louis Pollock. Bo: story by Louis Pollock. Prod/Dir: **AH**.

The Case of Mr. Pelham
Broadcast 12/4/55 (ep. 10).
25 mins. B&w. Shamley Productions.
Selected cast: Tom Ewell, Raymond Bailey, Kirby Smith, Kay Stewart, John Compton.
Selected credits: Scrp: Francis Cockrell. Bo: story by Anthony Armstrong. Prod/Dir: **AH**.

Back for Christmas
Broadcast 3/4/56 (ep. 23).
25 mins. B&w. Shamley Productions.
Selected cast: John Williams, Isabel Elsom, A. E. Gould-Porter, Gavin Muir, Katherine Warren.
Selected credits: Scrp: Francis Cockrell. Bo: story by John Collier. Prod/Dir: **AH**.

Wet Saturday
Broadcast 9/30/56 (ep. 40).
25 mins. B&w. Shamley Productions.
Selected cast: Sir Cedric Hardwicke, John Williams, Kathryn Givney, Jerry Barclay, Tita Purdom.
Selected credits: Scrp: Marian Cockrell. Bo: story by John Collier. Prod/Dir: **AH**.

Mr. Blanchard's Secret
Broadcast 12/23/56 (ep. 52).
25 mins. B&w. Shamley Productions.
Selected cast: Mary Scott, Robert Horton, Dayton Lummis, Meg Mundy, Eloise Hardt.
Selected credits: Scrp: Sarett Rudley. Bo: story by Emily Neff. Prod/Dir: **AH**.

One More Mile to Go
Broadcast 4/7/57 (ep. 67).
25 mins. B&w. Shamley Productions.
Selected cast: David Wayne, Louise Larrabee, Steve Brodie, Norman Leavitt.
Selected credits: Scrp: James P. Cavanagh. Bo: story by F. J. Smith. Prod/Dir: **AH**.

Four O'Clock (SUSPICION)
Broadcast 9/30/57 (ep. 1).
50 mins. B&w. Shamley Productions.
Selected cast: E. G. Marshall, Nancy Kelly, Richard Long, Tom Pittman, Harry Dean Stanton.
Selected credits: Scrp: Francis Cockrell. Bo: story by Cornell Woolrich. Prod/Dir: **AH**.

The Perfect Crime
Broadcast 10/20/57 (ep. 81).
25 mins. B&w. Shamley Productions.
Selected cast: Vincent Price, James Gregory, John Zaremba, Marianne Stewart, Gavin Gordon.
Selected credits: Scrp: Stirling Silliphant. Bo: story by Ben Ray Redman. Prod: Joan Harrison. Dir: **AH**.

Lamb to the Slaughter
Broadcast 4/13/58 (ep. 106).
25 mins. B&w. Shamley Productions.
Selected cast: Barbara Bel Geddes, Harold J. Stone, Allan Lane, Ken Clark, Robert C. Ross.

Selected credits: Scrp: Roald Dahl. Bo: story by Roald Dahl. Prod: Joan Harrison. Dir: **AH**.

Dip in the Pool
Broadcast 6/1/58 (ep. 113).
25 mins. B&w. Shamley Productions.
Selected cast: Keenan Wynn, Louise Platt, Philip Bourneuf, Fay Wray, Doreen Long.
Selected credits: Scrp: Robert C. Dennis, Francis Cockrell. Bo: story by Roald Dahl. Prod: Joan Harrison. Dir: **AH**.

Poison
Broadcast 10/5/58 (ep. 118).
25 mins. B&w. Shamley Productions.
Selected cast: Wendell Corey, James Donald, Arnold Moss, Weaver Levy.
Selected credits: Scrp: Casey Robinson. Bo: story by Roald Dahl. Prod: Joan Harrison. Dir: **AH**.

Banquo's Chair
Broadcast 5/3/59 (ep. 146).
25 mins. B&w. Shamley Productions.
Selected cast: John Williams, Kenneth Haigh, Reginald Gardiner, Max Adrian, Tom P. Dillon.
Selected credits: Scrp: Francis Cockrell. Bo: story by Rupert CroftCooke. Prod: Joan Harrison. Dir: **AH**.

Arthur
Broadcast 9/27/59 (ep. 154).
25 mins. B&w. Shamley Productions.
Selected cast: Laurence Harvey, Hazel Court, Robert Douglas, Barry G. Harvey, Patrick Macnee.
Selected credits: Scrp: James P. Cavanagh. Bo: story by Arthur Williams. Prod: Joan Harrison. Dir: **AH**.

The Crystal Trench
Broadcast 4/10/59 (ep. 155).
25 mins. B&w. Shamley Productions.
Selected cast: James Donald, Patricia Owens, Ben Astar, Werner Klemperer, Patrick Macnee.
Selected credits: Scrp: Stirling Silliphant. Bo: A. E. W. Mason. Prod: Joan Harrison. Dir: **AH**.

Incident at a Corner (FORD STAR-TIME)
Broadcast 4/5/60 (ep. 27).
50 mins. Color. Shamley Productions.
Selected cast: Paul Hartman, Vera Miles, George Peppard, Bob Sweeney, Leora Dana.
Selected credits: Scrp: Charlotte Armstrong. Bo: novel by Charlotte Armstrong. Prod: Joan Harrison. Dir: **AH**.

Mrs. Bixby and the Colonel's Coat
Broadcast 9/27/60 (ep. 191).
25 mins. B&w. Shamley Productions.
Selected cast: Audrey Meadows, Les Tremayne, Stephen Chase, Sally Hughes, Bernie Hamilton.
Selected credits: Scrp: Halsted Wells. Bo: story by Roald Dahl. Prod: Joan Harrison. Dir: **AH**.

The Horseplayer
Broadcast 3/14/61 (ep. 213).
25 mins. B&w. Shamley Productions.
Selected cast: Claude Rains, Ed Gardner, Percy Helton, Kenneth MacKenna, William Newell.
Selected credits: Scrp: Henry Slesar. Bo: story by Henry Slesar. Prod/Dir: **AH**.

Bang! You're Dead
Broadcast 10/17/61 (ep. 231).
25 mins. B&w. Shamley Productions.
Selected cast: Biff Elliott, Lucy Prentiss, Billy Mumy, Steve Dunne, Kelly Flynn.
Selected credits: Scrp: Harold Swanton. Bo: story by Margery Vosper. Prod: Joan Harrison. Dir: **AH**.

I Saw the Whole Thing (THE ALFRED HITCHCOCK HOUR)
Broadcast 10/11/62 (ep. 4).
50 mins. B&w. Shamley Productions.
Selected cast: John Forsythe, Kent Smith, John Fiedler, Philip Ober, William Newell.
Selected credits: Scrp: Henry Slesar. Bo: story by Henry Cecil. Prod: Joan Harrison. Dir: **AH**.

Note: Presently, ten of the half-hour Hitchcock–directed *Alfred Hitchcock Presents* shows are available on three commercial video releases. All the films can be viewed at the Museum of Television and Radio in New York City and Beverly Hills, California.

ALFRED HITCHCOCK PRESENTS

Approximately 25 mins. B&w.
Shamley Productions.
Prod: Joan Harrison and Norman Lloyd.

The series debuted on CBS, moving to NBC in September of 1960. The reader should be warned that syndicated reruns of the shows have been known to be edited versions.

1 "Revenge." 10/2/55; with Ralph Meeker and Vera Miles. Dir: **AH**.
2 "Premonition." 10/9/55; with Cloris Leachman and John Forsythe. Dir: Robert Stevens.
3 "Triggers in Leash." 10/16/55; with Darren McGavin and Gene Barry. Dir: Don Medford.
4 "Don't Come Back Alive." 10/23/55; with Sidney Blackmer. Dir: Robert Stevenson.
5 "Into Thin Air" (aka "The Vanishing Lady"). 10/30/55; with Patricia Hitchcock. Dir: Don Medford.
6 "Salvage." 11/6/55; with Gene Barry. Dir: Justus Addiss.
7 "Breakdown." 11/13/55; with Joseph Cotten. Dir: **AH**.
8 "Our Cook's a Treasure." 11/20/55; with Beulah Bondi and Everett Sloane. Dir: Robert Stevens.
9 "The Long Shot." 11/27/55; with John Williams. Dir: Robert Stevenson.
10 "The Case of Mr. Pelham." 12/4/55; with Tom Ewell. Dir: **AH**.
11 "Guilty Witness." 12/11/55; with Judith Evelyn and Joe Mantell. Dir: Robert Stevens.
12 "Santa Claus and the 10th Avenue Kid." 12/18/55; with Barry Fitzgerald. Dir: Don Weis.
13 "The Cheney Vase." 12/25/55; with Patricia Collinge and Darren McGavin. Dir: Robert Stevens.
14 "A Bullet for Baldwin." 1/1/56; with Sebastian Cabot. Dir: Justus Addiss.
15 "The Big Switch." 1/8/56; with George Mathews and George E. Stone. Dir: Don Weis.
16 "You Got to Have Luck." 1/15/56; with John Cassavetes. Dir: Robert Stevens.
17 "The Older Sister." 1/22/56; with Joan Lorring and Patricia Hitchcock. Dir: Robert Stevens.
18 "Shopping for Death." 1/29/56; with Robert H. Harris. Dir: Robert Stevens.
19 "The Derelicts." 2/5/56; with Philip Reed. Dir: Robert Stevenson.
20 "And So Died Riabouchinska." 2/12/56; with Claude Rains and Charles Bronson. Dir: Robert Stevenson.
21 "Safe Conduct." 2/19/56; with Claire Trevor and Jacques Bergerac. Dir: Justus Addiss.
22 "Place of Shadows." 2/26/56; with Everett Sloane. Dir: Robert Stevens.
23 "Back for Christmas." 3/4/56; with John Williams. Dir: **AH**.
24 "The Perfect Murder." 3/11/56; with Hurd Hatfield and Philip Coolidge. Dir: Robert Stevens.
25 "There Was an Old Woman." 3/18/56; with Estelle Winwood. Dir: Robert Stevens.
26 "Whodunit." 3/25/56; with John Williams and Alan Naples. Dir: Francis Cockrell.
27 "Help Wanted." 4/1/56; with Lorne Greene and John Qualen. Dir: James Neilson.
28 "Portrait of Jocelyn." 4/8/56; with Nancy Gates and John Baragrey. Dir: Robert Stevens.
29 "The Orderly World of Mr. Appleby." 4/15/56; with Robert H. Harris. Dir: James Neilson.
30 "Never Again." 4/22/56; with Phyllis Thaxter and Warren Stevens. Dir: Robert Stevens.
31 "The Gentleman from America." 4/29/56; with Biff McGuire. Dir: Robert Stevens.
32 "The Baby Sitter." 5/6/56; with Thelma Ritter and Carmen Mathews. Dir: Robert Stevens.
33 "The Belfry." 5/13/56; with Patricia Hitchcock and Dabbs Greer. Dir: Herschel Daugherty.
34 "The Hidden Thing." 5/20/56; with Robert H. Harris and Biff McGuire. Dir: Robert Stevens.
35 "The Legacy." 5/27/56; with Alan Hewitt and Leora Dana. Dir: James Neilson.
36 "Mink." 6/3/56; with Ruth Hussey and Vinton Hayworth. Dir: Robert Stevenson.
37 "Decoy." 6/10/56; with Robert Horton and Cara Williams. Dir: Arnold Laven.
38 "The Creeper." 6/17/56; with Constance Ford and Steve Brodie. Dir: Herschel Daugherty.

39 "Momentum." 6/24/56; with Joanne Woodward and Skippy Homeier. Dir: Robert Stevens.
40 "Wet Saturday." 9/30/56; with Sir Cedric Hardwicke. Dir: **AH**.
41 "Fog Closing In." 10/7/56; with Phyllis Thaxter and George Grizzard. Dir: Herschel Daugherty.
42 "De Mortuis." 10/14/56; with Philip Coolidge and Cara Williams. Dir: Robert Stevens.
43 "Kill With Kindness." 10/21/56; with Hume Cronyn. Dir: Robert Stevens.
44 "None Are So Blind." 10/28/56; with Hurd Hatfield and Mildred Dunnock. Dir: Robert Stevens.
45 "Toby." 11/4/56; with Jessica Tandy. Dir: Robert Stevens.
46 "Alibi Me." 11/11/56; with Shirley Smith and Herb Vigran. Dir: Jules Bricken.
47 "Conversation Over a Corpse." 11/18/56; with Ray Collins and Dorothy Stickney. Dir: Jules Bricken.
48 "Crack of Doom." 11/25/56; with Robert Horton and Robert Middleton. Dir: James Neilson.
49 "Jonathan." 12/2/56; with Corey Allen. Dir: John Meredyth Lucas.
50 "The Better Bargain." 12/9/56; with Henry Silva. Dir: Herschel Daugherty.
51 "The Rose Garden." 12/16/56; with John Williams and Evelyn Varden. Dir: Mirian Cockrell.
52 "Mr. Blanchard's Secret." 12/23/56; with Mary Scott. Dir: **AH**.
53 "John Brown's Body." 12/30/56; with Hugh Marlowe. Dir: Robert Stevens.
54 "Crackpot." 1/6/57; with Biff McGuire and Robert Emhardt. Dir: John Meredyth Lucas.
55 "Nightmare in 4-D." 1/13/57; with Virginia Gregg and Henry Jones. Dir: Justus Addiss.
56 "My Brother Richard." 1/20/57; with Harry Townes and Bobby Ellis. Dir: Herschel Daugherty.
57 "Manacled." 1/27/57; with Gary Merrill and William Redfield. Dir: Robert Stevens.
58 "A Bottle of Wine." 2/3/57; with Herbert Marshall. Dir: Herschel Daugherty.
59 "Malice Domestic." 2/10/57; with Ralph Meeker and Vinton Hayworth. Dir: John Meredyth Lucas.
60 "Number Twenty-Two." 2/17/57; with Rip Torn and Ray Teal. Dir: Robert Stevens.

61 "The End of Indian Summer." 2/24/57; with Gladys Cooper. Dir: Robert Stevens.
62 "One for the Road." 3/3/57; with John Baragrey. Dir: Robert Stevens.
63 "The Cream of the Jest." 3/10/57; with Claude Rains. Dir: Herschel Daugherty.
64 "I Killed the Count." (part one of three) 3/17/57; with Melville Cooper and John Williams. All three Dir: Robert Stevens. Note: This was a three-episode story, not one episode as has been claimed.
65 "I Killed the Count." (part two) 3/24/57.
66 "I Killed the Count." (part three) 3/31/57.
67 "One More Mile to Go." 4/7/57; with David Wayne and Norman Leavitt. Dir: **AH**.
68 "Vicious Circle." 4/14/57; with Dick York and George Macready. Dir: Paul Henreid.
69 "The Three Dreams of Mr. Findlater." 4/21/57; with John Williams. Dir: Jules Bricken.
70 "The Night the World Ended." 4/28/57; with Russell Collins. Dir: Justus Addiss.
71 "The Hands of Mr. Ottermole." 5/5/57; with Theodore Bikel. Dir: Robert Stevens.
72 "A Man Greatly Beloved." 5/12/57; with Hugh Marlowe and Sir Cedric Hardwicke. Dir: James Neilson.
73 "Martha Mason, Movie Star." 5/19/57; with Judith Evelyn and Vinton Hayworth. Dir: Justus Addiss.
74 "The West Warlock Time Capsule." 5/26/57; with Henry Jones and Mildred Dunnock. Dir: Justus Addiss.
75 "Father and Son." 6/2/57; with Edmund Gwenn and Charles Davis. Dir: Herschel Daugherty.
76 "The Indestructable Mr. Weems." 6/9/57; with Russell Collins and Ted Newton. Dir: Justus Addiss.
77 "A Little Sleep." 6/16/57; with Vic Morrow and Barbara Cook. Dir: Paul Henreid.
78 "The Dangerous People." 6/23/57; with Ken Clarke and Albert Salmi. Dir: Robert Stevens.
79 "The Glass Eye." 10/6/57; with William Shatner and Jessica Tandy. Dir: Robert Stevens. Note: Stevens won an Emmy for this episode.

80 "The Mail Order Prophet." 10/13/57; with E. G. Marshall. Dir: James Neilson.
81 "The Perfect Crime." 10/20/57; with Vincent Price and James Gregory. Dir: **AH**.
82 "Heart of Gold." 10/27/57; with Nehemiah Persoff. Dir: Robert Stevens.
83 "Silent Witness." 11/3/57; with Dolores Hart and Patricia Hitchcock. Dir: Paul Henreid.
84 "Reward to Finder." 11/10/57; with Oscar Homolka and Claude Akins. Dir: James Neilson.
85 "Enough Rope for Two." 11/17/57; with Jean Hagen and Steve Brodie. Dir: Paul Henreid.
86 "Last Request." 11/24/57; with Harry Guardino and Hugh Marlowe. Dir: Paul Henreid.
87 "The Young One." 12/1/57; with Carol Lynley and Vince Edwards. Dir: Robert Altman.
88 "The Diplomatic Corpse." 12/8/57; with Peter Lorre. Dir: Paul Henreid.
89 "The Deadly." 12/15/57; with Phyllis Thaxter and Craig Stevens. Dir: Don Taylor.
90 "Miss Paisley's Cat." 12/22/57; with Dorothy Stickney and Raymond Bailey. Dir: Marian Cockrell.
91 "Night of the Execution." 12/29/57; with Russell Collins and Pat Hingle. Dir: Bernard C. Schoenfeld.
92 "The Percentage." 1/5/58; with Carmen Mathews. Dir: James Neilson.
93 "Together." 1/12/58; with Joseph Cotten. Dir: Robert Altman.
94 "Sylvia." 1/19/58; with John McIntire and Ann Todd. Dir: Herschel Daugherty.
95 "The Motive." 1/26/58; with Skippy Homeier and William Redfield. Dir: Robert Stevens.
96 "Miss Bracegirdle Does Her Duty." 2/2/58; with Mildred Natwick. Dir: Marian Cockrell.
97 "The Equalizer." 2/9/58; with Leif Erickson and Martin Balsam. Dir: James Neilson.
98 "On the Nose." 2/16/58; with David Opatoshu. Dir: James Neilson.
99 "Guest for Breakfast." 2/23/58; with Scott McKay and Joan Tetzel. Dir: Paul Henreid.
100 "The Return of the Hero." 3/2/58; with Jacques Bergerac. Dir: Herschel Daugherty.

101 "The Right Kind of House." 3/9/58; with Jeanette Nolan and Robert Emhardt. Dir: Don Taylor.

102 "Foghorn." 3/16/58; with Barbara Bel Geddes and Bartlett Robinson. Dir: Robert Stevens.

103 "Flight to the East." 3/23/58; with Gary Merrill and Anthony George. Dir: Arthur Hiller.

104 "Bull in a China Shop." 3/30/58; with Dennis Morgan. Dir: James Neilson.

105 "Disappearing Trick." 4/6/58; with Robert Horton and Raymond Bailey. Dir: Arthur Hiller.

106 "Lamb to the Slaughter." 4/13/58; with Barbara Bel Geddes. Dir: **AH**.

107 "Fatal Figures." 4/20/58; with John McGiver. Dir: Don Taylor.

108 "Death Sentence." 4/27/58; with Katherine Bard and James Best. Dir: Paul Henreid.

109 "The Festive Season." 5/4/58; with Carmen Mathews. Dir: Arthur Hiller.

110 "Listen! Listen!" 5/11/58; with Edgar Stehli and Adam Williams. Dir: Don Taylor.

111 "Post Mortem." 5/18/58; with Edgar Peterson and Steve Forrest. Dir: Arthur Hiller.

112 "The Crocodile Case." 5/25/58; with Denholm Elliott and Hazel Court. Dir: Don Taylor.

113 "Dip in the Pool." 6/1/58; with Fay Wray and Keenan Wynn. Dir: **AH**. Note: Hitchcock makes a cameo appearance in this episode, seen on the cover of a magazine.

114 "The Safe Place." 6/8/58; with Wendell Holmes and Robert H. Harris. Dir: James Neilson.

115 "The Canary Sedan." 6/15/58; with Jessica Tandy and Owen Cunningham. Dir: Robert Stevens.

116 "The Impromptu Murder." 6/22/58; with Hume Cronyn and Doris Lloyd. Dir: Paul Henreid.

117 "Little White Frock." 6/29/58; with Herbert Marshall and Julie Adams. Dir: Herschel Daugherty.

118 "Poison." 10/5/58; with Wendell Corey and Arnold Moss. Dir: **AH**.

119 "Don't Interrupt." 10/12/58; with Cloris Leachman. Dir: Robert Stevens.

120 "The Jokester." 10/19/58; with Albert Salmi and Roscoe Ates. Dir: Arthur Hiller.

121 "The Crooked Road." 10/26/58; with Richard Kiley and Patricia Breslin. Dir: Paul Henreid.

122 "The $2,000,000 Defense." 11/2/58; with Barry Sullivan and Lori March. Dir: Norman Lloyd.

123 "Design for Loving." 11/9/58; with Norman Lloyd and Barbara Baxley. Dir: Robert Stevens.

124 "A Man with a Problem." 11/16/58; with Gary Merrill and Ken Lynch. Dir: Robert Stevens.

125 "Safety for the Witness." 11/23/58; with Art Carney and Doris Lloyd. Dir: Norman Lloyd.

126 "Murder Me Twice." 12/7/58; with Phyllis Thaxter and Alan Marshall. Dir: David Swift.

127 "Tea Time." 12/14/58; with Marsha Hunt and Murray Matheson. Dir: Robert Stevens.

128 "And The Desert Shall Blossom." 12/21/58; with Ben Johnson. Dir: Arthur Hiller.

129 "Mrs. Herman and Mrs. Fenimore." 12/28/58; with Mary Astor and Russell Collins. Dir: Arthur Hiller.

130 "Six People, No Music." 1/4/59; with John McGiver and Howard Smith. Dir: Norman Lloyd.

131 "The Morning After." 1/11/59; with Fay Wray and Robert Alda. Dir: Herschel Daughtery.

132 "A Personal Matter." 1/18/59; with Wayne Morris and Frank Silvera. Dir: Paul Henreid.

133 "Out There, Darkness." 1/25/59; with Bette Davis and Frank Albertson. Dir: Paul Henreid.

134 "Total Loss." 2/1/59; with Nancy Olson and Barbara Lord. Dir: Don Taylor.

135 "The Last Dark Step." 2/8/59; with Ray Spain and Robert Horton. Dir: Herschel Daugherty.

136 "The Morning of the Bride." 2/15/59; with Barbara Bel Geddes and Patricia Hitchcock. Dir: Arthur Hiller.

137 "The Diamond Necklace." 2/22/59; with Claude Rains and Betsy Von Furstenberg. Dir: Herschel Daugherty.

138 "Relative Value." 3/1/59; with Denholm Elliott and Torin Thatcher. Dir: Paul Almond.

139 "The Right Price." 3/8/59; with Eddie Foy Jr. Dir: Arthur Hiller.

140 "I"ll Take Care of You." 3/15/59; with Elisabeth Fraser and Ida Moore. Dir: Robert Stevens.

141 "The Avon Emeralds." 3/22/59; with Hazel Court. Dir: Robert Stevens.

142 "The Kind Waitress." 3/29/59; with Olive Deering and Celia Lovsky. Dir: Paul Henreid.

143 "Cheap is Cheap." 4/5/59; with Dennis Day. Dir: Bretaigne Windust.

144 "The Waxwork." 4/12/59; with Barry Sullivan and Everett Sloane. Dir: Robert Stevens.

145 "The Impossible Dream." 4/19/59; with Franchot Tone and Mary Astor. Dir: Robert Stevens.

146 "Banquo's Chair." 5/3/59; with John Williams. Dir: **AH**.

147 "A Night with the Boys." 5/10/59; with John Smith and Joyce Meadows. Dir: John Brahm.

148 "Your Witness." 5/17/59; with Brian Hutton and Brian Keith. Dir: Norman Lloyd.

149 "The Human Interest Story." 5/24/59; with Steve McQueen and Tyler McVey. Dir: Norman Lloyd.

150 "The Dusty Drawer." 5/31/59; with Dick York and Philip Coolidge. Dir: Herschel Daugherty.

151 "Curtains for Me" (aka "A True Account"). 6/7/59; with Kent Smith and Robert Webber. Dir: Leonard Horn.

152 "Touche." 6/14/59; with Hugh Marlowe and Robert Morse. Director is unknown.

153 "Invitation to an Accident." 6/21/59; with Gary Merrill and Joanna Moore. Dir: Don Taylor.

154 "Arthur." 9/27/59; with Laurence Harvey and Patrick Macnee. Dir: **AH**.

155 "The Crystal Trench." 10/4/59; with Patricia Owens and James Donald. Dir: **AH**.

156 "Appointment at Eleven." 10/11/59; with Clint Kimbrough and Michael J. Pollard. Dir: Robert Stevens.

157 "Coyote Moon." 10/18/59; with Macdonald Carey. Dir: Herschel Daugherty.

158 "No Pain." 10/25/59; with Brian Keith and Joanna Moore. Dir: Norman Lloyd.

159 "Anniversary Gift." 11/1/59; with Jackie Coogan and Harry Morgan. Dir: Norman Lloyd.

160 "Dry Run." 11/8/59; with Walter Matthau and Robert Vaughn. Dir: John Brahm.

161 "The Blessington Method." 11/15/59; with Henry Jones and Elizabeth Patterson. Dir: Herschel Daugherty.

162 "Dead Weight." 11/22/59; with Joseph Cotton and Julie Adams. Dir: Stuart Rosenberg.

163 "Special Delivery." 11/29/59; with Steve Dunne and Beatrice Straight. Dir: Norman Lloyd.

164 "Road Hog." 12/6/59; with Richard Chamberlain and Raymond Massey. Dir: Stuart Rosenberg.

165 "The Specialty of the House." 12/13/59; with Robert Morley. Dir: Robert Stevens.

166 "An Occurrence at Owl Creek Bridge." 12/20/59; with Ronald Howard and Juano Hernandez. Dir: Robert Stevenson.

167 "Graduating Class." 12/27/59; with Wendy Hiller and Gigi Perreau. Dir: Herschel Daugherty.

168 "Man From the South." 1/3/60; with Steve McQueen and Peter Lorre. Dir: Norman Lloyd.

169 "The Ikon of Elijah." 1/10/60; with Sam Jaffe and Oscar Homolka. Dir: Paul Almond.

170 "The Cure." 1/24/60; with Nehemiah Persoff and Cara Williams. Dir: Herschel Daugherty.

171 "Backward, Turn Backward." 1/31/60; with Paul Maxwell and Tom Tully. Dir: Stuart Rosenberg.

172 "Not the Running Type." 2/7/60; with Paul Hartman and Wendell Holmes. Dir: Arthur Hiller.

173 "The Day of the Bullet." 2/14/60; with John Graven and Barry Gordon. Dir: Norman Lloyd.

174 "Hitch Hike." 2/21/60; with John McIntire and Read Morgan. Dir: Paul Henreid.

175 "Across the Threshold." 2/28/60; with Barbara Baxley and George Grizzard. Dir: Arthur Hiller.

176 "Craig's Will." 3/6/60; with Dick Van Dyke and Paul Stewart. Dir: Gene Reynolds.

177 "Mme. Mystery." 3/27/60; with Joby Baker and Audrey Totter. Dir: John Brahm.

178 "The Little Man Who Was There." 4/3/60; with Norman Lloyd and Clegg Hoyt. Dir: George Stevens Jr.

179 "Mother, May I Go Out to Swim?" 4/10/60; with William Shatner and Jessie Royce Landis. Dir: Herschel Daugherty.

180 "The Cuckoo Clock." 4/17/60; with Beatrice Straight and Patricia Hitchcock. Dir: John Brahm.

181 "Forty Detectives Later." 4/24/60; with James Franciscus and Jack Weston. Dir: Arthur Hiller.

182 "The Hero." 5/1/60; with Oscar Homolka and Irene Tedrow. Dir: John Brahm.

183 "Insomnia." 5/8/60; with Dennis Weaver and Al Hodge. Dir: John Brahm.

184 "I Can Take Care of Myself." 5/15/60; with Pat Harrington and Linda Lawson. Dir: Alan Crosland Jr.

185 "One Grave Too Many." 5/22/60; with Jeremy Slate and Biff Elliott. Dir: Arthur Hiller.

186 "Party Line." 5/29/60; with Judy Canova and Arch Johnson. Dir: Hilton A. Green.

187 "Cell 227." 6/5/60; with Brian Keith and James Westerfield. Dir: Paul Henreid.

188 "The Schartz–Metterlume Method." 6/12/60; with Elspeth March and Patricia Hitchcock. Dir: Richard Dunlap.

189 "Letter of Credit." 6/19/60; with Bob Sweeney and Theodore Newton. Dir: Paul Henreid.

190 "Escape to Sonoita." 6/26/60; with Burt Reynolds and James Bell. Dir: Stuart Rosenberg.

191 "Hooked." 9/25/60; with Robert Horton and Anne Francis. Dir: Norman Lloyd.

192 "Mrs. Bixby and the Colonel's Coat." 9/27/60; with Audrey Meadows. Dir: **AH.**

193 "The Doubtful Doctor." 10/4/60; with Dick York and Michael Burns. Dir: Arthur Hiller.

194 "A Very Moral Theft." 10/11/60; with Walter Matthau and Sam Gilman. Dir: Norman Lloyd.

195 "The Contest of Aaron Gold." 10/18/60; with Barry Gordon and Frank Maxwell. Dir: Norman Lloyd.

196 "The Five Forty-Eight." 10/25/60; with Zachary Scott and Phyllis Thaxter. Dir: John Brahm.

197 "Pen Pal." 11/1/60; with Roy Montgomery and Clu Gulager. Dir: John Brahm.

198 "Outlaw in Town." 11/15/60; with Ricardo Montalban and Arch Johnson. Dir: Herschel Daugherty.

199 "Oh Youth and Beauty." 11/22/60; with David Lewis and Gary Merrill. Dir: Norman Lloyd.

200 "The Money." 11/29/60; with Wolfe Barzell and Doris Dowling. Dir: Ida Lupino.

201 "Sybilla." 12/6/60; with Barbara Bel Geddes and Alexander Scourby. Dir: Ida Lupino.

202 "The Man with Two Faces." 12/13/60; with Spring Byington. Dir: Stuart Rosenberg.

203 "The Baby Blue Expression." 12/20/60; with Sarah Marshall and Peter Walker. Dir: Arthur Hiller.

204 "The Man Who Found the Money." 12/27/60; with R.G. Armstrong and Lucy Prentis. Dir: Alan Crosland Jr.

205 "Change of Heart." 1/3/61; with Anne Helm and Abraham Sofaer. Dir: Robert Florey.

206 "Summer Shade." 1/10/61; with Julie Adams and John Hoyt. Dir: Herschel Daugherty.

207 "A Crime for Mothers." 1/24/61; with Patricia Smith and Howard McNear. Dir: Ida Lupino.

208 "The Last Escape." 1/31/61; with Keenan Wynn and Jan Sterling. Dir: Paul Henreid.

209 "The Greatest Monster of Them All." 2/14/61; with Robert H. Harris. Dir: Robert Stevens.

210 "The Landlady." 2/21/61; with Dean Stockwell and Laurie Main. Dir: Paul Henreid.

211 "The Throwback." 2/28/61; with Murray Matheson and Scott Marlowe. Dir: John Brahm.

212 "The Kiss-Off." 3/7/61; with Rip Torn and Bert Freed. Dir: Alan Crosland Jr.

213 "The Horseplayer." 3/14/61; with Claude Rains and Ed Gardner. Dir: **AH.**

214 "Incident in a Small Jail." 3/21/61; with John Fiedler and Ron Nicholas. Dir: Norman Lloyd.

215 "A Woman's Help." 3/28/61; with Geraldine Fitzgerald and Scott McKay. Dir: Arthur Hiller.

216 "Museum Piece." 4/4/61; with Myron McCormick and Bert Convy. Dir: Paul Henreid.

217 "Coming, Mama." 4/11/61; with Eileen Heckart and Don DeFore. Dir: George Stevens Jr.

218 "Deathmate." 4/18/61; with Gia Scala and Lee Philips. Dir: Alan Crosland Jr.

219 "Gratitude." 4/25/61; with Peter Falk and Clegg Hoyt. Dir: Alan Crosland Jr.

220 "The Pearl Necklace." 5/2/61; with Ernest Truex and Hazel Court. Dir: Don Weis.

221 "You Can't Trust a Man." 5/9/61; with Polly Bergen and Frank Albertson. Dir: Paul Henreid.

222 "The Gloating Place." 5/16/61; with Susan Harrison and King Calder. Dir: Alan Crosland Jr.

223 "Self-Defense." 5/23/61; with George Nader and Selmer Jackson. Dir: Paul Henreid.

224 "A Secret Life." 5/30/61; with Ronald Howard and Arte Johnson. Dir: Don Weis.

225 "Servant Problem." 6/6/61; with Jo Van Fleet and John Emery. Dir: Alan Crosland Jr.

226 "Coming Home." 6/13/61; with Gil Perkins. Dir: Alf Kjellin.

227 "Final Arrangements." 6/20/61; with Martin Balsam and Slim Pickens. Dir: Gordon Hessler.

228 "Make My Death Bed." 6/27/61; with Diana Van Der Vlis and James Best. Dir: Arthur Hiller.

229 "Ambition." 7/4/61; with Leslie Nielsen and Harry Landers. Dir: Paul Henreid.

230 "The Hat Box." 10/10/61; with Paul Ford and Billy Gray. Dir: Alan Crosland Jr.

231 "Bang! You're Dead." 10/17/61; with Billy Mumy and Marta Kristen. Dir: **AH.**

232 "Maria." 10/24/61; with Norman Lloyd and Kreg Martin. Dir: Boris Sagal.

233 "Cop for a Day." 10/31/61; with Walter Matthau and Susan Brown. Dir: Paul Henreid.

234 "Keep Me Company." 11/7/61; with Anne Francis and Jack Ging. Dir: Alan Crosland Jr.

235 "Beta Delta Gamma." 11/14/61; with Burt Brinkerhoff and Severn Darden. Dir: Alan Crosland Jr.

236 "You Can't Be a Little Girl All Your Life." 11/21/61; with Dick York and Ted de Corsia. Dir: Norman Lloyd.

237 "The Old Pro." 11/28/61; with Richard Conte and Sarah Shane. Dir: Paul Henreid.

238 "I, Spy." 12/5/61; with Kay Walsh and Eric Barker. Dir: Norman Lloyd.

239 "Services Rendered." 12/12/61; with Hugh Marlowe and Steve Dunne. Dir: Paul Henreid.

240 "The Right Kind of Medicine." 12/19/61; with Russell Collins and Robert Redford. Dir: Alan Crosland Jr.

241 "A Jury of Her Peers." 12/26/61; with Ann Harding and Robert Wray. Dir: Robert Florey.

242 "The Silk Petticoat." 1/2/62; with Michael Rennie. Dir: John Newland.

243 "Bad Actor." 1/9/62; with Robert Duvall and Carole Eastman. Dir: John Newland.

244 "The Door Without a Key." 1/16/62; with Claude Rains and Billy Mumy. Dir: Herschel Daugherty.

245 "The Chase of M. J. H." 1/23/62; with Richard Gaines and Barbara Baxley. Dir: Alan Crosland Jr.

246 "The Faith of Aaron Menefee." 1/30/62; with Robert Armstrong and Olan Soule. Dir: Norman Lloyd.

247 "The Woman Who Wanted to Live." 2/6/62; with Lola Albright and Charles Bronson. Dir: Alan Crosland Jr.

248 "Strange Miracle." 2/13/62; with David Opatoshu and Fran De Kova. Dir: Norman Lloyd.

249 "The Test." 2/20/62; with Brian Keith and Eduardo Ciannelli. Dir: Boris Sagal.

250 "Burglar Proof." 2/27/62; with Robert Webber and Whit Bissell. Dir: John Newland.

251 "The Big Score." 3/6/62; with Evan Evans and Tom Gilleran. Dir: Boris Sagal.

252 "Profit Sharing Plan." 3/13/62; with Henry Jones and Rebecca Sand. Dir: Bernard Girard.

253 "Apex." 3/20/62; with Patricia Breslin and George Kane. Dir: Alan Crosland Jr.

254 "The Last Remains." 3/27/62; with Ed Gardner and John Fiedler. Dir: Leonard Horn.

255 "Ten O'Clock Tiger." 4/3/62; with Frankie Darro and Karl Lukas. Dir: Bernard Girard.

256 "Act of Faith." 4/10/62; with George Grizzard and Dennis King. Dir: Bernard Girard.

257 "The Kerry Blue." 4/17/62; with Carmen Mathews and Rob Reiner. Dir: Paul Henreid.

258 "The Matched Pearl." 4/24/62; with John Ireland and Ernest Truex. Dir: Bernard Girard.

259 "What Frightened You Fred?" 5/1/62; with Ed Asner and Adam Williams. Dir: Paul Henreid.

260 "Most Likely to Succeed." 5/8/62; with Joanna Moore. Dir: Richard Whorf.

261 "Victim Four." 5/15/62; with John Lupton and Peggy Ann Garner. Dir: Paul Henreid.

262 "Golden Opportunity." 5/22/62; with Richard Long and Rebecca Sand. Dir: Robert Florey.

263 "The Twelve Hour Caper." 5/29/62; with Dick York and Sarah Marshall. Dir: John Newland.

264 "The Children of Aldo Nuova." 6/5/62; with Jack Carson and Christopher Dark. Dir: Robert Florey.

265 "First-Class Honeymoon." 6/12/62; with Robert Webber and Marjorie Bennett. Dir: Don Weis.

266 "The Big Kick." 6/19/62; with Anne Helm and Wayne Rogers. Dir: Alan Crosland Jr.

267 "Where Beauty Lies." 6/26/62; with Cloris Leachman and George Nader. Dir: Robert Florey.

268 "The Sorcerer's Apprentice." Not broadcast in original run; with Diana Dors and Brandon De Wilde. Dir: Joseph Leytis. Based on the short story of the same name by Robert Bloch. Note: NBC officials objected to the horrifying ending, which left a young retarded boy cutting a real woman in half with a magician's buzz saw. This episode has been shown in syndicated reruns.

THE ALFRED HITCHCOCK HOUR

Approximately 50 mins. B&w.
Shamley Productions.
Prod: Joan Harrison and Norman Lloyd.

The Hitchcock program moved back to CBS when the hour-long version premiered, and returned to NBC beginning in October of 1964.

1 "Piece of the Action." 9/20/62; with Gig Young and Robert Redford. Dir: Bernard Girard.

2 "Don't Look Behind You." 9/27/62; with Vera Miles and Jeffrey Hunter. Dir: John Brahm.

3 "Night of the Owl." 10/4/62; with Brian Keith and Philip Coolidge. Dir: Alan Crosland Jr.

4 "I Saw the Whole Thing." 10/11/62; with John Forsythe and Kent Smith. Dir: **AH.**

5 "Captive Audience." 10/18/62; with Ed Nelson and James Mason. Dir: Alf Kjellin.

6 "Final Vow." 10/25/62; with Carol Lynley and Clu Gulager. Dir: Norman Lloyd.

7 "Annabel." 11/1/62; with Susan Oliver and Dean Stockwell. Dir: Paul Henreid.

8 "House Guest." 11/8/62; with Macdonald Carey and Billy Mumy. Dir: Alan Crosland Jr.

9 "The Black Curtain." 11/15/62; with Richard Basehart and Lee Philips. Dir: Sydney Pollack.

10 "Day of the Reckoning." 11/22/62; with Claude Akins and Louis Hayward. Dir: Jerry Hopper.

11 "Ride the Nightmare." 11/29/62; with Gail Bonney and Olan Soule. Dir: Bernard Girard.

12 "Hangover." 12/6/62; with Jayne Mansfield and Tony Randall. Dir: Bernard Girard.

13 "Bonfire." 12/13/62; with Peter Falk and Craig Duncan. Dir: Joseph Pevney.

14 "The Tender Poisoner." 12/20/62; with Howard Duff and Dan Dailey. Dir: Leonard Horn.

15 "The 31st of February." 1/4/63; with William Conrad and David Wayne. Dir: Alf Kjellin.

16 "What Really Happened?" 1/11/63; with Anne Francis and Gladys Cooper. Dir: Jack Smight.

17 "Forecast: Low Clouds and Coastal Fog." 1/18/63; with Dan O'Herlihy and Inger Stevens. Dir: Charles Haas.

18 "A Tangled Web." 1/25/63; with Barry Morse and Robert Redford. Dir: Alf Kjellin.

19 "To Catch a Butterfly." 2/1/63; with Bradford Dillman. Dir: David Lowell Rich.

20 "The Paragon." 2/8/63; with Gary Merrill and Joan Fontaine. Dir: Jack Smight.

21 "I'll Be the Judge, I'll Be the Jury." 2/15/63; with Peter Graves and Albert Salmi. Dir: James Sheldon.

22 "Diagnosis: Danger." 3/1/63; with Charles McGraw and Michael Parks. Dir: Sydney Pollack.

23 "The Lonely Hour." 3/8/63; with Nancy Kelly and Juanita Moore. Dir: Jack Smight.

24 "The Star Juror." 3/15/63; with Dean Jagger and Betty Field. Dir: Herschel Daugherty.

25 "The Long Silence." 3/22/62; with Michael Rennie and Phyllis Thaxter. Dir: Robert Douglas.

26 "An Out for Oscar." 4/5/63; with Linda Christian and Larry Storch. Dir: Bernard Girard.

27 "Death and the Joyful Woman." 4/12/63; with Laraine Day and Gilbert Roland. Dir: John Brahm.

28 "Last Seen Wearing Bluejeans." 4/19/63; with Randy Boone and Katherine Crawford. Dir: Alan Crosland Jr.

29 "The Dark Pool." 5/3/63; with Madlyn Rhue and Anthony George. Dir: Jack Smight.

30 "Dear Uncle George." 5/10/63; with Dabney Coleman and Gene Barry. Dir: Joseph Newman.

31 "Run for Doom." 5/17/63; with John Gavin and Diana Dors. Dir: Bernard Girard.

32 "Death of a Cop." 5/24/63; with Richard Jaeckel and Victor Jory. Dir: Joseph Newman.

33 "A Home Away from Home." 9/27/63; with Ray Milland and Claire Griswald. Dir: Herschel Daugherty.

34 "A Nice Touch." 10/4/63; with Anne Baxter and Harry Townes. Dir: Joseph Pevney.

35 "Terror at Northfield." 10/11/63; with Dick York and Jacqueline Scott. Dir: Harvey Hart.

36 "You'll Be the Death of Me." 10/18/63; with Robert Loggia and Barry Atwater. Dir: Robert Douglas.

37 "Blood Bargain." 10/25/63; with Anne Francis and Richard Kiley. Dir: Bernard Girard.

38 "Nothing Ever Happens in Linvale." 11/8/63; with Gary Merrill and Fess Parker. Dir: Herschel Daugherty.

39 "Starring the Defense." 11/15/63; with Richard Basehart and Teno Pollick. Dir: Joseph Pevney.

40 "The Cadaver." 11/29/63; with Michael Parks and Joby Baker. Dir: Alf Kjellin.

41 "The Dividing Wall." 12/6/63; with James Gregory and Simon Scott. Dir: Bernard Girard.

42 "Good-Bye, George." 12/13/63; with Robert Culp and Patricia Barry. Dir: Robert Stevens.

43 "How to Get Rid of Your Wife." 12/20/63; with Bill Quinn and Bob Newhart. Dir: Alf Kjellin.

44 "Three Wives Too Many." 1/3/64; with Teresa Wright and Dan Duryea. Dir: Joseph Newman.

45 "The Magic Shop." 1/10/64; with Leslie Nielsen and David Opatoshu. Dir: Robert Stevens.

46 "Beyond the Sea of Death." 1/24/64; with Mildred Dunnock and Diana Hyland. Dir: Alf Kjellin.

47 "Night Caller." 1/31/64; with Bruce Dern and David White. Dir: Alf Kjellin.

48 "The Evil of Adelaide Winters." 2/7/64; with Kim Hunter and John Larkin. Dir: Laslo Benedek.

49 "The Jar." 2/14/64; with James Best. Dir: Norman Lloyd.

50 "Final Escape." 2/21/64; with Edd Byrnes and Robert Keith. Dir: William Whitney.

51 "Murder Case." 3/6/64; with John Cassavetes and Ben Wright. Dir: John Brahm.

52 "Anyone for Murder?" 3/13/64; with Barry Nelson and Dick Dawson. Dir: Leo Penn.

53 "Beast in View." 3/20/64; with Joan Hackett and Kevin McCarthy. Dir: Joseph Newman.

54 "Behind the Locked Door." 3/27/64; with Gloria Swanson and James McArthur. Dir: Robert Douglas.

55 "A Matter of Murder." 4/3/64; with Telly Savalas and Darren McGavin. Dir: David Lowell Rich.

56 "The Gentleman Caller." 4/10/64; with Roddy McDowall and Diane Sayer. Dir: Joseph Newman.

57 "The Ordeal of Mrs. Snow." 4/17/64; with Patricia Collinge and June Vincent. Dir: Robert Stevens.

58 "Ten Minutes From Now." 5/1/64; with Donnelly Rhodes and Lou Jacobi. Dir: Alf Kjellin.

59 "Sign of Satan." 5/8/64; with Christopher Lee and Gia Scala. Dir: Robert Douglas.

60 "Who Needs an Enemy?" 5/15/64; with Steven Hill and Richard Anderson. Dir: Harry Morgan.

61 "Bed of Roses." 5/22/64; with Patrick O'Neal and Torin Thatcher. Dir: Philip Leacock.

62 "Second Verdict." 5/29/64; with Martin Landau and Frank Gorshin. Dir: Lewis Teague.

63 "Isabel." 6/5/64; with Les Tremayne and Bradford Dillman. Dir: Alf Kjellin.

64 "Body in the Barn." 7/3/64; with Lillian Gish and Kent Smith. Dir: Joseph Newman.
65 "The Return of Verge Likens." 10/5/64; with Peter Fonda and Sam Reese. Dir: Arnold Laven.
66 "Change of Address." 10/12/64; with Arthur Kennedy and Phyllis Thaxter. Dir: David Friedkin.
67 "Water's Edge." 10/19/64; with John Cassavetes and Ann Sothern. Dir: Bernard Hirard.
68 "The Life Work of Juan Diaz." 10/26/64; with Alejandro Rey and Larry Donasin. Dir: Norman Lloyd.
69 "See the Monkey Dance." 11/9/64; with Efrem Zimbalist Jr. and Patricia Medina. Dir: Joseph Newman.
70 "Lonely Place." 11/16/64; with Teresa Wright and Bruce Dern. Dir: Harvey Hart.
71 "The McGregor Affair." 11/23/64; with Andrew Duggan and John Hoyt. Dir: David Friedkin.
72 "Misadventure." 12/7/64; with Lola Albright and George Kennedy. Dir: Joseph Newman.
73 "Triumph." 12/14/64; with Ed Begley and Jeanette Nolan. Dir: Harvey Hart.
74 "Memo from Purgatory." 12/21/64; with James Caan and Walter Koenig. Dir: Joseph Pevney.
75 "Consider Her Ways." 12/28/64; with Barbara Barrie and Gladys Cooper. Dir: Robert Stevens.
76 "The Crimson Witness." 1/4/65; with Peter Lawford and Alan Baxter. Dir: David Friedkin.
77 "Where the Woodbine Twineth." 1/11/65; with Margaret Leighton and Juanita Moore. Dir: Alf Kjellin.
78 "Final Performance." 1/18/65; with Franchot Tone and Roger Perry. Dir: John Brahm.
79 "Thanatos Palace Hotel." 2/1/65; with Steven Hill and Angie Dickinson. Dir: Laslo Benedek.
80 "One of the Family." 2/8/65; with Lilia Skala and Olive Deering. Dir: Joseph Pevney.
81 "An Unlocked Window." 2/15/65; with Dana Wynter and John Kerr. Dir: Joseph Newman.
82 "The Trap." 2/22/65; with Donnelly Rhodes and Anne Francis. Dir: John Brahm.
83 "Wally the Beard." 3/1/65; with Larry Blyden and Katherine Squire. Dir: James Brown.

84 "Death Scene." 3/8/65; with Vera Miles and John Carradine. Dir: Harvey Hart.
85 "The Photographer and the Undertaker." 3/15/65; with Jack Cassidy and Harry Townes. Dir: Alex March.
86 "Thou Still Unravished Bride." 3/22/65; with Ron Randell and David Carradine. Dir: David Friedkin.
87 "Completely Foolproof." 3/29/65; with J. D. Cannon and Patricia Barry. Dir: Alf Kjellin.
88 "Power of Attorney." 4/5/65; with Richard Johnson and Geraldine Fitzgerald. Dir: Harvey Hart.
89 "The World's Oldest Motive." 4/12/65; with Henry Jones and Kathleen Freeman. Dir: Joseph Newman.
90 "The Monkey's Paw — A Retelling." 4/19/65; with Jane Wyatt and Lee Majors. Dir: Joseph Newman.
91 "The Second Wife." 4/26/65; with June Lockhart and John Anderson. Dir: Joseph Newman.
92 "Night Fever." 5/3/65; with Colleen Dewhurst and Richard Bull. Dir: Herbert Coleman. Note: Coleman also produced some of Hitchcock's films.
93 "Off Season." 5/10/65; with John Gavin and Tom Drake. Dir: William Friedkin.

SUSPICION

Approximately 50 mins. B&w.
Shamley Productions.
Exec prod: **AH**. Assoc prod: Joan Harrison.

This series aired sporadically on NBC on Monday nights. It ran from 9/30/57 to 9/22/58 (including repeats). A brief second series, not from Shamley Productions —though re-screening some of the Shamley–produced episodes—aired later, and was hosted by Walter Abel. It ran on Sundays from 6/14/59 to 9/6/59.

1 "Four O'Clock." 9/30/57; with E. G. Marshall, Nancy Kelly. Dir: **AH**.
2 "Rainy Day." 12/2/57; with George Willi, Robert Flemyng. Dir: James Neilson.
3 "Lord Arthur Savile's Crime." 1/13/58; with Sebastian Cabot, Ronald Howard. Dir: Robert Stevens.

4 "Heartbeat." 2/3/58; with David Wayne. Dir: Robert Stevens.
5 "Meeting In Paris." 2/10/58; with Jane Greer, Rory Calhoun. Dir: James Neilson.
6 "The Eye Of Truth." 3/17/58; with Joseph Cotten. Dir: Robert Stevens.
7 "The Bull Skinner." 4/7/58; with John Beal, Rod Steiger. Dir: Lewis Milestone.
8 "The Way Up To Heaven." 4/28/58; with Sebastian Cabot, Marian Lorne. Dir: Herschel Daugherty.
9 "The Voice In The Night." 5/25/58; with James Donald, Barbara Rush. Dir: Arthur Hiller.
10 "The Woman Who Turned To Salt." 6/16/58; with Pamela Brown, Michael Rennie. Dir: Stirling Silliphant.

ALFRED HITCHCOCK PRESENTS (REVIVAL SERIES)

Approximately 25 mins. Color.

These new episodes were first broadcast on NBC, beginning with a two-hour made-for-television movie featuring four half-hour tales. The movie was an experimental pilot, in an attempt to see if television viewers would be interested in a newer version of the classic show. The resulting series was later broadcast on the USA cable network after being dropped by NBC after twenty-six episodes; USA mixed new episodes with ones previously broadcast on NBC. Computer colorized versions of Hitch's original opening and closing comments were featured. This technically made Hitchcock the first dead man to host a television series.

"Alfred Hitchcock Presents: The Movie." Broadcast on 5/5/85; consisted of the following four presentations:
1 "Incident in a Small Jail," with Ned Beatty and Tony Frank.
2 "The Man From the South," with John Huston, Kim Novak, and Tippi Hedren.
3 "Bang! You're Dead," with Billy Mumy and Bianca Rose.
4 "An Unlocked Window," with Annette O'Toole and Bruce Davison.
Note: These four half-hour presentations are often shown in syndication as four separate episodes instead of one.
5 "Revenge." 9/25/85; with David Clennon and Linda Purl.

6 "Night Fever." 10/6/85; with Robert Carradine and Tim Cunningham.

7 "Wake Me When I'm Dead." 10/20/85; with Barbara Hershey and Buck Henry.

8 "Final Escape." 10/27/85; with Season Hubley and David Roberts.

9 "The Night Caller." 11/3/85; with Michael O'Keefe and Linda Fiorentino.

10 "Method Actor." 11/10/85; with Parker Stevenson and Martin Sheen.

11 "The Human Interest Story." 11/17/85; with James Callahan and John Shea.

12 "Breakdown." 12/1/85; with Andy Garcia and John Heard.

13 "Prisoners." 12/8/85; with Steve Eastin and Yaphet Kotto.

14 "Gigolo." 12/15/85; with Sandy Dennis and Brad Davis.

15 "The Gloating Place." 1/5/86; with Isabelle Walker.

16 "The Right Kind of Medicine." 1/12/86; with Jack Thibeau and Robert Prosky.

17 "Beast in View." 1/19/86; with Cliff Potts and Tom Atkins.

18 "A Very Happy Ending." 2/16/86; with Dan Dayton and Myrna White.

19 "The Canary Sedan." 3/2/86; with Kathleen Quinlan and Peter Haskell.

20 "Enough Rope for Two." 3/9/86; with Tim Daly and Jeff Fahey.

21 "The Creeper." 3/16/86; with Karen Allen and Lori Butler.

22 "Happy Birthday." 3/23/86; with Arsenio Hall and Bruce Gray.

23 "The Jar." 4/6/86; with Griffin Dunne and Stephen Shellen. Dir: Tim Burton.

24 "Deadly Honeymoon." 4/13/86; with David Dukes and Victoria Tennant.

25 "Four O'Clock." 5/4/86; with Richard Cox and Kenneth McMillan. Note: This show was a remake of the Hitchcock-directed episode of *Suspicion.*

26 "Road Hog." 5/11/86; with Burt Young and Ronny Cox.

27 "The Initiation." 1/24/87; with Marion Ross and Peter Spence.

28 "Conversation Over a Corpse." 1/31/87; with Barbara Babcock.

29 "Man on the Edge." 2/7/87; with Mark Hamill and Michael Ironside.

30 "If the Shoe Fits." 2/14/87; with Ted Shackelford and Lawrence Dane.

31 "The Mole." 2/21/87; with Edward Herrmann and Ann Ward.

32 "Anniversary Gift." 2/28/87; with Pamela Sue Martin and Peter Dvorsky.

33 "The Impatient Patient." 3/7/87; with E. G. Marshall and Patricia Hamilton.

34 "When This Man Dies." 3/14/87; with Adrian Zmed and Brenda Bazinet.

35 "The Specialty of the House." 3/21/87; with John Saxon and Neil Munro.

36 "The Final Twist." 3/28/87; with Martin Landau and Robert Wisden.

37 "Tragedy Tonight." 4/4/87; with Catherine Mary Stewart and Bob Collins.

38 "World's Oldest Motive." 4/11/87; with Dwight Schultz and Dave Nichols.

39 "Deathmate." 4/18/87; with Wayne Best and Richard Monette.

40 "Very Careful Rape." 2/6/88; with Melissa Sue Anderson and Cedric Smith.

41 "Animal Lovers." 2/13/88; with Ron White and Susan Anton.

42 "Prism." 2/20/88; with Lindsay Wagner and Brent Strait.

43 "A Stolen Heart." 2/27/88; with William Katt and Marco Bianco.

44 "Houdini on Channel 4." 3/5/88; with Nick Lewin and Carolyn Dunn.

45 "Killer Takes All." 3/12/88; with Van Johnson and Shelley Peterson.

46 "Hippocratic Oath." 3/19/88; with Mavor Moore and Shaun Cassidy.

47 "Prosecutor." 3/26/88; with Parker Stevenson and Lawrence Dane.

48 "If Looks Could Kill." 4/23/88; with Michelle Phillips and Duncan Regehr.

49 "You'll Die Laughing." 4/30/88; with Anthony Newley.

50 "Murder Party." 5/7/88; with David McCallum and David Hemblen.

51 "Twist." 5/14/88; with Stella Stevens and Clive Revill.

52 "User Deadly." 5/21/88; with Harry Guardino and Geordie Johnson.

53 "Career Move." 5/28/88; with David Cassidy and Robert Wisden.

54 "Full Disclosure." 6/18/88; with Robert Lansing and Al Waxman.

55 "Kandinsky's Vault." 6/25/88; with Eli Wallach and Robin Ward.

56 "There Was a Little Girl . . ." 7/2/88; with Michael Tucker and Kate Vernon.

57 "Twisted Sisters." 7/9/88; with Mia Sara and Carolyn Dunn.

58 "The Thirteenth Floor." 7/16/88; with Anthony Franciosa and Laura Robinson.

59 "The Hunted." (part one of two) 7/30/88; with Edward Woodward and Kate Trotter.

60 "The Hunted." (part two of two) 8/6/88; with Edward Woodward and Kate Trotter.

61 "Fogbound." 10/8/88; with Kathleen Quinlan and Stephen Mendel.

62 "Pen Pal." 10/15/88; with Jean Simms and Page Fletcher.

63 "Ancient Voices." 11/12/88; with Richard Anderson and Doug McClure.

64 "Survival of the Fittest." 11/19/88; with Patrick Macnee and Nigel Bennett.

65 "The Big Spin." 1/6/89; with Erik Estrada and Kathy Laskey.

66 "Don't Sell Yourself Short." 1/14/89; with David Soul and Harvey Atkin.

67 "For Art's Sake." 1/21/89; with Simon Williams and Michele Scarabelli.

68 "Murder in Mind." 1/28/89; with Melissa Sue Anderson and Noel Harrison.

69 "Mirror, Mirror." 4/2/89; with Elizabeth Ashley and Robert Collins.

70 "Skeleton in the Closet." 2/11/89; with Mimi Kuzyk and Jeff Wincott.

71 "In the Driver's Seat." 2/18/89; with Greg Evigan, David Elliott and Bill MacDonald.

72 "Driving Under the Influence." 2/25/89; with Mike Connors and John Novak.

73 "In the Name of Science." 3/10/89; with Dirk Benedict and Catherine Disher.

74 "Romance Machine." 3/25/89; with Rich Hall and Art Hindle.

75 "Diamonds Aren't Forever." 4/14/89; with George Lazenby and Jack Blum. Note: Lazenby plays a British secret service agent—take a guess who.

76 "My Dear Watson." 4/21/89; with Brian Bedford and Patrick Monckton.

77 "Night Creatures." 4/28/89; with Brett Cullen and Louise Vallance.

78 "The Man Who Knew Too Little." 7/8/89; with Lewis Collins and Cynthia Belliveau.

79 "Reunion." 7/15/89; with James Blendick and Patricia Collins.

80 "South by Southeast." 7/22/89; with Patrick Wayne and Cedric Smith. Note: As the final original broadcast, this was more of a salute to Hitchcock, involving a fictional "lost" film script Hitch was interested in filming.

The following is a selection of the Hitchcock films that were dramatized on radio programs. (See also page 85.)

The Lux Radio Theatre (2/3/41). *Rebecca* with Ronald Colman and Ida Lupino.

The Lux Radio Theatre (6/9/41). *Mr. and Mrs. Smith* with Bob Hope and Carole Lombard.

The Philip Morris Playhouse (12/19/41). *The Lady Vanishes* with Flora Robson and Errol Flynn.

The Gulf Screen Guild Theater (2/8/42). *Mr. and Mrs. Smith* with Errol Flynn and Lana Turner.

The Philip Morris Playhouse (11/6/42). *Rebecca* with Herbert Marshall.

The Lux Radio Theatre (1/3/44). *Shadow of a Doubt* with William Powell and Teresa Wright.

The Lux Radio Theatre (9/18/44). *Suspicion* with William Powell and Olivia de Havilland.

Matinee Theater (11/26/44). *Mr. and Mrs. Smith* with Victor Jory and guests Gertrude Warner and Betty Winkler.

Matinee Theater (1/21/45). *Rebecca* with Victor Jory and guests Gertrude Warner and Blanche Yurka.

Theater of Romance (4/30/46). *Shadow of a Doubt* with Brian Donlevy.

Hollywood Startime (7/20/46). *Mr. and Mrs. Smith* with Robert Montgomery.

Academy Award Theater (7/24/46). *Foreign Correspondent* with Joseph Cotten.

Hour of Mystery (9/1/46). *The 39 Steps* with David Niven.

Hollywood Players (10/1/46). *Rebecca* with Joseph Cotten and Joan Fontaine.

Academy Award Theater (10/30/46). *Suspicion* with Cary Grant and Ann Todd. Note: Nigel Bruce was originally scheduled to reprise his film role in this broadcast, but was prevented by illness.

The Lux Radio Theatre (1/26/48). *Notorious* with Joseph Cotten, Gerald Mohr, and Ingrid Bergman.

The Lux Radio Theatre (3/8/48). *Spellbound* with Joseph Cotten and Valli.

The Camel Screen Guild Players (6/21/48). *Shadow of a Doubt* with Vanessa Brown and Joseph Cotten.

The Ford Theater (2/18/49). *Shadow of a Doubt* with Ray Milland and Ann Blyth.

The Lux Radio Theatre (5/9/49). *The Paradine Case* with Joseph Cotten.

The Prudential Family Hour of Stars (7/24/49). *Rebecca* with Audrey Totter.

The Lux Radio Theatre (11/6/50). *Rebecca* with Laurence Olivier and Vivien Leigh. Note: Leigh was Olivier's choice for the female lead in Hitchcock's film. In this *Lux* presentation, Leigh stars in the role both she and her real-life husband wanted back in 1940.

Hollywood Sound Stage (1/10/52). *Shadow of a Doubt* with Ann Blyth and Jeff Chandler.

The Philip Morris Playhouse on Broadway (5/25/52). *Rebecca* with Melvyn Douglas.

(Television and Radio anthology information compiled by Martin Grams Jr., author of the forthcoming *The Alfred Hitchcock Presents Companion*.)

SELECTED BIBLIOGRAPHY

Anobile, Richard J., ed. *Alfred Hitchcock's* Psycho. London: Pan Books/Macmillan, 1974.

Armes, Roy. *A Critical History of British Cinema*. New York: Oxford University Press, 1978.

Auiler, Dan. *Hitchcock's Notebooks*. New York: Spike, 1999.

Auiler, Dan. Vertigo: *The Making of a Hitchcock Classic*. New York: St. Martin's Press, 1998.

Barr, Charles. *"Blackmail*: Silent & Sound." *Sight and Sound* (Spring 1983): 122–126.

Behlmer, Rudy, ed. *Memo From: David O. Selznick*. New York: Avon Books, 1972.

Boyd, David, ed. *Perspectives on Alfred Hitchcock*. New York: GK Hall & Co., 1995.

Cardiff, Jack. *Magic Hour: The Life of a Cameraman*. London: Faber & Faber, 1996.

Carey, John. *The Violent Effigy: A Study of Dickens's Imagination*. London: Faber & Faber, 1979.

Counts, Kylie B. "The Making of Alfred Hitchcock's *The Birds*." *Cinefantastique* Vol. 10 No. 2 (Fall 1980): 14–35.

Durgnat, Raymond. *The Strange Case of Alfred Hitchcock*. London: Faber & Faber, 1974.

Elley, Derek, ed. *Variety Movie Guide*. London: Hamlyn, 1993.

Gottlieb, Sidney, ed. *Hitchcock on Hitchcock: Selected Writings and Interviews*. London: Faber & Faber, 1995.

Gross, Edward. "*Psycho* Time: Joseph Stefano remembers writing Hitchcock's original shower of blood!" *Fangoria* 55 (n.d.): 65.

Harris, Robert A., and Michael S. Lasky. *The Films of Alfred Hitchcock*. Secaucus: Citadel Press, 1976.

Haver, Ronald. *David O. Selznick's Hollywood*. New York: Bonanza Books, 1980.

Hayes, John Michael. "The Hayes Office: John Michael Hayes interviewed by Richard Valley." *Scarlet Street* 21 (n.d.): 90–97; *Scarlet Street* 22 (n.d.): 84–88, 97.

"Q&A Alfred Hitchcock." *Herald Examiner* (6/25/72).

Higham, Charles, and Roy Moseley. *Cary Grant: The Lonely Heart*. London: New English Library, 1989.

Humphries, Patrick. *The Films of Alfred Hitchcock*. London: Bison Books, 1986.

Hurley, Neil P. *Soul in Suspense: Hitchcock's Fright and Delight*. Metuchen: The Scarecrow Press, 1993.

Janaway, Christopher. *Schopenhauer*. (Oxford: Oxford University Press, 1994.

Kuhns, J. L. "Hitchcock's *The Mountain Eagle*." *Hitchcock Annual* (1998–99): 31–108.

Leff, Leonard J. *Hitchcock and Selznick: The Rich and Strange Collaboration of Alfred Hitchcock and David O. Selznick in Hollywood*. New York: Weidenfeld & Nicolson, 1987.

Leigh, Janet, with Christopher Nickens. Psycho: *Behind the Scenes of the Classic Thriller*. New York: Harmony Books, 1995.

Lloyd, N. *Stages: Of Life in Theatre, Film and Television*. New York: Scarecrow Press, 1990; New York: Limelight Editions, 1993.

Magee, Bryan. *The Philosophy of Schopenhauer*. New York: Oxford University Press, 1983.

Maltin, Leonard. *Leonard Maltin's Movie & Video Guide*. 1998 ed. New York: Signet, 1997.

McCann, Graham. *Cary Grant: A Class Apart*. London: Fourth Estate, 1997.

McCarty, J., and B. Kelleher. *Alfred Hitchcock Presents*. New York: St. Martin's Press, 1985.

McGilligan, Pat, ed. *Backstory: Interviews with Screenwriters of Hollywood's Golden Age*. Berkeley: University of California Press, 1986.

Millichap, Joseph R. *Steinbeck and Film*. New York: Frederick Ungar Publishing Co., 1983.

Mogg, Ken. "The Man Who Knew Too Little: Alfred Hitchcock's *The Wrong Man* (1957) compared with Charles Dickens's *Bleak House* (1853)." *The MacGuffin* 20 (n.d.): 15–26.

Moorehead, Caroline. *Sidney Bernstein: A Biography*. London: Jonathan Cape, 1984.

Naremore, James, ed. *North by Northwest*. New Brunswick: Rutgers University Press, 1993.

Nightingale, Benedict. *An Introduction to Fifty Modern British Plays*. London: Pan Books, 1982.

Paglia, Camille. *Sexual Personae: Art and Decadence from Nefertiti to Emily Dickinson*. London: Penguin Books, 1991.

Peary, Danny, ed. *Close–Ups: The Movie Star Book*. N.p., 1979.

Perry, George. *The Films of Alfred Hitchcock*. London: E. P. Dutton, 1965.

Prawer, S. S. *Caligari's Children: The Film as Tale of Terror*. Oxford: Oxford University Press, 1980.

Priestley, J. B. *The English*. Harmondsworth: Penguin Books, 1975.

Prouty, H. H. *The Alfred Hitchcock Teleguide*. Unpublished reference guide available at the Library of the Academy of Motion Pictures Arts and Sciences, 1984.

Rebello, Stephen. *Alfred Hitchcock and the Making of* Psycho. New York: Harper Collins, 1991.

Richards, Stanley, ed. *Dial M for Murder. Best Mystery and Suspense Plays of the Modern Theatre*. New York: Avon Books, 1971.

Rohmer, Eric, and Claude Chabrol. *Hitchcock: The First Forty–four Films*. Oxford: Roundhouse, 1979.

Rothman, William. *Hitchcock: The Murderous Gaze*. Cambridge: Harvard University Press, 1982.

Roud, Richard, ed. *Cinema: A Critical Dictionary*. London: Secker & Warburg, 1980.

Ryall, Tom. *Alfred Hitchcock & the British Cinema*. London: Croom Helm, 1986.

Samuels, Charles Thomas. *Encountering Directors*. New York: Putnam's, 1972.

Samuels, Robert. *Hitchcock's Bi–Textuality: Lacan, Feminisms, and Queer Theory*. New York: State University of New York Press, 1998.

Schickel, Richard. *The Men Who Made the Movies*. New York: Atheneum, 1975.

Sikov, Ed. *Laughing Hysterically: American Screen Comedy of the 1950s*. New York: Columbia University Press, 1994.

Sinyard, Neil. *The Films of Alfred Hitchcock*. New York: Gallery Books, 1986.

Sloan, Jane E. *Alfred Hitchcock: A Filmography and Bibliography*. Berkeley: University of California, 1993.

Smith, Steven C. *A Heart at Fire's Center: The Life and Music of Bernard Herrmann*. Berkeley: University of California Press, 1991.

Solomon, Robert C. *Continental Philosophy Since 1750: The Rise and Fall of the Self*. Oxford: Oxford University Press, 1988.

Spoto, Donald. *Notorious: The Life of Ingrid Bergman*. New York: HarperCollins, 1997.

———. *The Art of Alfred Hitchcock: Fifty Years of His Motion Pictures*. New York: Anchor Books, 1992.

———. *The Life of Alfred Hitchcock: The Dark Side of Genius*. London: Collins, 1983.

Stam, Robert, and Pearson, Roberta. "Hitchcock's *Rear Window*: Reflexivity and the Critique of Voyeurism." In *A Hitchcock Reader*, edited by M. Deutelbaum and L. Poague, 193–206. Ames: Iowa State University Press, 1986.

Steinberg, Cobbett. *Reel Facts: The Movie Book of Records*. Updated ed., New York: Vintage, 1982.

Symons, Julian. *Crime and Detection: An Illustrated History From 1840*. London: Panther Books, 1968.

Taylor, John Russell. *Hitch: The Life and Work of Alfred Hitchcock*. London: Faber & Faber, 1978.

Truffaut, François. *Hitchcock*. London: Secker & Warburg, 1968.

Valley, Richard. "The Trouble With Hitchcock." *Scarlet Street* 21 (n.d.): 61–65.

Walker, John, ed. *Halliwell's Film and Video Guide*. 1998 ed. London: HarperCollins, 1997.

———. *Halliwell's Filmgoer's Companion*. 12th ed. London: HarperCollins, 1997.

Welles, Orson, and Peter Bogdanovich. *This is Orson Welles*. New York: Da Capo, 1998.

Wilson, Colin, and Pat Pitman. *Encyclopaedia of Murder*. London: Pan Books, 1984.

Wood, Robin. *Hitchcock's Films Revisited*. New York: Columbia University Press, 1989.

Yacowar, Maurice. *Hitchcock's British Films*. Hamden: Archon Books, 1977.

PICTURE CREDITS

Grateful acknowledgment is made to the studios and distributors whose stills and posters illustrate this book for the purposes of review:

ABC, Alfred Hitchcock Productions, Amer-Anglo Corp, Tom Arnold, Artlee Independent Distributors, Associated British, Aywon Independent Distributors, British Film Institute, British International Pictures, Emelka GBA, FilWite Productions, First National, Gainsborough, Gaumont-British, Geoffrey Stanley Inc., The Kobal Collection, Frank Lloyd, Mayflower Pictures, Metro-Goldwyn-Mayer, Oak (Hilton A. Green), Paramount, Patron Inc., Phoenix, Powers Pictures, The Rank Organization, RKO, Selznick International, Shamley Productions Inc., Skirball Productions, Sono Art World Pictures, Transatlantic Pictures, 20th Century Fox, Ufa Eastern Division, United Artists, Universal, Vanguard Films Inc., W and F of London, Walter Wanger, Wardour, Warner Brothers, World Wide Distributors.

Any omissions will be corrected in future editions.

Many people helped with sourcing the visual material for this book. The publisher's thanks and gratitude go to:

Allpoints/Image-Is-Everything Collection, Peter Baumann, BFI Films: Stills, Posters, and Designs (Mandy Rowson), Tim Daley, Martin Dawber, Richard Ducar, The Tony Hillman Collection, Roger Huber, The Kinema Collection, The Kobal Collection, Dr. Ulrich Rüdel, Hans Signer.

Ad on p. 168 courtesy of Technicolor.

Cover on p. 171 by permission of *Esquire* magazine. ©Hearst Communications, Inc. Also, *Esquire* is a trademark of Hearst Magazines Property, Inc. All rights reserved.

AUTHOR'S ACKNOWLEDGMENTS

I must be brief. Special thanks to Freda. To Harry and Ron. And to David and Adam at Titan. Now here's a "checklist" of some of the many people who have helped in the preparation of this book. Gratitude to them all . . .

Dan Auiler, Charles Barr, David Barraclough, Nandor Bokor, Gillian Christie, Bruce Christopher, Ron Conway, Donette Crow, Steven L. DeRosa, Freda Freiberg, Tag Gallagher, Sid Gottlieb, Martin Grams, Jr., Tony Hillman, Fergal Hughes, Bob Kelly, Philip Kemp, J. Lary Kuhns, Adrian Martin, Aysen Mustafa, Adam Newell, Danny Nissim, Stephen Rebello, Ulrich Ruedel, Robert Schoen, Leslie Shepard, Chris Teather, Harry Tsarvenkos, Richard Valley, Katy Wild.

The publishers would also like to thank Kristi Kittendorf, Marcus Hearn, and Alan Barnes, and especially Janet Leigh for providing the introduction.

CONTRIBUTING AUTHORS

Dan Auiler is the author of *Hitchcock's Notebooks*, Titan Books' *Vertigo: The Making of a Hitchcock Classic,* and co-author (with Stephen Rebello) of the forthcoming *North by Northwest: The Making of Hitchcock's Classic Thriller.* Auiler teaches cinema and drama courses, and lives in Los Angeles.

David Barraclough is an editor living in London, and author of *Hollywood Heaven* and *Movie Recordbreakers.*

Steven L. DeRosa is a New York–based writer and filmmaker, author of the forthcoming *Writing with Hitchcock: The Collaboration of Alfred Hitchcock and John Michael Hayes,* and is currently completing a volume on Hitchcock's unrealized projects.

Martin Grams Jr. is the author of *Suspense: Twenty Years of Thrills and Chills, The History of the Cavalcade of America,* and co-author of *The CBS Radio Mystery Theater: An Episode Guide and Handbook to Nine Years of Broadcasting, 1974–82.* He is currently completing a book documenting the entire history of *Have Gun, Will Travel* and *The Alfred Hitchcock Presents Companion.*

Philip Kemp is a freelance writer and film historian based in London, and a regular contributor to *Sight and Sound* magazine. He is currently working on a biography of Michael Balcon.

J. Lary Kuhns is a mathematician who has also been a student of Hitchcock's films. He has recently published an illustrated analysis of the "lost" film *The Mountain Eagle.*